TOTAL FREEDOM

The Essential Krishnamurti

Also by J. Krishnamurti

The Awakening of Intelligence

The Book of Life: Daily Meditations with Krishnamurti

Education and the Significance of Life

The Ending of Time (with David Bohm)

Exploration into Insight

The First and Last Freedom

The Flame of Attention

The Flight of the Eagle

Freedom from the Known

The Future of Humanity (with David Bohm)

Krishnamurti's Notebook

Krishnamurti to Himself

Life Ahead

Meeting Life

The Network of Thought

On Conflict

On Fear

On Freedom

On God

On Learning and Knowledge

On Living and Dying

On Love and Loneliness

On Mind and Thought

On Nature and the Environment

On Relationship

On Right Livelihood

On Truth

Think on These Things

Truth and Actuality (with David Bohm)

The Wholeness of Life (with David Bohm)

TOTAL FREEDOM

The Essential Krishnamurti

J. Krishnamurti

HarperSanFrancisco
An Imprint of HarperCollins*Publishers*

Information about the Krishnamurti Foundations, Schools, and Study Centers can be obtained from:

Krishnamurti Foundation of America
P.O. Box 1560
Ojai, CA 93024 U.S.A.
and
Krishnamurti Foundation Trust, Ltd.
Brockwood Park, Bramdean, Hants SO24 OLQ, U.K.

Sources and Acknowledgments can be found on page 361.

Edited by Mary Cadogan, Alan Kishbaugh, Mark Lee, and Ray McCoy.

FIRST EDITION

Library of Congress Cataloging-in-Publication Data

Krishnamurti, J. (Jiddu).
Total freedom : the essential Krishnamurti /
J. Krishnamurti. — 1st ed.
Includes bibliographical references and index.
ISBN 0-06-064880-5 (pbk.)
1. Liberty. I. Title.
B5134.K75T73 1996
181'.4—dc20 96-20115

04 05 ❖ RRD (H) 19 18

CONTENTS

FOREWORD

Great sages of history have been ill-served in the preservation of their wisdom. The best of these saints and savants—ancient Hindu and Jewish holy men, the Buddha, Confucius, Socrates, Jesus Christ, the Prophet Mohammed—left few significant writings. Their truths were unfolded in profound discourses and sagacious dialogues—oral expositions transmitted to us in incomplete renderings. Thus, only some of the verities are known; many have been lost. Those who seek the complete scheme, as originally presented, have to depend on unreliable intermediaries such as faith, interpretation, interpolation, and reconstruction.

As we move closer to our time, this problem is inverted. Knowledge overtakes wisdom and culture surrenders to technology. Recordings are comprehensive, but what is recorded is often of lesser value. There is, it seems, a shortage of authentic sages. By the numbers there are plenty who purvey wisdom and pseudowisdom, teachers claiming to possess and provide transcendent insights. However, very few of them survive the tests that surely define a real spiritual pathfinder—the ability to convey a message that is universal and liberating, nondiscriminating and free of hatred; a message that is capable of disinterested enrichment of minds and lives, and is also within the understanding of everyone. By any or all of these yardsticks, J. Krishnamurti was truly a modern master.

Krishnamurti's entire life was focused on realizing and explaining the human quest. For six decades, until his death in 1986 at the age of ninety, he traveled the world bringing his thoughts to those who would listen. Millions did. His popularity sometimes fluctuated, but Krishnamurti persisted in his efforts to "set man absolutely, unconditionally free." Toward the end of his life, new generations—children of our technetronic age—rediscovered Krishnamurti. In an era of hot shots and holy rollers, razzle-dazzle religion and pulpit rap, he retained the aura of an old-fashioned prophet. Philosophic fads came and went; Krishnamurti endured.

There are two reasons for this apparent timelessness. The most obvious is, of course, the personality of Krishnamurti. His public persona radiated a kind of undemonstrative charisma, the attraction of luminous restraint. Add to this a speaking manner and tone that could evoke a personal intimacy in the midst of even the largest audiences. It is not surprising that the writer Aldous Huxley, no slouch when it came to critical observation, declaimed: "It was like listening to a discourse of the Buddha—such power, such intrinsic authority."

Yet, in the end, personality alone is an unsatisfactory explanation. Many who did not see or hear Krishnamurti were and still are drawn to his thoughts. So, to appreciate the appeal we must go to the philosophic source—the ideas he articulated and their main themes. A careful examination of this body of work will reveal both consistency and changes. While certain central concepts remain fundamental, Krishnamurti did not hesitate to adapt and evolve to new historical circumstances and spiritual quests.

Again and again, Krishnamurti declared that people do not need guidance, they need awakening. This high confidence in human potential was rooted in the belief that each individual has no limit on development, if he can eschew the cultural barnacles that load his being: "A theory based on another man's experience in matters of the psyche or of an inward life has no meaning at all. . . . We have to let it go completely because we have to stand alone." With this denial of the transferability of experience and the rejection of all spiritual guidance, including his own, Krishnamurti breaks with most world religions—all of which have spiritual paradigms and instructors whose examples we can emulate. It was not his purpose to attack other faiths, but he frequently warns against the misleading power of religions, institutions, and rituals—and above all, the divisiveness of sectarianism.

As the years passed, Krishnamurti's philosophic and intellectual membranes expanded beyond his core themes. Increasingly, we see him addressing the evils of civil and religious power, the futility of existing social structures, the inertia of conformity, and the failure of temporizing reform. By the mid–1950s, Krishnamurti had developed notions about education, human relations, and communications that are not found in his earlier discourses. The teacher was also learning—not only answering the questions of others but also extending his own questions. Yet, the range of his expositions grows to embrace a number of new concerns—nationalism, war, ecological despoliation, unemployment, and hunger. With an almost contemporary sensitivity, social issues that were once on the periphery of his perceptions come closer to center stage. References to the significance of meditation become more frequent. A note of impatience, an urgency, begins to surface. Krishnamurti senses the peril of the times and the compelling demand for action. As if to respond in style as well as substance, his talks become more focused and his dialogues less elliptical. And yet, the essential message is unchanged: "When one sees life as it is, when one sees oneself as one is, [only] from there can one move [ahead]."

Of all the sages and significant spiritual figures of modern times, Krishnamurti has had the longest exposure—about sixty-five years on the stage of eminence. Yet, it is difficult to assess his historical stature. He is too close to us and it is too early to know the full effect of his teachings. After all, for several decades subsequent to his crucifixion, there was little sign that Jesus Christ would make a major mark on history. At the moment of their death and for quite some time after, who could have predicted the long-term influence of the Buddha, Confucius, or even Karl Marx? If Krishnamurti's ideas become more widely accepted in the future, it will be because they resonate with the yearnings of people—because they speak intently to individuals disillusioned with all-knowing and socially transforming macroideologies. Should this outcome take place, it will be because Krishnamurti's discourses resonate across boundaries of time and place. His voice is silent but its message never ceases to speak.

Ralph Buultjens, Ph.D.
Professor of Social Sciences, New York University,
former Nehru Professor at Cambridge University, U.K.

PREFACE

From obscure beginnings in a small town in India, Krishnamurti emerged as an uncompromising and unclassifiable teacher, whose talks and writings were not linked to any specific religion and were neither of the East nor the West but *for* the whole world.

For some sixty years he spoke to vast audiences in words that were of vital, catalytic relevance to every individual and every society. He had frequent discussions with distinguished writers, philosophers, scientists, educators, and national leaders. With extraordinary immediacy and directness, and without any frameworks or dependencies, he was able to reach the core of problems with which humanity has grappled for centuries.

Krishnamurti's books have been published all over the world and translated into more than twenty languages. His works are also available on audio and video recordings and electronic disks. Much of this material is now used in over 150 colleges and universities.

Faced with this volume of material, we have chosen a broad range of previously published works as well as unpublished ones to give a sense of the depth and breadth of Krishnamurti's teaching. Readers are, of course, encouraged to look beyond this selection to the whole body of his talks and writings.

The full text of "Truth Is a Pathless Land," the talk which set in motion his break with Theosophy, is included as it embodies the theme that informed his life's work. The rest of the book has four, more or less chronologically arranged, parts.

Part 1 contains material from talks given in the years following his dissociation from Theosophy. Part 2 is drawn from accounts of his conversations with various individuals, an early work on education, and the more private *Journal* and *Krishnamurti to Himself*.

Part 3 presents, from records of public meetings, discussions with students and talks with Foundation Trustees, an indication of the great variety of questions that Krishnamurti dealt with during his years of traveling and meeting people.

The final part opens with Krishnamurti's own statement of *The Core* of his teaching, followed by talks from the later years, which explore the themes of *The Core* and recall his earlier declaration of truth as a pathless land that is total freedom, love, and intelligence.

Mary Cadogan, Alan Kishbaugh, Mark Lee, Ray McCoy

INTRODUCTION

When first privileged to meet Krishnamurti, I was deeply struck by the intensity of his quietude. The intensity bespoke great energy and his quietude expressed a settled tranquility. Such a combination is rare; indeed, so rare that on encountering it nothing can be taken for granted.

Our meeting was, as we say loosely, accidental. It was in a sound studio. I had neither met him before nor read any of his books. Yet, amazingly, he invited me on the spot to undertake a videotaped dialogue with him. He seemed not in the least concerned that, in the ordinary sense, he did not know me from Adam. I inferred that he was either a great gambler or so attuned to the present instant that his action was exact, a paragon of timeliness. There was something profoundly impersonal in that invitation without his being aloof or indifferent.

The next shock came with his asking me, "What would you like to talk about?" I replied, "How about hearing and seeing?" He accepted the topic joyously. And so immediately began, impromptu, a conversation on inward hearing and inward seeing. Two years later, again utterly unexpectedly, he invited me to undertake a series of dialogues that would encompass the kernel of his teaching. Though years before I had been in radio broadcasting—announcing and newscasting—and so had some professional acquaintance with studio programming, none of that experience was decisive for the movement of the dialogues. They developed without any rehearsal, prearrangement, contrivance, or hands-on fashioning. Both his ease and intensity of focus were amazing.

Krishnamurti was an exact embodiment of his doctrine of "choiceless awareness." Here, the word *choiceless* might suggest only a mode of subjectivity. On the contrary, choiceless awareness, while reflected in the persona, is in no way reducible to it and so eludes a psychological reduction. Choicelessness is the mind's equivalent of the silence out of which intelligible utterance arises, of "that emptiness in which the things of the mind can exist but the things are not the mind . . . that emptiness has no center and so is capable of infinite movement. Creation is born out of this emptiness but it is not the creation of man putting things together. That creation of emptiness is love and death." This last sentence points directly and immediately to the character of the instant for both self-awakening and self-misunderstanding. Unless there is a psychological death to our self-identification with memory and upon the same instant a total understanding of need, we remain collapsed into the content of thought and a timely response to the instant eludes us:

> "When there is a total understanding of need, the outward and the inner, then desire is not a torture. Then it has a quite different meaning, a significance far beyond the content of thought and it goes beyond feeling, with its emotions, myths and illusions. With the total understanding of need, not the mere quantity or the quality of it, desire then is a flame and not a torture. Without this flame life itself is lost. It is this flame that burns away the pettiness of its object, the frontiers, the fences that have been imposed upon it. Then call it by whatever name you will, love, death, beauty. Then it is there without an end."

Some might think it untoward to begin a short introduction to sagely works with a personal anecdote. One thinks of Krishnamurti's repeated caution to his audiences: "The speaker is unimportant." Then there is Chuang Tzu's: "The Perfect man has no self; the Holy man has no merit; the Sage has no fame." (All three being the same.) True enough and almost never pondered, let alone embodied. Yet to find in such words an invitation to ignore the personal presence of a great teacher (whether in the flesh or remembered) betrays a shallow readiness to try to go beyond where one has not begun. Krishnamurti admonishes us that "Meditation is not something different from daily life . . . it is the seeing of *what is* and going beyond it." If one has not seen *what is,* how can one go beyond it?

Unfortunately, academic practice shows little or no understanding of "seeing *what is*" in the context of genuine self-inquiry. Rather, academic life is a journey through the forest of abstractions. Experimental science has the advantage of requiring laboratory demonstration of its theoretical conclusions. Even so, this procedure is pursued within the dual structure of perceiver and perceived. Perception without the perceiver, as in meditation, is unheard of:

> "This perception is entirely different from seeing an object without an observer, because in the perception of meditation there is no object and therefore no experience. What meaning has such medita-

tion? There is no meaning; there is no utility. But in that meditation there is a movement of great ecstasy. It is the ecstasy which gives to the eye, to the brain, and to the heart the quality of innocency. Without seeing life as something totally new, it is a routine, a boredom, a meaningless affair. So meditation is of the greatest importance. It opens the door to the incalculable, to the measureless."

This ecstatic pointer of Krishnamurti's so escapes our contemporary mind-set as to be practically unintelligible. Yet it is supremely intelligent. How so? Because it implies a radical distinction between consciousness and awareness. In our time, philosophy and depth psychology have virtually absolutized consciousness. They fail to discern that consciousness is not self-correcting. How can it be so since consciousness is ever tied to change? It is only as awareness has an object that consciousness comes into play. In itself awareness is both independent of objects and changeless. On that account it is the door to the incalculable and measureless.

Krishnamurti invites us to begin the most radical self-inquiry since it opens out upon the infinite space of awareness. Self-inquiry begins by asking not what am I but what am I not? Such a no-nonsense question has no need of theoretical structures, the conceptual paraphernalia of our depth psychologies, philosophies, and theologies and belief systems. The question is astonishingly yet frighteningly simple; frightening because it entails the deepest sense of aloneness, since none but oneself can ask the question nor answer it. Yet, with the patience, courage, and radical trust to hang in there without bolting from it one discovers the unlonely aloneness of that "meditation which is absolutely no effort, no achievement, no thinking, the brain is quiet, not made quiet by will, by intention, by conclusion and all that nonsense; it is quiet. And, being quiet, it has infinite space."

In this short introduction, I have deliberately avoided taking an academic approach to Krishnamurti's teaching. To have done so would have falsified his spirit and quite missed the mark of his message. He was not concerned with the career of ideas and the ongoing palaver that is believed to express the finest examples of the life of the mind. In his last talk (January 1986) he put the matter cogently and succinctly:

"It would be useless for you and the speaker to listen to a lot of words, but if we could together take a very long journey, not in

> terms of time, not in terms of belief or conclusions or theories, but in examining very carefully the way of our lives, fear, uncertainty, insecurity and all the inventions that man has made, including the extraordinary computers. If we take a long journey into this, where are we at the end of two million years? Where are we going, not as some theory, not what some wretched book says, however holy it is, but where are we all going? And where have we begun? They're both related to each other: where we are going, where we begin. The beginning may be the ending. Don't agree. Find out."

Right away, one hears the cry: "How? How find out?!" The very word, how, betrays a belief in the power of process and procedure to produce an effect; and indeed, they do in the material order. But here, the directive to find out addresses a different sphere, the sphere of one's misrelation to oneself. The attempt to impose upon this disorder any discipline according to a pattern only hardens the misrelation, binding it further to time, belief, conclusions, and theories. There is no how to making a pure act of attention to what is at hand. There is nothing mysterious about this. In fact, in the normal course of daily living we make, perhaps, a few such acts but quickly fall out of them. Why? The answer to that question comes only through self-examination—not through theories of the unconscious or from learned disquisitions on the nature of man. The pure act of attention is spontaneous and free; the hearer and the heard, the perceiver and perceived drop away leaving only listening and seeing. "Only when the mind is blissful, quiet, without any movement of its own, without projection of thought, conscious or unconscious—only then does the eternal come into being."

During this century we have taken in with our mother's milk the enervating dogma that the hallmarks of human nature are anxiety (angst) and estrangement, a secularized version of the dogma of original sin. But through meditation, as Krishnamurti revealed it, and self-inquiry, one discovers one's original nature, original innocence and the natural state. Is this, then, the heart of the matter? Yes, since the heart of the matter is a matter of the heart.

Allan W. Anderson
Professor Emeritus of Religious Studies
San Diego University

TRUTH IS A PATHLESS LAND

The Dissolution of the Order of the Star

The Order of the Star in the East was founded in 1911 to proclaim the coming of the World Teacher. Krishnamurti was made Head of the Order. On August 2, 1929, the opening day of the annual Star Camp at Ommen, Holland, Krishnamurti dissolved the Order before three thousand members. This is the full text of the talk he gave on that occasion.

We are going to discuss this morning the dissolution of the Order of the Star. Many people will be delighted, and others will be rather sad. It is a question neither for rejoicing nor for sadness, because it is inevitable, as I am going to explain.

You may remember the story of how the devil and a friend of his were walking down the street when they saw ahead of them a man stoop down and pick up something from the ground, look at it, and put it away in his pocket. The friend said to the devil, "What did that man pick up?" "He picked up a piece of Truth," said the devil. "That is a very bad business for you, then," said his friend. "Oh, not at all," the devil replied, "I am going to let him organize it."

I maintain that Truth is a pathless land, and you cannot approach it by any path whatsoever, by any religion, by any sect. That is my point of view, and I adhere to that absolutely and unconditionally. Truth, being limitless, unconditioned, unapproachable by any path whatsoever, cannot be organized; nor should any organization be formed to lead or to coerce people along any particular path. If you first understand that, then you will see how impossible it is to organize a belief. A belief is purely an individual matter, and you cannot and must not organize it. If you do, it becomes dead, crystalized; it becomes a creed, a sect, a religion, to be imposed on others. This is what everyone throughout the world is attempting to do. Truth is narrowed down and made a plaything for those who are weak, for those who are only momentarily discontented. Truth cannot be brought down; rather, the individual must make the effort to ascend to it. You cannot bring the mountaintop to the valley. If you would attain to the mountaintop you must pass through the valley, climb the steeps, unafraid of the dangerous precipices. You must climb toward the

Truth, it cannot be "stepped down" or organized for you. Interest in ideas is mainly sustained by organizations, but organizations only awaken interest from without. Interest, which is not born out of love of Truth for its own sake, but aroused by an organization, is of no value. The organization becomes a framework into which its members can conveniently fit. They no longer strive after Truth or the mountaintop, but rather carve for themselves a convenient niche in which they put themselves, or let the organization place them, and consider that the organization will thereby lead them to Truth.

So that is the first reason, from my point of view, why the Order of the Star should be dissolved. In spite of this, you will probably form other Orders, you will continue to belong to other organizations searching for Truth. I do not want to belong to any organization of a spiritual kind, please understand this. I would make use of an organization which would take me to London, for example; this is quite a different kind of organization, merely mechanical, like the post or the telegraph. I would use a motorcar or a steamship to travel; these are only physical mechanisms which have nothing whatever to do with spirituality. Again, I maintain that no organization can lead man to spirituality.

If an organization be created for this purpose, it becomes a crutch, a weakness, a bondage, and must cripple the individual, and prevent him from growing, from establishing his uniqueness, which lies in the discovery for himself of that absolute, unconditioned Truth. So that is another reason why I have decided, as I happen to be the Head of the Order, to dissolve it. No one has persuaded me to this decision.

This is no magnificent deed, because I do not want followers, and I mean this. The moment you follow someone you cease to follow Truth. I am not concerned whether you pay attention to what I say or not. I want to do a certain thing in the world and I am going to do it with unwavering concentration. I am concerning myself with only one essential thing: to set man free. I desire to free him from all cages, from all fears, and not to found religions, new sects, nor to establish new theories and new philosophies. Then you will naturally ask me why I go the world over, continually speaking. I will tell you for what reason I do this: not because I desire a following, not because I desire a special group of special disciples. (How men love to be different from their fellowmen, however ridiculous, absurd, and trivial their distinctions may be!

I do not want to encourage that absurdity.) I have no disciples, no apostles, either on earth or in the realm of spirituality.

Nor is it the lure of money, nor the desire to live a comfortable life, which attracts me. If I wanted to lead a comfortable life I would not come to a camp or live in a damp country! I am speaking frankly because I want this settled once and for all. I do not want these childish discussions year after year.

One newspaper reporter, who interviewed me, considered it a magnificent act to dissolve an organization in which there were thousands and thousands of members. To him it was a great act because, he said: "What will you do afterwards, how will you live? You will have no following, people will no longer listen to you." If there are only five people who will listen, who will live, who have their faces turned toward eternity, it will be sufficient. Of what use is it to have thousands who do not understand, who are fully embalmed in prejudice, who do not want the new, but would rather translate the new to suit their own sterile, stagnant selves? If I speak strongly, please do not misunderstand me; it is not through lack of compassion. If you go to a surgeon for an operation, is it not kindness on his part to operate even if he causes you pain? So, in like manner, if I speak straightly, it is not through lack of real affection, on the contrary.

As I have said, I have only one purpose: to make man free, to urge him toward freedom, to help him to break away from all limitations, for that alone will give him eternal happiness, will give him the unconditioned realization of the self.

Because I am free, unconditioned, whole—not the part, not the relative, but the whole Truth that is eternal—I desire those, who seek to understand me, to be free; not to follow me, not to make out of me a cage which will become a religion, a sect. Rather should they be free from all fears—from the fear of religion, from the fear of salvation, from the fear of spirituality, from the fear of love, from the fear of death, from the fear of life itself. As an artist paints a picture because he takes delight in that painting, because it is his self-expression, his glory, his well-being, so I do this and not because I want anything from anyone.

You are accustomed to authority, or to the atmosphere of authority, which you think will lead you to spirituality. You think and hope that another can, by his extraordinary powers—a miracle—transport you to this realm of eternal freedom, which is Happiness. Your whole outlook on life is based on that authority.

You have listened to me for three years now, without any change taking place except in the few. Now analyze what I am saying, be critical, so that you may understand thoroughly, fundamentally. When you look for an authority to lead you to spirituality, you are bound automatically to build an organization around that authority. By the very creation of that organization, which, you think, will help this authority to lead you to spirituality, you are held in a cage.

If I talk frankly, please remember that I do so, not out of harshness, not out of cruelty, not out of the enthusiasm of my purpose, but because I want you to understand what I am saying. That is the reason why you are here, and it would be a waste of time if I did not explain clearly, decisively, my point of view.

For eighteen years you have been preparing for this event, for the Coming of the World Teacher. For eighteen years you have organized, you have looked for someone who would give a new delight to your hearts and minds, who would transform your whole life, who would give you a new understanding; for someone who would raise you to a new plane of life, who would give you a new encouragement, who would set you free—and now look what is happening! Consider, reason with yourselves, and discover in what way that belief has made you different—not with the superficial difference of the wearing of a badge, which is trivial, absurd. In what manner has such a belief swept away all the unessential things of life? That is the only way to judge: In what way are you freer, greater, more dangerous to every Society which is based on the false and the unessential? In what way have the members of this organization of the Star become different?

As I said, you have been preparing for eighteen years for me. I do not care if you believe that I am the World Teacher or not. That is of very little importance. Since you belong to the organization of the Order of the Star, you have given your sympathy, your energy, acknowledging that Krishnamurti is the World Teacher partially or wholly: wholly for those who are really seeking, only partially for those who are satisfied with their own half-truths.

You have been preparing for eighteen years, and look how many difficulties there are in the way of your understanding, how many complications, how many trivial things. Your prejudices, your fears, your authorities, your churches new and old—all these, I maintain, are a barrier to understanding. I cannot make myself clearer than this. I do not want you to agree with me. I do not want you to follow me. I want you to understand what I am saying.

This understanding is necessary because your belief has not transformed you but only complicated you, and because you are not willing to face things as they are. You want to have your own gods—new gods instead of the old, new religions instead of the old, new forms instead of the old—all equally valueless, all barriers, all limitations, all crutches. Instead of old spiritual distinctions you have new spiritual distinctions, instead of old worships you have new worships. You are all depending for your spirituality on someone else, for your happiness on someone else, for your enlightenment on someone else; and although you have been preparing for me for eighteen years, when I say all these things are unnecessary, when I say that you must put them all away and look within yourselves for the enlightenment, for the glory, for the purification, and for the incorruptibility of the self, not one of you is willing to do it. There may be a few, but very, very few.

So why have an organization?

Why have false, hypocritical people following me, the embodiment of Truth? Please remember that I am not saying something harsh or unkind, but we have reached a situation when you must face things as they are. I said last year that I would not compromise. Very few listened to me then. This year I have made it absolutely clear. I do not know how many thousands throughout the world—members of the Order—have been preparing for me for eighteen years, and yet now they are not willing to listen unconditionally, wholly, to what I say.

So why have an organization?

As I said before, my purpose is to make men unconditionally free, for I maintain that the only spirituality is the incorruptibility of the self, which is eternal, is the harmony between reason and love. This is the absolute, unconditioned Truth, which is Life itself. I want, therefore, to set man free, rejoicing as the bird in the clear sky, unburdened, independent, ecstatic in that freedom. And I, for whom you have been preparing for eighteen years, now say that you must be free of all these things, free from your complications, your entanglements. For this you need not have an organization based on spiritual belief. Why have an organization for five or ten people in the world who understand, who are struggling, who have put aside all trivial things? And for the weak people, there can be no organization to help them to find the Truth, because Truth is in everyone; it is not far, it is not near; it is eternally there.

Organizations cannot make you free. No man from outside can make you free; nor can organized worship, nor the immolation of yourselves for a cause, make you free; nor can forming yourselves into an organization, nor throwing yourselves into works, make you free. You use a typewriter to write letters, but you do not put it on an altar and worship it. But that is what you are doing when organizations become your chief concern. "How many members are there in it?" That is the first question I am asked by all newspaper reporters. "How many followers have you? By their number we shall judge whether what you say is true or false." I do not know how many there are. I am not concerned with that. As I said, if there were even one man who had been set free, that is enough.

Again, you have the idea that only certain people hold the key to the Kingdom of Happiness. No one holds it. No one has the authority to hold that key. That key is your own self, and in the development and the purification and in the incorruptibility of that self alone is the Kingdom of Eternity.

So you will see how absurd is the whole structure that you have built, looking for external help, depending on others for your comfort, for your happiness, for your strength. These can only be found within yourselves.

So why have an organization?

You are accustomed to being told how far you have advanced, what is your spiritual status. How childish! Who but yourself can tell you if you are beautiful or ugly within? Who but yourself can tell you if you are incorruptible? You are not serious in these things.

So why have an organization?

But those who really desire to understand, who are looking to find that which is eternal, without beginning and without an end, will walk together with a greater intensity, will be a danger to everything that is unessential, to unrealities, to shadows. And they will concentrate, they will become the flame, because they understand. Such a body we must create, and that is my purpose. Because of that real understanding there will be true friendship. Because of that true friendship—which you do not seem to know—there will be real cooperation on the part of each one. And this not because of authority, not because of salvation, not because of immolation for a cause, but because you really understand, and hence are capable of living in the eternal. This is a greater thing than all pleasure, than all sacrifice.

So these are some of the reasons why, after careful consideration for two years, I have made this decision. It is not from a momentary impulse. I have not been persuaded to it by anyone. I am not persuaded in such things. For two years I have been thinking about this, slowly, carefully, patiently, and I have now decided to disband the Order, as I happen to be its Head. You can form other organizations and expect someone else. With that I am not concerned, nor with creating new cages, new decorations for those cages. My only concern is to set men absolutely, unconditionally free.

PART 1

Early Works

Jiddu Krishnamurti was born in 1895 into a modest Brahmin home in Madanapalle, India. His mother died when he was ten, and during his childhood he was delicate and frequently ill. When his father retired from government employment, he arranged with Annie Besant, the President of the International Theosophical Society, to work for this organization of which he had been a member for some years. Krishnamurti, then in his fourteenth year, moved with three of his brothers and his father to the Theosophical headquarters in Madras.

A deeply affectionate bond formed between Mrs. Besant and Krishnamurti, and she became his legal guardian. The theosophists had been awaiting the advent of a "World Teacher," to prepare for whose coming they had formed a group known as the Order of the Star in the East, with Krishnamurti at its Head. In 1912 Krishnamurti was formally proclaimed the World Teacher, but in 1929 he disbanded the Order with his spiritually radical speech "Truth Is a Pathless Land." By doing so he rejected estates, money, power, and all claims to authority or guru status.

For the rest of his life he traveled extensively, giving talks to all who cared to listen in Europe, India, the United States, South America, Australia, and New Zealand. Thousands from all walks of life came to hear him.

This part comprises a selection from his talks given in the mid-1930s. It includes one given in Mexico City and a series given in 1934 in Ojai, California, where Krishnamurti later spent the years of World War II (1939 to 1945).

WHAT I WANT TO DO

You may ask, "What is it that you want to do? If you don't want us to join any society or accept certain theories, what is it then that you want to do?"

What I want to do is to help you, the individual, to cross the stream of suffering, confusion and conflict, through deep and complete fulfillment. This fulfillment does not come through egotistic self-expression, nor through compulsion and imitation. Not through some fantastic sentiment and conclusions, but through clear thinking, through intelligent action, we shall cross this stream of pain and sorrow. There is a reality which can be understood only through deep and true fulfillment.

Before we can understand the richness and the beauty of fulfillment, mind must free itself from the background of tradition, habit, and prejudice. For example, if you belong to a particular political party, you naturally regard all your political considerations from the narrow, limited point of view of that party. If you have been brought up, nursed, conditioned in a certain religion, you look at life through its veil of prejudice and darkness. That background of tradition prevents the complete understanding of life, and so causes confusion and suffering.

I would beg of you to listen to what I have to say, freeing yourself for this hour at least from the background in which you have been brought up, with its traditions and prejudices, and think simply and directly about the many human problems.

To be truly critical is not to be in opposition. Most of us have been trained to oppose and not to criticize. When a man merely opposes, it generally indicates that he has some vested interest which he desires to protect, and that is not deep penetration through critical examination. True criticism lies in trying to understand the full significance of values without the hindrance of defensive reactions.

We see throughout the world extremes of poverty and riches, abundance and at the same time starvation; we have class distinction and racial hatred, the stupidity of nationalism and the appalling cruelty of war. There is exploitation of man by man; religions with their vested interests have become the means of exploitation, also dividing man from man. There is anxiety, confusion, hopelessness, frustration.

We see all this. It is part of our daily life. Caught up in the wheel of suffering, if you are at all thoughtful you must have asked yourself how these human problems can be solved. Either you are conscious of the chaotic state of the world, or you are completely asleep, living in a fantastic world, in an illusion. If you are aware, you must be grappling with these problems. In trying to solve them, some turn to experts for their solution, and follow their ideas and theories. Gradually they form themselves into an exclusive body, and thus they come into conflict with other experts and their parties; and the individual merely becomes a tool in the hands of the group or of the expert. Or you try to solve these problems by following a particular system, which, if you carefully examine it, becomes merely another means of exploiting the individual. Or you think that to change all this cruelty and horror there must be a mass movement, a collective action.

Now the idea of a mass movement becomes merely a catchword if you, the individual, who are part of the mass, do not understand your true function. True collective action can take place only when you, the individual, who are also the mass, are awake and take the full responsibility for your action without compulsion.

Please bear in mind that I am not giving you a system of philosophy which you can follow blindly, but I am trying to awaken the desire for true and intelligent fulfillment, which alone can bring about happy order and peace in the world.

There can be fundamental and lasting change in the world, there can be love and intelligent fulfillment, only when you wake up and begin to free yourself from the net of illusions, the many illusions which you have created about yourself through fear. When the mind frees itself from these hindrances, when there is that deep, inward, voluntary change, then only can there be true, lasting, collective action, in which there can be no compulsion.

Please understand that I am talking to you as an individual, not to a collective group or to a particular party. If you do not awaken to your full responsibility, to your fulfillment, then your function as a human being in society must be frustrated, limited, and in that lies sorrow.

So the question is: How can there be this profound individual revolution? If there is this true, voluntary revolution on the part of the individual, then you will create the right environment for all, without the distinction of class or race. Then the world will be a single human unit.

How are you going to awaken as individuals to this profound revolution? Now what I am going to say is not complicated, it is simple; and because of its very simplicity, I am afraid you will reject it as not being positive. What you call positive is to be given a definite plan, to be told exactly what to do. But if you can understand for yourself what are the hindrances that are preventing your deep and true fulfillment, then you will not become a mere follower and be exploited. All following is detrimental to completeness.

To have this profound revolution, you must become fully conscious of the structure which you have created about yourself and in which you are now caught. That is, we have now certain values, ideals, beliefs, which act as a net to hold the mind, and by questioning and understanding all their significance, we shall realize how they have come into existence. Before you can act fully and truly, you must know the prison in which you are living, how it has been created; and in examining it without any self-defense you will find out for yourself its true significance, which no other can convey to you. Through your own awakening of intelligence, through your own suffering you will discover the manner of true fulfillment.

Each one of us is seeking security, certainty, through egotistic thought and action, objectively and subjectively. If you are conscious of your own thought, you will see that you are pursuing your own egotistic certainty and security, both outwardly and inwardly. In reality, there is no such absolute division of life as the objective and the subjective world. I make this division only for convenience.

Objectively, this search for egotistic security and certainty expresses itself through family, which becomes a center of exploitation, based on acquisitiveness. If you examine it, you will see that what you call the love of family is nothing but possessiveness.

That search for security again expresses itself through class divisions, which develop into the stupidity of nationalism and imperialism, breeding hatred, racial antagonism, and the ultimate cruelty of war. So through our own egotistic desires we have created a world of nationalities and conflicting sovereign governments, whose function is to prepare for war and force man against man.

Then there is the search for egotistic security, certainty, through what we call religion. You like fondly to believe that divine beings have created these organized forms of belief which we call religions. You yourself have created them for your own convenience; through ages they have become sanctified, and you have now become enslaved to them. There can never be ideal religions, so let us not waste our time discussing them. They can exist only in theory, not in reality. Let us examine how we have created religions and in what manner we are enslaved to them. If you deeply examine them as they are, you will see that they are nothing but the vested interest of organized belief—holding, separating, and exploiting man. As you are objectively seeking security, so also you are seeking subjectively a different kind of security, certainty, which you call immortality. You crave egotistic continuance in the hereafter, calling it immortality. Later in my talks I will explain what to me is true immortality.

In your search for that security, fear is born, and so you submit yourself to another who promises you that immortality. Through fear you create a spiritual authority, and to administer that authority there are priests who exploit you through belief, dogma, and creed, through show, pomp, and pageantry, which throughout the world is called religion. It is essentially based on fear, though you may call it the love of God or truth; it is, if you examine it intelligently, nothing but the result of fear and, therefore, it must become one of the means of exploiting man. Through your own desire for immortality, for selfish continuance, you have built this illusion which you call religion, and you are unconsciously or consciously caught in it. Or you may not belong to any particular religion, but you may belong to some sect which subtly promises a reward, a subtle inflation of the ego in the hereafter. Or you may not belong to any society or sect, but there may be an inward desire, hidden and concealed, to seek your own immortality. So long as there is a desire for self-continuance in any form, there must be fear, which creates authority, and from this there come the subtle cruelty and stupidity of submitting oneself to exploitation. This exploitation is so subtle, so refined, that one becomes enamored of it, calling it spiritual progress and advancement toward perfection.

Now you, the individual, must become conscious of all this intricate structure, conscious of the source of fear, and be willing to eradicate it, whatever be the consequence. This means coming into conflict individually with the existing ideals and values; and when the mind frees itself from the false, there can be the creation of right environment for the whole.

Your first concern is to become conscious of the prison; then you will see that your own thought is continually trying to avoid coming into conflict with the values of the prison. This escape creates ideals which, however beautiful, are but illusions. It is one of the tricks of the mind to escape into an ideal, because if it does not escape, it must come directly into conflict with the prison, with the environment. That is, the mind wants to escape into an illusion rather than face the suffering which will inevitably arise when it begins to question the values, the morality, the religion of the prison.

So what matters is to come into conflict with the traditions and values of the society and religion in which you are caught, and not intellectually escape through an ideal. When you begin to question these values, you begin to awaken that true intelligence which alone can solve the many human problems.

As long as the mind is caught up in false values, there cannot be fulfillment. Completeness alone will reveal truth, the movement of eternal life.

Mexico City, October 20, 1935

WHAT ARE YOU SEEKING?

It is my purpose during these talks not so much to give a system of thought as to awaken thought, and to do that I am going to make certain statements, naturally not dogmatic, which I hope you will consider. As you consider them, there will arise many questions; if you will kindly put these to me, I will try to answer them, and thus we can discuss further what I have to say.

I wonder why most of you come here? Presumably you are seeking something. And what are you seeking? You cannot answer that question, naturally, because your search varies, the object of your search varies; the object of your search is constantly changing, so you do not definitely know what you seek, what you want. But you have established, unfortunately, a habit of going from one supposed spiritual teacher to another supposed spiritual teacher, of joining various organizations, societies, and of following systems; in other words, trying to find out what gives you greater and greater satisfaction, excitement.

This process of going from one school of thought to another, from one system of thought to another, from one teacher to another, you call the search for truth. In other words, you are going from one idea to another idea, from one system of thought to another, accumulating, hoping to understand life, trying to fathom its significance, its struggles, each time declaring that you have found something.

Now, I hope you won't say at the end of my talks that you have found something, because the moment you have found something you are already lost; it is an anchor to which mind clings and, therefore, that eternal movement, this true search of which I am going to speak, ceases. And most minds are looking for a definite aim, with this definite desire to find, and when once there is established this desire, you will find something. But it won't be something living; it will be a dead thing that you will find and, therefore, you will put that away to turn to another; and this process of continually choosing, continually discarding, you call acquiring wisdom, experience, or truth.

Probably most of you have come here with this attitude, consciously or unconsciously, so your thought is expended merely on the search for schemes and confirmations, on the desire to join a movement or form groups, without the clarity of the fundamental or trying to understand what these fundamental things of life mean. So as I said, I am not putting forward an ideal to be imitated, a goal to be found; but my purpose is, rather, to awaken that thought by which the mind can liberate itself from these things which we have established, which we have taken for granted as being true.

Now, each one tries to immortalize the product of environment; that thing which is the result of the environment we try to make eternal. That is, the various fears, hopes, longings, prejudices, likes, and personal views which we glorify as our temperament are, after all, the result, the product, of environment; and this bundle of memories, which is the result of environment, the product of the reactions to environment, becomes that consciousness which we call the "I." Is that not so? The whole struggle is between the result of environment, with which mind identifies itself and becomes the "I," between that and environment. After all, the "I," the consciousness with which the mind identifies itself, is the result of environment. The struggle takes place between that "I" and the constantly changing environment.

You are continually seeking immortality for this "I." In other words, falsehood tries to become the real, the eternal. When you understand the significance of the environment, there is no reaction and, therefore, no conflict between the reaction, that is, between what we call the "I" and the creator of the reaction, which is the environment. So this seeking for immortality, this craving to be certain, to be lasting, is called the process of evolution, the process of acquiring truth or God or the understanding of life. And anyone who helps you toward this, who helps you to immortalize reaction, which we call the "I," you make of him your redeemer, your savior, your master, your teacher, and you follow his system. You follow him with thought, or without thought; with thought when you think that you are following him with intelligence because he is going to lead you to immortality, to the realization of that ecstasy. That is, you want another to immortalize for you that reaction which is the outcome of environment, which is in itself inherently false. Out of the desire to immortalize that which is false you create religions, sociological systems and divisions, political methods, economic panaceas, and moral standards. So gradually in this process of developing systems to make the individual immortal, lasting, secure, the individual is completely lost, and he comes into conflict with the creations of his own search, with the creations which are born out of his longing to be secure and which he calls immortality.

After all, why should religions exist? Religions as divisions of thought have grown, have been glorified and nourished by sets of beliefs because there is this desire that you shall realize, that you shall attain, that there shall be immortality.

And again, moral standards are merely the creations of society, so that the individual may be held within its bondage. To me, morality cannot be standardized. There cannot be at the same time morality and standards. There can only be intelligence, which is not, which cannot be, standardized. But we shall go into that in my later talks.

So this continual search in which each one of us is caught up, the search for happiness, for truth, for reality, for health—this continual desire is cultivated by each one of us in order that we may be secure, permanent. And out of that search for permanency, there must be conflict, conflict between the result of environment, that is, the "I," and the environment itself.

Now if you come to think of it, what is the "I"? When you talk about "I," "mine," my house, my enjoyment, my wife, my child, my love, my temperament, what is that? It is nothing but the result of environment, and there is a conflict between that result, the "I," and the environment itself. Conflict can only, and must inevitably, exist between the false and the false, not between truth and the false. Isn't that so? There cannot be conflict between what is true and what is false. But there can be conflict and there must be conflict between two false things, between the degrees of falseness, between the opposites.

So do not think this struggle between the self and the environment, which you call the true struggle, is true. Isn't there a struggle taking place in each one of you between yourself and your environment, your surroundings, your husband, your wife, your child, your neighbor, your society, your political organizations? Is there not a constant battle going on? You consider that battle necessary in order to help you to realize happiness, truth, immortality, or ecstasy. To put it differently: What you consider to be the truth is but self-consciousness, the "I," which is all the time trying to become immortal, and the environment, which I say is the continual movement of the false. This movement of the false becomes your ever-changing environment, which is called progress, evolution.

So to me, happiness, or truth, or God, cannot be found as the outcome of the result of environment, the "I," the continually changing conditions.

I will try to put it again, differently. There is conflict, of which each one of you is conscious, between yourself and the environment, the conditions. Now, you say to yourself, "If I can conquer environment, overcome it, dominate it, I shall find out, I shall understand"; so there is this continual battle going on between yourself and environment.

Now, what is the "yourself"? It is but the result, the product, of environment. So what are you doing? You are fighting one false thing with another false thing, and environment will be false so long as you do not understand it. Therefore, the environment is producing that consciousness which you call the "I," which is continually trying to become immortal. And to make it immortal there must be many ways, there must be means, and therefore you have religions, systems, philosophies, all the nuisances and barriers that you have created. Hence, there must be conflict between the result of environment and environment itself; and, as I said, there can be conflict only between the false and the false; never between truth and the false, whereas in your minds there is this firmly established idea that in this struggle between the result of environment, which is the "I," and the environment itself, lies power, wisdom, the path to eternity, to reality, truth, happiness.

Our vital concern should be with this environment, not with the conflict, not how to overcome it, not how to run away from it. By questioning the environment and trying to understand its significance, we shall find out its true worth. Isn't that so? Most of us are enmeshed, caught up in the process of trying to overcome, to run away from circumstances, environment; we are not trying to find out what it means, what is its cause, its significance, its value. When you see the significance of environment, it means drastic action, a tremendous upheaval in your life, a complete, revolutionary change of ideas, in which there is no authority, no imitation. But very few are willing to see the significance of environment, because it means change, a radical change, a revolutionary change, and very few people want that. So most people, vast numbers of people, are concerned with the evasion of environment; they cover it up, or try to find new substitutions by getting rid of Jesus Christ and setting up a new savior; by seeking new teachers in place of the old, but they do not ever inquire whether they need a guide at all. This alone would help, this alone would give the true significance of that particular demand.

So where there is a search for substitution, there must be authority, the following of leadership, and hence the individual becomes but a cog in the social and religious machinery of life. If you look closely you will see that your search is nothing but a search for comfort and security and escape; not a search for understanding, not a search for truth, but rather a search for an evasion and, therefore, a search for the conquering of all obstacles; after all, all conquering is but substitution, and in substitution there is no understanding.

There are escapes through religions, with their edicts, moral standards, fears, authorities; and escapes through self-expression; what you call self-expression, what the vast majority of people call self-expression, is but the reaction against environment, is but the effort to express oneself through reaction against that environment—self-expression through art, through science, through various forms of action. Here I am not including the true, spontaneous expressions of beauty, of art, of science; they in themselves are complete. I am talking of the man who is seeking these things as a means of self-expression. A real artist does not talk about his self-expression, he is expressing that which he intensely feels; but there are so many spurious artists, like the spurious spiritual people, who are all the time seeking self-expression as a means of getting something, some satisfaction which they cannot find in the environment in which they live.

Through this search for security and permanency, we have established religions—with all their inanities, divisions, exploitations—as means of escape; and these means of escape become so vital, so important, because, to tackle environment, that is, the conditions about us, demands tremendous action, voluntary, dynamic action, and very few are willing to take that action. On the contrary, you are willing to be forced to an action by environment, by circumstances; that is, if a man becomes highly moral and virtuous through depression, you say what a nice man he is, how he has changed. For that change you depend upon environment; and so long as there is the dependence on environment for righteous action, there must be means of escape, substitutions, call it religion or what you will, whereas for the true artist, who is also truly spiritual, there is spontaneous expression, which in itself is sufficient, complete, whole.

So what are you doing? What is happening to each one of you? What are you trying to do in your lives? You are seeking; and what are you seeking? There is a conflict between yourself and the constant movement of environment. You are seeking a means to overcome that environment, so as to perpetuate your own self, which is but the result of that environment; or, because you have been thwarted so often by environment, which prevents you from self-expressing, as you call it, you seek a new means of self-expression through service to humanity, through economic adjustments, and all the rest of it.

Each one has to find out for what he is searching; if he is not searching, then there is satisfaction and decay. If there is conflict, there is the desire to overcome that conflict, to escape from that conflict, to dominate it. And as I have said, conflict can exist only between two false things, between that supposed reality which you call the "I," which to me is nothing else but the result of environment, and the environment itself. If your mind is merely concerned with the overcoming of that struggle, then you are perpetuating falseness and hence, there is more conflict, more sorrow. But if you understand the significance of environment, that is, wealth, poverty, exploitation, oppression, nationalities, religions, and all the inanities of social life in modern existence, not trying to overcome them but seeing their significance, then there must be individual action, and complete revolution of ideas and thought. Then there is no longer a struggle, but rather light dispelling darkness. There is no conflict between light and darkness. There is no conflict between truth and that which is false. There is only conflict where there are opposites.

Ojai, California, June 16, 1934

THE SIGNIFICANCE OF ENVIRONMENT

You may remember that yesterday I was talking about the birth of conflict, and how the mind seeks a solution for it. I want to deal this morning with the whole idea of conflict and disharmony, and show the utter futility of mind trying to seek a solution for conflict, because the mere search for the solution will not do away with the conflict itself. When you seek a solution, a means of dissolving the conflict, you merely try to superimpose, or substitute in its place, a new set of ideas, a new set of theories, or you try to run away from conflict altogether. When people desire a solution for their conflict, that is what they seek.

If you observe, you will see that when there is conflict, you are at once seeking a solution for it. You want to find a way out of that conflict, and you generally do find a way out; but you have not solved the conflict, you have merely shifted it by substituting a new environment, a new condition, which will in turn produce further conflict. So let us look into this whole idea of conflict, from where it arises, and what we can do with it.

Now, conflict is the result of environment, isn't it? To put it differently, what is environment? When are you conscious of environment? Only when there is conflict and a resistance to that environment. So, if you observe, if you look into your lives, you will see that conflict is continually twisting, perverting, shaping your lives; and intelligence, which is the perfect harmony of mind and heart, has no part in your lives at all. That is, environment is continually shaping, molding your lives to action, and naturally out of that continual twisting, molding, shaping, perversion, conflict is born. So where there is this constant process of conflict there cannot be intelligence. And yet we think that by continually going through conflict we shall arrive at that intelligence, that fullness, and that plenitude of ecstasy. But by the accumulation of conflict we cannot find out how to live intelligently; you can find out how to live intelligently only when you understand the environment which is creating conflict, and mere substitution, that is, the introduction of new conditions, is not going to solve the conflict. And yet if you observe, you will see that when there is conflict, mind is seeking a substitution. We either say, "It is heredity, economic conditions, past environment," or we assert our belief in karma, reincarnation, evolution; so we are trying to give excuses for the present conflict in which the mind is caught, and are not trying to find out what is the cause of conflict itself, which is to inquire into the significance of environment.

Conflict then can exist only between environment—environment being economic and social conditions, political domination, neighbors—between that environment, and the result of environment, which is the "I." Conflict can exist only so long as there is reaction to that environment which produces the "I," the self. The majority of people are unconscious of this conflict—the conflict between one's self, which is but the result of the environment, and the environment itself; very few are conscious of this continuous battle. One becomes conscious of that conflict, that disharmony, that struggle between the false creation of the environment, which is the "I," and the environment itself, only through suffering. Isn't that so? It is only through acuteness of suffering, acuteness of pain, acuteness of disharmony, that you become conscious of the conflict.

What happens when you become conscious of the conflict? What happens when in that intensity of suffering you become fully conscious of the battle, the struggle which is going on? Most people want an immediate relief, an immediate answer. They want to shelter themselves from that suffering and, therefore, they find various means of escape such as religions, excitements, inanities, and the many mysterious avenues of escape which we have created through our desire to protect ourselves from this struggle. Suffering makes one conscious of this conflict, and yet suffering will not lead man to that fullness, to that richness, that plenitude, that ecstasy of life, because after all, suffering can only awaken the mind to great intensity. And when the mind is acute, then it begins to question—the environment, the conditions, and in that questioning, intelligence is functioning; and it is only intelligence that will lead man to the fullness of life and to the discovery of the significance of sorrow. Intelligence begins to function in the moment of acuteness of suffering, when mind and heart are no longer escaping, escaping through the various avenues which you have so cleverly made, which are so apparently reasonable, factual, real. If you observe carefully, without prejudice, you will see that so long as there is an escape you are not solving, you are not coming face-to-face with conflict and, therefore, your suffering is merely the accumulating of ignorance. That is, when one ceases to escape, through the well-known channels, then in that acuteness of suffering, intelligence begins to function.

Please, I do not want to give you examples and similes, because I want you to think it out, and if I give examples I do all the thinking and you merely listen, whereas if you begin to think about what I am saying, you will see, you will observe for yourself how mind, being accustomed to so many substitutions, authorities, escapes, never comes to that point of acuteness of suffering which demands that intelligence must function. And it is only when intelligence is fully functioning that there can be the utter dissolution of the cause of conflict.

Whenever there is the lack of understanding of environment there must be conflict. Environment gives birth to conflict, and so long as we do not understand environment, conditions, surroundings, and are merely seeking substitutions for these conditions, we are evading one conflict and meeting another. But if in that acuteness of suffering which brings forth in its fullness a conflict, if in that state we begin to question environment, then we shall understand the true worth of environment, and intelligence then functions naturally. Hitherto mind has identified itself with conflict, with environment, with evasions and, therefore, with suffering; that is, you say, "I suffer," whereas in that state of acuteness of suffering, in that intensity of suffering in which there is no longer escape, mind itself becomes intelligence.

To put it again differently, so long as we are seeking solutions, so long as we are seeking substitutions, authorities for the cause and the alleviation of conflict, there must be identification of the mind with the particular; whereas if the mind is in that state of intense suffering in which all the avenues of escape are blocked, then intelligence will be awakened, will function naturally and spontaneously.

Please, if you experiment with this, you will see that I am not giving you theories, but something with which you can work, something which is practical. You have so many environments, which have been imposed on you by society, by religion, by economic conditions, by social distinctions, by exploitation, and political oppressions. The "I" has been created by that imposition, by that compulsion; there is the "I" in you which is fighting the environment and hence, there is conflict. It is no use creating a new environment, because the same thing will still exist. But if in that conflict there is conscious sorrow and suffering—and there is always suffering in all conflict, only man wants to run away from that struggle and he therefore seeks substitutes—if in that acuteness of suffering you stop searching for substitutes and really face the facts, you will see that mind, which is the summation of intelligence, begins to discover the true worth of environment, and then you will realize that mind is free of conflict. In the very acuteness of suffering lies its own dissolution. So therein is the understanding of the cause of conflict.

Also, one should bear in mind that what we call accumulation of sorrows does not lead to intensity, nor does the multiplication of suffering lead to its own dissolution; for acuteness of mind in suffering comes only when the mind has ceased to escape. And no conflict will awaken that suffering, that acuteness of suffering, when the mind is trying to escape, for in escape there is no intelligence.

To put it briefly again, before I answer the questions that have been given to me: First of all, everyone is caught up in suffering and conflict, but most people are unconscious of that conflict; they are merely seeking substitutions, solutions, and escapes, whereas if they cease seeking escapes and begin to question the environment which causes that conflict, then mind becomes acute, alive, intelligent. In that intensity mind becomes intelligence and, therefore, sees the full worth and significance of the environment, which creates conflict.

Please, I am sure half of you don't understand this, but it doesn't matter. What you can do, if you will, is to think this over, really think over it, and see if what I am saying is not true. But to think over it is not to intellectualize it, that is, to sit down and make it vanish away through the intellect. To find out if what I am saying is true, you have to put it into action, and to put it into action you must question the environment. That is, if you are in conflict, naturally you must question the environment, but most minds have become so perverted that they are not aware that they are seeking solutions, escapes through their marvelous theories. They reason perfectly, but their reasoning is based on the search for escape, of which they are wholly unconscious.

So if there is conflict, and if you want to find out the cause of that conflict, naturally the mind must discover it through acuteness of thought and, therefore, the questioning of all that which environment places about you—your family, your neighbors, your religions, your political authorities; and by questioning there will be action against the environment. There is the family, the neighbor and the state, and by questioning their significance you will see that intelligence is spontaneous, not to be acquired, not to be cultivated. You have sown the seed of awareness and that produces the flower of intelligence.

QUESTIONER: You say that the "I" is the product of environment. Do you mean that a perfect environment could be created which would not develop the "I" consciousness? If so, the perfect freedom of which you speak is a matter of creating the right environment. Is this correct?

KRISHNAMURTI: Wait a minute. Can there ever be right environment, perfect environment? There cannot. So let us reason together, go into it fully.

What is environment? Environment is created, this whole human structure has been created, by human fears, longings, hopes, desires, attainments. Now, you cannot make a perfect environment because each man is creating, according to his fancies and desires, new sets of conditions; but having an intelligent mind, you can pierce through all these false environments and, therefore, be free of that "I" consciousness. Please, the "I" consciousness, the sense of "mine," is the result of environment, isn't it? I don't think we need discuss it because it is pretty obvious.

If the state gave you your house and everything you required, there would be no need of "my house"; there might be some other sense of "mine," but we are discussing the particular. As that has not been the case with you, there is the sense of "mine," possessiveness. That is the result of environment; that "I" is but the false reaction to environment, whereas if the mind begins to question the environment itself, there is no longer a reaction to environment. Therefore, we are not concerned with the possibility of there ever being a perfect environment.

After all, what is perfect environment? Each man will tell you what to him is a perfect environment. The artist will say one thing, the financier another, the cinema actress another; each man asks for a perfect environment which satisfies him, in other words, which does not create conflict in him. Therefore, there cannot be a perfect environment. But if there is intelligence, then environment has no value, no significance, because intelligence is then freed from circumstance; it is functioning fully.

The question is not whether we can create a perfect environment, but rather how to awaken that intelligence which shall be free of environment, imperfect or perfect. I say you can awaken that intelligence by questioning the full value of any environment in which your mind is caught up. Then you will see that you are free of any particular environment, because then you are functioning intelligently, not being twisted, perverted, shaped by environment.

Q: Surely you cannot mean what your words seem to convey. When I see vice rampant in the world, I feel an intense desire to fight against that vice and against all the suffering it creates in the lives of my fellow human beings. This means great conflict, for when I try to help I am often viciously opposed. How then can you say that there is no conflict between the false and the true?

K. I said yesterday that there can be struggle only between two false things, conflict between the environment and the result of environment, which is the "I." Now between these two lie innumerable avenues of escape, which the "I" has created, which we call vice, goodness, morality, moral standards, fears, and all the many opposites; and the struggle can exist only between the two, between the false creation of the environment, which is the "I," and the environment itself. But there cannot be struggle between truth and that which is false. Surely that is obvious, isn't it? You may be viciously opposed because the other man is ignorant. It doesn't mean you mustn't fight—but don't assume the righteousness of fighting. Please, you know there is a natural way of doing things, a spontaneous, sweet way of doing things, without this aggressive, vicious righteousness.

First of all, in order to fight, you must know what you are fighting, so there must be understanding of the fundamental, not of the divisions between the false things. Now we are so conscious, we are so fully conscious of the divisions between the false things, between the result and the environment, that we fight them and, therefore, we want to reform, we want to change, we want to alter, without fundamentally changing the whole structure of human life. That is, we still want to preserve the "I" consciousness which is the false reaction to environment; we want to preserve that and yet want to alter the world. In other words, you want to have your own bank account, your own possessions; you want to preserve the sense of "mine," and yet you want to alter the world so that there shall not be this idea of "mine" and "yours."

So what one has to do is to find out if one is dealing with the fundamental, or merely with the superficial. And to me the superficial will exist so long as you are merely concerned with the alteration of environment so as to alleviate conflict. That is, you still want to cling to the "I" consciousness as "mine," but yet desire to alter the circumstances so that they will not create conflict in that "I." I call that superficial thought, and from that there naturally is superficial action, whereas if you think fundamentally, that is, question the very result of the environment, which is the "I" and, therefore, question the environment itself, then you are acting fundamentally and, therefore, lastingly. And in that there is an ecstasy, in that there is a joy of which now you do not know because you are afraid to act fundamentally.

Q: In your talk yesterday you spoke of environment as the movement of the false. Do you include in environment all the creations of nature, including human forms?

K: Doesn't environment continually change? Doesn't it? For most people it doesn't change because change implies continual adjustment and, therefore, continual awareness of mind, and most people are concerned with the static condition of the environment. Yet environment is moving because it is beyond your control, and it is false so long as you do not understand its significance.

Does environment include human forms? Why set them apart from nature? We are not concerned so much with nature, because we have almost brought nature under control, but we have not understood the environment created by human beings. Look at the relationship between peoples, between two human beings, and all the conditions which human beings have created that we have not understood, even though we have largely understood and conquered nature through science.

So we are not concerned with the stability, with the continuance, of an environment which we understand, because the moment we understand it there is no conflict. That is, we are seeking security, emotional and mental, and we are happy so long as that security is assured and, therefore, we never question environment, and hence the constant movement of environment is a false thing which is creating disturbance in each one. As long as there is conflict, it indicates that we have not understood the conditions placed about us; and that movement of environment remains false so long as we do not inquire into its significance, and we can only discover it in that state of acute consciousness of suffering.

Q: It is perfectly clear to me that the "I" consciousness is the result of environment, but do you not see that the "I" did not originate for the first time in this life? From what you say it is obvious that the "I" consciousness, being the result of environment, must have begun in the distant past and will continue in the future.

K: I know this is a question to catch me about reincarnation. But that doesn't matter. Now let's look into it. First of all, you will admit, if you think about it, that the "I" is the result of environment. Now to me it doesn't matter whether it is the past environment or present environment. After all, environment is of the past also. You have done something which you haven't understood, you did something yesterday which you haven't understood, and that pursues you until you understand it. You cannot solve that past environment till you are fully conscious in the present. So it doesn't matter whether the mind is crippled by past or present conditions. What matters is that you shall understand the environment and this will liberate the mind from conflict.

Some people believe that the "I" has had a birth in the distant past and will continue in the future. It is irrelevant to me, it has no significance at all. I will show you why. If the "I" is the result of the environment, if the "I" is but the essence of conflict, then the mind must be concerned not with that continuance of conflict, but with freedom from that conflict. So it does not matter whether it is the past environment which is crippling the mind, or the present which is perverting it, or whether the "I" has had a birth in the distant past. What matters is that in that state of suffering, in that consciousness, that conscious acuteness of suffering, there is the dissolution of the "I."

This brings in the idea of karma. You know what it means, that you have a burden in the present, the burden of the past in the present. That is, you bring with you the environment of the past into the present, and because of that burden, you control the future, you shape the future. If you come to think of it, it must be so, that if your mind is perverted by the past, naturally the future must also be twisted, because if you have not understood the environment of yesterday it must be continued today and, therefore, as you don't understand today, naturally you will not understand tomorrow either. That is, if you have not seen the full significance of an environment or of an action, this perverts your judgment of today's environment, of today's action born of environment, which will again pervert you tomorrow. So one is caught up in this vicious circle, and hence the idea of continual rebirth, rebirth of memory, or rebirth of the mind continued by environment.

But I say mind can be free of the past, of past environment, past hindrances and, therefore, you can be free of the future, because then you are living dynamically in the present, intensely, supremely. In the present is eternity, and to understand that, mind must be free of the burden of the past; and to free the mind of the past there must be an intense questioning of the present, not the considering of how the "I" will continue in the future.

Ojai, California, June 17, 1934

Today, we are going to answer questions.

QUESTIONER: What is the difference between self-discipline and suppression?

KRISHNAMURTI: I don't think there is much difference between the two because both deny intelligence. Suppression is the gross form of the subtler self-discipline, which is also repression; that is, both suppression as well as self-discipline are mere adjustments to environment. One is the gross form of adjustment, which is suppression, and the other, self-discipline, is the subtle form. Both are based on fear: suppression, on an obvious fear; the other, self-discipline, on fear born of loss, or on fear which expresses itself through gain.

Self-discipline—what you call self-discipline—is merely an adjustment to an environment which we have not completely understood; therefore, in that adjustment there must be the denial of intelligence. Why has one ever to discipline one's self? Why does one discipline, force one's self to mold after a particular pattern? Why do so many people belong to the various schools of disciplines, supposed to lead to spirituality, to greater understanding, greater unfoldment of thought? You will see that the more you discipline the mind, train the mind, the greater its limitations. Please, one has to think this over carefully and with delicate perception and not get confused by introducing other issues. Here I am using the word *self-discipline* as in the question, that is, disciplining one's self after a certain pattern, preconceived or preestablished and, therefore, with the desire to attain, to gain, whereas to me the very process of discipline, this continual twisting of mind to a particular preestablished pattern, must eventually cripple the mind. The mind, which is really intelligent, is free of self-discipline, for intelligence is born out of the questioning of environment and the discovery of the true significance of environment. In that discovery is true adjustment, not the adjustment to a particular pattern or condition, but the adjustment through understanding, which is, therefore, free of the particular condition.

Take a primitive man; what does he do? In him there is no discipline, no control, no suppression. He does what he desires to do, this primitive. The intelligent man also does what he desires, but with intelligence. Intelligence is not born out of self-discipline or suppression. In the one instance it is wholly the pursuit of desire, the primitive man pursuing the object he desires. In the other instance, the intelligent man sees the significance of desire and sees the conflict; the primitive man does not, he pursues anything he desires and creates suffering and pain. So to me self-discipline and suppression are both alike—they both deny intelligence.

Please experiment with what I have said about discipline, self-discipline. Don't reject it, don't say you must have self-discipline, because there will be chaos in the world—as if there were not already chaos; and again, don't merely accept what I say, agreeing that it is true. I am telling you something with which I have experimented and which I have found to be true. Psychologically I think it is true, because self-discipline implies a mind that is tethered to a particular thought or belief or ideal, a mind that is held by a condition; and as an animal that is tethered to a post can only wander within the distance of its rope, so does the mind which is tethered to a belief, which is perverted through self-discipline, wander only within the limitation of that condition. Therefore, such a mind is not mind at all, it is incapable of thought. It may be capable of adjustment between the limitations of the post and the farthest point of its reach; but such a mind, such a heart cannot really think and feel. The mind and the heart are disciplined, crippled, perverted, through denying thought, denying affection. So you must observe, become aware how your own thought, how your own feelings are functioning, without wanting to guide them in any particular direction. First of all, before you guide them, find out how they are functioning. Before you try to change and alter thought and feeling, find out the manner of their working, and you will see that they are continually adjusting themselves within the limitations established by that point fixed by desire and the fulfillment of that desire. In awareness there is no discipline.

Let me take an example. Suppose that you are class-minded, class-conscious, snobbish. You don't know that you are snobbish, but you want to find out if you are; how will you find out? By becoming conscious of your thought and your emotions. Then what happens? Suppose that you discover that you are snobbish, then that very discovery creates a disturbance, a conflict, and that very conflict dissolves snobbishness, whereas if you merely discipline the mind not to be snobbish, you are developing a different characteristic which is the opposite of being a snob, and being deliberate, therefore false, is equally pernicious.

So, because we have established various patterns, various goals, aids, which we are continually—consciously or unconsciously—pursuing, we discipline our minds and hearts toward them and, therefore, there must be control, perversion, whereas if you begin to inquire into the conditions that create conflict, and thereby awaken intelligence, then that intelligence itself is so supreme that it is continually in movement and, therefore, there is never a static point which can create conflict.

Q: Granted that the "I" is made up of reactions from environment, by what method can one escape its limitations; or how does one go about the process of reorientation, in order to avoid conflict between the two false things?

K: First of all, you want to know the method of escape from the limitations. Why? Why do you ask? Please, why do you always ask for a method, for a system? What does it indicate, this desire for a method? Every demand for a method indicates the desire to escape. You want me to lay down a system so that you may imitate that system. In other words, you want a system invented for you to superimpose on those conditions which are creating conflict, so that you can escape from all conflict. In other words you merely seek to adjust yourselves to a pattern, in order to escape from conflict or from your environment. That is the desire behind the demand for a method, for a system. You know life is not Pelmanism. The desire for a method indicates essentially the desire to escape.

How does one go about the process of reorientation in order to avoid constant conflict between the two false things? First of all, are you aware that you are in conflict, before you want to know how to get away from it? Or, being aware of conflict, are you merely seeking a refuge, a shelter which will not create further conflict? So let us decide whether you want a shelter, a safety zone, which will no longer yield conflict, whether you want to escape from the present conflict to enter a condition in which there shall be no conflict; or whether you are unaware, unconscious of this conflict in which you exist. If you are unconscious of the conflict, that is, the battle that is taking place between that self and the environment, if you are unconscious of that battle, then why do you seek further remedies? Remain unconscious. Let the conditions themselves produce the necessary conflict, without your rushing after, invoking artificially, falsely, a conflict which does not exist in your mind and heart. And you create artificially a conflict because you are afraid you are missing something. Life will not miss you. If you think it does, something is wrong with you. Perhaps you are neurotic, not normal.

If you are in conflict, you will not ask me for a method. Were I to give you a method you would merely be disciplining yourself according to that method, trying to imitate an ideal, a pattern which I have laid down and, therefore, destroying your own intelligence, whereas if you are really conscious of that conflict, in that consciousness suffering will become acute and in that acuteness, in that intensity, you will dissolve the cause of suffering, which is the lack of understanding of the environment.

You know we have lost all sense of living normally, simply, directly. To get back to that normality, that simplicity, that directness, you cannot follow methods, you cannot merely become automatic machines; and I am afraid most of us are seeking methods because we think that through them we shall realize fullness, stability, and permanency. To me methods lead to slow stagnation and decay and they have nothing to do with real spirituality, which is, after all, the summation of intelligence.

Q: You speak of the necessity of a drastic revolution in the life of the individual. If he does not want to revolutionize his outward personal environment because of the suffering it would cause to his family and friends, will inward revolution lead him to the freedom from all conflict?

K: First of all, sirs, don't you also feel that a drastic revolution in the life of the individual is necessary? Or are you merely satisfied with things as they are, with your ideas of progress, evolution, and your desire for attainment, with your longings and fluctuating pleasures? You know, the moment you begin to think, really begin to feel, you must have this burning desire for a drastic change, drastic revolution, complete reorientation of thinking. Now, if you feel that that is necessary, then neither family nor friends will stand in the way. Then there is neither an outward revolution nor an inward revolution; there is only revolution, change. But the moment you begin to limit it by saying, "I must not hurt my family, my friends, my priest, my capitalistic exploiter or state exploiter," then you really don't see the necessity for radical change, you merely seek a change of environment. In that there is merely lethargy, which creates further false environment and continues the conflict.

I think we give the rather false excuse that we must not hurt our families and our friends. You know when you want to do something vital, you do it, irrespective of your family and friends, don't you? Then you don't consider that you are going to hurt them. It is beyond your control; you feel so intensely, you think so completely that it carries you beyond the limitation of family circles, classified bondages. But you begin to consider family, friends, ideals, beliefs, traditions, the established order of things, only when you are still clinging to a particular safety, when there is not that inward richness, but merely the dependence on external stimulation for that inward richness. So if there is that full consciousness of suffering, brought about by conflict, then you are not held in the bondage of any particular orthodoxy, friends, or family. You want to find out the cause of that suffering, you want to find out the significance of the environment which creates that conflict; then in that there is no personality, no limited thought of the "I." But it is only when you cling to that limited thought of the "I" that you have to consider how far you shall wander and how far you shall not wander.

Surely truth, or that Godhead of understanding, is not to be found by clinging either to family or tradition or habit. It is to be found only when you are completely naked, stripped of your longings, hopes, securities; and in that direct simplicity is the richness of life.

Q: Can you explain why environment started being false instead of true? What is the origin of all this mess and trouble?

K: Who do you think created environment? Some mysterious God? Please, just a minute; who created environment, the social structure, the economic, the religious structure? We. Each one has contributed individually, until it has become collective, and the individual who has helped to create the collective now is lost in the collective, for it has become his mold, his environment. Through the desire for security—financial, moral, and spiritual—you have created a capitalistic environment in which there is nationality, class distinction, and exploitation. We have created it, you and I. This thing hasn't miraculously come into being. You will again create another capitalistic, acquisitive system of a different kind, with a different nuance, with a different color, so long as you are seeking security. You may abolish this present pattern, but so long as there is possessiveness, you will create another capitalistic state, with a new phraseology, a new jargon.

And the same thing applies to religions, with all their absurd ceremonies, exploitations, fears. Who has created them? You and I. Throughout the centuries we have created these things and yielded to them through fear. It is the individual who has created false environment everywhere. And he has become a slave, and that false condition has resulted in a false search for the security of that self-consciousness which you call the "I," and hence, the constant battle between the "I" and the false environment.

You want to know who has created this environment and all this appalling mess and trouble, because you want a redeemer to lift you out of that trouble and set you in a new heaven. Clinging to all your particular prejudices, hopes, fears, and preferences, you have individually created this environment, so individually you must break it down and not wait for a system to come and sweep it away. A system will probably come and sweep it away and then you will merely become slaves to that system. The communistic system may come in, and then probably you will be using new words, but having the same reactions, only in a different manner, with a different tempo.

That is why I said the other day that if environment is driving you to a certain action, it is no longer righteous. It is only when there is action born out of the understanding of that environment that there is righteousness.

So individually we must become conscious. I assure you, you will then individually create something immense, not a society which is merely holding to an ideal and, therefore, decaying, but a society that is constantly in movement, not coming to a culmination and dying. Individuals establish a goal, strive after its attainment, and after attaining, collapse. They try all the time to reach some goal and stay at that stage which they have attained. As the individual so the state—the state is trying all the time to reach an ideal, a goal, whereas to me the individual must be in constant movement, must ever be becoming, not seeking a culmination, not pursuing a goal. Then self-expression, which is society, will be ever in constant movement.

Q: Do you consider that karma is the interaction between the false environment and the false "I"?

K: You know *karma* is a Sanskrit word which means to act, to do, to work, and also it implies cause and effect. Now karma is the bondage, the reaction born out of the environment, which the mind has not understood. As I tried to explain yesterday, if we do not understand a particular condition, naturally the mind is burdened with that condition, with that lack of understanding; and with that lack of understanding we function and act and, therefore, create further burdens, greater limitations.

So one has to find out what creates this lack of understanding, what prevents the individual from gathering the full significance of the environment, whether it be the past environment or the present. And to discover that significance, mind must really be free of prejudice. It is one of the most difficult things to be really free of a bias, of a temperament, of a twist; and to approach environment with a fresh openness, a directness, demands a great deal of perception. Most minds are biased through vanity, through the desire to impress others by being somebody, or through the desire to attain truth, or to escape from their environment, or expand their own consciousness—only they call this by a special spiritual name—or through their national prejudices. All these desires prevent the mind from perceiving directly the full worth of the environment; and as most minds are prejudiced, the first thing that one has to become conscious of is one's own limitations. And when you begin to be conscious, there is conflict in that consciousness. When you know that you are really brutally proud or conceited, in the very consciousness of conceit it begins to dissipate, because you perceive the absurdity of it; but if you begin merely to cover it up, it creates further diseases, further false reactions.

So to live each moment now without the burden of the past or of the present, without that crippling memory created by the lack of understanding, mind must ever meet things anew. It is fatal to meet life with the burden of certainty, with the conceit of knowledge, because, after all, knowledge is merely a thing of the past. So when you come to that life with a freshness, then you will know what it is to live without conflict, without this continual straining effort. Then you wander far on the floods of life.

Ojai, California, June 18, 1934

To me there is a reality, an immense living truth; and to comprehend that, there must be utter simplicity of thought. What is simple is infinitely subtle, what is simple is greatly delicate. There is a great subtlety, an infinite subtlety and delicacy, and if you use words merely as a means of getting to that delicacy, to that simplicity of thought, then I am afraid you will not comprehend what I want to convey. But if you would use the significance of words as a bridge to cross, then words will not become an illusion in which the mind is lost.

I say there is this living reality, call it God, truth, or what you like, and it cannot be found or realized through search. Where there is the implication of search, there must be contrast and duality; whenever mind is seeking, it must inevitably imply a division, a distinction, a contrast, which does not mean that mind must be contented, mind must be stagnant. There is that delicate poise, which is neither contentment, nor this ceaseless effort born of search, of this desire to attain, to achieve; and in that delicacy of poise lies simplicity, not the simplicity of having but few clothes or few possessions. I am not talking of such simplicity, which is merely a crude form, but of simplicity born of this delicacy of thought, in which there is neither search nor contentment.

As I said, search implies duality, contrast. Now where there is contrast, duality, there must be identification with one of the opposites, and from this there arises compulsion. When we say we search, our mind is rejecting something and seeking a substitute that will satisfy it, and thereby it creates duality, and from this there arises compulsion. That is, the choice of the one is the overcoming of the other, isn't it?

When we say we seek out or cultivate a new value, it is but the overcoming of that in which the mind is already caught up, which is its opposite. This choice is based on attraction to one or fear of the other, and this clinging through attraction, or rejection through fear, creates influence over the mind. Influence then is the negation of understanding and can exist only where there is division, the psychological division from which there arise distinctions such as class, national, religious, sex. That is, when the mind is trying to overcome, it must create duality, and that very duality negates understanding and creates the distinctions. That duality influences the mind, and hence a mind influenced by duality cannot understand the significance of environment or the significance of the cause of conflict. These psychological influences are merely reactions to environment from that center of "I" consciousness, of like and dislike, or antitheses, and naturally where there are antitheses, opposites, there can be no comprehension. From this distinction there arises the classification of influences as beneficial and evil. So as long as mind is influenced—and influence is born of attraction, opposites, antitheses—there must be the domination or compulsion of love, of intellect, of society; and this influence must be a hindrance to that understanding which is beauty, truth, and love itself.

Now, if you can become aware of this influence, then you can discern its cause. Most people seem to be aware superficially, not at the greatest depth. It is only when there is awareness at the greatest depth of consciousness, of thought and emotion, that you can discern the division that is created through influence, which negates understanding.

QUESTIONER: After listening to your talk about memory, I have completely lost mine, and I find I cannot remember my huge debts. I feel blissful. Is this liberation?

KRISHNAMURTI: Ask the person to whom you owe the money. I am afraid that there is some confusion with regard to what I have been trying to say concerning memory. If you rely on memory as a guide to conduct, as a means of activity in life, then that memory must impede your action, your conduct, because then that action or conduct is merely the result of calculation and, therefore, it has no spontaneity, no richness, no fullness of life. It does not mean that you must forget your debts. You cannot forget the past. You cannot blot it out of your mind. That is an impossibility. Subconsciously it will exist, but if that subconscious, dormant memory is influencing you unconsciously, is molding your action, your conduct, your whole outlook on life, then that influence must ever be creating further limitations, imposing further burdens on the functioning of intelligence.

For example, I have recently come from India; I have been to Australia and New Zealand, where I met various people, had many ideas and saw many sights. I can't forget these, though the memory of them may fade. But the reaction to the past may impede my full comprehension in the present; it may hinder the intelligent functioning of my mind. That is, if my experiences and remembrances of the past are becoming hindrances in the present through their reaction, then I cannot comprehend or live fully, intensely, in the present.

You react to the past because the present has lost its significance, or because you want to avoid the present; so you go back to the past and live in that emotional thrill, in that reaction of surging memory, because the present has little value. So when you say, "I have completely lost my memory," I am afraid you are fit for only one place. You cannot lose memory, but by living completely in the present, in the fullness of the moment, you become conscious of all the subconscious entanglements of memory, the dormant hopes and longings which surge forward and prevent you from functioning intelligently in the present. If you are aware of that, if you are aware of that hindrance, aware of it at its depth, not superficially, then the dormant subconscious memory, which is but the lack of understanding and incompleteness of living, disappears and, therefore, you meet each movement of environment, each swiftness of thought, anew.

Q: You say that the complete understanding of the outer and inner environment of the individual releases him from bondage and sorrow. Now, even in that state, how can one free himself from the indescribable sorrow which in the nature of things is caused by the death of someone he really loves?

K: What is the cause of suffering in this case? And what is it that we call suffering? Isn't suffering merely a shock to the mind to awaken it to its own insufficiency? The recognition of that insufficiency creates what we call sorrow. Suppose that you have been relying on your son or your husband or your wife to satisfy that insufficiency, that incompleteness; by the loss of that person whom you love, there is created the full consciousness of that emptiness, of that void, and out of that consciousness comes sorrow, and you say, "I have lost somebody."

So through death there is, first of all, the full consciousness of emptiness, which you have been carefully evading. Hence, where there is dependence there must be emptiness, shallowness, insufficiency and, therefore, sorrow and pain. We don't want to recognize that; we don't see that that is the fundamental cause. So we begin to say, "I miss my friend, my husband, my wife, my child. How am I to overcome this loss? How am I to overcome this sorrow?"

Now, all overcoming is but substitution. In that there is no understanding and, therefore, there can only be further sorrow, though momentarily you may find a substitution that will completely put the mind to sleep. If you don't seek an overcoming, then you turn to seances, mediums, or take shelter in the scientific proof that life continues after death. So you begin to discover various means of escape and substitution, which momentarily relieve you from suffering, whereas if there were the cessation of this desire to overcome and if there were really the desire to understand—to find out, fundamentally—what causes pain and sorrow, then you would discover that so long as there is loneliness, shallowness, emptiness, insufficiency, which in its outer expression is dependence, there must be pain. And you cannot fill that insufficiency by overcoming obstacles, by substitutions, by escaping or by accumulating, which is merely the cunning of the mind lost in the pursuit of gain.

Suffering is merely that high, intense clarity of thought and emotion which forces you to recognize things as they are. But this does not mean acceptance, resignation. When you see things as they are in the mirror of truth, which is intelligence, then there is a joy, an ecstasy; in that there is no duality, no sense of loss, no division. I assure you this is not theoretical. If you consider what I am now saying, with my answer to the first question about memory, you will see how memory creates greater and greater dependence, the continual looking back to an event emotionally, to get a reaction from it, which prevents the full expression of intelligence in the present.

Q: What suggestion or advice would you give to one who is hindered by strong sexual desire?

K: After all, where there is no creative expression of life, we give undue importance to sex, which becomes an acute problem. So the question is not what advice or suggestion I would give, or how one can overcome passion, sexual desire, but how to release that creative living, and not merely tackle one part of it, which is sex; that is, how to understand the wholeness, the completeness of life.

Now, through modern education, through circumstances and environment, you are driven to do something which you hate. You are repelled, but you are forced to do it because of your lack of proper equipment, proper training. In your work you are being prevented by circumstances, by conditions, from expressing yourself fundamentally, creatively, and so there must be an outlet; and this outlet becomes the sex problem or the drink problem or some idiotic, inane problem. All these outlets become problems.

Or you are artistically inclined. There are very few artists, but you may be inclined, and that inclination is continually being perverted, twisted, thwarted, so that you have no means of real self-expression and thus, undue importance comes to be given either to sex or to some religious mania. Or your ambitions are thwarted, curtailed, hindered, and so again undue importance is given to those things that should be normal. So, until you understand comprehensively your religious, political, economic, and social desires, and their hindrances, the natural functions of life will be of immense importance, and the first place in your life. Hence, all the innumerable problems of greed, of possessiveness, of sex, of social and racial distinctions have their false measure and false value. But if you were to deal with life, not in parts but as a whole, comprehensively, creatively, with intelligence, then you would see that these problems, which are enervating the mind and destroying creative living, disappear, and then intelligence functions normally, and in that there is an ecstasy.

Q: I have been under the impression that I have been putting your ideas into action; but I have no joy in life, no enthusiasm for any pursuit. My attempts at awareness have not cleared my confusion, nor have they brought any change or vitality into my life. My living has no more meaning for me now than it had when I started to listen to you seven years ago. What is wrong with me?

K: I wonder if the questioner has, first of all, understood what I have been saying before trying to put my ideas into action. And why should he put my ideas into action? And what are my ideas? And why are they my ideas? I am not giving you a mold or a code by which you can live, or a system which you can follow. All that I am saying is, that to live creatively, enthusiastically, intelligently, vitally, intelligence must function. That intelligence is perverted, hindered, by what one calls memory, and I have explained what I mean by that, so I won't go into it again. So long as there is this constant battle to achieve, so long as mind is influenced, there must be duality, and hence, pain, struggle; and our search for truth or for reality is but an escape from that pain.

And so I say, become aware that your effort, your struggle, your impinging memories are destroying your intelligence. To become aware is not to be superficially conscious, but to go into the full depth of consciousness so as not to leave undiscovered one unconscious reaction. All this demands thought; all this demands an alertness of mind and heart, not a mind that is cluttered up with beliefs, creeds, and ideals. Most minds are burdened with these and with the desire to follow. As you become conscious of your burden, don't say you mustn't have ideals, you mustn't have creeds, and repeat all the rest of the jargon. The very "must" creates another doctrine, another creed; merely become conscious and in the intensity of that consciousness, in the intensity of awareness, in that flame you will create such crisis, such conflict, that that very conflict itself will dissolve the hindrance.

I know some people come here year after year, and I try to explain these ideas in different ways each year, but I am afraid there is very little thought among the people who say, "We have been listening to you for seven years." I mean by thought, not mere intellectual reasoning, which is but ashes, but that poise between emotion and reason, between affection and thought; and that poise is not influenced, is not affected, by the conflict of the opposites. But if there is neither the capacity to think clearly, nor the intensity of feeling, how can you awaken, how can there be poise, how can there be this alertness, this awareness? So life becomes futile, inane, worthless.

Hence, the very first thing to do, if I may suggest it, is to find out why you are thinking in a certain way, and why you are feeling in a certain manner. Don't try to alter it, don't try to analyze your thoughts and your emotions; but become conscious of why you are thinking in a particular groove and from what motive you act. Although you can discover the motive through analysis, although you may find out something through analysis, it will not be real; it will be real only when you are intensely aware at the moment of the functioning of your thought and emotion; then you will see their extraordinary subtlety, their fine delicacy. So long as you have a "must" and a "must not," in this compulsion you will never discover that swift wandering of thought and emotion. And I am sure you have been brought up in the school of "must" and "must not" and hence, you have destroyed thought and feeling. You have been bound and crippled by systems, methods, by your teachers. So leave all those "musts" and "must nots." This does not mean that there shall be licentiousness, but become aware of a mind that is ever saying, "I must," and "I must not." Then as a flower blossoms forth of a morning, so intelligence happens, is there, functioning, creating comprehension.

Q: The artist is sometimes mentioned as one who has this understanding of which you speak, at least while working creatively.

But if someone disturbs or crosses him, he may react violently, excusing his reaction as a manifestation of temperament. Obviously he is not living completely at the moment. Does he really understand if he so easily slips back into self-consciousness?

K: Who is that person whom you call an artist? A man who is momentarily creative? To me he is not an artist. The man who merely at rare moments has this creative impulse and expresses that creativeness through perfection of technique, surely you would not call him an artist. To me, the true artist is one who lives completely, harmoniously, who does not divide his art from living, whose very life is that expression, whether it be a picture, music, or his behavior; who has not divorced his expression on a canvas or in music or in stone from his daily conduct, daily living. That demands the highest intelligence, highest harmony. To me the true artist is the man who has that harmony. He may express it on canvas, or he may talk, or he may paint; or he may not express it at all, he may feel it. But all this demands that exquisite poise, that intensity of awareness and, therefore, his expression is not divorced from the daily continuity of living.

Ojai, California, June 29, 1934

What we call happiness or ecstasy is, to me, creative thinking. And creative thinking is the infinite movement of thought, emotion, and action. That is, when thought, which is emotion, which is action itself, is unimpeded in its movement, is not compelled or influenced or bound by an idea, and does not proceed from the background of tradition or habit, then that movement is creative. So long as thought—and I won't repeat each time emotion and action—so long as thought is circumscribed, held by a fixed idea, or merely adjusts itself to a background or condition and, therefore, becomes limited, such thought is not creative.

So the question which every thoughtful person puts to himself is how can he awaken this creative thinking; because when there is this creative thinking, which is infinite movement, then there can be no idea of a limitation, a conflict.

Now this movement of creative thinking does not seek in its expression a result, an achievement; its results and expressions are not its culmination. It has no culmination or goal, for it is eternally in movement. Most minds are seeking a culmination, a goal, an achievement, and are molding themselves upon the idea of success, and such thought, such thinking is continually limiting itself, whereas if there is no idea of achievement but only the continual movement of thought as understanding, as intelligence, then that movement of thought is creative. That is, creative thinking ceases when mind is crippled by adjustment through influence, or when it functions with the background of a tradition which it has not understood, or from a fixed point, like an animal tied to a post. So long as this limitation, this adjustment, exists, there cannot be creative thinking, intelligence, which alone is freedom.

This creative movement of thought never seeks a result or comes to a culmination, because result or culmination is always the outcome of alternate cessation and movement, whereas if there is no search for a result, but only continual movement of thought, then that is creative thinking.

Again, creative thinking is free of division, which creates conflict between thought, emotion, and action. And division exists only when there is the search for a goal, when there is adjustment and the complacency of certainty.

Action is this movement which is itself thought and emotion, as I explained. This action is the relationship between the individual and society. It is conduct, work, cooperation, which we call fulfillment. That is, when mind is functioning without seeking a culmination, a goal, and, therefore, thinking creatively, that thinking is action, which is the relationship between the individual and society. Now if this movement of thought is clear, simple, direct, spontaneous, profound, then there is no conflict in the individual against society, for action then is the very expression of this living, creative movement.

So to me there is no art of thinking, there is only creative thinking. There is no technique of thinking, but only spontaneous creative functioning of intelligence, which is the harmony of reason, emotion, and action, not divided or divorced from each other.

Now this thinking and feeling, without a search for a reward, a result, is true experiment, isn't it? In real experiencing, real experimenting, there cannot be the search for result, because this experimenting is the movement of creative thought. To experiment, mind must be continually freeing itself from the environment with which it conflicts in its movement, the environment which we call the past. There can be no creative thinking if mind is hindered by the search for a reward, by the pursuit of a goal.

When the mind and heart are seeking a result or a gain, thereby complacency and stagnation, there must be practice, an overcoming, a discipline, out of which comes conflict. Most people think that by practicing a certain idea they will release creative thinking. Now, practice, if you come to observe it, ponder over it, is nothing but the result of duality. And an action born of this duality must perpetuate that distinction between mind and heart, and such action becomes merely the expression of a calculated, logical, self-protective conclusion. If there is this practice of self-discipline, or this continual domination or influence by circumstances, then practice is merely an alteration, a change toward an end; it is merely action within the confines of the limited thought which you call self-consciousness. So practice does not bring about creative thinking.

To think creatively is to bring about harmony between mind, emotion, and action. That is, if you are convinced of an action, without the search of a reward at the end, then that action, being the result of intelligence, releases all hindrances that have been placed on the mind through the lack of understanding.

Where the mind and heart are held by fear, by lack of understanding, by compulsion, such a mind, though it can think within the confines, within the limitations of that fear, is not really thinking, and its action must ever throw up new barriers. Therefore, its capacity to think is ever being limited. But if the mind frees itself through the understanding of circumstances and, therefore, acts, then that very action is creative thinking.

QUESTIONER: Will you please give an example of the practical exercise of constant awareness and choice in everyday life?

KRISHNAMURTI: Would you ask that question if there were a poisonous snake in your room? Then you wouldn't ask, "How am I to keep awake? How am I to be intensely aware?" You ask that question only when you are not sure that there is a poisonous snake in your room. Either you are wholly unconscious of it, or you want to play with that snake, you want to enjoy its pain and its delights.

Please follow this. There cannot be awareness, that alertness of mind and emotion, so long as mind is still caught up in both pain and pleasure. That is, when an experience gives you pain and at the same time gives you pleasure, you do nothing about it. You act only when the pain is greater than the pleasure, but if the pleasure is greater, you do nothing at all about it, because there is no acute conflict. It is only when pain overbalances pleasure, is more acute than pleasure, that you demand an action.

Most people wait for the increase of pain before they act, and during this waiting period they want to know how to be aware. No one can tell them. They are waiting for the increase of pain before they act; that is, they wait for pain through its compulsion to force them to act, and in that compulsion there is no intelligence. It is merely environment which forces them to act in a particular way, not intelligence. Therefore when a mind is caught up in this stagnation, in this lack of tenseness, there will naturally be more pain, more conflict.

By the look of things political, war may break out again. It may break out in two years, in five years, in ten years. An intelligent man can see this and intelligently act. But the man who is stagnating, who is waiting for pain to force him to action, looks to greater chaos, greater suffering to give him impetus to act and hence, his intelligence is not functioning. There is awareness only when the mind and heart are taut, are in great tenseness.

For example, when you see that possessiveness must lead to incompleteness, when you see that insufficiency, lack of richness, shallowness, must ever produce dependence, when you recognize that, what happens to your mind and heart? The immediate craving is to fill that shallowness; but apart from that, when you see the futility of continual accumulation, you begin to be aware of how your mind is functioning. You see that in mere accumulation there cannot be creative thinking; and yet mind is pursuing accumulation. Therefore, in becoming aware of that, you create a conflict, and that very conflict will dissolve the cause of accumulation.

Q: In what way could a statesman who understood what you are saying give it expression in public affairs? Or is it not more likely that he would retire from politics when he understood their false bases and objectives?

K: If he understood what I am saying, he would not separate politics from life in its completeness; and I don't see why he should retire. After all, politics now are merely instruments of exploitation; but if he considered life as a whole, not politics only—and by politics he means only his country, his people, and the exploitation of others—and regarded human problems not as national but as world problems, not as American, Hindu, or German problems, then, if he understood what I am talking about, he would be a true human being, not a politician. And to me, that is the most important thing, to be a human being, not an exploiter, or merely an expert in one particular line. I think that is where the mischief lies. The politician deals with politics only; the moralist with morals, the so-called spiritual teacher with the spirit, each thinking that he is the expert, and excluding all others. Our whole structure of society is based on that, and so these leaders of the various departments create greater havoc and greater misery, whereas if we as human beings saw the intimate connection between all these, between politics, religion, economics, and social life, if we saw the connection, then we would not think and act separatively, individualistically.

In India, for example, there are millions starving. The Hindu who is a nationalist says, "Let us first become intensely national; then we shall be able to solve this problem of starvation," whereas to me, the way to solve the problem of starvation is not to become nationalistic, but the contrary; starvation is a world problem, and this process of isolation but further increases starvation. So if the politician deals with the problems of human life merely as a politician, then such a man creates greater havoc, greater mischief; but if he considers the whole of life without differentiation between races, nationalities, and classes, then he is truly a human being, though he may be a politician.

Q: You have said that with two or three others who understand, you could change the world. Many believe that they themselves understand, and that there are others likewise, such as artists and men of science, and yet the world is not changed. Please speak of the way in which you would change the world. Are you not now changing the world, perhaps slowly and subtly, but nevertheless definitely, through your speaking, your living, and the influence you will undoubtedly have on human thought in the years to come? Is this the change you had in mind, or was it something immediately affecting the political, economic, and racial structure?

K: I am afraid I have never thought of the immediacy of action and its effect. To have a lasting, true result, there must be behind action great observation, thought, and intelligence, and very few people are willing to think creatively, or be free from influence and bias. If you begin to think individually, you will then be able to cooperate intelligently; and as long as there is no intelligence there cannot be cooperation, but only compulsion and hence, chaos.

Q: To what extent can a person control his own actions? If we are, at any one time, the sum of our previous experience, and there is no spiritual self, is it possible for a person to act in any other way than that which is determined by his original inheritance, the sum of his past training, and the stimuli which play upon him at the time? If so, what causes the changes in the physical processes, and how?

K: "To what extent can a person control his own actions?" A person does not control his own actions if he has not understood environment. Then he is only acting under the compulsion, the influence, of environment; such an action is not action at all, but is merely reaction or self-protectiveness. But when a person begins to understand environment, sees its full significance and worth, then he is master of his own actions, then he is intelligent; and therefore, no matter what the condition he will function intelligently.

"If we are, at any one time, the sum of our previous experience, and there is no spiritual self, is it possible for a person to act in any other way than that which is determined by his original inheritance, the sum of his past training, and the stimuli which play upon him at the time?"

Again, what I have said applies to this. That is, if he is merely acting from the burden of the past, whether it be his individual or racial inheritance, such action is merely the reaction of fear; but if he understands the subconscious, that is, his past accumulations, then he is free of the past and, therefore, he is free of the compulsion of the environment.

After all, environment is of the present as well as of the past. One does not understand the present because of the clouding of the mind by the past; and to free the mind from the subconscious, the unconscious hindrances of the past, is not to roll memory back into the past, but to be fully conscious in the present. In that consciousness, in that full consciousness of the present, all the past hindrances come into activity, surge forward, and in that surging forward, if you are aware, you will see the full significance of the past and, therefore, understand the present.

"If so, what causes the changes in the physical processes, and how?" As far as I understand the questioner, he wants to know what produces this action, this action which is forced upon him by environment. He acts in a particular manner, compelled by environment, but if he understood environment intelligently, there would be no compulsion whatever; there would be understanding, which is action itself.

Q: I live in a world of chaos, politically, economically, and socially, bound by laws and conventions which restrict my freedom. When my desires conflict with these impositions, I must break the law and take the consequences, or repress my desires. Where then, in such a world, is there any escape from self-discipline?

K: Self-discipline is merely an adjustment to environment, brought about through conflict. That is what I call self-discipline. You have established a pattern, an ideal, which acts as a compulsion, and you are forcing the mind to adjust itself to that environment, forcing it, modifying it, controlling it. What happens when you do that? You are really destroying creativeness; you are perverting, suppressing, creative affection. But if you begin to understand environment, then there is no longer repression or mere adjustment to environment, which you call self-discipline.

How then can you understand environment? How can you understand its full worth, significance? What prevents you from seeing its significance? First of all, fear. Fear is the cause of the search for protection or security, security which is either physical, spiritual, religious, or emotional. So long as there is that search there must be fear, which then creates a barrier between your mind and your environment, and thereby creates conflict; and that conflict you cannot dissolve as long as you are only concerned with adjustment, modification, and never with the discovery of the fundamental cause of fear.

So where there is this search for security, for a certainty, for a goal, preventing creative thinking, there must be adjustment, called self-discipline, which is but compulsion, the imitation of a pattern, whereas when the mind sees that there is no such thing as security in the piling up of things or of knowledge, then mind is released from fear and, therefore, mind is intelligence, and that which is intelligence does not discipline itself. There is self-discipline only where there is no intelligence. Where there is intelligence, there is understanding, free from influence, from control and domination.

Q: How is it possible to awaken thought in an organism wherein the mechanism requisite for the apprehension of abstract ideas is absent?

K: By the simple process of suffering; by the process of continual experience. But you see, we have taken such shelter behind false values that we have ceased to think at all, and then we ask, "What are we to do? How are we to awaken thought?" We have cultivated fears which have become glorified as virtues and ideals, behind which mind takes shelter, and all action proceeds from that shelter, from that mold. Therefore, there is no thinking. You have conventions, and the adjusting of oneself to these conventions is called thought and action, which is not at all thought or action, because it is born of fear and, therefore, cripples the mind.

How can you awaken thought? Circumstances, or the death of someone you love, or a catastrophe, or depression, force you into conflict. Outer circumstances force you to act, and in that compulsion there cannot be the awakening of thought, because you are acting through fear. And if you begin to see that you cannot wait for circumstances to force you to act, then you begin to observe the very circumstances themselves; then you begin to penetrate and understand the circumstances, the environment. You don't wait for depression to make you into a virtuous person, but you free your mind from possessiveness, from compulsion.

The acquisitive system is based on the idea that you can possess, and that it is legal to possess. Possession glorifies you. The more you have, the better, the nobler, you are considered. You have created that system, and you have become a slave to that system. You can create another society, not based on acquisitiveness, and that society can compel you as individuals to conform to its conventions, just as this society compels you to conform to its acquisitiveness. What is the difference? None whatever. You as individuals are merely being forced by circumstances or law to act in a particular direction and, therefore, there is no creative thinking at all; whereas if intelligence is beginning to function, then you are not a slave to either society, the acquisitive or the nonacquisitive. But to free the mind, there must be great intensity; there must be this continual alertness, observation, which itself creates conflict. This alertness itself produces a disturbance, and when there is that crisis, that intensity of conflict, then mind, if it is not escaping, begins to think anew, to think creatively, and that very thinking is eternity.

Ojai, California, June 30, 1934

I think most people have lost the art of listening. They come with their particular problems, and think that by listening to my talk their problems will be solved. I am afraid this will not happen; but if you know how to listen, then you will begin to understand the whole, and your mind will not be entangled by the particular.

So, if I may suggest it, don't try to seek from this talk a solution for your particular problem, or an alleviation of your suffering. I can help you or rather, you will help yourself only if you think anew, creatively. Regard life not as several isolated problems, but comprehensively, as a whole, with a mind that is not suffocated by the search for solutions. If you will listen without the burden of problems, and take a comprehensive outlook, then you will see that your particular problem has a different significance; and although it may not be solved at once, you will begin to see the true cause of it. In thinking anew, in relearning how to think, there will come the dissolution of the problems and conflicts with which one's mind and heart are burdened, and from which arise all disharmony, pain, and suffering.

Now, each one, more or less, is consumed by desires whose objects vary according to environment, temperament, and inheritance. According to your particular condition, to your particular education and upbringing, religious, social, and economic, you have established certain objectives whose attainment you are ceaselessly pursuing, and this pursuit has become paramount in your lives.

Once you have established these objectives, there naturally arise the specialists who act as your guides toward the attainment of your desires. Hence, the perfection of technique, specialization, becomes merely the means to gain your end; and in order to gain this end, which you have established through your religious, economic, and social conditioning, you must have specialists. So your action loses its significance, its value, because you are concerned with the attainment of an objective, not with the fulfillment of intelligence which is action; you are concerned with the arrival, not with that which is fulfillment itself. Living becomes merely the means to an end, and life a school in which you learn to attain an end. Action, therefore, becomes but a medium through which you can come to that objective which you have established through your various environments and conditions. So life becomes a school of great conflict and struggle, never a thing of fulfillment, of richness, of completeness.

Then you begin to ask, what is the end, the purpose of living? This is what most people ask; this is what is in the minds of most people here. Why are we living? What is the end? What is the goal? What is the purpose? You are concerned with the purpose, with the end, rather than with living in the present; whereas a man who fulfills never inquires into the end because fulfillment itself is sufficient. But as you do not know how to fulfill, how to live completely, richly, sufficiently, you begin to inquire into the purpose, the goal, the end, because you think you can then meet life, knowing the end—at least you think you can know the end—then, knowing the end, you hope to use experience as a means toward that end; hence, life becomes a medium, a measure, a value to come to that attainment.

Consciously or unconsciously, surreptitiously or openly, one begins to inquire into the purpose of life, and each one receives an answer from the so-called specialists. The artist, if you ask him what is the purpose of life, will tell you that it is self-expression through painting, sculpture, music, or poetry; the economist, if you ask him, will tell you that it is work, production, cooperation, living together, functioning as a group, as society; and if you ask the religionist he will tell you the purpose of life is to seek and to realize God, to live according to the laws laid down by teachers, prophets, saviors, and that by living according to their laws and edicts you may realize that truth which is God. Each specialist gives you his answer about the purpose of life, and according to your temperament, fancies, and imagination you begin to establish these purposes, these ends, as your ideals.

Such ideals and ends have become merely a haven of refuge because you use them to guide and protect yourself in this turmoil. So you begin to use these ideals to measure your experiences, to inquire into the conditions of your environment. You begin, without the desire to understand or to fulfill, merely to inquire into the purpose of environment; and in discovering that purpose, according to your conditioning, your preconceptions, you merely avoid the conflict of living without understanding.

So mind has divided life into ideals, purposes, culminations, attainments, ends; and turmoil, conflict, disturbance, disharmony; and you, yourself, the self-consciousness. That is, mind has separated life into these three divisions. You are caught up in turmoil and so through this turmoil, this conflict, this disturbance which is but sorrow, you work toward an end, a purpose. You wade through, plough through this turmoil to the goal, to the end, to the haven of refuge, to the attainment of the ideal; and these ideals, ends, refuges have been designed by economic, religious, and spiritual experts.

Thus, you are, at one end, wading through conditions and environment, and creating conflict while trying to realize ideals, purposes, and attainments which have become refuges and shelters at the other. The very inquiry into the purpose of life indicates the lack of intelligence in the present; and the man who is fully active—not lost in activities, as most Americans are, but fully active, intelligently, emotionally, fully alive—has fulfilled himself. Therefore, the inquiry into an end is futile, because there is no such thing as an end and a beginning; there is but the continual movement of creative thinking, and what you call problems are the results of your ploughing through this turmoil toward a culmination. That is, you are concerned with how to overcome this turmoil, how to adjust yourselves to environment in order to arrive at an end. With that your whole life is concerned, not with yourself and the goal. You are not concerned with that, you are concerned with the turmoil, how to go through it, how to dominate it, how to overcome it and, therefore, how to evade it. You want to arrive at that perfect evasion which you call ideals, at that perfect refuge which you call the purpose of life, which is but an escape from the present turmoil.

Naturally, when you seek to overcome, to dominate, to evade, and to arrive at that ultimate goal, there arises the search for systems and their leaders, guides, teachers, and experts; to me all these are exploiters. The systems, the methods, and their teachers, and all the complications of their rivalries, enticements, promises, and deceits, create divisions in life known as sects and cults.

That is what is happening. When you are seeking an attainment, a result, an overcoming of the turmoil, and not considering the "you," the "I" consciousness, and the end which you are ceaselessly and consciously, or unconsciously, pursuing, naturally you must create exploiters, either of the past or the present; and you are caught up in their pettinesses, their jealousies, their disciplines, their disharmonies, and their divisions. So the mere desire to go through this turmoil ever creates further problems, for there is no consideration of the actor or the manner of his action, but merely the consideration of the scene of turmoil as a means to get to an end.

Now to me, the turmoil, the end, and the "you" are the same; there is no division. This division is artificial, and it is created by the desire to gain, by the pursuit of acquisitive accumulation, which is born of insufficiency.

In becoming conscious of emptiness, of shallowness, one begins to realize the utter insufficiency of one's own thinking and feeling, and so in one's thought there arises the idea of accumulation, and from that is born this division between "you," the self-consciousness, and the end. To me, as I said, there can be no such distinction, because the moment you fulfill there can no longer be the actor and the act, but only that creative movement of thought which does not seek a result, and so there is a continual living, which is immortality.

But you have divided life. Let us consider what this "I," this actor, this observer, this center of conflict, is. It is but a long, continuous scroll of memory. This "I" is a scroll of memory in which there are accentuations. These accentuations or depressions we call complexes, and from these we act. That is, mind, being conscious of insufficiency, pursues a gain and, therefore, creates a distinction, a division. Such a mind cannot understand environment, and as it cannot understand it, it must rely on the accumulation of memory for guidance; for memory is but a series of accumulations which act as a guide toward an end. That is the purpose of memory. Memory is the lack of comprehension; that lack of comprehension is your background, and from that proceeds your action.

This memory is acting as a guide toward an end, and that end, being preestablished, is merely a self-protective refuge which you call ideals, attainment, truth, God, or perfection. The beginning and the end, the "you" and the goal, are the results of this self-protective mind.

I have explained how a self-protective mind comes into being; it comes into being as the result of the consciousness or awareness of emptiness, of void. Therefore, it begins to think in terms of achievement, acquisition, and from that it begins to function, dividing life and restricting its actions. So the end and the "you" are the result of this self-protective mind; and turmoil, conflict, and disharmony are but the process of self-protection, and are born out of this self-protection, spiritual and economic.

Spiritually and economically you are seeking security, because you rely on accumulation for your richness, for your comprehension, for your fullness, for your fulfillment. And so the cunning, in the spiritual as well as in the economic world, exploit you, for both seek power by glorifying self-protection. So each mind is making a tremendous effort to protect itself, and the end, the means, and the "you" are nothing else but the process of self-protection. What happens when there is this process of self-protection? There must be conflict with circumstances, which we call society; there is the "you" trying to protect itself against the collective, the group, the society.

Now, the reverse of that isn't true. That is, don't think that if you cease to protect yourself you will be lost. On the contrary, you will be lost if you are protecting yourself due to the insufficiency, due to the shallowness of thought and affection. But if you merely cease to protect yourself because you think through that you are going to find truth, again it will be but another form of protection.

So, as we have built up through centuries, generation after generation, this wheel of self-protection, spiritual and economic, let us find out if spiritual or economic self-protection is real. Perhaps economically you may assert self-protection for a while. The man who has money and many possessions, and who has secured comforts and pleasures for his body, is generally, if you will observe, most insufficient and unintelligent, and is groping after so-called spiritual protection.

Let us inquire however if there really is spiritual self-protection, because economically we see there is no security. The illusion of economic security is shown throughout the world by these depressions, crises, wars, calamities, and chaos. We recognize this, and so turn to spiritual security. But to me there is no security, there is no self-protection, and there never can be any. I say there is only wisdom, which is understanding, not protection. That is, security, self-protection, is the outcome of insufficiency, in which there is no intelligence, in which there is no creative thinking, in which there is constant battle between the "you" and society, and in which the cunning exploit you ruthlessly. As long as there is the pursuit of self-protection there must be conflict, and so there can be no understanding, no wisdom. And as long as this attitude exists, your search for spirituality, for truth, or for God is vain, useless, because it is merely the search for greater power, greater security.

It is only when the mind, which has taken shelter behind the walls of self-protection, frees itself from its own creations that there can be that exquisite reality. After all, these walls of self-protection are the creations of the mind which, conscious of its insufficiency, builds these walls of protection, and behind them takes shelter. One has built up these barriers unconsciously or consciously, and one's mind is so crippled, bound, held, that action brings greater conflict, further disturbances.

So the mere search for the solution of your problems is not going to free the mind from creating further problems. As long as this center of self-protectiveness, born of insufficiency, exists, there must be disturbances, tremendous sorrow, and pain; and you cannot free the mind of sorrow by disciplining it not to be insufficient. That is, you cannot discipline yourself, or be influenced by conditions and environment, in order not to be shallow. You say to yourself, "I am shallow; I recognize the fact, and how am I going to get rid of it?" I say, do not seek to get rid of it, which is merely a process of substitution, but become conscious, become aware of what is causing this insufficiency. You cannot compel it; you cannot force it; it cannot be influenced by an ideal, by a fear, by the pursuit of enjoyment and powers. You can find out the cause of insufficiency only through awareness. That is, by looking into environment and piercing into its significance there will be revealed the cunning subtleties of self-protection.

After all, self-protection is the result of insufficiency, and as the mind has been trained, caught up in its bondage for centuries, you cannot discipline it, you cannot overcome it. If you do, you lose the significance of the deceits and subtleties of thought and emotion behind which mind has taken shelter; and to discover these subtleties you must become conscious, aware.

Now to be aware is not to alter. Our mind is accustomed to alteration which is merely modification, adjustment, becoming disciplined to a condition; whereas if you are aware, you will discover the full significance of the environment. Therefore there is no modification, but entire freedom from that environment.

Only when all these walls of protection are destroyed in the flame of awareness, in which there is no modification or alteration or adjustment, but complete understanding of the significance of environment with all its delicacies and subtleties—only through that understanding is there the eternal; because in that there is no "you" functioning as a self-protective focus. But as long as that self-protecting focus which you call the "I" exists, there must be confusion, there must be disturbance, disharmony, and conflict. You cannot destroy these hindrances by disciplining yourself or by following a system or by imitating a pattern; you can understand them with all their complications only through the full awareness of mind and heart. Then there is an ecstasy, there is that living movement of truth, which is not an end, not a culmination, but an ever-creative living, an ecstasy which cannot be described, because all description must destroy it. So long as you are not vulnerable to truth, there is no ecstasy, there is no immortality.

Ojai, California, July 1, 1934

PART 2

Insights into Everyday Life

People have often wondered how Krishnamurti, whom they believe lived in protected and luxurious circumstances, could have had the remarkable insights into the often trouble-fraught lives of ordinary people that he demonstrated in his writings and talks. Without knowing of the illnesses of his childhood, his suffering at the time of his brother's death, or his lifelong physical pain and sensitivity, they have marveled at his ability to see through the eyes of a mother living in poverty in an Indian village, of a laborer toiling on a dusty road, of a rich man or a troubled young student.

During the 1930s and '40s, Krishnamurti gave private interviews to people from almost every social background who asked to speak with him about their personal problems. Perceiving the unity of human existence, he was able to convey revealing insights into issues affecting all men and women. He described the essence of these probing discussions in books which also expressed his deep appreciation of the natural landscape and his intense, long-standing concern for the environment.

This part presents some of these writings, which have been published in three volumes as *The Commentaries on Living.* Here, too, are extracts from his writings on education and to the young (*Education and the Significance of Life* and *Life Ahead*) and on freedom, in a book with an introduction by Aldous Huxley, *The First and Last Freedom*. Possibly some of the most intimate and revealing passages are those selected from his *Journal* and from *Krishnamurti to Himself* in which (as in *Krishnamurti's Notebook*) he often touches on the deepest mystical sources of his lifetime of teaching.

To communicate with one another, even if we know each other very well, is extremely difficult. I may use words that may have to you a significance different from mine. Understanding comes when we, you and I, meet on the same level at the same time. That happens only when there is real affection between people, between husband and wife, between intimate friends. That is real communion. Instantaneous understanding comes when we meet on the same level at the same time.

It is very difficult to commune with one another easily, effectively, and with definitive action. I am using words which are simple, which are not technical, because I do not think that any technical type of expression is going to help us solve our difficult problems; so I am not going to use any technical terms, either of psychology or of science. I have not read any books on psychology or any religious books, fortunately. I would like to convey, by the very simple words which we use in our daily life, a deeper significance; but that is very difficult if you do not know how to listen.

There is an art of listening. To be able really to listen, one should abandon or put aside all prejudices, preformulations, and daily activities. When you are in a receptive state of mind, things can be easily understood; you are listening when your real attention is given to something. But unfortunately most of us listen through a screen of resistance. We are screened with prejudices, whether religious or spiritual, psychological, or scientific; or with our daily worries, desires, and fears. And with these for a screen, we listen. Therefore, we listen really to our own noise, to our own sound, not to what is being said. It is extremely difficult to put aside our training, our prejudices, our inclination, our resistance, and, reaching beyond the verbal expression, to listen so that we understand instantaneously. That is going to be one of our difficulties.

If, during this discourse, anything is said which is opposed to your way of thinking and belief, just listen; do not resist. You may be right and I may be wrong; but by listening and considering together we are going to find out what is the truth. Truth cannot be given to you by somebody. You have to discover it; and to discover, there must be a state of mind in which there is direct perception. There is no direct perception when there is a resistance, a safeguard, a protection. Understanding comes through being aware of *what is.* To know exactly *what is,* the real, the actual, without interpreting it, without condemning or justifying it, is, surely, the beginning of wisdom. It is only when we begin to interpret, to translate according to our conditioning, according to our prejudice, that we miss the truth. After all, it is like research. To know what something is, what it is exactly, requires research—you cannot translate it according to your moods. Similarly, if we can look, observe, listen, be aware of, *what is,* exactly, then the problem is solved. And that is what we are going to do in all these discourses. I am going to point out to you *what is,* and not translate it according to my fancy; nor should you translate it or interpret it according to your background or training.

Is it not possible, then, to be aware of everything as it is? Starting from there, surely, there can be an understanding. To acknowledge, to be aware of, to get at that which is, puts an end to struggle. If I know that I am a liar, and it is a fact which I recognize, then the struggle is over. To acknowledge, to be aware of what one is, is already the beginning of wisdom, the beginning of understanding, which releases you from time. To bring in the quality of time—time, not in the chronological sense, but as the medium, as the psychological process, the process of the mind—is destructive, and creates confusion.

So, we can have understanding of *what is* when we recognize it without condemnation, without justification, without identification. To know that one is in a certain condition, in a certain state, is already a process of liberation; but a man who is not aware of his condition, of his struggle, tries to be something other than he is, which brings about habit. So, then, let us keep in mind that we want to examine *what is*, to observe and be aware of exactly what is the actual, without giving it any slant, without giving it an interpretation. It takes an extraordinarily astute mind, an extraordinarily pliable heart, to be aware of and to follow *what is;* because *what is* is constantly moving, constantly undergoing a transformation, and if the mind is tethered to belief, to knowledge, it ceases to pursue, it ceases to follow the swift movement of *what is. What is* is not static, surely it is constantly moving, as you will see if you observe it very closely. To follow it, you need a very swift mind and a pliable heart—which are denied when the mind is static, fixed in a belief, in a prejudice, in an identification; and a mind and heart that are dry cannot follow easily, swiftly, that which is.

One is aware, I think, without too much discussion, too much verbal expression, that there is individual as well as collective chaos, confusion, and misery. It is not only in India, but right throughout the world; in China, America, England, Germany, all over the world, there is confusion, mounting sorrow. It is not only national, it is not particularly here, it is all over the world. There is extraordinarily acute suffering, and it is not individual only but collective. So it is a world catastrophe, and to limit it merely to a geographical area, a colored section of the map, is absurd; because then we shall not understand the full significance of this world-wide as well as individual suffering. Being aware of this confusion, what is our response today? How do we react?

There is suffering—political, social, religious; our whole psychological being is confused, and all the leaders, political and religious, have failed us; all the books have lost their significance. You may go to the Bhagavad Gita or the Bible or the latest treatise on politics or psychology, and you will find that they have lost that ring, that quality of truth; they have become mere words. You yourself, who are the repeater of those words, are confused and uncertain, and mere repetition of words conveys nothing. Therefore, the words and the books have lost their value; that is, if you quote the Bible, or Marx, or the Bhagavad Gita, as you who quote it are yourself uncertain, confused, your repetition becomes a lie; because what is written there becomes mere propaganda, and propaganda is not truth. So when you repeat, you have ceased to understand your own state of being. You are merely covering with words of authority your own confusion. But what we are trying to do is to understand this confusion and not cover it up with quotations; so what is your response to it? How do you respond to this extraordinary chaos, this confusion, this uncertainty of existence? Be aware of it, as I discuss it. Follow not my words, but the thought which is active in you. Most of us are accustomed to being spectators and not to partake in the game. We read books but we never write books. It has become our tradition, our national and universal habit, to be the spectators, to look on at a football game, to watch the public politicians and orators. We are merely the outsiders, looking on, and we have lost the creative capacity. Therefore, we want to absorb and partake.

But if you are merely observing, if you are merely spectators, you will lose entirely the significance of this discourse, because I am not going to give you information which you can pick up in an encyclopedia. What we are trying to do is to follow each other's thoughts, to pursue as far as we can, as profoundly as we can, the intimations, the responses, of our own feelings. So please find out what your response is to this cause, to this suffering; not what somebody else's words are, but how you yourself respond. Your response is one of indifference if you benefit by the suffering, by the chaos, if you derive profit from it, either economic, social, political, or psychological. Therefore, you do not mind if this chaos continues. Surely, the more trouble there is in the world, the more chaos, the more one seeks security. Haven't you noticed it? When there is confusion in the world, psychologically and in every way, you enclose yourself in some kind of security, either that of a bank account or that of an ideology; or else you turn to prayer, you go to the temple, which is really escaping from what is happening in the world. More and more sects are being formed, more and more "isms" are springing up all over the world. Because the more confusion there is, the more you want a leader, somebody who will guide you out of this mess, so you turn to the religious books, or to one of the latest teachers; or else you act and respond according to a system which appears to solve the problem, a system either of the left or of the right. That is exactly what is happening.

The moment you are aware of confusion, of exactly *what is,* you try to escape from it. Those sects which offer you a system for the solution of suffering—economic, social, or religious—are the worst; because then system becomes important and not man—whether it be a religious system, or a system of the left or of the right. System becomes important—the philosophy, the idea, becomes important—and not man; and for the sake of the idea, of the ideology, you are willing to sacrifice all mankind, which is exactly what is happening in the world. This is not merely my interpretation; if you observe, you will find that is exactly what is happening. The system has become important. Therefore, as the system has become important, men, you and I, lose significance; and the controllers of the system, whether religious or social, whether of the left or of the right, assume authority, assume power and, therefore, sacrifice you, the individual. That is exactly what is happening.

Now what is the cause of this confusion, this misery? How did this misery come about, this suffering, not only inwardly but outwardly, this fear and expectation of war, the third World War that is breaking out? What is the cause of it? Surely it indicates the collapse of all moral, spiritual, values, and the glorification of all sensual values, of the value of things made by the hand or by the mind. What happens when we have no other values except the value of the things of the senses, the value of the products of the mind, of the hand, or of the machine? The more significance we give to the sensual value of things, the greater the confusion, is it not? Again, this is not my theory. You do not have to quote books to find out that your values, your riches, your economic and social existence are based on things made by the hand or by the mind. So we live and function and have our being steeped in sensual values, which means that things, the things of the mind, the things of the hand and of the machine, have become important; and when things become important, belief becomes predominantly significant—which is exactly what is happening in the world, is it not?

Thus, giving more and more significance to the values of the senses brings about confusion; and, being in confusion, we try to escape from it through various forms, whether religious, economic or social, or through ambition, through power, through the search for reality. But the real is near, you do not have to seek it; and a man who seeks truth will never find it. Truth is in *what is*—and that is the beauty of it. But the moment you conceive it, the moment you seek it, you begin to struggle; and a man who struggles cannot understand. That is why we have to be still, observant, passively aware. We see that our living, our action, is always within the field of destruction, within the field of sorrow; like a wave, confusion and chaos always overtake us. There is no interval in the confusion of existence.

Whatever we do at present seems to lead to chaos, seems to lead to sorrow and unhappiness. Look at your own life and you will see that our living is always on the border of sorrow. Our work, our social activity, our politics, the various gatherings of nations to stop war, all produce further war. Destruction follows in the wake of living; whatever we do leads to death. That is what is actually taking place.

Can we stop this misery at once, and not go on always being caught by the wave of confusion and sorrow? That is, great teachers, whether the Buddha or the Christ, have come; they have accepted faith, making themselves, perhaps, free from confusion and sorrow. But they have never prevented sorrow, they have never stopped confusion. Confusion goes on, sorrow goes on. If you, seeing this social and economic confusion, this chaos, this misery, withdraw into what is called the religious life and abandon the world, you may feel that you are joining these great teachers; but the world goes on with its chaos, its misery and destruction, the everlasting suffering of its rich and poor. So, our problem, yours and mine, is whether we can step out of this misery instantaneously. If, living in the world, you refuse to be a part of it, you will help others out of this chaos—not in the future, not tomorrow, but now. Surely that is our problem. War is probably coming, more destructive, more appalling in its form. Surely we cannot prevent it, because the issues are much too strong and too close. But you and I can perceive the confusion and misery immediately, can we not? We must perceive them, and then we shall be in a position to awaken the same understanding of truth in another. In other words, can you be instantaneously free? Because that is the only way out of this misery. Perception can take place only in the present; but if you say, "I will do it tomorrow," the wave of confusion overtakes you, and you are then always involved in confusion.

Now is it possible to come to that state when you yourself perceive the truth instantaneously and, therefore, put an end to confusion? I say that it is, and that it is the only possible way. I say it can be done and must be done, not based on supposition or belief. To bring about this extraordinary revolution—which is not the revolution to get rid of the capitalists and install another group—to bring about this wonderful transformation, which is the only true revolution, is the problem. What is generally called revolution is merely the modification or the continuance of the right according to the ideas of the left. The left, after all, is the continuation of the right in a modified form. If the right is based on sensual values, the left is but a continuance of the same sensual values, different only in degree or expression. Therefore, true revolution can take place only when you, the individual, become aware in your relationship to another. Surely what you are in your relationship to another, to your wife, your child, your boss, your neighbor, is society. Society by itself is nonexistent. Society is what you and I, in our relationship, have created; it is the outward projection of all our own inward psychological states. So if you and I do not understand ourselves, merely transforming the outer, which is the projection of the inner, has no significance whatsoever; that is, there can be no significant alteration or modification in society so long as I do not understand myself in relationship to you. Being confused in my relationship, I create a society which is the replica, the outward expression, of what I am. This is an obvious fact, which we can discuss. We can discuss whether society, the outward expression, has produced me, or whether I have produced society.

Is it not, therefore, an obvious fact that what I am in my relationship to another creates society, and that without radically transforming myself, there can be no transformation of the essential function of society? When we look to a system for the transformation of society, we are merely evading the question, because a system cannot transform man; man always transforms the system, which history shows. Until I, in my relationship to you, understand myself, I am the cause of chaos, misery, destruction, fear, brutality. Understanding myself is not a matter of time; I can understand myself at this very moment. If I say, "I shall understand myself tomorrow," I am bringing in chaos and misery, my action is destructive. The moment I say that I "shall" understand, I bring in the time element and so am already caught up in the wave of confusion and destruction. Understanding is now, not tomorrow. Tomorrow is for the lazy mind, the sluggish mind, the mind that is not interested. When you are interested in something, you do it instantaneously, there is immediate understanding, immediate transformation. If you do not change now, you will never change, because the change that takes place tomorrow is merely a modification, it is not transformation. Transformation can only take place immediately; the revolution is now, not tomorrow.

When that happens, you are completely without a problem, for then the self is not worried about itself; then you are beyond the wave of destruction.

AMBITION

The baby had been crying all night, and the poor mother had been doing her best to quiet him. She sang to him, she scolded him, she petted and rocked him; but it was no good. The baby must have been teething, and it was a weary night for the whole family. But now the dawn was coming over the dark trees, and at last the baby became quiet. There was a peculiar stillness as the sky grew lighter and lighter. The deep branches were clear against the sky, slender and naked; a child called, a dog barked, a lorry rattled by, and another day had begun. Presently the mother came out carrying the baby, carefully wrapped, and walked along the road past the village, where she waited for a bus. Presumably she was taking him to the doctor. She looked so tired and haggard after that sleepless night, but the baby was fast asleep.

Soon the sun was over the treetops, and the dew sparkled on the green grass. Far away a train whistled, and the distant mountains looked cool and shadowy. A large bird flew noisily away, for we had disturbed her brooding. Our approach must have been very sudden, for she hadn't had time to cover her eggs with dry leaves. There were over a dozen of them. Even though uncovered they were hardly visible, she had so cleverly concealed them, and now she was watching from a distant tree. We saw the mother with her brood a few days later, and the nest was empty.

It was shady and cool along the path, which led through the damp woods to the distant hilltop, and the wattle was in bloom. It had rained heavily a few days before, and the earth was soft and yielding. There were fields of young potatoes, and far down in the valley was the town. It was a beautiful, golden morning. Beyond the hill the path led back, to the house.

She was very clever. She had read all the latest books, had seen the latest plays, and was well-informed about some philosophy which had become the latest craze. She had been analyzed and had apparently read a great deal of psychology, for she knew the jargon. She made a point of seeing all the important people, and had casually met someone who brought her along. She talked easily and expressed herself with poise and effect. She had been married, but had had no children; and one felt that all that was behind her, and that now she was on a different journey. She must have been rich, for she had about her that peculiar atmosphere of the wealthy. She began right away by asking, "In what way are you helping the world in this present crisis?" It must have been one of her stock questions. She went on to ask, more eagerly, about the prevention of war, the effects of communism, and the future of man.

Are not wars, the increasing disasters and miseries, the outcome of our daily life? Are we not, each one of us, responsible for this crisis? The future is in the present; the future will not be very different if there is no comprehension of the present. But do you not think that each one of us is responsible for this conflict and confusion?

"It may be so; but where does this recognition of responsibility lead? What value has my little action in the vast destructive action? In what way is my thought going to affect the general stupidity of man? What is happening in the world is sheer stupidity, and my intelligence is in no way going to affect it. Besides, think of the time it would take for individual action to make any impression on the world."

Is the world different from you? Has not the structure of society been built up by people like you and me? To bring about a radical change in the structure, must not you and I fundamentally transform ourselves? How can there be a deep revolution of values if it does not begin with us? To help in the present crisis, must one look for a new ideology, a new economic plan? Or must one begin to understand the conflict and confusion within oneself, which, in its projection, is the world? Can new ideologies bring unity between man and man? Do not beliefs set man against man? Must we not put away our ideological barriers—for all barriers are ideological—and consider our problems, not through the bias of conclusion and formulas, but directly and without prejudice? We are never directly in relationship with our problems, but always through some belief or formulation. We can solve our problems only when we are directly in relationship with them. It is not our problems which set man against man, but our ideas about them. Problems bring us together, but ideas separate us. If one may ask, why are you so apparently concerned about the crisis?

"Oh, I don't know. I see so much suffering, so much misery, and I feel something must be done about it."

Are you really concerned, or are you merely ambitious to do something?

"When you put it that way, I suppose I am ambitious to do something in which I shall succeed."

So few of us are honest in our thinking. We want to be successful, either directly for ourselves, or for the ideal, the belief with which we have identified ourselves. The ideal is our own projection, it is the product of our mind, and our mind experiences according to our conditioning. For these self-projections we work, we slave away and die. Nationalism, like the worship of God, is only the glorification of oneself. It is oneself that is important, actually or ideologically, and not the disaster and the misery. We really do not want to do anything about the crisis; it is merely a new topic for the clever, a field for the socially active and for the idealist.

Why are we ambitious?

"If we were not, nothing would get done in the world. If we were not ambitious we would still be driving about in horse carriages. Ambition is another name for progress. Without progress, we would decay, wither away."

In getting things done in the world, we are also breeding wars and untold miseries. Is ambition progress? For the moment we are not considering progress, but ambition. Why are we ambitious? Why do we want to succeed, to be somebody? Why do we struggle to be superior? Why all this effort to assert oneself, whether directly, or through an ideology or the State? Is not this self-assertion the main cause of our conflict and confusion? Without ambition, would we perish? Can we not physically survive without being ambitious?

"Who wants to survive without success, without recognition?"

Does not this desire for success, for applause, bring conflict both within and without? Would being free of ambition mean decay? Is it stagnation to have no conflict? We can drug ourselves, put ourselves to sleep with beliefs, with doctrines, and so have no deep conflicts. For most of us, some kind of activity is the drug. Obviously, such a state is one of decay, disintegration. But when we are aware of the false as the false, does it bring death? To be aware that ambition in any form, whether for happiness, for God, or for success, is the beginning of conflict both within and without, surely does not mean the end of all action, the end of life.

Why are we ambitious?

"I would be bored if I were not occupied in striving to achieve some kind of result. I used to be ambitious for my husband, and I suppose you would say it was for myself through my husband; and now I am ambitious for myself through an idea. I have never thought about ambition, I have just been ambitious."

Why are we clever and ambitious? Is not ambition an urge to avoid *what is?* Is not this cleverness really stupid, which is what we are? Why are we so frightened of *what is?* What is the good of running away if whatever we are is always there? We may succeed in escaping, but what we are is still there, breeding conflict and misery. Why are we so frightened of our loneliness, of our emptiness? Any activity away from *what is* is bound to bring sorrow and antagonism. Conflict is the denial of *what is* or the running away from *what is;* there is no conflict other than that. Our conflict becomes more and more complex and insoluble because we do not face *what is*. There is no complexity in *what is,* but only in the many escapes that we seek.

"Our life here in India is more or less shattered; we want to make something of it again, but we don't know where to begin. I can see the importance of mass action, and also its dangers. I have pursued the ideal of nonviolence, but there has been bloodshed and misery. Since the Partition, this country has had blood on its hands, and now we are building up the armed forces. We talk of nonviolence and yet prepare for war. I am as confused as the political leaders. In prison I used to read a great deal, but it has not helped me to clarify my own position.

"Can we take one thing at a time and somewhat go into it? First, you lay a great deal of emphasis on the individual, but is not collective action necessary?"

The individual is essentially the collective, and society is the creation of the individual. The individual and society are interrelated, are they not? They are not separate. The individual builds the structure of society, and society or environment shapes the individual. Though environment conditions the individual, he can always free himself, break away from his background. The individual is the maker of the very environment to which he becomes a slave; but he has also the power to break away from it and create an environment that will not dull his mind or spirit. The individual is important only in the sense that he has the capacity to free himself from his conditioning and understand reality. Individuality that is merely ruthless in its own conditioning builds a society whose foundations are based on violence and antagonism. The individual exists only in relationship, otherwise he is not; and it is the lack of understanding of this relationship that is breeding conflict and confusion. If the individual does not understand his relationship to people, to property, and to ideas or beliefs, merely to impose upon him a collective or any other pattern only defeats its own end. To bring about the imposition of a new pattern will require so-called mass action; but the new pattern is the invention of a few individuals, and the mass is mesmerized by the latest slogans, the promises of a new utopia. The mass is the same as before, only now it has new rulers, new phrases, new priests, new doctrines. This mass is made up of you and me, it is composed of individuals; the mass is fictitious, it is a convenient term for the exploiter and the politician to play with. The many are pushed into action, into war, and so on, by the few; and the few represent the desires and urges of the many. It is the transformation of the individual that is of the highest importance, but not in terms of any pattern. Patterns always condition, and a conditioned entity is always in conflict within himself and so with society. It is comparatively easy to substitute a new pattern of conditioning for the old; but for the individual to free himself from all conditioning is quite another matter.

"This requires careful and detailed thought, but I think I am beginning to understand it. You lay emphasis on the individual, but not as a separate and antagonistic force within society. Now the second point. I have always worked for an ideal, and I don't understand your denial of it. Would you mind going into this problem?"

Our present morality is based on the past or the future, on the traditional, or the what *ought* to be. The what *ought* to be is the ideal in opposition to what has been, the future in conflict with the past. Nonviolence is the ideal, the what *should* be; and the what has been is violence. The what has been projects the what *should* be; the ideal is homemade, it is projected by its own opposite, the actual. The antithesis is an extension of the thesis; the opposite contains the element of its own opposite. Being violent, the mind projects its opposite, the ideal of nonviolence. It is said that the ideal helps to overcome its own opposite; but does it? Is not the ideal an avoidance, an escape from the what has been, or from *what is*? The conflict between the actual and the ideal is obviously a means of postponing the understanding of the actual, and this conflict only introduces another problem which helps to cover up the immediate problem. The ideal is a marvelous and respectable escape from the actual. The ideal of nonviolence, like the collective utopia, is fictitious; the ideal, the what *should* be, helps us to cover up and avoid *what is.*

The pursuit of the ideal is the search for reward. You may shun the worldly rewards as being stupid and barbarous, which they are; but your pursuit of the ideal is the search for reward at a different level, which is also stupid. The ideal is a compensation, a fictitious state which the mind has conjured up. Being violent, separate, and out for itself, the mind projects the gratifying compensation, the fiction which it calls the ideal, the utopia, the future, and vainly pursues it. That very pursuit is conflict, but it is also a pleasurable postponement of the actual. The ideal, the what *should* be, does not help in understanding *what is;* on the contrary, it prevents understanding.

"Do you mean to say that our leaders and teachers have been wrong in advocating and maintaining the ideal?"

What do you think?

"If I understand correctly what you say—"

Please, it is not a matter of understanding what another may say, but of finding out what is true. Truth is not opinion; truth is not dependent on any leader or teacher. The weighing of opinions only prevents the perception of truth. Either the ideal is a home-made fiction which contains its own opposite, or it is not. There are no two ways about it. This does not depend on any teacher, you must perceive the truth of it for yourself.

"If the ideal is fictitious, it revolutionizes all my thinking. Do you mean to say that our pursuit of the ideal is utterly futile?"

It is a vain struggle, a gratifying self-deception, is it not?

"This is very disturbing, but I am forced to admit that it is. We have taken so many things for granted that we have never allowed ourselves to observe closely what is in our hand. We have deceived ourselves, and what you point out upsets completely the structure of my thought and action. It will revolutionize education, our whole way of living and working. I think I see the implications of a mind that is free from the ideal, from the what *should* be. To such a mind, action has a significance quite different from that which we give it now. Compensatory action is not action at all, but only a reaction—and we boast of action! But without the ideal, how is one to deal with the actual, or with the what has been?"

The understanding of the actual is possible only when the ideal, the what *should* be, is erased from the mind; that is, only when the false is seen as the false. The what *should* be is also the what should *not* be. As long as the mind approaches the actual with either positive or negative compensation, there can be no understanding of the actual. To understand the actual you must be in direct communion with it; your relationship with it cannot be through the screen of the ideal, or through the screen of the past, of tradition, of experience. To be free from the wrong approach is the only problem. This means, really, the understanding of conditioning, which is the mind. The problem is the mind itself, and not the problems it breeds; the resolution of the problems bred by the mind is merely the reconciliation of effects, and that only leads to further confusion and illusion.

"How is one to understand the mind?"

The way of the mind is the way of life—not the ideal life, but the actual life of sorrow and pleasure, of deception and clarity, of conceit and the pose of humility. To understand the mind is to be aware of desire and fear.

"Please, this is getting a bit too much for me. How am I to understand my mind?"

To know the mind, must you not be aware of its activities? The mind is only experience, not just the immediate, but also the accumulated. The mind is the past in response to the present, which makes for the future. The total process of the mind has to be understood.

"Where am I to begin?"

From the only beginning: relationship. Relationship is life; to be is to be related. Only in the mirror of relationship is the mind to be understood, and you have to begin to see yourself in that mirror.

"Do you mean in my relationship with my wife, with my neighbor, and so on? Is that not a very limited process?"

What may appear to be small, limited, if approached rightly, reveals the fathomless. It is like a funnel, the narrow opens into the wide. When observed with passive watchfulness, the limited reveals the limitless. After all, at its source the river is small, hardly worth noticing.

"So I must begin with myself and my immediate relationships."

Surely. Relationship is never narrow or small. With the one or with the many, relationship is a complex process, and you can approach it pettily, or freely and openly. Again, the approach is dependent on the state of the mind. If you do not begin with yourself, where else will you begin? Even if you begin with some peripheral activity, you are in relationship with it, the mind is the center of it. Whether you begin near or far, you are there. Without understanding yourself, whatever you do will inevitably bring about confusion and sorrow. The beginning is the ending.

"I have wandered far afield. I have seen and done many things, I have suffered and laughed like so many others, and yet I have had to come back to myself. I am like that *sannyasi* who set out in search of truth. He spent many years going from teacher to teacher, and each pointed out a different way. At last he wearily returned to his home, and in his own house was the jewel! I see how foolish we are, searching the universe for that bliss which is to be found only in our own hearts when the mind is purged of its activities. You are perfectly right. I begin from where I started. I begin with what I am."

We were steadily climbing, without any perceptible movement. Below us was a vast sea of clouds, white and dazzling, wave upon wave as far as the eye could see. They looked so astonishingly solid and inviting. Occasionally, as we climbed higher in a wide circle there were breaks in this brilliant foam, and far below was the green earth. Above us was the clear blue sky of winter, soft and immeasurable. A massive range of snow-covered mountains stretched from north to south, sparkling in the brilliant sun. These mountains reached an elevation of over fourteen thousand feet, but we had risen above them and were still climbing. They were a familiar range of peaks, and they looked so near and serene. The higher peaks lay to the north, and we shot off to the south, having reached the required altitude of twenty thousand feet.

The passenger in the next seat was very talkative. He was unfamiliar with those mountains, and had dozed as we climbed; but now he was awake and eager for a talk. It appeared that he was going out on some business for the first time; he seemed to have many interests, and spoke with considerable information about them. The sea was now below us, dark and distant, and a few ships were dotted here and there. There was not a tremor of the wings, and we passed one lighted town after another along the coast. He was saying how difficult it was not to have fear, not particularly of a crash, but of all the accidents of life. He was married and had children, and there was always fear—not of the future alone, but of everything in general. It was a fear that had no particular object, and though he was successful, this fear made his life weary and painful. He had always been rather apprehensive, but now it had become extremely persistent and his dreams were of a frightening nature. His wife knew of his fear, but she was not aware of its seriousness.

Fear can exist only in relation to something. As an abstraction, fear is a mere word, and the word is not the actual fear. Do you know specifically of what you are afraid?

"I have never been able to lay my finger on it, and my dreams too are very vague; but threading through them all there is fear. I have talked to friends and doctors about it, but they have either laughed it off or otherwise not been of much help. It has always eluded me, and I want to be free of the beastly thing."

Do you really want to be free, or is that just a phrase?

"I may sound casual, but I would give a great deal to be rid of this fear. I am not a particularly religious person, but strangely enough I have prayed to have it taken away from me. When I am interested in my work, or in a game, it is often absent; but like some monster it is ever waiting, and soon we are companions again."

Have you that fear now? Are you aware now that it is somewhere about? Is the fear conscious or hidden?

"I can sense it, but I do not know whether it is conscious or unconscious."

Do you sense it as something far away or near—not in space or distance, but as a feeling?

"When I am aware of it, it seems to be quite close. But what has that got to do with it?"

Fear can come into being only in relation to something. That something may be your family, your work, your preoccupation with the future, with death. Are you afraid of death?

"Not particularly, though I would like to have a quick death and not a long drawn-out one. I don't think it is my family that I have this anxiety about, nor is it my job."

Then it must be something deeper than the superficial relationships that is causing this fear. One may be able to point out what it is, but if you can discover it for yourself it will have far greater significance. Why are you not afraid of the superficial relationships?

"My wife and I love each other; she wouldn't think of looking at another man, and I am not attracted to other women. We find completeness in each other. The children are an anxiety, and what one can do, one does; but with all this economic mess in the world, one cannot give them financial security, and they will have to do the best they can. My job is fairly secure, but there is the natural fear of anything happening to my wife."

So you are sure of your deeper relationship. Why are you so certain?

"I don't know, but I am. One has to take some things for granted, hasn't one?"

That's not the point. Shall we go into it? What makes you so sure of your intimate relationship? When you say that you and your wife find completeness in each other, what do you mean?

"We find happiness in each other: companionship, understanding, and so on. In the deeper sense, we depend on each other. It would be a tremendous blow if anything happened to either of us. We are in that sense dependent."

What do you mean by dependent? You mean that without her you would be lost, you would feel utterly alone, is that it? She would feel the same; so you are mutually dependent.

"But what is wrong with that?"

We are not condemning or judging, but only inquiring. Are you sure you want to go into all this? You are quite sure? All right, then let's go on.

Without your wife, you would be alone, you would be lost in the deepest sense; so she is essential to you, is she not? You depend on her for your happiness, and this dependence is called love. You are afraid to be alone. She is always there to cover up the fact of your loneliness, as you cover up hers; but the fact is still there, is it not? We use each other to cover up this loneliness; we run away from it in so many ways, in so many different forms of relationship, and each such relationship becomes a dependence. I listen to the radio because music makes me happy, it takes me away from myself; books and knowledge are also a very convenient escape from myself. And on all these things we depend.

"Why should I not escape from myself? I have nothing to be proud of, and by being identified with my wife, who is much better than I am, I get away from myself."

Of course, the vast majority escape from themselves. But by escaping from yourself, you have become dependent. Dependence grows stronger, escapes more essential, in proportion to the fear of *what is*. The wife, the book, the radio, become extraordinarily important; escapes come to be all-significant, of the greatest value. I use my wife as a means of running away from myself, so I am attached to her. I must possess her, I must not lose her; and she likes to be possessed, for she is also using me. There is a common need to escape, and mutually we use each other. This usage is called love. You do not like what you are, and so you run away from yourself, from *what is*.

"That is fairly clear. I see something in that, it makes sense. But why does one run away? What is one escaping from?"

From your own loneliness, your own emptiness, from what you are. If you run away without seeing *what is,* you obviously cannot understand it; so first you have to stop running, escaping, and only then can you watch yourself as you are. But you cannot observe *what is* if you are always criticizing it, if you like or dislike it. You call it loneliness and run away from it; and the very running away from *what is* is fear. You are afraid of this loneliness, of this emptiness, and dependence is the covering of it. So fear is constant; it is constant as long as you are running away from *what is.* To be completely identified with something, with a person or an idea, is not a guarantee of final escape, for this fear is always in the background. It comes through dreams, when there is a break in identification; and there is always a break in identification, unless one is unbalanced.

"Then my fear arises from my own hollowness, my insufficiency. I see that all right, and it is true; but what am I to do about it?"

You cannot do anything about it. Whatever you do is an activity of escape. That is the most essential thing to realize. Then you will see that you are not different or separate from that hollowness. You are that insufficiency. The observer is the observed emptiness. Then if you proceed further, there is no longer calling it loneliness; the terming of it has ceased. If you proceed still further, which is rather arduous, the thing known as loneliness is not; there is a complete cessation of loneliness, emptiness, of the thinker as the thought. This alone puts an end to fear.

"Then what is love?"

Love is not identification; it is not thought about the loved. You do not think about love when it is there; you think about it only when it is absent, when there is distance between you and the object of your love. When there is direct communion, there is no thought, no image, no revival of memory; it is when the communion breaks, at any level, that the process of thought, of imagination, begins. Love is not of the mind. The mind makes the smoke of envy, of holding, of missing, of recalling the past, of longing for tomorrow, of sorrow and worry; and this effectively smothers the flame. When the smoke is not, the flame is. The two cannot exist together; the thought that they exist together is merely a wish. A wish is a projection of thought, and thought is not love.

TIME AND TRANSFORMATION

I would like to talk a little about time, because I think the enrichment, the beauty and significance of that which is timeless, of that which is true, can be experienced only when we understand the whole process of time. After all, we are seeking, each in his own way, a sense of happiness, of enrichment. Surely a life that has significance, the riches of true happiness, is not of time. Like love, such a life is timeless; and to understand that which is timeless, we must not approach it through time but rather understand time. We must not utilize time as a means of attaining, realizing, apprehending, the timeless. That is what we are doing most of our lives: spending time trying to grasp that which is timeless, so it is important to understand what we mean by time, because I think it is possible to be free of time. It is very important to understand time as a whole and not partially.

It is interesting to realize that our lives are mostly spent in time—time, not in the sense of chronological sequence, of minutes, hours, days, and years, but in the sense of psychological memory. We live by time, we are the result of time. Our minds are the product of many yesterdays and the present is merely the passage of the past to the future. Our minds, our activities, our being, are founded on time; without time we cannot think, because thought is the result of time, thought is the product of many yesterdays and there is no thought without memory. Memory is time, for there are two kinds of time, the chronological and the psychological. There is time as yesterday by the watch and as yesterday by memory. You cannot reject chronological time; it would be absurd—you would miss your train. But is there really any time at all apart from chronological time? Obviously there is time as yesterday but is there time as the mind thinks of it? Is there time apart from the mind? Surely time, psychological time, is the product of the mind. Without the foundation of thought there is no time—time merely being memory as yesterday in conjunction with today, which molds tomorrow. That is, memory of yesterday's experience in response to the present is creating the future, which is still the process of thought, a path of the mind. The thought process brings about psychological progress in time but is it real, as real as chronological time? And can we use that time which is of the mind as a means of understanding the eternal, the timeless? As

I said, happiness is not of yesterday, happiness is not the product of time, happiness is always in the present, a timeless state. I do not know if you have noticed that when you have ecstasy, a creative joy, a series of bright clouds surrounded by dark clouds, in that moment there is no time: there is only the immediate present. The mind, coming in after the experiencing in the present, remembers and wishes to continue it, gathering more and more of itself, thereby creating time. So time is created by the "more"; time is acquisition and time is also detachment, which is still an acquisition of the mind. Therefore, merely disciplining the mind in time, conditioning thought within the framework of time, which is memory, surely does not reveal that which is timeless.

Is transformation a matter of time? Most of us are accustomed to thinking that time is necessary for transformation: I am something, and to change what I am into what I should be requires time. I am greedy, with greed's results of confusion, antagonism, conflict, and misery; to bring about the transformation, which is nongreed, we think time is necessary. That is to say, time is considered as a means of evolving something greater, of becoming something. The problem is this: One is violent, greedy, envious, angry, vicious, or passionate. To transform *what is,* is time necessary? First of all, why do we want to change *what is,* or bring about a transformation? Why? Because what we are dissatisfies us; it creates conflict, disturbance, and disliking that state we want something better, something nobler, more idealistic. Therefore, we desire transformation because there is pain, discomfort, conflict. Is conflict overcome by time? If you say it will be overcome by time, you are still in conflict. You may say it will take twenty days or twenty years to get rid of conflict, to change what you are, but during that time you are still in conflict and, therefore, time does not bring about transformation. When we use time as a means of acquiring a quality, a virtue, or a state of being, we are merely postponing or avoiding *what is;* and I think it is important to understand this point. Greed or violence cause pain, disturbance in the world of our relationship with another, which is society; and being conscious of this state of disturbance, which we term greed or violence, we say to ourselves, "I will get out of it in time. I will practice nonviolence, I will practice non-envy, I will practice peace." Now, you want to practice nonviolence because violence is a state of disturbance, conflict, and you think that in time you will gain nonviolence and overcome the conflict. What is actually happening? Being in a state of conflict you want to achieve a state in which there is no conflict. Now is that state of no conflict the result of time, of a duration? Obviously not, because while you are achieving a state of nonviolence, you are still being violent and are, therefore, still in conflict.

Our problem is, can a conflict, a disturbance, be overcome in a period of time, whether it be days, years, or lives? What happens when you say, "I am going to practice nonviolence" during a certain period of time? The very practice indicates that you are in conflict, does it not? You would not practice if you were not resisting conflict; you say the resistance to conflict is necessary in order to overcome conflict and for that resistance you must have time. But the very resistance to conflict is itself a form of conflict. You are spending your energy in resisting conflict in the form of what you call greed, envy, or violence but your mind is still in conflict, so it is important to see the falseness of the process of depending on time as a means of overcoming violence and thereby being free of that process. Then you are able to be what you are: a psychological disturbance which is violence itself.

To understand anything, any human or scientific problem, what is important, what is essential? A quiet mind, is it not? A mind that is intent on understanding. It is not a mind that is exclusive, that is trying to concentrate, which again is an effort of resistance. If I really want to understand something, there is immediately a quiet state of mind. When you want to listen to music or look at a picture which you love, which you have a feeling for, what is the state of your mind? Immediately there is a quietness, is there not? When you are listening to music, your mind does not wander all over the place; you are listening. Similarly, when you want to understand conflict, you are no longer depending on time at all; you are simply confronted with *what is,* which is conflict. Then immediately there comes a quietness, a stillness of mind. When you no longer depend on time as a means of transforming *what is* because you see the falseness of that process, then you are confronted with *what is,* and as you are interested to understand *what is,* naturally you have a quiet mind. In that alert yet passive state of mind there is understanding. So long as the mind is in conflict, blaming, resisting, condemning, there can be no understanding. If I want to understand you, I must not condemn you, obviously. It is that quiet mind, that still mind, which brings about transformation. When the mind is no longer resisting, no longer avoiding, no longer discarding or blaming *what is* but is simply passively aware, then in that passivity of the mind you will find, if you really go into the problem, that there comes a transformation.

Revolution is only possible now, not in the future; regeneration is today, not tomorrow. If you will experiment with what I have been saying, you will find that there is immediate regeneration, a newness, a quality of freshness; because the mind is always still when it is interested, when it desires or has the intention to understand. The difficulty with most of us is that we have not the intention to understand, because we are afraid that, if we understood, it might bring about a revolutionary action in our life and, therefore, we resist. It is the defense mechanism that is at work when we use time or an ideal as a means of gradual transformation.

Thus, regeneration is only possible in the present, not in the future, not tomorrow. A man who relies on time as a means through which he can gain happiness or realize truth or God is merely deceiving himself; he is living in ignorance and, therefore, in conflict. A man who sees that time is not the way out of our difficulty and who is, therefore, free from the false, such a man naturally has the intention to understand; therefore, his mind is quiet spontaneously, without compulsion, without practice. When the mind is still, tranquil, not seeking any answer or any solution, neither resisting nor avoiding—it is only then that there can be a regeneration, because then the mind is capable of perceiving what is true; and it is truth that liberates, not your effort to be free.

At this time of the year, in this warm climate, it was spring. The sun was exceptionally mild, for a light wind was coming from the north where the mountains were fresh in the snow. A tree beside the road, bare a week ago, was now covered with new green leaves which sparkled in the sun. The new leaves were so tender, so delicate, so small in the vast space of the mind, of the earth and the blue sky; yet within a short time they seemed to fill the space of all thought. Further along the road there was a flowering tree which had no leaves, but only blossoms. The breeze had scattered the petals on the ground, and several children were sitting among them. They were the children of the chauffeurs and other servants. They would never go to school; they would always be the poor people of the earth, but among the fallen petals beside the tarred road, those children were part of the earth. They were startled to see a stranger sitting there with them, and they became suddenly silent; they stopped playing with the petals, and for a few seconds they were as still as statues. But their eyes were alive with curiosity, friendliness, and apprehension.

In a small, sunken garden by the roadside there were quantities of bright flowers. Among the leaves of a tree in that garden a crow was shading itself from the midday sun. Its whole body was resting on the branch, the feathers covering its claws. It was calling or answering other crows, and within a period of ten minutes there were five or six different notes in its cawing. It probably had many more notes, but now it was satisfied with a few. It was very black, with a gray neck; it had extraordinary eyes which were never still, and its beak was hard and sharp. It was completely at rest and yet completely alive. It was strange how the mind was totally with that bird. It was not observing the bird, though it had taken in every detail; it was not the bird itself, for there was no identification with it. It was with the bird, with its eyes and its sharp beak, as the sea is with the fish; it was with the bird, and yet it went through and beyond it. The sharp, aggressive, and frightened mind of the crow was part of the mind that spanned the seas and time. This mind was vast, limitless, beyond all measure, and yet it was aware of the slightest movement of the eyes of that black crow among the new, sparkling leaves. It was aware of the falling petals, but it had no focus of attention, no point from which to attend. Unlike space, which has always something in it—a particle of dust, the earth, or the heavens—it was wholly empty, and being empty it could attend without a cause. Its attention had neither root nor branch. All energy was in that empty stillness. It was not the energy that is built up with intent, and which is soon dissipated when pressure is taken away. It was the energy of all beginning; it was life that had no time as ending.

Sorrow from Self-Pity

Several people had come together, and as each one tried to state some problem, the others began to explain it and to compare it with their own trials. But sorrow is not to be compared. Comparison breeds self-pity, and then misfortune ensues. Adversity is to be met directly, not with the idea that yours is greater than another's.

They were all silent now, and presently one of them began.

"My mother has been dead for some years. Quite recently I have lost my father also, and I am full of remorse. He was a good father, and I ought to have been many things which I was not. Our ideas clashed; our respective ways of life kept us apart. He was a religious man, but my religious feeling is not so obvious. The relationship between us was often strained, but at least it was a relationship, and now that he is gone I am stricken with sorrow. My sorrow is not only remorse, but also the feeling of suddenly being left alone. I have never had this kind of sorrow before, and it is quite acute. What am I to do? How am I to get over it?"

If one may ask, do you suffer for your father, or does sorrow arise from having no longer the relationship to which you had grown accustomed?

"I don't quite understand what you mean."

Do you suffer because your father is gone or because you feel lonely?

"All I know is that I suffer, and I want to get away from it. I really don't understand what you mean. Will you please explain?"

It is fairly simple, is it not? Either you are suffering on behalf of your father, that is, because he enjoyed living and wanted to live, and now he is gone; or you are suffering because there has been a break in a relationship that had significance for so long, and you are suddenly aware of loneliness. Now, which is it? You are suffering surely, not for your father, but because you are lonely, and your sorrow is that which comes from self-pity.

"What exactly is loneliness?"

Have you never felt lonely?

"Yes, I have often taken solitary walks. I go for long walks alone, especially on my holidays."

Isn't there a difference between the feeling of loneliness and being alone as on a solitary walk?

"If there is, then I don't think I know what loneliness means."

"I don't think we know what anything means, except verbally," someone added.

Have you never experienced for yourself the feeling of loneliness, as you might a toothache? When we talk of loneliness, are we experiencing the psychological pain of it, or merely employing a word to indicate something which we have never directly experienced? Do we really suffer, or only think we suffer?

"I want to know what loneliness is," he replied.

You mean you want a description of it. It's an experience of being completely isolated; a feeling of not being able to depend on anything, of being cut off from all relationship. The "me," the ego, the self, by its very nature, is constantly building a wall around itself; all its activity leads to isolation. Becoming aware of its isolation, it begins to identify itself with virtue, with God, with property, with a person, country, or ideology; but this identification is part of the process of isolation. In other words, we escape by every possible means from the pain of loneliness, from this feeling of isolation, and so we never directly experience it. It's like being afraid of something round the corner and never facing it, never finding out what it is, but always running away and taking refuge in somebody or something, which only breeds more fear. Have you never felt lonely in this sense of being cut off from everything, completely isolated?

"I have no idea at all what you are talking about."

Then, if one may ask, do you really know what sorrow is? Are you experiencing sorrow as strongly and urgently as you would a toothache? When you have a toothache, you act; you go to the dentist. But when there is sorrow you run away from it through explanation, belief, drink, and so on. You act, but your action is not the action that frees the mind from sorrow, is it?

"I don't know what to do, and that's why I'm here."

Before you can know what to do, must you not find out what sorrow actually is? Haven't you merely formed an idea, a judgment, of what sorrow is? Surely, the running away, the evaluation, the fear, prevents you from experiencing it directly. When you are suffering from a toothache you don't form ideas and opinions about it; you just have it and you act. But here there is no action, immediate or remote, because you are really not suffering. To suffer and to understand suffering, you must look at it, you must not run away.

"My father is gone beyond recall, and so I suffer. What must I do to go beyond the reaches of suffering?"

We suffer because we do not see the truth of suffering. The fact and our ideation about the fact are entirely distinct, leading in two different directions. If one may ask, are you concerned with the fact, the actuality, or merely with the idea of suffering?

"You are not answering my question, sir. What am I to do?"

Do you want to escape from suffering, or to be free from it? If you merely want to escape, then a pill, a belief, an explanation, an amusement, may "help," with the inevitable consequences of dependence, fear, and so on. But if you wish to be free from sorrow, you must stop running away and be aware of it without judgment, without choice; you must observe it, learn about it, know all the intimate intricacies of it. Then you will not be frightened of it, and there will no longer be the poison of self-pity. With the understanding of sorrow there is freedom from it. To understand sorrow there must be the actual experiencing of it, and not the verbal fiction of sorrow.

"May I just ask just one question?" put in one of the others. "In what manner should one live one's daily life?"

As though one were living for that single day, for that single hour.

"How?"

If you had only one hour to live, what would you do?

"I really don't know," he replied anxiously.

Would you not arrange what is necessary outwardly, your affairs, your will, and so on? Would you not call your family and friends together and ask their forgiveness for the harm that you might have done to them, and forgive them for whatever harm they might have done to you? Would you not die completely to the things of the mind, to desires, and to the world? And if it can be done for an hour then it can also be done for the days and years that may remain.

"Is such a thing really possible, sir?"

Try it and you will find out.

When one travels around the world, one notices to what an extraordinary degree human nature is the same, whether in India or America, in Europe or Australia. This is especially true in colleges and universities. We are turning out, as if through a mold, a type of human being whose chief interest is to find security, to become somebody important, or to have a good time with as little thought as possible.

Conventional education makes independent thinking extremely difficult. Conformity leads to mediocrity. To be different from the group or to resist environment is not easy and is often risky as long as we worship success. The urge to be successful, which is the pursuit of reward whether in the material or in the so-called spiritual sphere, the search for inward or outward security, the desire for comfort—this whole process smothers discontent, puts an end to spontaneity and breeds fear; and fear blocks the intelligent understanding of life. With increasing age, dullness of mind and heart sets in.

In seeking comfort, we generally find a quiet corner in life where there is a minimum of conflict, and then we are afraid to step out of that seclusion. This fear of life, this fear of struggle and of new experience, kills in us the spirit of adventure; our whole upbringing and education have made us afraid to be different from our neighbor, afraid to think contrary to the established pattern of society, falsely respectful of authority and tradition.

Fortunately, there are a few who are in earnest, who are willing to examine our human problems without the prejudice of the right or of the left; but in the vast majority of us, there is no real spirit of discontent, of revolt. When we yield uncomprehendingly to environment, any spirit of revolt that we may have had dies down, and our responsibilities soon put an end to it.

Revolt is of two kinds: there is violent revolt, which is mere reaction, without understanding, against the existing order; and there is the deep psychological revolt of intelligence. There are many who revolt against the established orthodoxies only to fall into new orthodoxies, further illusions and concealed self-indulgences. What generally happens is that we break away from one group or set of ideals and join another group, take up other ideals, thus creating a new pattern of thought against which we will again have to revolt. Reaction only breeds opposition, and reform needs further reform.

But there is an intelligent revolt which is not reaction, and which comes with self-knowledge through the awareness of one's own thought and feeling. It is only when we face experience as it comes and do not avoid disturbance that we keep intelligence highly awakened; and intelligence highly awakened is intuition, which is the only true guide in life.

Now, what is the significance of life? What are we living and struggling for? If we are being educated merely to achieve distinction, to get a better job, to be more efficient, to have wider domination over others, then our lives will be shallow and empty. If we are being educated only to be scientists, to be scholars wedded to books, or specialists addicted to knowledge, then we shall be contributing to the destruction and misery of the world.

Though there is a higher and wider significance to life, of what value is our education if we never discover it? We may be highly educated, but if we are without deep integration of thought and feeling, our lives are incomplete, contradictory, and torn with many fears; and as long as education does not cultivate an integrated outlook on life, it has very little significance.

In our present civilization we have divided life into so many departments that education has very little meaning, except in learning a particular technique or profession. Instead of awakening the integrated intelligence of the individual, education is encouraging him to conform to a pattern and so is hindering his comprehension of himself as a total process. To attempt to solve the many problems of existence at their respective levels, separated as they are into various categories, indicates an utter lack of comprehension.

The individual is made up of different entities, but to emphasize the differences and to encourage the development of a definite type leads to many complexities and contradictions. Education should bring about the integration of these separate entities, for without integration, life becomes a series of conflicts and sorrows. Of what value is it to be trained as lawyers if we perpetuate litigation? Of what value is knowledge if we continue in our confusion? What significance has technical and industrial capacity if we use it to destroy one another? What is the point of our existence if it leads to violence and utter misery? Though we may have money or are capable of earning it, though we have our pleasures and our organized religions, we are in endless conflict.

We must distinguish between the personal and the individual. The personal is the accidental; and by the accidental I mean the circumstances of birth, the environment in which we happen to have been brought up, with its nationalism, superstitions, class distinctions and prejudices. The personal or accidental is but momentary, though that moment may last a lifetime; and as the present system of education is based on the personal, the accidental, the momentary, it leads to perversion of thought and the inculcation of self-defensive fears.

All of us have been trained by education and environment to seek personal gain and security, and to fight for ourselves. Though we cover it over with pleasant phrases, we have been educated for various professions within a system based on exploitation and acquisitive fear. Such a training must inevitably bring confusion and misery to ourselves and to the world, for it creates in each individual those psychological barriers which separate and hold him apart from others.

Education is not merely a matter of training the mind. Training makes for efficiency, but it does not bring about completeness. A mind that has merely been trained is the continuation of the past, and such a mind can never discover the new. That is why, to find out what is right education, we will have to inquire into the whole significance of living.

To most of us, the meaning of life as a whole is not of primary importance, and our education emphasizes secondary values, merely making us proficient in some branch of knowledge. Though knowledge and efficiency are necessary, to lay chief emphasis on them only leads to conflict and confusion.

There is an efficiency inspired by love which goes far beyond and is much greater than the efficiency of ambition; and without love, which brings an integrated understanding of life, efficiency breeds ruthlessness. Is this not what is actually taking place all over the world? Our present education is geared to industrialization and war, its principal aim being to develop efficiency; and we are caught in this machine of ruthless competition and mutual destruction. If education leads to war, if it teaches us to destroy or be destroyed, has it not utterly failed?

To bring about right education, we must obviously understand the meaning of life as a whole, and for that we have to be able to think, not consistently, but directly and truly. A consistent thinker is a thoughtless person, because he conforms to a pattern;

he repeats phrases and thinks in a groove. We cannot understand existence abstractly or theoretically. To understand life is to understand ourselves, and that is both the beginning and the end of education.

Education is not merely acquiring knowledge, gathering and correlating facts; it is to see the significance of life as a whole. But the whole cannot be approached through the part, which is what governments, organized religions, and authoritarian parties are attempting to do.

The function of education is to create human beings who are integrated and, therefore, intelligent. We may take degrees and be mechanically efficient without being intelligent. Intelligence is not mere information; it is not derived from books, nor does it consist of clever self-defensive responses and aggressive assertions. One who has not studied may be more intelligent than the learned. We have made examinations and degrees the criterion of intelligence and have developed cunning minds that avoid vital human issues. Intelligence is the capacity to perceive the essential, the *what is;* and to awaken this capacity, in oneself and in others, is education.

Education should help us to discover lasting values so that we do not merely cling to formulas or repeat slogans; it should help us to break down our national and social barriers, instead of emphasizing them, for they breed antagonism between man and man. Unfortunately, the present system of education is making us subservient, mechanical, and deeply thoughtless; though it awakens us intellectually, inwardly it leaves us incomplete, stultified, and uncreative.

Without an integrated understanding of life, our individual and collective problems will only deepen and extend. The purpose of education is not to produce mere scholars, technicians, and job hunters, but integrated men and women who are free of fear; for only between such human beings can there be enduring peace.

It is in the understanding of ourselves that fear comes to an end. If the individual is to grapple with life from moment to moment, if he is to face its intricacies, its miseries and sudden demands, he must be infinitely pliable and, therefore, free of theories and particular patterns of thought.

Education should not encourage the individual to conform to society or to be negatively harmonious with it, but help him to discover the true values which come with unbiased investigation and self-awareness. When there is no self-knowledge, self-expression becomes self-assertion, with all its aggressive and ambitious conflicts. Education should awaken the capacity to be self-aware and not merely indulge in gratifying self-expression.

What is the good of learning if in the process of living we are destroying ourselves? As we are having a series of devastating wars, one right after another, there is obviously something radically wrong with the way we bring up our children. I think most of us are aware of this, but we do not know how to deal with it.

Systems, whether educational or political, are not changed mysteriously; they are transformed when there is a fundamental change in ourselves. The individual is of first importance, not the system; and as long as the individual does not understand the total process of himself, no system, whether of the left or of the right, can bring order and peace to the world.

It seems to me that a totally different kind of morality and conduct, and an action that springs from the understanding of the whole process of living, have become an urgent necessity, in our world of mounting crises and problems. We try to deal with these issues through political and organizational methods, through economic readjustment and various reforms; but none of these things will ever resolve the complex difficulties of human existence, though they may offer temporary relief. All reforms, however extensive and seemingly lasting, are in themselves merely productive of further confusion and further need of reformation. Without understanding the whole complex being of man, mere reformation will bring about only the confusing demand for further reforms. There is no end to reform; and there is no fundamental solution along these lines.

Political, economic, or social revolutions are not the answer either, for they have produced appalling tyrannies, or the mere transfer of power and authority into the hands of a different group. Such revolutions are not at any time the way out of our confusion and conflict.

But there is a revolution which is entirely different and which must take place if we are to emerge from the endless series of anxieties, conflicts, and frustrations in which we are caught. This revolution has to begin not with theory and ideation, which eventually prove worthless, but with a radical transformation in the mind itself. Such a transformation can be brought about only through right education and the total development of the human being. It is a revolution that must take place in the whole of the mind and not merely in thought. Thought, after all, is only a result and not the source. There must be radical transformation of the source and not mere modification of the result. At present we are tinkering with results, with symptoms. We are not bringing about a vital change, uprooting the old ways of thought, freeing the mind from traditions and habits. It is with this vital change we are concerned and only right education can bring it into being.

To inquire and to learn is the function of the mind. By learning I do not mean the mere cultivation of memory or the accumulation of knowledge, but the capacity to think clearly and sanely without illusion, to start from facts and not from beliefs and ideals. There is no learning if thought originates from conclusions. To merely acquire information or knowledge is not to learn. Learning implies the love of understanding and the love of doing a thing for itself. Learning is possible only when there is no coercion of any kind. And coercion takes many forms, does it not? There is coercion through influence, through attachment or threat, through persuasive encouragement or subtle forms of reward.

Most people think that learning is encouraged through comparison, whereas the contrary is the fact. Comparison brings about frustration and merely encourages envy, which is called competition. Like other forms of persuasion, comparison prevents learning and breeds fear. Ambition also breeds fear. Ambition, whether personal or identified with the collective, is always antisocial. So-called noble ambition in relationship is fundamentally destructive.

It is necessary to encourage the development of a good mind—a mind which is capable of dealing with the many issues of life as a whole, and which does not try to escape from them and so become self-contradictory, frustrated, bitter, or cynical. And it is essential for the mind to be aware of its own conditioning, its own motives and pursuits.

Since the development of a good mind is one of our chief concerns, how one teaches becomes very important. There must be a cultivation of the totality of the mind, and not merely the giving of information. In the process of imparting knowledge, the educator has to invite discussion and encourage the students to inquire and to think independently.

Authority, as "the one who knows," has no place in learning. The educator and the student are both learning through their special relationship with each other, but this does not mean that the educator disregards the orderliness of thought. Orderliness of thought is not brought about by discipline in the form of assertive statements of knowledge; but it comes into being naturally when the educator understands that in cultivating intelligence there must be a sense of freedom. This does not mean freedom to do whatever one likes, or to think in the spirit of mere contradiction. It is the freedom in which the student is being helped to be aware of his own urges and motives, which are revealed to him through his daily thought and action.

A disciplined mind is never a free mind, nor can a mind that has suppressed desire ever be free. It is only through understanding the whole process of desire that the mind can be free. Discipline always limits the mind to a movement within the framework of a particular system of thought or belief, does it not? And such a mind is never free to be intelligent. Discipline brings about submission to authority. It gives the capacity to function within the pattern of a society which demands functional ability, but it does not awaken the intelligence which has its own capacity. The mind that has cultivated nothing but capacity through memory is like the modern electronic computer which, though it functions with astonishing ability and accuracy, is still only a machine. Authority can persuade the mind to think in a particular direction. But being guided to think along certain lines, or in terms of a foregone conclusion, is not to think at all; it is merely to function like a human machine, which breeds thoughtless discontent, bringing with it frustration and other miseries.

We are concerned with the total development of each human being, helping him to realize his own highest and fullest capacity—not some fictitious capacity which the educator has in view as a concept or an ideal. Any spirit of comparison prevents this full flowering of the individual, whether he is to be a scientist or a gardener. The fullest capacity of the gardener is the same as the fullest capacity of the scientist when there is no comparison; but when comparison comes in, then there is the disparagement and the envious reactions which create conflict between man and man. Like sorrow, love is not comparative; it cannot be compared with the greater or the lesser. Sorrow is sorrow, as love is love, whether it be in the rich or in the poor.

The fullest development of every individual creates a society of equals. The present social struggle to bring about equality on the economic or some spiritual level has no meaning at all. Social reforms aimed at establishing equality breed other forms of antisocial activity, but with right education, there is no need to seek equality through social and other reforms, because envy, with its comparison of capacities, ceases.

We must differentiate here between function and status. Status, with all its emotional and hierarchical prestige, arises only through the comparison of functions as the high and the low. When each individual is flowering to his fullest capacity, there is then no comparison of functions; there is only the expression of capacity as a teacher, or a prime minister, or a gardener, and so status loses its sting of envy.

Functional or technical capacity is now recognized through having a degree after one's name; but if we are truly concerned with the total development of the human being, our approach is entirely different. An individual who has the capacity may take a degree and add letters after his name, or he may not, as he pleases. But he will know for himself his own deep capabilities, which will not be framed by a degree, and their expression will not bring about that self-centered confidence which mere technical capacity usually breeds. Such confidence is comparative and, therefore, antisocial. Comparison may exist for utilitarian purpose; but it is not for the educator to compare the capacities of his students and give greater or lesser evaluation.

Since we are concerned with the total development of the individual, the student may not be allowed in the beginning to choose his own subjects, because his choice is likely to be based on passing moods and prejudices, or on finding the easiest thing to do; or he may choose according to the immediate demands of a particular need. But if he is helped to discover by himself and to cultivate his innate capacities, then he will naturally choose not the easiest subjects, but those through which he can express his capacities to the fullest and highest extent. If the student is helped from the very beginning to look at life as a whole, with all its psychological, intellectual, and emotional problems, he will not be frightened by it.

Intelligence is the capacity to deal with life as a whole; and giving grades or marks to the student does not assure intelligence. On the contrary, it degrades human dignity. This comparative evaluation cripples the mind, which does not mean that the teacher must not observe the progress of every student and keep a record of it. Parents, naturally anxious to know the progress of their children, will want a report; but if, unfortunately, they do not understand what the educator is trying to do, the report will become an instrument of coercion to produce the results they desire, and so undo the work of the educator.

Parents should understand the kind of education the school intends to give. Generally they are satisfied to see their children preparing to get a degree of some kind which will assure them of a livelihood. Very few are concerned with more than this. Of course, they wish to see their children happy, but beyond this vague desire very few give any thought to their total development. As most parents desire above all else that their children should have a successful career, they frighten or affectionately bully them into acquiring knowledge, and so the book becomes very important; and with it there is the mere cultivation of memory, the mere repetition without the quality of real thought behind it.

Perhaps the greatest difficulty the educator has to face is the indifference of parents to a wider and deeper education. Most parents are concerned only with the cultivation of some superficial knowledge that will secure their children respectable positions in a corrupt society. So the educator not only has to educate the children in the right way, but also to see to it that the parents do not undo whatever good may have been done at the school. Really the school and the home should be joint centers of right education, and should in no way be opposed to each other, with the parents desiring one thing and the educator doing something entirely different. It is very important that the parents be fully acquainted with what the educator is doing and be vitally interested in the total development of their children. It is as much the responsibility of the parents to see that this kind of education is carried out as it is of the teachers, whose burden is already sufficiently heavy. A total development of the child can be brought about only when there is the right relationship between the teacher, the student, and the parents. As the educator cannot yield to the passing fancies or obstinate demands of the parents, it is necessary for them to understand the educator and cooperate with him, and not bring about conflict and confusion in their children.

The child's natural curiosity, the urge to learn, exists from the very beginning, and surely this should be intelligently encouraged continually, so that it remains vital and without distortion, and will gradually lead him to the study of a variety of subjects. If this eagerness to learn is encouraged in the child at all times, then his study of mathematics, geography, history, science, or any other subject, will not be a problem to the child or to the educator. Learning is facilitated when there is an atmosphere of happy affection and thoughtful care.

Emotional openness and sensitivity can be cultivated only when the student feels secure in his relationship with his teachers. The feeling of being secure in relationship is a primary need of children. There is a vast difference between the feeling of being secure and the feeling of dependency. Consciously or unconsciously, most educators cultivate the feeling of dependency, and thereby subtly encourage fear, which the parents also do in their own affectionate or aggressive manner. Dependency in the child is brought about by authoritarian or dogmatic assertions on the part of parents and teachers as to what the child must be and do. With dependency there is always the shadow of fear, and this fear compels the child to obey, to conform, to accept without thought the edicts and sanctions of his elders. In this atmosphere of dependency, sensitivity is crushed, but when the child knows and feels that he is secure, his emotional flowering is not thwarted by fear.

This sense of security in the child is not the opposite of insecurity. It is the feeling of being at ease, whether in his own home or at school, the feeling that he can be what he is, without being compelled in any way; that he can climb a tree and not be scolded if he falls. He can have this sense of security only when the parents and the educators are deeply concerned with the total welfare of the child.

It is important in a school that the child should feel at ease, completely secure from the very first day. This first impression is of the highest importance. But if the educator artificially tries by various means to gain the child's confidence and allows him to do what he likes, then the educator is cultivating dependency; he is not giving the child the feeling of being secure, the feeling that he is in a place where there are people who are deeply concerned with his total welfare.

The very first impact of this new relationship based on confidence, which the child may never have had before, will help toward a natural communication, without the young regarding the elders as a threat to be feared. A child who feels secure has his own natural ways of expressing the respect which is essential for learning. This respect is denuded of all authority and fear. When he has a feeling of security, the child's conduct or behavior is not something imposed by an elder, but becomes part of the process of learning. Because he feels secure in his relationship with the teacher, the child will naturally be considerate; and it is only in this atmosphere of security that emotional openness and sensitivity can flower. Being at ease, feeling secure, the child will do what he likes; but in doing what he likes, he will find out what is the right thing to do, and his conduct then will not be due to resistance, or obstinacy, or suppressed feelings, or the mere expression of a momentary urge.

Sensitivity means being sensitive to everything around one—to the plants, the animals, the trees, the skies, the waters of the river, the bird on the wing; and also to the moods of the people around one, and to the stranger who passes by. This sensitivity brings about the quality of uncalculated, unselfish response, which is true morality and conduct. Being sensitive, the child in his conduct will be open and not secretive; therefore, a mere suggestion on the part of the teacher will be accepted easily, without resistance or friction.

As we are concerned with the total development of the human being, we must understand his emotional urges, which are very much stronger than intellectual reasoning; we must cultivate emotional capacity and not help to suppress it. When we understand and are, therefore, capable of dealing with emotional as well as intellectual issues, there will be no sense of fear in approaching them. For the total development of the human being, solitude as a means of cultivating sensitivity becomes a necessity. One has to know what it is to be alone, what it is to meditate, what it is to die; and the implications of solitude, of meditation, of death, can be known only by seeking them out. These implications cannot be taught, they must be learned. One can indicate, but learning by what is indicated is not the experiencing of solitude or meditation. To experience what is solitude and what is meditation, one must be in a state of inquiry; only a mind that is in a state of inquiry is capable of learning. But when inquiry is suppressed by previous knowledge, or by the authority and experience of another, then learning becomes mere imitation, and imitation causes a human being to repeat what is learned without experiencing it.

Teaching is not the mere imparting of information but the cultivation of an inquiring mind. Such a mind will penetrate into the question of what is religion, and not merely accept the established religions with their temples and rituals. The search for God, or truth, or whatever one may like to name it—and not the mere acceptance of belief and dogma—is true religion.

Just as the student cleans his teeth every day, bathes every day, learns new things every day, so also there must be the action of sitting quietly with others or by himself. This solitude cannot be brought about by instruction, or urged by the external authority of tradition, or induced by the influence of those who want to sit quietly but are incapable of being alone. Solitude helps the mind to see itself clearly, as in a mirror, and to free itself from the vain endeavor of ambition with all its complexities, fears, and frustrations, which are the outcome of self-centered activity. Solitude gives to the mind a stability, a constancy which is not to be measured in terms of time. Such clarity of mind is character. The lack of character is the state of self-contradiction.

To be sensitive is to love. The word *love* is not love. And love is not to be divided as the love of God and the love of man, nor is it to be measured as the love of the one and of the many. Love gives itself abundantly as a flower gives its perfume; but we are always measuring love in our relationship and thereby destroying it.

Love is not a commodity of the reformer or the social worker; it is not a political instrument with which to create action. When the politician and the reformer speak of love, they are using the word and do not touch the reality of it; for love cannot be employed as a means to an end, whether in the immediate or in the far-off future. Love is of the whole earth and not of a particular field or forest. The love of reality is not encompassed by any religion; and when organized religions use it, it ceases to be. Societies, organized religions, and authoritarian governments, sedulous in their various activities, unknowingly destroy the love that becomes passion in action.

In the total development of the human being through right education, the quality of love must be nourished and sustained from the very beginning. Love is not sentimentality, nor is it devotion. It is as strong as death. Love cannot be bought through knowledge; and a mind that is pursuing knowledge without love is a mind that deals in ruthlessness and aims merely at efficiency.

So the educator must be concerned from the very beginning with this quality of love, which is humility, gentleness, consideration, patience, and courtesy. Modesty and courtesy are innate in the man of right education; he is considerate to all, including the animals and plants, and this is reflected in his behavior and manner of talking.

The emphasis on this quality of love frees the mind from its absorption in its ambition, greed, and acquisitiveness. Does not love have about it a refinement which expresses itself as respect and good taste? Does it not also bring about the purification of the mind, which otherwise has a tendency to strengthen itself in pride? Refinement in behavior is not a self-imposed adjustment or the result of an outward demand; it comes spontaneously with this quality of love. When there is the understanding of love, then sex and all the complications and subtleties of human relationship can be approached with sanity and not with excitement and apprehension.

The educator to whom the total development of the human being is of primary importance must understand the implications of the sexual urge which plays such an important part in our life, and be able from the very beginning to meet the children's natural curiosity without arousing a morbid interest. Merely to impart biological information at the adolescent age may lead to experimental lust if the quality of love is not felt. Love cleanses the mind of evil. Without love and understanding on the part of the educator, merely to separate the boys from the girls, whether by barbed wire or by edicts, only strengthens their curiosity and stimulates that passion which is bound to degenerate into mere satisfaction. So it is important that boys and girls be educated together rightly.

This quality of love must express itself also in doing things with one's hands, such as gardening, carpentry, painting, handicrafts; and through the senses, as seeing the trees, the mountains, the richness of the earth, the poverty that men have created amongst themselves; and in healing music, the song of the birds, the murmur of running waters.

We are concerned not only with the cultivation of the mind and the awakening of emotional sensitivity, but also with a well-rounded development of the physique, and to this we must give considerable thought. For if the body is not healthy, vital, it will inevitably distort thought and make for insensitivity. This is so obvious that we need not go into it in detail. It is necessary that the body be in excellent health, that it be given the right kind of food and have sufficient sleep. If the senses are not alert, the body will impede the total development of the human being. To have grace of movement and well-balanced control of the muscles, there must be various forms of exercise, dancing, and games. A body that is not kept clean, that is sloppy and does not hold itself in good posture, is not conducive to sensitivity of mind and emotions. The body is not the instrument of the mind, but body, emotions, and mind make up the total human being, and unless they live together harmoniously, conflict is inevitable.

Conflict makes for insensitivity. The mind may dominate the body and suppress the senses, but it thereby makes the body insensitive; and an insensitive body becomes a hindrance to the full flight of the mind. The mortification of the body is definitely not conducive to the seeking out of the deeper layers of consciousness; for this is possible only when the mind, the emotions, and the body are not in contradiction with each other, but are integrated and in unison, effortlessly, without being driven by any concept, belief, or ideal.

In the cultivation of the mind, our emphasis should not be on concentration, but on attention. Concentration is a process of forcing the mind to narrow down to a point, whereas attention is without frontiers. In that process the mind is always limited by a frontier or boundary, but when our concern is to understand the totality of the mind, mere concentration becomes a hindrance. Attention is limitless, without the frontiers of knowledge. Knowledge comes through concentration, and any extension of knowledge is still within its own frontiers. In the state of attention the mind can and does use knowledge, which of necessity is the result of concentration; but the part is never the whole, and adding together the many parts does not make for the perception of the whole. Knowledge, which is the additive process of concentration, does not bring about the understanding of the immeasurable. The total is never within the brackets of a concentrated mind.

So attention is of primary importance, but it does not come through the effort of concentration. Attention is a state in which the mind is ever learning without a center around which knowledge gathers as accumulated experience. A mind that is concentrated upon itself uses knowledge as a means of its own expansion; and such activity becomes self-contradictory and antisocial.

Learning in the true sense of the word is possible only in that state of attention in which there is no outer or inner compulsion. Right thinking can come about only when the mind is not enslaved by tradition and memory. It is attention that allows silence to come upon the mind, which is the opening of the door to creation. That is why attention is of the highest importance.

Knowledge is necessary at the functional level as a means of cultivating the mind, and not as an end in itself. We are concerned not with the development of just one capacity, such as that of a mathematician, or a scientist, or a musician, but with the total development of the student as a human being.

How is the state of attention to be brought about? It cannot be cultivated through persuasion, comparison, reward, or punishment, all of which are forms of coercion. The elimination of fear is the beginning of attention. Fear must exist as long as there is an urge to be or to become, which is the pursuit of success, with all its frustrations and tortuous contradictions. You can teach concentration, but attention cannot be taught, just as you cannot possibly teach freedom from fear; but we can begin to discover the causes that produce fear, and in understanding these causes there is the elimination of fear. So attention arises spontaneously when around the student there is an atmosphere of well-being, when he has the feeling of being secure, of being at ease, and is aware of the disinterested action that comes with love. Love does not compare, and so the envy and torture of becoming cease.

The general discontent which all of us experience, whether young or old, soon finds a way to satisfaction, and thus our minds are put to sleep. Discontent is awakened from time to time through suffering, but the mind again seeks a gratifying solution. In this wheel of dissatisfaction and gratification the mind is caught, and the constant awakening through pain is part of our discontent. Discontent is the way of inquiry, but there can be no inquiry if the mind is tethered to tradition, to ideals. Inquiry is the flame of attention.

By discontent I mean that state in which the mind understands *what is,* the actual, and constantly inquires to discover further. Discontent is a movement to go beyond the limitations of *what is;* and if you find ways and means of smoothing or overcoming discontent, then you will accept the limitations of self-centered activity and of the society in which you find yourself.

Discontent is the flame which burns away the dross of satisfaction, but most of us seek to dissipate it in various ways. Our discontent then becomes the pursuit of the more, the desire for a bigger house, a better car, and so on, all of which are within the field of envy; and it is envy that sustains such discontent. But I am talking of a discontent in which there is no envy, no greed for "the more," a discontent that is not sustained by any desire for satisfaction. This discontent is an unpolluted state which exists in each one of us, if it is not deadened through wrong education, through gratifying solutions, through ambition, or through the pursuit of an ideal. When we understand the nature of real discontent, we shall see that attention is part of this burning flame, which consumes the pettiness and leaves the mind free of the limitations of self-enclosing pursuits and gratifications.

So attention comes into being only when there is inquiry not based on self-advancement or gratification. This attention must be cultivated in the child, right from the beginning. You will find that when there is love—which expresses itself through humility, courtesy, patience, gentleness—you are already free of the barriers which insensitivity builds; and so you are helping to bring about in the child this state of attention from a very tender age.

Attention is not something to be learned, but you can help to awaken it in the student by not creating around him that sense of compulsion which produces a self-contradictory existence. Then his attention can be focused at any moment on any given subject, and it will not be the narrow concentration brought about through the compulsive urge of acquisition or achievement.

A generation educated in this manner will be free of acquisitiveness and fear, the psychological inheritance of their parents and of the society in which they are born; and because they are so educated, they will not depend on the inheritance of property. This matter of inheritance destroys real independence and limits intelligence; for it breeds a false sense of security, giving a self-assurance which has no basis and creating a darkness of the mind in which nothing new can flourish. But a generation educated in this totally different manner we have been considering will create a new society; for they will have the capacity born of that intelligence which is not hedged about by fear.

Since education is the responsibility of the parents as well as of the teachers, we must learn the art of working together, and this is possible only when each one of us perceives what is true. It is perception of the truth that brings us together, and not opinion, belief, or theory. There is a vast difference between the conceptual and the factual. The conceptual may bring us together temporarily, but there will again be separation if our working together is only a matter of conviction. If the truth is seen by each one of us, there may be disagreement in detail but there will be no urge to separate. It is the foolish who break away over some detail. When the truth is seen by all, the detail can never become an issue over which there is dissension.

Most of us are used to working together along the lines of established authority. We come together to work for a concept, or to advance an ideal, and this requires conviction, persuasion, propaganda, and so on. Such working together for a concept, for an ideal, is totally different from the cooperation which comes from seeing the truth and the necessity of putting that truth into action. Working under the stimulus of authority—whether it be the authority of an ideal, or the authority of a person who represents that ideal—is not real cooperation. A central authority who knows a great deal, or who has a strong personality and is obsessed with certain ideas, may force or subtly persuade others to work with him for what he calls the ideal; but surely this is not the working together of alert and vital individuals, whereas when each one of us understands for himself the truth of any issue, then our common understanding of that truth leads to action, and such action is cooperation. He who cooperates because he sees the truth as the truth, the false as the false, and the truth in the false, will also know when not to cooperate, which is equally important.

If each one of us realizes the necessity of a fundamental revolution in education and perceives the truth of what we have been considering, then we shall work together without any form of persuasion. Persuasion exists only when someone takes a stand from which he is unwilling to move. When he is merely convinced of an idea or entrenched in an opinion, he brings about opposition, and then he or the other has to be persuaded, influenced, or induced to think differently. Such a situation will never arise when each one of us sees the truth of the matter for himself. But if we do not see the truth and act on the basis of merely verbal conviction or intellectual reasoning, then there is bound to be contention, agreement or disagreement, with all the associated distortion and useless effort.

It is essential that we work together, and it is as if we were building a house. If some of us are building and others are tearing down, the house will obviously never be built. So we must individually be very clear that we really see and understand the necessity of bringing about the kind of education that will produce a new generation capable of dealing with the issues of life as a whole, and not as isolated parts unrelated to the whole.

To be able to work together in this really cooperative way, we must meet often and be alert not to get submerged in detail. Those of us who are seriously dedicated to the bringing about of the right kind of education have the responsibility not only of carrying out in action all that we have understood, but also of helping others to come to this understanding. Teaching is the noblest profession—if it can be called a profession at all. It is an art that requires, not just intellectual attainments, but infinite patience and love. To be truly educated is to understand our relationship to all things—to money, to property, to people, to nature—in the vast field of our existence.

Beauty is part of this understanding, but beauty is not merely a matter of proportion, form, taste, and behavior. Beauty is that state in which the mind has abandoned the center of self in the passion of simplicity. Simplicity has no end; and there can be simplicity only when there is an austerity which is not the outcome of calculated discipline and self-denial. This austerity is self-abandonment, which love alone can bring about. When we have no love we create a civilization in which beauty of form is sought without the inner vitality and austerity of simple self-abandonment. There is no self-abandonment if there is an immolation of oneself in good works, in ideals, in beliefs. These activities appear to be free of the self, but in reality the self is still working under the cover of different labels. Only the innocent mind can inquire into the unknown. But the calculated innocence which may wear a loincloth or the robe of a monk is not that passion of self-abandonment from which come courtesy, gentleness, humility, patience—the expressions of love.

Most of us know beauty only through that which has been created or put together—the beauty of a human form, or of a temple. We say a tree, or a house, or the widely curving river, is beautiful. And through comparison we know what ugliness is—at least we think we do. But is beauty comparable? Is beauty that which has been made evident, manifest? We consider beautiful a particular picture, poem, or face, because we already know what beauty is from what we have been taught, or from what we are familiar with and about which we have formed an opinion. But does not beauty cease with comparison? Is beauty merely a familiarity with the known, or is it a state of being in which there may or may not be the created form?

We are always pursuing beauty and avoiding the ugly, and this seeking of enrichment through the one and avoidance of the other must inevitably breed insensitivity. Surely, to understand or to feel what beauty is, there must be sensitivity to both the so-called beautiful and the so-called ugly. A feeling is not beautiful or ugly, it is just a feeling. But we look at it through our religious and social conditioning and give it a label; we say it is a good feeling or a bad feeling, and so we distort or destroy it. When feeling is not given a label it remains intense, and it is this passionate intensity that is essential to the understanding of that which is neither ugliness nor manifested beauty. What has the greatest importance is sustained feeling, that passion which is not the mere lust of self-gratification; for it is this passion that creates beauty and, not being comparable, it has no opposite.

In seeking to bring about a total development of the human being, we must obviously take into full consideration the unconscious mind as well as the conscious. Merely to educate the conscious mind without understanding the unconscious brings self-contradiction into human lives, with all its frustrations and miseries. The hidden mind is far more vital than the superficial. Most educators are concerned only with giving information or knowledge to the superficial mind, preparing it to acquire a job and adjust itself to society. So the hidden mind is never touched. All that so-called education does is to superimpose a layer of knowledge and technique, and a certain capacity to adjust to environment.

The hidden mind is far more potent than the superficial mind, however well-educated and capable of adjustment; and it is not something very mysterious. The hidden or unconscious mind is the repository of racial memories. Religion, superstition, symbol, peculiar traditions of a particular race, the influence of literature both sacred and profane, aspirations, frustrations, mannerisms, and varieties of food—all these are rooted in the unconscious. The open and secret desires, with their motivations, hopes, and fears, their sorrows and pleasures, and the beliefs which are sustained through the urge for security, translating itself in various ways—these things also are contained in the hidden mind, which not only has this extraordinary capacity to hold the residual past, but also the capacity to influence the future. Intimations of all this are given to the superficial mind through dreams and in various other ways when it is not wholly occupied with everyday events.

The hidden mind is nothing sacred and nothing to be frightened of, nor does it demand a specialist to expose it to the superficial mind. But because of the hidden mind's enormous potency, the superficial mind cannot deal with it as it would wish. The superficial mind is to a great extent impotent in relation to its own hidden part. However much it may try to dominate, shape, or control the hidden, because of its immediate social demands and pursuits, the superficial can only scratch the surface of the hidden; and so there is a cleavage or contradiction between the two. We try to bridge this chasm through discipline, through various practices, sanctions, and so on; but it cannot so be bridged.

The conscious mind is occupied with the immediate, the limited present, whereas the unconscious is under the weight of centuries, and cannot be stemmed or turned aside by an immediate necessity. The unconscious has the quality of deep time, and the conscious mind, with its recent culture, cannot deal with it according to its passing urgencies. To eradicate self-contradiction, the superficial mind must understand this fact and be quiescent, which does not mean giving scope to the innumerable urges of the hidden. When there is no resistance between the open and the hidden, then the hidden, because it has the patience of time, will not violate the immediate.

The hidden, unexplored, and un-understood mind, with its superficial part which has been "educated," comes into contact with the challenges and demands of the immediate present. The superficial may respond to the challenge adequately; but because there is a contradiction between the superficial and the hidden, any experience of the superficial only increases the conflict between itself and the hidden. This brings about still further experience, again widening the chasm between the present and the past. The superficial mind, experiencing the outer without understanding the inner, the hidden, only produces deeper and wider conflict.

Experience does not liberate or enrich the mind, as we generally think it does. As long as experience strengthens the experiencer, there must be conflict. In having experiences, a conditioned mind only strengthens its conditioning, and so perpetuates contradiction and misery. Only for the mind that is capable of understanding the total ways of itself can experiencing be a liberating factor.

Once there is perception and understanding of the power and capacities of the many layers of the hidden, then the details can be looked into wisely and intelligently. What is important is the understanding of the hidden, and not the mere education of the superficial mind to acquire knowledge, however necessary. This understanding of the hidden frees the total mind from conflict, and only then is there intelligence.

We must awaken the full capacity of the superficial mind that lives in everyday activity, and also understand the hidden. In understanding the hidden there is a total living in which self-contradiction, with its alternating sorrow and happiness, ceases. It is essential to be acquainted with the hidden mind and aware of its workings; but it is equally important not to be occupied with it or give it undue significance. It is only when the mind understands the superficial and the hidden that it can go beyond its own limitations and discover that bliss which is not of time.

FREEDOM FROM THE KNOWN

1

If you think it is important to know about yourself only because I or someone else has told you it is important, then I am afraid all communication between us comes to an end. But if we agree that it is vital that we understand ourselves completely, then you and I have quite a different relationship, then we can explore together with a happy, careful, and intelligent inquiry.

I do not demand your faith; I am not setting myself up as an authority. I have nothing to teach you—no new philosophy, no new system, no new path to reality; there is no path to reality any more than to truth. All authority of any kind, especially in the field of thought and understanding, is the most destructive, evil thing. Leaders destroy the followers and followers destroy the leaders. You have to be your own teacher and your own disciple. You have to question everything that man has accepted as valuable, as necessary.

If you do not follow somebody you feel very lonely. Be lonely then. Why are you frightened of being alone? Because you are faced with yourself as you are and you find that you are empty, dull, stupid, ugly, guilty, and anxious—a petty, shoddy, secondhand entity. Face the fact; look at it, do not run away from it. The moment you run away fear begins.

In inquiring into ourselves we are not isolating ourselves from the rest of the world. It is not an unhealthy process. Man throughout the world is caught up in the same daily problems as ourselves, so in inquiring into ourselves we are not being in the least neurotic because there is no difference between the individual and the collective. That is an actual fact. I have created the world as I am. So don't let us get lost in this battle between the part and the whole.

I must become aware of the total field of my own self, which is the consciousness of the individual and of society. It is only then, when the mind goes beyond this individual and social consciousness, that I can become a light to myself that never goes out.

Now where do we begin to understand ourselves? Here am I, and how am I to study myself, observe myself, see what is actually taking place inside myself? I can observe myself only in relationship because all life is relationship. It is no use sitting in a corner meditating about myself. I cannot exist by myself. I exist only in relationship to people, things, and ideas, and in studying my relationship to outward things and people, as well as to inward things, I begin to understand myself. Every other form of understanding is merely an abstraction and I cannot study myself in abstraction. I am not an abstract entity; therefore, I have to study myself in actuality—as I am, not as I wish to be.

Understanding is not an intellectual process. Acquiring knowledge about yourself and learning about yourself are two different things, for the knowledge you accumulate about yourself is always of the past and a mind that is burdened with the past is a sorrowful mind. Learning about yourself is not like learning a language or a technology or a science—then you obviously have to accumulate and remember; it would be absurd to begin all over again—but in the psychological field, learning about yourself is always in the present and knowledge is always in the past, and as most of us live in the past and are satisfied with the past, knowledge becomes extraordinarily important to us. That is why we worship the erudite, the clever, the cunning. But if you are learning all the time, learning every minute, learning by watching and listening, learning by seeing and doing, then you will find that learning is a constant movement without the past.

If you say you will learn gradually about yourself, adding more and more, little by little, you are not studying yourself now as you are but through acquired knowledge. Learning implies a great sensitivity. There is no sensitivity if there is an idea, which is of the past, dominating the present. Then the mind is no longer quick, pliable, alert. Most of us are not sensitive, even physically. We overeat, we do not bother about the right diet, we oversmoke and drink so that our bodies become gross and insensitive; the quality of attention in the organism itself is made dull. How can there be a very alert, sensitive, clear mind if the organism itself is dull and heavy? We may be sensitive about certain things that touch us personally but to be completely sensitive to all the implications of life demands that there be no separation between the organism and the psyche. It is a total movement.

To understand anything you must live with it, you must observe it, you must know all its content, its nature, its structure, its movement. Have you ever tried living with yourself? If so, you will begin to see that your self is not a static state, it is a fresh living thing. And to live with a living thing your mind must also be alive. And it cannot be alive if it is caught in opinions, judgments, and values.

In order to observe the movement of your own mind and heart, of your whole being, you must have a free mind, not a mind that agrees and disagrees, taking sides in an argument, disputing over mere words but rather, following with an intention to understand—a very difficult thing to do because most of us don't know how to look at, or listen to, our own being any more than we know how to look at the beauty of a river or listen to the breeze among the trees.

When we condemn or justify we cannot see clearly, nor can we when our minds are endlessly chattering; then we do not observe *what is,* we look only at the projections we have made of ourselves. Each of us has an image of what we think we are or what we should be, and that image, that picture, entirely prevents us from seeing ourselves as we actually are.

It is one of the most difficult things in the world to look at anything simply. Because our minds are very complex we have lost the quality of simplicity. I don't mean simplicity in clothes or food, wearing only a loincloth or breaking a record fasting or any of that immature nonsense the saints cultivate, but the simplicity that can look directly at things without fear—that can look at ourselves as we actually are without any distortion, to say when we lie we lie, not cover it up or run away from it.

Also in order to understand ourselves we need a great deal of humility. If you start by saying, "I know myself," you have already stopped learning about yourself; or if you say, "There is nothing much to learn about myself because I am just a bundle of memories, ideas, experiences, and traditions," then you have also stopped learning about yourself. The moment you have achieved anything you cease to have that quality of innocence and humility; the moment you have a conclusion or start examining from knowledge, you are finished, for then you are translating every living thing in terms of the old, whereas if you have no foothold, if there is no certainty, no achievement, there is freedom—to look, to achieve. And when you look with freedom it is always new. A confident man is a dead human being.

But how can we be free to look and learn when our minds, from the moment we are born to the moment we die, are shaped by a particular culture in the narrow pattern of the "me"? For centuries we have been conditioned by nationality, caste, class, tradition, religion, language, education, literature, art, custom, convention, propaganda of all kinds, economic pressure, the food we eat, the climate we live in, our family, our friends, our experiences—every influence you can think of—and, therefore, our responses to every problem are conditioned.

Are you aware that you are conditioned? That is the first thing to ask yourself, not how to be free of your conditioning. You may never be free of it, and if you say, "I must be free of it," you may fall into another trap of another form of conditioning. So are you aware that you are conditioned? Do you know that even when you look at a tree and say, "That is an oak tree," or "That is a banyan tree," the naming of the tree, which is botanical knowledge, has so conditioned your mind that the word comes between you and actually seeing the tree? To come in contact with the tree you have to put your hand on it and the word will not help you to touch it.

How do you know you are conditioned? What tells you? What tells you you are hungry?—not as a theory but the actual fact of hunger? In the same way, how do you discover the actual fact that you are conditioned? Isn't it by your reaction to a problem, a challenge? You respond to every challenge according to your conditioning and your conditioning, being inadequate, will always react inadequately.

When you become aware of it, does this conditioning of race, religion, and culture bring a sense of imprisonment? Take only one form of conditioning, nationality, become seriously, completely aware of it and see whether you enjoy it or rebel against it, and if you rebel against it, whether you want to break through all conditioning. If you are satisfied with your conditioning you will obviously do nothing about it, but if you are not satisfied, when you become aware of it you will realize that you never do anything without it. Never! And, therefore, you are always living in the past with the dead.

You will be able to see for yourself how you are conditioned only when there is a conflict in the continuity of pleasure or the avoidance of pain. If everything is perfectly happy around you, your wife loves you, you love her, you have a nice house, nice children and plenty of money, then you are not aware of your conditioning at all. But when there is a disturbance—when your wife looks at someone else or you lose your money or are threatened with war or any other pain or anxiety—then you know you are conditioned. When you struggle against any kind of disturbance or defend yourself against any outer or inner threat, then you know you are conditioned. And as most of us are disturbed most of the time, either superficially or deeply, that very disturbance indicates that we are conditioned. So long as the animal is petted he reacts nicely, but the moment he is antagonized the whole violence of his nature comes out.

We are disturbed about life, politics, the economic situation, the horror, the brutality, the sorrow in the world as well as in ourselves, and from that we realize how terribly narrowly conditioned we are. And what shall we do? Accept that disturbance and live with it as most of us do? Get used to it as one gets used to living with a backache? Put up with it?

There is a tendency in all of us to put up with things, to get used to them, to blame them on circumstances. "Ah, if things were right I would be different," we say, or, "Give me the opportunity and I will fulfill myself," or, "I am crushed by the injustice of it all," always blaming our disturbances on others or on our environment or on the economic situation.

If one gets used to disturbance it means that one's mind has become dull, just as one can get so used to beauty around one that one no longer notices it. One gets indifferent, hard and callous, and one's mind becomes duller and duller. If we do not get used to it we try to escape from it by taking some kind of drug, joining a political group, shouting, writing, going to a football match or to a temple or church, or finding some other form of amusement.

Why is it that we escape from actual facts? We are afraid of death—I am just taking that as an example—and we invent all kinds of theories, hopes, beliefs, to disguise the fact of death, but the fact is still there. To understand a fact we must look at it, not run away from it. Most of us are afraid of living as well as of dying. We are afraid for our family, afraid of public opinion, of losing our job, our security, and hundreds of other things. The simple fact is that we are afraid, not that we are afraid of this or that. Now why cannot we face that fact?

You can face a fact only in the present and if you never allow it to be present because you are always escaping from it, you can never face it, and because we have cultivated a whole network of escapes we are caught in the habit of escape.

Now, if you are at all sensitive, at all serious, you will not only be aware of your conditioning but you will also be aware of the dangers it results in, what brutality and hatred it leads to. Why, then, if you see the danger of your conditioning, don't you act? Is it because you are lazy, laziness being lack of energy? Yet you will not lack energy if you see an immediate physical danger like a snake in your path, or a precipice, or a fire. Why, then, don't you act when you see the danger of your conditioning? If you saw the danger of nationalism to your own security, wouldn't you act?

The answer is you don't see. Through an intellectual process of analysis you may see that nationalism leads to self-destruction but there is no emotional content in that. Only when there is an emotional content do you become vital.

If you see the danger of your conditioning merely as an intellectual concept, you will never do anything about it. In seeing a danger as a mere idea there is conflict between the idea and action and that conflict takes away your energy. It is only when you see the conditioning and the danger of it immediately, and as you would see a precipice, that you act. So seeing is acting.

Most of us walk through life inattentively, reacting unthinkingly according to the environment in which we have been brought up, and such reactions create only further bondage, further conditioning, but the moment you give your total attention to your conditioning you will see that you are free from the past completely, that it falls away from you naturally.

2

We said in a previous chapter that joy was something entirely different from pleasure, so let us find out what is involved in pleasure and whether it is at all possible to live in a world that does not contain pleasure but a tremendous sense of joy, of bliss.

We are all engaged in the pursuit of pleasure in some form or other—intellectual, sensuous or cultural pleasure, the pleasure of reforming, telling others what to do, of modifying the evils of society, of doing good—the pleasure of greater knowledge, greater physical satisfaction, greater experience, greater understanding of life, all the clever, cunning things of the mind; and the ultimate pleasure is, of course, to have God.

Pleasure is the structure of society. From childhood until death we are secretly, cunningly, or obviously pursuing pleasure. So whatever our form of pleasure is, I think we should be very clear about it because it is going to guide and shape our lives. It is, therefore, important for each one of us to investigate closely, hesitantly, and delicately this question of pleasure, for to find pleasure, and then nourish and sustain it, is a basic demand of life and without it existence becomes dull, stupid, lonely, and meaningless.

You may ask why then should life not be guided by pleasure? For the very simple reason that pleasure must bring pain, frustration, sorrow and fear, and, out of fear, violence. If you want to live that way, live that way. Most of the world does anyway, but if you want to be free from sorrow you must understand the whole structure of pleasure.

To understand pleasure is not to deny it. We are not condemning it or saying it is right or wrong, but if we pursue it, let us do so with our eyes open, knowing that a mind that is all the time seeking pleasure must inevitably find its shadow, pain. They cannot be separated, although we run after pleasure and try to avoid pain.

Now, why is the mind always demanding pleasure? Why is it that we do noble and ignoble things with the undercurrent of pleasure? Why is it we sacrifice and suffer on the thin thread of pleasure? What is pleasure and how does it come into being? I wonder if any of you have asked yourself these questions and followed the answers to the very end?

Pleasure comes into being through four stages—perception, sensation, contact, and desire. I see a beautiful motorcar, say; then I get a sensation, a reaction, from looking at it; then I touch it or imagine touching it, and then there is the desire to own and show myself off in it. Or I see a lovely cloud, or a mountain clear against the sky, or a leaf that has just come in springtime, or a deep valley full of loveliness and splendor, or a glorious sunset, or a beautiful face, intelligent, alive, not self-conscious and, therefore, no longer beautiful. I look at these things with intense delight and as I observe them there is no observer but only sheer beauty like love. For a moment I am absent with all my problems, anxieties, and miseries—there is only that marvelous thing. I can look at it with joy and the next moment forget it, or else the mind steps in, and then the problem begins; my mind thinks over what it has seen and thinks how beautiful it was; I tell myself I should like to see it again many times. Thought begins to compare, judge, and say "I must have it again tomorrow." The continuity of an experience that has given delight for a second is sustained by thought.

It is the same with sexual desire or any other form of desire. There is nothing wrong with desire. To react is perfectly normal. If you stick a pin in me I shall react unless I am paralyzed. But then thought steps in and chews over the delight and turns it into pleasure. Thought wants to repeat the experience, and the more you repeat, the more mechanical it becomes; the more you think about it, the more strength thought gives to pleasure. So thought creates and sustains pleasure through desire, and gives it continuity; and, therefore, the natural reaction of desire to any beautiful thing is perverted by thought. Thought turns it into a memory and memory is then nourished by thinking about it over and over again.

Of course, memory has a place at a certain level. In everyday life we could not function at all without it. In its own field it must be efficient, but there is a state of mind where it has very little place. A mind which is not crippled by memory has real freedom.

Have you ever noticed that when you respond to something totally, with all your heart, there is very little memory? It is only when you do not respond to a challenge with your whole being that there is a conflict, a struggle, and this brings confusion and pleasure or pain. And the struggle breeds memory. That memory is added to all the time by other memories and it is those memories which respond. Anything that is the result of memory is old and, therefore, never free. There is no such thing as freedom of thought. It is sheer nonsense.

Thought is never new, for thought is the response of memory, experience, knowledge. Thought, because it is old, makes this thing which you have looked at with delight and felt tremendously for the moment, old. From the old you derive pleasure, never from the new. There is no time in the new.

So if you can look at all things without allowing pleasure to creep in—at a face, a bird, the color of a sari, the beauty of a sheet of water shimmering in the sun, or anything that gives delight—if you can look at it without wanting the experience to be repeated, then there will be no pain, no fear and, therefore, tremendous joy.

It is the struggle to repeat and perpetuate pleasure which turns it into pain. Watch it in yourself. The very demand for the repetition of pleasure brings about pain, because it is not the same as it was yesterday. You struggle to achieve the same delight, not only to your aesthetic sense but the same inward quality of the mind, and you are hurt and disappointed because it is denied to you.

Have you observed what happens to you when you are denied a little pleasure? When you don't get what you want you become anxious, envious, hateful. Have you noticed when you have been denied the pleasure of drinking or smoking or sex or whatever it is, have you noticed what battles you go through? And all that is a form of fear, isn't it? You are afraid of not getting what you want or of losing what you have. When some particular faith or ideology which you have held for years is shaken or torn away from you by logic or life, aren't you afraid of standing alone? That belief has for years given you satisfaction and pleasure, and when it is taken away you are left stranded, empty, and the fear remains until you find another form of pleasure, another belief.

It seems to me so simple and because it is so simple we refuse to see its simplicity. We like to complicate everything. When your wife turns away from you, aren't you jealous? Aren't you angry? Don't you hate the man who has attracted her? And what is all that but fear of losing something which has given you a great deal of pleasure, a companionship, a certain quality of assurance and the satisfaction of possession?

So if you understand that where there is a search for pleasure there must be pain, live that way if you want to, but don't just slip into it. If you want to end pleasure, though, which is to end pain, you must be totally attentive to the whole structure of pleasure, not cut it out as monks and sannyasis do, never looking at a woman because they think it is a sin and thereby destroying the vitality of their understanding—but seeing the whole meaning and significance of pleasure. Then you will have tremendous joy in life. You cannot think about joy. Joy is an immediate thing and by thinking about it, you turn it into pleasure. Living in the present is the instant perception of beauty and the great delight in it without seeking pleasure from it.

3

Fear, pleasure, sorrow, thought, and violence are all interrelated. Most of us take pleasure in violence, in disliking somebody, hating a particular race or group of people, having antagonistic feelings toward others. But in a state of mind in which all violence has come to an end there is a joy that is very different from the pleasure of violence, with its conflicts, hatreds, and fears.

Can we go to the very root of violence and be free from it? Otherwise we shall live everlastingly in battle with each other. If that is the way you want to live—and apparently most people do—then carry on; if you say, "Well, I'm sorry, violence can never end," then you and I have no means of communication, you have blocked yourself; but if you say there might be a different way of living, then we shall be able to communicate with each other.

So let us consider together, those of us who can communicate, whether it is at all possible totally to end every form of violence in ourselves and still live in this monstrously brutal world. I think it is possible. I don't want to have a breath of hate, jealousy, anxiety, or fear in me. I want to live completely at peace. Which doesn't mean that I want to die. I want to live on this marvelous earth, so full, so rich, so beautiful. I want to look at the trees, flowers, rivers, meadows, women, boys and girls, and at the same time live completely at peace with myself and with the world. What can I do?

If we know how to look at violence, not only outwardly in society—the wars, the riots, the national antagonisms and class conflicts—but also in ourselves, then perhaps we shall be able to go beyond it.

Here is a very complex problem. For centuries upon centuries man has been violent; religions have tried to tame him throughout the world and none of them have succeeded. So if we are going into the question we must, it seems to me, be at least very serious about it because it will lead us into quite a different domain, but if we want merely to play with the problem for intellectual entertainment we shall not get very far.

You may feel that you yourself are very serious about the problem but that as long as so many other people in the world are not serious and are not prepared to do anything about it, what is the good of your doing anything? I don't care whether they take it seriously or not. I take it seriously, that is enough. I am not my brother's keeper. I myself, as a human being, feel very strongly about this question of violence and I will see to it that in myself I am not violent, but I cannot tell you or anybody else, "Don't be violent." It has no meaning—unless you yourself want it. So if you yourself really want to understand this problem of violence let us continue on our journey of exploration together.

Is this problem of violence out there or here? Do you want to solve the problem in the outside world or are you questioning violence itself as it is in you? If you are free of violence in yourself the question is, "How am I to live in a world full of violence, acquisitiveness, greed, envy, brutality? Will I not be destroyed?"

That is the inevitable question which is invariably asked. When you ask such a question it seems to me you are not actually living peacefully.

If you live peacefully you will have no problem at all. You may be imprisoned because you refuse to join the army or shot because you refuse to fight—but that is not a problem; you will be shot. It is extraordinarily important to understand this.

We are trying to understand violence as a fact, not as an idea, as a fact which exists in the human being, and the human being is myself. And to go into the problem I must be completely vulnerable, open, to it. I must expose myself to myself—not necessarily expose myself to you because you may not be interested—but I must be in a state of mind that demands to see this thing right to the end and at no point stops and says I will go no further.

Now it must be obvious to me that I am a violent human being. I have experienced violence in anger, violence in my sexual demands, violence in hatred, creating enmity, violence in jealousy, and so on. I have experienced it, I have known it, and I say to myself, "I want to understand this whole problem, not just one fragment of it expressed in war, but this aggression in man which also exists in the animals and of which I am a part."

Violence is not merely killing another. It is violence when we use a sharp word, when we make a gesture to brush away a person, when we obey because there is fear. So violence isn't merely organized butchery in the name of God, in the name of society or country. Violence is much more subtle, much deeper, and we are inquiring into the very depths of violence.

When you call yourself an Indian or a Muslim or a Christian or a European, or anything else, you are being violent. Do you see why it is violent? Because you are separating yourself from the rest of mankind. When you separate yourself by belief, by nationality, by tradition, it breeds violence. So a man who is seeking to understand violence does not belong to any country, to any religion, to any political party or partial system; he is concerned with the total understanding of mankind.

Now, there are two primary schools of thought with regard to violence: one which says, "Violence is innate in man" and the other which says, "Violence is the result of the social and cultural heritage in which man lives." We are not concerned with which school we belong to—it is of no importance. What is important is the fact that we are violent, not the reason for it.

One of the most common expressions of violence is anger. When my wife or sister is attacked I say I am righteously angry; when my country is attacked, my ideas, my principles, my way of life, I am righteously angry. I am also angry when my habits are attacked or my petty little opinions. When you tread on my toes or insult me I get angry, or if you run away with my wife and I get jealous, that jealousy is called righteous because she is my property. And all this anger is morally justified. But to kill for my country is also justified. So when we are talking about anger, which is a part of violence, do we look at anger in terms of righteous and unrighteous anger according to our own inclinations and environmental drive, or do we see only anger? Is there righteous anger ever? Or is there only anger? There is no good influence or bad influence, only influence, but when you are influenced by something which doesn't suit me I call it an evil influence. The moment you protect your family, your country, a bit of colored rag called a flag, a belief, an idea, a dogma, the thing that you demand or that you hold, that very protection indicates anger. So can you look at anger without any explanation or justification, without saying, "I must protect my goods," or "I was right to be angry," or "How stupid of me to be angry"?

Can you look at anger as if it were something by itself? Can you look at it completely objectively, which means neither defending it nor condemning it? Can you? Can I look at you if I am antagonistic to you or if I am thinking what a marvelous person you are? I can see you only when I look at you with a certain care in which neither of these things is involved. Now, can I look at anger in the same way, which means that I am vulnerable to the problem, I do not resist it, I am watching this extraordinary phenomenon without any reaction to it?

It is very difficult to look at anger dispassionately because it is a part of me, but that is what I am trying to do. Here I am, a violent human being, whether I am black, brown, white, or purple. I am not concerned with whether I have inherited this violence or whether society has produced it in me; all I am concerned with is whether it is at all possible to be free from it. To be free from violence means everything to me. It is more important to me than sex, food, position, for this thing is corrupting me. It is destroying me and destroying the world, and I want to understand it, I want to be beyond it. I feel responsible for all this anger and violence in the world. I feel responsible—it isn't just a lot of words—and I say to myself, "I can do something only if I am beyond anger myself, beyond violence, beyond nationality." And this feeling I have that I must understand the violence in myself brings tremendous vitality and passion to find out.

But to be beyond violence I cannot suppress it, I cannot deny it, I cannot say, "Well, it is a part of me and that's that," or "I don't want it." I have to look at it, I have to study it, I must become very intimate with it and I cannot become intimate with it if I condemn it or justify it. We do condemn it, though; we do justify it. Therefore, I am saying, stop for the time being condemning it or justifying it.

Now, if you want to stop violence, if you want to stop wars, how much vitality, how much of yourself, do you give to it? Isn't it important to you that your children are killed, that your sons go into the army where they are bullied and butchered? Don't you care? My God, if that doesn't interest you, what does? Guarding your money? Having a good time? Taking drugs? Don't you see that this violence in yourself is destroying your children? Or do you see it only as some abstraction?

All right then, if you are interested, attend with all your heart and mind to find out. Don't just sit back and say, "Well, tell us all about it." I point out to you that you cannot look at anger nor at violence with eyes that condemn or justify, and that if this violence is not a burning problem to you, you cannot put those two things away. So first you have to learn; you have to learn how to look at anger, how to look at your husband, your wife, your children; you have to listen to the politician, you have to learn why you are not objective, why you condemn or justify. You have to learn that you condemn and justify because it is part of the social structure you live in, your conditioning as a German or an Indian or a Negro or an American or whatever you happen to have been born, with all the dulling of the mind that this conditioning results in. To learn, to discover, something fundamental you must have the capacity to go deeply. If you have a blunt instrument, a dull instrument, you cannot go deeply. So what we are doing is sharpening the instrument, which is the mind—the mind which has been made dull by all this justifying and condemning. You can penetrate deeply only if your mind is as sharp as a needle and as strong as a diamond. It is no good just sitting back and asking, "How am I to get such a mind?" You have to want it as you want your next meal, and to have it you must see that what makes your mind dull and stupid is this sense of invulnerability which has built walls round itself and which is part of this condemnation and justification. If the mind can be rid of that, then you can look, study, penetrate, and perhaps come to a state that is totally aware of the whole problem.

So let us come back to the central issue—is it possible to eradicate violence in ourselves? It is a form of violence to say, "You haven't changed, why haven't you?" I am not doing that. It doesn't mean a thing to me to convince you of anything. It is your life, not my life. The way you live is your affair. I am asking whether it is possible for a human being living psychologically in any society to clear violence from himself inwardly? If it is, the very process will produce a different way of living in this world.

Most of us have accepted violence as a way of life. Two dreadful wars have taught us nothing except to build more and more barriers between human beings, that is, between you and me. But for those of us who want to be rid of violence, how is it to be done? I do not think anything is going to be achieved through analysis, either by ourselves or by a professional. We might be able to modify ourselves slightly, live a little more quietly, with a little more affection, but in itself it will not give total perception. But I must know how to analyze, which means that in the process of analysis my mind becomes extraordinarily sharp, and it is that quality of sharpness, of attention, of seriousness, which will give total perception. One hasn't the eyes to see the whole thing at a glance; this clarity of the eye is possible only if one can see the details, then jump. Some of us, in order to rid ourselves of violence, have used a concept, an ideal called nonviolence, and we think by having an ideal of the opposite to violence, nonviolence, we can get rid of the fact, the actual—but we cannot. We have had ideals without number, all the sacred books are full of them, yet we are still violent—so why not deal with violence itself and forget the word altogether?

If you want to understand the actual you must give your whole attention, all your energy, to it. That attention and energy are distracted when you create a fictitious, ideal world. So can you completely banish the ideal? The man who is really serious, with the urge to find out what truth is, what love is, has no concept at all. He lives only in *what is*.

To investigate the fact of your own anger you must pass no judgment on it, for the moment you conceive of its opposite you condemn it and, therefore, you cannot see it as it is. When you say you dislike or hate someone that is a fact, although it sounds terrible. If you look at it, go into it completely, it ceases, but if you say, "I must not hate; I must have love in my heart," then you are living in a hypocritical world with double standards. To live completely, fully, in the moment is to live with *what is,* the actual, without any sense of condemnation or justification—then you understand it so totally that you are finished with it. When you see clearly the problem is solved.

But can you see the face of violence clearly—the face of violence not only outside you but inside you, which means that you are totally free from violence because you have not admitted ideology through which to get rid of it? This requires very deep meditation, not just a verbal agreement or disagreement. You have now read a series of statements but have you really understood? Your conditioned mind, your way of life, the whole structure of the society in which you live, prevent you from looking at a fact and being entirely free from it immediately. You say, "I will think about it; I will consider whether it is possible to be free from violence or not. I will try to be free." That is one of the most dreadful statements you can make, "I will try." There is no trying, no doing your best. Either you do it or you don't do it. You are admitting time while the house is burning. The house is burning as a result of the violence throughout the world and in yourself and you say, "Let me think about it. Which ideology is best to put out the fire?" When the house is on fire, do you argue about the color of the hair of the man who brings the water?

4

None of the agonies of suppression, nor the brutal discipline of conforming to a pattern, has led to truth. To come upon truth the mind must be completely free, without a spot of distortion.

But first let us ask ourselves if we really want to be free.

When we talk of freedom are we talking of complete freedom or of freedom from some inconvenient or unpleasant or undesirable thing? We would like to be free from painful and ugly memories and unhappy experiences but keep our pleasurable, satisfying ideologies, formulas, and relationships. But to keep the one without the other is impossible, for, as we have seen, pleasure is inseparable from pain.

So it is for each one of us to decide whether or not we want to be completely free. If we say we do, then we must understand the nature and structure of freedom.

Is it freedom when you are free from something—free from pain, free from some kind of anxiety? Or is freedom itself something entirely different? You can be free from jealousy, say, but isn't that freedom a reaction and, therefore, not freedom at all? You can be free from dogma very easily, by analyzing it, by kicking it out, but the motive for that freedom from dogma has its own reaction because the desire to be free from a dogma may be that it is no longer fashionable or convenient. Or you can be free from nationalism because you believe in internationalism or because you feel it is no longer economically necessary to cling to this silly nationalistic dogma with its flag and all that rubbish. You can easily put that away. Or you may react against some spiritual or political leader who has promised you freedom as a result of discipline or revolt. But has such rationalism, such logical conclusion, anything to do with freedom?

If you say you are free from something, it is a reaction which will then become another reaction which will bring about another conformity, another form of domination. In this way you can have a chain of reactions and accept each reaction as freedom. But it is not freedom; it is merely a continuity of a modified past, which the mind clings to.

The youth of today, like all youth, are in revolt against society, and that is a good thing in itself, but revolt is not freedom because when you revolt it is a reaction and that reaction sets up its own pattern and you get caught in that pattern. You think it is something new. It is not; it is the old in a different mold. Any social or political revolt will inevitably revert to the good old bourgeois mentality.

Freedom comes only when you see and act, never through revolt. The seeing is the acting and such action is as instantaneous as when you see danger. Then there is no cerebration, no discussion or hesitation; the danger itself compels the act and, therefore, to see is to act and to be free.

Freedom is a state of mind—not freedom from something but a sense of freedom, a freedom to doubt and question everything and, therefore, so intense, active, and vigorous that it throws away every form of dependence, slavery, conformity, and acceptance. Such freedom implies being completely alone. But can the mind brought up in a culture so dependent on environment and its own tendencies ever find that freedom which is complete solitude and in which there is no leadership, no tradition, and no authority?

This solitude is an inward state of mind, which is not dependent on any stimulus or any knowledge and is not the result of any experience or conclusion. Most of us, inwardly, are never alone. There is a difference between isolation, cutting oneself off, and aloneness, solitude. We all know what it is to be isolated, building a wall around oneself in order never to be hurt, never to be vulnerable, or cultivating detachment, which is another form of agony, or living in some dreamy ivory tower of ideology. Aloneness is something quite different.

You are never alone because you are full of all the memories, all the conditioning, all the mutterings of yesterday; your mind is never clear of all the rubbish it has accumulated. To be alone you must die to the past. When you are alone, totally alone, not belonging to any family, any nation, any culture, any particular continent, there is that sense of being an outsider. The man who is completely alone in this way is innocent and it is this innocence that frees the mind from sorrow.

We carry about with us the burden of what thousands of people have said and the memories of all our misfortunes. To abandon all that totally is to be alone, and the mind that is alone is not only innocent but young—not in time or age, but young, innocent, alive at whatever age—and only such a mind can see that which is truth and that which is not measurable by words.

In this solitude you will begin to understand the necessity of living with yourself as you are, not as you think you should be or as you have been. See if you can look at yourself without any tremor, any false modesty, any fear, any justification, or condemnation—just live with yourself as you actually are. It is only when you live with something intimately that you begin to understand it. But the moment you get used to it—get used to your own anxiety or envy or whatever it is—you are no longer living with it. If you live by a river, after a few days you do not hear the sound of the water anymore, or if you have a picture in the room which you see every day you lose it after a week. It is the same with the mountains, the valleys, the trees—the same with your family, your husband, your wife. But to live with something like jealousy, envy, or anxiety you must never get used to it, never accept it. You must care for it as you would care for a newly planted tree, protect it against the sun, against the storm. You must care for it, not condemn it or justify it. Therefore, you begin to love it. When you care for it, you are beginning to love it. It is not that you love being envious or anxious, as so many people do, but rather that you care for watching.

So can you—can you and I—live with what we actually are, knowing ourselves to be dull, envious, fearful, believing we have tremendous affection when we have not, getting easily hurt, easily flattered, and bored—can we live with all that, neither accepting it nor denying it, but just observing it without becoming morbid, depressed, or elated?

Now let us ask ourselves a further question. Is this freedom, this solitude, this coming into contact with the whole structure of what we are in ourselves—is it to be come upon through time? That is, is freedom to be achieved through a gradual process? Obviously not, because as soon as you introduce time you are enslaving yourself more and more. You cannot become free gradually. It is not a matter of time.

The next question is, can you become conscious of that freedom?

If you say, "I am free," then you are not free. It is like a man saying, "I am happy." The moment he says, "I am happy," he is living in a memory of something that has gone. Freedom can only come about naturally, not through wishing, wanting, longing. Nor will you find it by creating an image of what you think it is. To come upon it the mind has to learn to look at life, which is a vast movement, without the bondage of time, for freedom lies beyond the field of consciousness.

5

The demand to be safe in relationship inevitably breeds sorrow and fear. This seeking for security is inviting insecurity. Have you ever found security in any of your relationships? Have you? Most of us want the security of loving and being loved, but is there love when each one of us is seeking his own security, his own particular path? We are not loved because we don't know how to love.

What is love? The word is so loaded and corrupted that I hardly like to use it. Everybody talks of love—every magazine and newspaper and every missionary talks everlastingly of love. I love my country, I love my king, I love some book, I love that mountain, I love pleasure, I love my wife, I love God. Is love an idea? If it is, it can be cultivated, nourished, cherished, pushed around, twisted in any way you like. When you say you love God what does it mean? It means that you love a projection of your own imagination, a projection of yourself clothed in certain forms of respectability according to what you think is noble and holy; so to say, "I love God," is absolute nonsense. When you worship God you are worshiping yourself—and that is not love.

Because we cannot solve this human thing called love we run away into abstractions. Love may be the ultimate solution to all man's difficulties, problems, and travails, so how are we going to find out what love is? By merely defining it? The church has defined it one way, society another and there are all sorts of deviations and perversions. Adoring someone, sleeping with someone, the emotional exchange, the companionship—is that what we mean by love? That has been the norm, the pattern, and it has become so tremendously personal, sensuous, and limited that religions have declared that love is something much more than this. In what they call human love they see there is pleasure, competition, jealousy, the desire to possess, to hold, to control and to interfere with another's thinking, and knowing the complexity of all this they say there must be another kind of love: divine, beautiful, untouched, uncorrupted.

Throughout the world, so-called holy men have maintained that to look at a woman is something totally wrong: they say you cannot come near to God if you indulge in sex; therefore, they push it aside although they are eaten up with it. But by denying sexuality they put out their eyes and cut out their tongues for they deny the whole beauty of the earth. They have starved their hearts and minds; they are dehydrated human beings; they have banished beauty because beauty is associated with woman.

Can love be divided into the sacred and the profane, the human and the divine, or is there only love? Is love of the one and not of the many? If I say, "I love you," does that exclude the love of the other? Is love personal or impersonal? Moral or immoral? Family or nonfamily? If you love mankind can you love the particular? Is love sentiment? Is love emotion? Is love pleasure and desire? All these questions indicate, don't they, that we have ideas about love, ideas about what it should or should not be, a pattern or a code developed by the culture in which we live.

So to go into the question of what love is we must first free it from the encrustation of centuries, put away all ideals and ideologies of what it should or should not be. To divide anything into what should be and *what is* is the most deceptive way of dealing with life.

Now how am I going to find out what this flame is which we call love—not how to express it to another but what it means in itself? I will first reject what the church, what society, what my parents and friends, what every person and every book, has said about it because I want to find out for myself what it is. Here is an enormous problem that involves the whole of mankind. There have been a thousand ways of defining it and I myself am caught in some pattern or other according to what I like or enjoy at the moment—so shouldn't I, in order to understand it, first free myself from my own inclinations and prejudices? I am confused, torn by my own desires, so I say to myself, "First clear up your own confusion. Perhaps you may be able to discover what love is through what it is not."

The government says go and kill for the love of your country. Is that love? Religion says give up sex for the love of God. Is that love? Is love desire? Don't say no. For most of us it is desire with pleasure, the pleasure that is derived through the senses, through sexual attachment and fulfillment. I am not against sex, but see what is involved in it. What sex gives you momentarily is the total abandonment of yourself, then you are back again with your turmoil, so you want a repetition over and over again of that state in which there is no worry, no problem, no self. You say you love your wife. In that love is involved sexual pleasure, the pleasure of having someone in the house to look after your children, to cook. You depend on her; she has given you her body, her emotions, her encouragement, a certain feeling of security and well-being. Then she turns away from you; she gets bored or goes off with someone else, and your whole emotional balance is destroyed, and this disturbance, which you don't like, is called jealousy. There is pain in it, anxiety, hate and violence. So what you are really saying is, "As long as you belong to me I love you but the moment you don't I begin to hate you. As long as I can rely on you to satisfy my demands, sexual and otherwise, I love you, but the moment you cease to supply what I want I don't like you." So there is antagonism between you, there is separation, and when you feel separate from another there is no love. But if you can live with your wife without thought creating all these contradictory states, these endless quarrels in yourself, then perhaps—perhaps—you will know what love is. Then you are completely free and so is she, whereas if you depend on her for all your pleasure you are a slave to her. So when one loves there must be freedom, not only from the other person but from oneself.

This belonging to another, being psychologically nourished by another, depending on another—in all this there must always be anxiety, fear, jealousy, guilt; and so long as there is fear there is no love; a mind ridden with sorrow will never know what love is; sentimentality and emotionalism have nothing whatsoever to do with love. And so love is not to do with pleasure and desire.

Love is not the product of thought, which is the past. Thought cannot possibly cultivate love. Love is not hedged about and caught in jealousy, for jealousy is of the past. Love is always active, present. It is not "I will love" or "I have loved." If you know love you will not follow anybody. Love does not obey. When you love there is neither respect nor disrespect.

Don't you know what it means really to love somebody, to love without hate, without jealousy, without anger, without wanting to interfere with what he is doing or thinking, without condemning, without comparing—don't you know what it means? Where there is love is there comparison? When you love someone with all your heart, with all your mind, with all your body, with your entire being, is there comparison? When you totally abandon yourself to that love there is not the other.

Does love have responsibility and duty, and will it use those words? When you do something out of duty is there any love in it? In duty there is no love. The structure of duty in which the human being is caught is destroying him. So long as you are compelled to do something because it is your duty you don't love what you are doing. When there is love there is no duty and no responsibility.

Most parents, unfortunately, think they are responsible for their children and their sense of responsibility takes the form of telling them what they should do and what they should not do, what they should become and what they should not become. The parents want their children to have a secure position in society. What they call responsibility is part of that respectability they worship; and it seems to me that where there is respectability there is no order; they are concerned only with becoming a perfect bourgeois. When they prepare their children to fit into society they are perpetuating war, conflict, and brutality. Do you call that care and love?

Really to care is to care as you would for a tree or a plant, watering it, studying its needs, the best soil for it, looking after it with gentleness and tenderness—but when you prepare your children to fit into society you are preparing them to be killed. If you loved your children you would have no war.

When you lose someone you love you shed tears; are your tears for yourself or for the one who is dead? Are you crying for yourself or for another? Have you ever cried for another? Have you ever cried for your son who was killed on the battlefield? You have cried, but do those tears come out of self-pity or have you cried because a human being has been killed? If you cry out of self-pity your tears have no meaning because you are concerned about yourself. If you are crying because you are bereft of one in whom you have invested a great deal of affection, it was not really affection. When you cry for your brother who dies, cry for him. It is very easy to cry for yourself because he is gone. Apparently you are crying because your heart is touched, but it is not touched for him, it is only touched by self-pity and self-pity makes you hard, encloses you, makes you dull and stupid.

When you cry for yourself, is it love? Crying because you are lonely, because you have been left, because you are no longer powerful—complaining of your lot, your environment—always you in tears? If you understand this, which means to come in contact with it as directly as you would touch a tree or a pillar or a hand, then you will see that sorrow is self-created, sorrow is created by thought, sorrow is the outcome of time. I had my brother three years ago, now he is dead, now I am lonely, aching, there is no one to whom I can look for comfort or companionship, and it brings tears to my eyes.

You can see all this happening inside yourself if you watch it. You can see it fully, completely, in one glance, not take analytical time over it. You can see in a moment the whole structure and nature of this shoddy little thing called "me," my tears, my family, my nation, my belief, my religion—all that ugliness, it is all inside you. When you see it with your heart, not with your mind, when you see it from the very bottom of your heart, then you have the key that will end sorrow. Sorrow and love cannot go together, but in the Christian world they have idealized suffering, put it on a cross and worshiped it, implying that you can never escape from suffering except through that one particular door, and this is the whole structure of an exploiting religious society.

So when you ask what love is, you may be too frightened to see the answer. It may mean complete upheaval; it may break up the family; you may discover that you do not love your wife or husband or children—do you?—you may have to shatter the house you have built, you may never go back to the temple.

But if you still want to find out, you will see that fear is not love, dependence is not love, jealousy is not love, possessiveness and domination are not love, responsibility and duty are not love, self-pity is not love, the agony of not being loved is not love, love is not the opposite of hate any more than humility is the opposite of vanity. So if you can eliminate all these, not by forcing them but by washing them away as the rain washes the dust of many days from a leaf, then perhaps you will come upon this strange flower, which man always hungers after.

If you have not got love—not just in little drops but in abundance—if you are not filled with it, the world will go to disaster. You know intellectually that the unity of mankind is essential and that love is the only way, but who is going to teach you how to love? Will any authority, any method, any system, tell you how to love? If anyone tells you, it is not love. Can you say, "I will practice love. I will sit down day after day and think about it. I will practice being kind and gentle and force myself to pay attention to others"? Do you mean to say that you can discipline yourself to love, exercise the will to love? When you exercise discipline and will to love, love goes out of the window. By practicing some method or system of loving you may become extraordinarily clever or more kindly or get into a state of nonviolence, but that has nothing whatsoever to do with love.

In this torn desert world there is no love because pleasure and desire play the greatest roles, yet without love your daily life has no meaning. And you cannot have love if there is no beauty. Beauty is not something you see—not a beautiful tree, a beautiful picture, a beautiful building, or a beautiful woman. There is beauty only when your heart and mind know what love is. Without love and that sense of beauty there is no virtue, and you know very well that, do what you will—improve society, feed the poor—you will only be creating more mischief, for without love there is only ugliness and poverty in your own heart and mind.

But when there is love and beauty, whatever you do is right, whatever you do is in order. If you know how to love, then you can do what you like because it will solve all other problems.

So we reach the point: Can the mind come upon love without discipline, without thought, without enforcement, without any book, any teacher or leader—come upon it as one comes upon a lovely sunset? It seems to me that one thing is absolutely necessary and that is passion without motive—passion that is not the result of some commitment or attachment, passion that is not lust. A man who does not know what passion is will never know love because love can come into being only when there is total self-abandonment.

A mind that is seeking is not a passionate mind and to come upon love without seeking it is the only way to find it—to come upon it unknowingly and not as the result of any effort or experience. Such a love, you will find, is not of time; such a love is both personal and impersonal, is both the one and the many. Like a flower that has perfume, you can smell it or pass it by. That flower is for everybody and for the one who takes trouble to breathe it deeply and look at it with delight. Whether one is very near in the garden or very far away, it is the same to the flower because it is full of that perfume and, therefore, it is sharing with everybody.

Love is something that is new, fresh, alive. It has no yesterday and no tomorrow. It is beyond the turmoil of thought. It is only the innocent mind which knows what love is, and the innocent mind can live in the world, which is not innocent. To find this extraordinary thing which man has sought endlessly through sacrifice, through worship, through relationship, through sex, through every form of pleasure and pain, is only possible when thought comes to understand itself and comes naturally to an end. Then love has no opposite, then love has no conflict.

You may ask, "If I find such a love, what happens to my wife, my children, my family? They must have security." When you put such a question you have never been outside the field of thought, the field of consciousness. When once you have been outside that field you will never ask such a question because then you will know what love is in which there is no thought and, therefore, no time. You may read this mesmerized and enchanted, but actually to go beyond thought and time—which means going beyond sorrow—is to be aware that there is a different dimension called love.

But you don't know how to come to this extraordinary fount, so what do you do? If you don't know what to do, you do nothing, don't you? Absolutely nothing. Then inwardly you are completely silent. Do you understand what that means? It means that you are not seeking, not wanting, not pursuing; there is no center at all. Then there is love.

Freedom from the Known

February 25, 1983

There is a tree by the river and we have been watching it day after day for several weeks when the sun is about to rise. As the sun rises slowly over the horizon, over the trees, this particular tree becomes all of a sudden golden. All the leaves are bright with life and as you watch it as the hours pass by, that tree whose name does not matter—what matters is that beautiful tree—an extraordinary quality seems to spread all over the land, over the river. And as the sun rises a little higher the leaves begin to flutter, to dance. And each hour seems to give to that tree a different quality. Before the sun rises it has a somber feeling, quiet, far away, full of dignity. And as the day begins, the leaves with the light on them dance and give it that peculiar feeling that one has of great beauty. By midday its shadow has deepened and you can sit there protected from the sun, never feeling lonely, with the tree as your companion. As you sit there, there is a relationship of deep abiding security and a freedom that only trees can know.

Toward the evening when the western skies are lit up by the setting sun, the tree gradually becomes somber, dark, closing in on itself. The sky has become red, yellow, green, but the tree remains quiet, hidden, and is resting for the night.

If you establish a relationship with it then you have relationship with mankind. You are responsible then for that tree and for the trees of the world. But if you have no relationship with the living things on this earth you may lose whatever relationship you have with humanity, with human beings. We never look deeply into the quality of a tree; we never really touch it, feel its solidity, its rough bark, and hear the sound that is part of the tree. Not the sound of wind through the leaves, not the breeze of a morning that flutters the leaves, but its own sound, the sound of the trunk and the silent sound of the roots. You must be extraordinarily sensitive to hear the sound. This sound is not the noise of the world, not the noise of the chattering of the mind, not the vulgarity of human quarrels and human warfare, but sound as part of the universe.

It is odd that we have so little relationship with nature, with the insects and the leaping frog and the owl that hoots among the hills calling for its mate. We never seem to have a feeling for all living things on the earth. If we could establish a deep abiding relationship with nature we would never kill an animal for our appetite, we would never harm, vivisect, a monkey, a dog, a guinea pig for our benefit. We would find other ways to heal our wounds, heal our bodies. But the healing of the mind is something totally different. That healing gradually takes place if you are with nature, with that orange on the tree, and the blade of grass that pushes through the cement, and the hills covered, hidden, by the clouds.

This is not sentiment or romantic imagination but a reality of a relationship with everything that lives and moves on the earth. Man has killed millions of whales and is still killing them. All that we derive from their slaughter can be had through other means. But apparently man loves to kill things—the fleeting deer, the marvelous gazelle, and the great elephant. We love to kill each other. This killing of other human beings has never stopped throughout the history of man's life on this earth. If we could, and we must, establish a deep long abiding relationship with nature, with the actual trees, the bushes, the flowers, the grass, and the fast moving clouds, then we would never slaughter another human being for any reason whatsoever. Organized murder is war, and though we demonstrate against a particular war, nuclear, or any other kind of war, we have never demonstrated against war. We have never said that to kill another human being is the greatest sin on earth.

February 28, 1983

Flying at forty-one thousand feet from one continent to another you see nothing but snow, miles of snow; all the mountains and the hills are covered with snow, and the rivers too are frozen. You see them wandering, meandering, all over the land. And far below, the distant farms are covered with ice and snow. It is a long, tiresome flight of eleven hours. The passengers were chattering away. There was a couple behind one and they never stopped talking, never looked at the glory of those marvelous hills and mountains, never looked at the other passengers. Apparently they were absorbed in their own thoughts, in their own problems, in their chatterings. And at last, after a tedious, calm flight, in the dead of winter, you land at the town on the Pacific.

After the noise and the bustle, you leave that ugly, sprawling, vulgar, shouting city and the endless shops selling almost all the same things. You leave all that behind as you go round the coast highway of the blue Pacific, following the seashore, on a beautiful road, wandering through the hills, meeting the sea often; and as you leave the Pacific behind and enter into the country, winding over various small hills, peaceful, quiet, full of that strange dignity of the country, you enter the valley. You have been there for the last sixty years, and each time you are astonished to enter into this valley. It is quiet, almost untouched by man. You enter into this valley, which is almost like a vast cup, a nest. Then you leave the little village and climb to about fourteen hundred feet, passing rows and rows of orange orchards and groves. The air is perfumed with orange blossom. The whole valley is filled with that scent. And the smell of it is in your mind, in your heart, in your whole body. It is the most extraordinary feeling of living in a perfume that will last for about three weeks or more. And there is a quietness in the mountains, a dignity. And each time you look at those hills and the high mountain, which is over six thousand feet, you are really surprised that such a country exists. Each time you come to this quiet, peaceful valley there is a feeling of strange aloofness, of deep silence and the vast spreading of slow time.

Man is trying to spoil the valley but it has been preserved. And the mountains that morning were extraordinarily beautiful. You could almost touch them. The majesty, the vast sense of permanency is there in them. And you enter quietly into the house where you have lived for over sixty years and the atmosphere, the air, is, if one can use that word, *holy;* you can feel it. You can almost touch it. As it has rained considerably, for it is the rainy season, all the hills and the little folds of the mountain are green, flourishing, full—the earth is smiling with such delight, with some deep quiet understanding of its own existence.

You have said over and over again that the mind, or if you prefer it, the brain, must be quiet, must empty itself of all the knowledge it has gathered, not only to be free but to comprehend something that is not of time or thought or of any action. You have said this in different ways in most of your talks and I find this awfully difficult, not only to grasp the idea, the depth of it, but the feeling of quiet emptiness, if I can use that word. I never could feel my way into it. I have tried various methods to end the chattering of the mind, the endless occupation with something or other, this very occupation creating its problems. And as one lives one is caught up in all this. This is our daily life, the tedium, the talk that goes on in a family, and if there isn't talking there is always the television or a book. The mind seems to demand that it should be occupied, that it should move from one thing to another, from knowledge to knowledge, from action to action with the everlasting movement of thought.

As we pointed out, thought cannot be stopped by determination, by a decision of the will, or the urgent pressing desire to enter into that quality of quiet, still emptiness.

I find myself envious for something which I think, which I feel, to be true, which I would like to have, but it has always eluded me, it has always gone beyond my grasp. I have come, as I have often come, to talk with you. Why in my daily life, in my business life, is there not the stability, the endurance, of that quietness? Why isn't this in my life? I have asked myself what am I to do. I also realize I cannot do much, or I can't do anything at all about it. But it is there nagging. I can't leave it alone. If only I could experience it once, then that very memory will nourish me, then that very remembrance will give a significance to a really rather silly life. So I have come to inquire, to probe into this matter: why does the mind—perhaps the word *brain* may be better—demand that it should be occupied?'

March 10, 1983

The other day as one was walking along a secluded wooded lane far from the noise and the brutality and the vulgarity of civilization, right away from everything that was put together by man, there was a sense of great quietness, enveloping all things—serene, distant, and full of the sound of the earth. As you walked along quietly, not disturbing the things of the earth around you, the bushes, the trees, the crickets, and the birds, suddenly round a bend there were two small creatures quarreling with each other, fighting in their small way. One was trying to drive off the other. The other was intruding, trying to get into the other's little hole, and the owner was fighting it off. Presently the owner won and the other ran off. Again there was quietness, a sense of deep solitude. And as you looked up, the path climbed high into the mountains, the waterfall was gently murmuring down the side of the path; there was great beauty and infinite dignity, not the dignity achieved by man that seems so vain and arrogant. The little creature had identified itself with its home, as we human beings do. We are always trying to identify ourselves with our race, with our culture, with those things which we believe in, with some mystical figure, or some savior, some kind of super authority. Identifying with something seems to be the nature of man. Probably we have derived this feeling from that little animal.

One wonders why this craving, longing, for identification exists. One can understand the identification with one's physical needs, the necessary things—clothes, food, shelter, and so on. But inwardly, inside the skin as it were, we try to identify ourselves with the past, with tradition, with some fanciful romantic image, a symbol much cherished. And surely in this identification there is a sense of security, safety, a sense of being owned and of possessing. This gives great comfort. One takes comfort, security, in any form of illusion. And man apparently needs many illusions.

In the distance there is the hoot of an owl and there is a deep-throated reply from the other side of the valley. It is still dawn. The noise of the day has not begun and everything is quiet. There is something strange and holy where the sun arises. There is a prayer, a chant to the dawn, to that strange quiet light. That early morning, the light was subdued, there was no breeze and all the vegetation, the trees, the bushes, were quiet, still, waiting. Waiting for the sun to arise. And perhaps the sun would not come up for another half hour or so, and the dawn was slowly covering the earth with a strange stillness.

Gradually, slowly, the topmost mountain was getting brighter and the sun was touching it, golden, clear, and the snow was pure, untouched by the light of day.

As you climbed, leaving the little village paths down below, the noise of the earth—the crickets, the quails and other birds began their morning song, their chant, their rich worship of the day. And as the sun arose you were part of that light and had left behind everything that thought had put together. You completely forgot yourself. The psyche was empty of its struggles and its pains. And as you walked, climbed, there was no sense of separateness, no sense of being even a human being.

The morning mist was gathering slowly in the valley, and that mist was you, getting more and more thick, more and more into the fancy, the romance, the idiocy of one's own life. And after a long period of time you came down. There was the murmur of the wind, insects, the calls of many birds. And as you came down the mist was disappearing. There were streets, shops, and the glory of the dawn was fast fading away. And you began your daily routine, caught in the habit of work, the contentions between man and man, the divisions of identification, the division of ideologies, the preparations for wars, your own inward pain, and the everlasting sorrow of man.

March 18, 1983

At the bird feeder there were a dozen or more birds chirping away, pecking at the grains, struggling, fighting each other, and when another big bird came they all fluttered away. When the big bird left again they all came back, chattering, quarreling, chirping, making quite a lot of noise. Presently a cat went by and there was a flurry, a screeching and a great to-do. The cat was chased away—it was one of those wild cats, not a pet cat; there are a great many of those wild ones around here of different sizes, shapes, and colors. At the feeder all day long there were birds, little ones and big ones, and then a blue jay came scolding everybody, the whole universe, and chased the other birds away—or rather, they left when it came. They were very watchful for cats. And as the evening drew close all the birds went away and there was silence, quiet, peaceful. The cats came and went, but there were no birds.

That morning the clouds were full of light and there was promise in the air of more rain. For the past few weeks it had been raining. There is an artificial lake and the waters were right to the top. All the green leaves and the shrubs and the tall trees were waiting for the sun, which hadn't appeared bright as the Californian sun is; it had not shown its face for many a day.

One wonders what is the future of mankind, the future of all those children you see shouting, playing—such happy, gentle, nice faces—what is their future? The future is what we are now. This has been so historically for many thousands of years—the living and dying, and all the travail of our lives. We don't seem to pay much attention to the future. You see on television endless entertainment from morning until late in the night, except for one or two channels, but they are very brief and not too serious. The children are entertained. The commercials all sustain the feeling that you are being entertained. And this is happening practically all over the world. What will be the future of these children? There is the entertainment of sport—thirty, forty thousand people watching a few people in the arena and shouting themselves hoarse. And you also go and watch some ceremony being performed in a great cathedral, some ritual, and that too is a form of entertainment, only you call that holy, religious, but it is still an entertainment—a sentimental, romantic experience, a sensation of religiosity. Watching all this in different parts of the world, watching the mind being occupied with amusement, entertainment, sport, one must inevitably ask, if one is in any way concerned: What is the future? More of the same in different forms? A variety of amusements?

So you have to consider, if you are at all aware of what is happening to you, how the worlds of entertainment and sport are capturing your mind, shaping your life. Where is all this leading to? Or perhaps you are not concerned at all? You probably don't care about tomorrow. Probably you haven't given it thought, or, if you have, you may say it is too complex, too frightening, too dangerous to think of the coming years—not of your particular old age but of the destiny, if we can use that word, the result, of our present way of life, filled with all kinds of romantic, emotional, sentimental feelings and pursuits, and the whole world of entertainment impinging on your mind. If you are at all aware of all this, what is the future of mankind?

As we said earlier, the future is what you are now. If there is no change, not superficial adaptations, superficial adjustments to any pattern—political, religious, or social—but the change that is far deeper, demanding your attention, your care, your affection—if there is not a fundamental change, then the future is what we are doing every day of our life in the present. Change is rather a difficult word. Change to what? Change to another pattern? To another concept? To another political or religious system? Change from this to that? That is still within the realm, or within the field of *what is.* Change to that is projected by thought, formulated by thought, materialistically determined.

So one must inquire carefully into this word *change.* Is there a change if there is a motive? Is there a change if there is a particular direction, a particular end, a conclusion that seems sane, rational? Or perhaps a better phrase is "the ending of *what is.*" The ending, not the movement of *what is* to "what should be." That is not change. But if the ending has a motive, a purpose, is a matter of decision, then it is merely a change from this to that. The word *decision* implies the action of will: "I will do this; I won't do that." When desire enters into the act of the ending, that desire becomes the cause of ending. Where there is a cause there is a motive and so there is no real ending at all.

The twentieth century has had a tremendous lot of changes produced by two devastating wars, and the dialectical materialism, and the skepticism of religious beliefs, activities, and rituals, and so on, apart from the technological world, which has brought about a great many changes, and there will be further changes when the computer is fully developed—you are just at the beginning of it. Then when the computer takes over, what is going to happen to our human minds? That is a different question, which we should go into another time.

When the industry of entertainment takes over, as it is gradually doing now, when the young people, the students, the children, are constantly instigated to pleasure, to fancy, to romantic sensuality, the words *restraint* and *austerity* are pushed away, never even given a thought. The austerity of the monks, the *sannyasis,* who deny the world, who clothe their bodies with some kind of uniform or just a cloth—this denial of the material world is surely not austerity. You probably won't even listen to this, to what the implications of austerity are. When you have been brought up from childhood to amuse yourself and escape from yourself through entertainment, religious or otherwise, and when most of the psychologists say that you must express everything you feel and that any form of holding back or restraint is detrimental, leading to various forms of neuroticism, you naturally enter more and more into the world of sport, amusement, entertainment, all helping you to escape from yourself, from what you are.

The understanding of the nature of what you are, without any distortions, without any bias, without any reactions to what you discover you are, is the beginning of austerity. The watching, the awareness, of every thought, every feeling, not to restrain it, not to control it, but to watch it, like watching a bird in flight, without any of your own prejudices and distortions—that watching brings about an extraordinary sense of austerity that goes beyond all restraint, all the fooling around with oneself and all this idea of self-improvement, self-fulfillment. That is all rather childish. In this watching there is great freedom and in that freedom there is the sense of the dignity of austerity. But if you said all this to a modern group of students or children, they would probably look out of the window in boredom because this world is bent on its own pursuit of pleasure.

A large, fawn-colored squirrel came down the tree and went up to the feeder, nibbled at a few grains, sat there on top of it, looked around with its large beady eyes, its tail up, curved, a marvelous thing. It sat there for a moment or so, came down, went along the few rocks and then dashed to the tree and up and disappeared.

It appears that man has always escaped from himself, from what he is, from where he is going, from what all this is about—the universe, our daily life, the dying and the beginning. It is strange that we never realize that however much we may escape from ourselves, however much we may wander away—consciously, deliberately, or unconsciously, subtly—the conflict, the pleasure, the pain, the fear, and so on, are always there. They ultimately dominate. You may try to suppress them, you may try to put them away deliberately with an act of will but they surface again. And pleasure is one of the factors that predominates; it too has the same conflicts, the same pain, the same boredom. The weariness of pleasure and the fret are part of this turmoil of our life. You can't escape it, my friend. You can't escape from this deep unfathomed turmoil unless you really give thought to it, not only thought but see by careful attention, diligent watching, the whole movement of thought and the self. You may say all this is too tiresome, perhaps unnecessary. But if you do not pay attention to this, give heed, the future is not only going to be more destructive, more intolerable, but without much significance. All this is not a dampening, depressing point of view; it is actually so. What you are now is what you will be in the coming days. You can't avoid it. It is as definite as the sun rising and setting. This is the share of all man, of all humanity, unless we all change, each one of us, change to something that is not projected by thought.

May 9, 1983

You are already fairly high up, looking down into the valley, and if you climb a mile or more up and up the winding path, passing all kinds of vegetation—live oaks, sage, poison oak—and past a stream that is always dry in the summer, you can see the blue sea far away in the distance, across range after range. Up here it is absolutely quiet. It is so still there isn't a breath of air. You look down and the mountains look down on you. You can go on climbing up the mountain for many hours, down into another valley and up again. You have done it several times before, twice reaching the very top of those rocky mountains. Beyond them to the north is a vast plain of desert. Down there it is very hot, here it is quite cold; you have to put something on in spite of the hot sun.

And as you come down, looking at the various trees, plants, and little insects, suddenly you hear the rattle of a rattlesnake. And you jump, fortunately, away from the rattler. You are only about ten feet away from it. It is still rattling. You look at each other and watch. Snakes have no eyelids. This one was not very long but quite thick, as thick as your arm. You keep your distance and you watch it very carefully, its pattern, its triangular head, and its black tongue flickering in and out. You watch each other. It doesn't move and you don't move. But presently, its head and its tail toward you, it slithers back and you step forward. Again it coils up and rattles and you watch each other. And again, with its head and tail toward you, it begins to go back and again you move forward; and again it coils and rattles. You do this for several minutes, perhaps ten minutes or more; then it gets tired. You see that it is motionless, waiting, but as you approach it, it doesn't rattle. It has temporarily lost its energy. You are quite close to it. Unlike the cobra which stands up to strike, this snake strikes lunging forward. But there was no movement. It was too exhausted, so you leave it. It was really quite a poisonous, dangerous thing. Probably you could touch it but you are disinclined to, though not frightened. You feel that you would rather not touch it and you leave it alone.

And as you come further down you almost step on a quail with about a dozen or more babies. They scatter into the nearby bushes, and the mother too disappears into a bush and they all call to each other. You go down and wait, and if you have the patience to watch, you presently see them all come together under the mother's wing. It is cool up there and they are waiting for the sun to warm the air and the earth.

You come down across the little stream, past a meadow which is almost losing its green, and return to your room rather tired but exhilarated by the walk and by the morning sun. You see the orange trees with their bright yellow oranges, the rose bushes and the myrtle, and the tall eucalyptus trees. It is all very peaceful in the house.

It was a pleasant morning, full of strange activities on the earth. All those little things alive, rushing about, seeking their morning food—the squirrel, the gopher. They eat the tender roots of plants and are quite destructive. A dog can kill them so quickly with a snap. It is very dry, the rains are over and gone, to return again perhaps in four months or more. All the valley below is still glistening. It is strange how there is a brooding silence over the whole earth. In spite of the noise of towns and the traffic, there is something almost palpable, something holy. If you are in harmony with nature, with all the things around you, then you are in harmony with all human beings. If you have lost your relationship with nature you will inevitably lose your relationship with human beings.

A whole group of us sitting at table toward the end of the meal began a serious conversation, as has happened several times before. It was about the meaning of words, the weight of the word, the content of the word, not merely the superficial meaning of the word but the depth of it, the quality of it, the feeling of it. Of course the word is never the actual thing. The description, the explanation, is not that which is described, nor that about which there is an explanation. The word, the phrase, the explanation are not the actuality. But the word is used as a communication of one's thought, one's feeling, and the word, though it is not communicated to another, holds the feeling inside oneself. The actual never conditions the brain, but the theory, the conclusion, the description, the abstraction, do condition it. The table never conditions the brain but god does, whether it is the god of the Hindus, Christians, or Muslims. The concept, the image, conditions the brain, not that which is actually happening, taking place.

To the Christian, the word *Jesus* or *Christ* has great significance, great meaning; it evokes a deep sentiment, a sensation. Those words have no meaning to the Hindu, to the Buddhist, or to the Muslim. Those words are not the actual. So those words, which have been used for two thousand years, have conditioned the brain. The Hindu has his own gods, his own divinities. Those divinities, like the Christians', are the projections of thought, out of fear, out of pleasure, and so on.

It seems that language really doesn't condition the brain; what does is the theory of the language, the abstraction of a certain feeling and the abstraction taking the form of an idea, a symbol, a person—not the actual person but a person imagined, or hoped for, or projected by thought. All those abstractions, those ideas, conclusions, however strong, condition the brain. But the actual, like the table, never does.

Take a word like *suffering.* That word has a different meaning for the Hindu and the Christian. But suffering, however described by words, is shared by all of us. Suffering is the fact, the actual. But when we try to escape from it through some theory, or through some idealized person, or through a symbol, those forms of escape mold the brain. Suffering as a fact doesn't, and this is important to realize.

Like the word *attachment;* to see the word, to hold it as if in your hand and watch it, feel the depth of it, the whole content of it, the consequences of it, the fact that we are attached—the fact, not the word; that feeling doesn't shape the brain, put it into a mold, but the moment one moves away from it, that is, when thought moves away from the fact, that very movement away, movement of escape, is not only a time factor, but the beginning of shaping the brain in a certain mold.

To the Buddhist the word *Buddha,* the impression, the image, creates great reverence, great feeling, devotion; he seeks refuge in the image which thought has created. And as the thought is limited, because all knowledge is always limited, that very image brings about conflict—the feeling of reverence to a person, or to a symbol, or to a certain long-established tradition—but the feeling of reverence itself, divorced from all the external images, symbols, and so on, is not a factor of conditioning the brain.

There, sitting in the next chair, was a modified Christian. And when across the table one mentioned Christ one could immediately feel the restrictive, reverential reserve. That word has conditioned the brain. It is quite extraordinary to watch this whole phenomenon of communication with words, each race giving different significance and meaning to the word and thereby creating a division, a limitation, to the feeling which mankind suffers. The suffering of mankind is common, is shared by all human beings. The Russian may express it in one way, the Hindu, the Christian in another, and so on, but the fact of suffering, the actual feeling of pain, grief, loneliness, that feeling never shapes or conditions the brain. So one becomes very attentive to, aware of, the subtleties of the word, the meaning, the weight of it.

The universal, the global feeling of all human beings and their interrelationship, can only come into being when the words *nation, tribe, religion,* have all disappeared. Either the word has depth, significance, or none at all. For most of us words have very little depth, they have lost their weight. A river is not a particular river. The rivers of America or England or Europe or India are all rivers, but the moment there is identification through a word, there is division. And this division is an abstraction of the river, the quality of water, the depth of the water, the volume, the flow, the beauty of the river.

May 30, 1983

It has been raining here every day for over a month. When you come from a climate like California where the rains stopped over a month ago, where the green fields were drying up and turning brown and the sun was very hot, it is rather startling and surprising to see the green grass, the marvelous green trees and the copper beeches, which are a spreading, light brown, becoming gradually darker and darker. To see them now among the green trees is a delight. They are going to be very dark as the summer comes on. And this earth is very beautiful. Earth, whether it is desert or filled with orchards and green, bright fields, is always beautiful.

To go for a walk in the fields with the cattle and the young lambs, and in the woods with the song of birds, without a single thought in your mind, only watching the earth, the trees, the sheep and hearing the cuckoo calling and the wood pigeons; to walk without any emotion, any sentiment, to watch the trees and all the earth—when you so watch, you learn your own thinking, are aware of your own reactions and do not allow a single thought to escape you without understanding why it came, what was the cause of it. If you are watchful, never letting a thought go by, then the brain becomes very quiet. Then you watch in great silence and that silence has immense depth, a lasting incorruptible beauty.

The boy was good at games, really quite good. He was also good at his studies; he was serious. So one day he came to his teacher and said, "Sir, could I have a talk with you?" The educator said, "Yes, we can have a talk; let us go out for a walk." So they had a dialogue. It was a conversation between the teacher and the taught, a conversation in which there was some respect on both sides, and as the educator was also serious, the conversation was pleasant, friendly, and they had forgotten that he was a teacher with a student; the rank was forgotten, the importance of one who knows, the authority, and the other who is curious.

"Sir, I wonder if you know what all this is about, why I am getting an education, what part will it play when I grow up, what role have I in this world, why do I have to study, why do I have to marry and what is my future? Of course, I realize I have to study and pass some sort of exams and I hope I will be able to pass them. I will probably live for some years, perhaps fifty, sixty, or more, and in all those years to come what will be my life and the life of those people around me? What am I going to be and what is the point of these long hours over books and hearing the teachers? There might be a devastating war; we might all be killed. If death is all that lies ahead, then what is the point of all this education? Please, I am asking these questions quite seriously because I have heard the other teachers and you too pointing out many of these things."

"I would like to take one question at a time. You have asked many questions, you have put several problems before me, so first let us look at perhaps the most important question: What is the future of mankind and of yourself? As you know, your parents are fairly well-off and of course they want to help you in any way they can. Perhaps if you get married they might give you a house, buy a house with all the things necessary in it, and you might have a nice wife—might. So what is it you are going to be? The usual mediocre person? Get a job, settle down with all the problems around you and in you—is that your future? Of course a war may come, but it may not happen; let us hope it does not happen. Let us hope man may come to realize that wars of any kind will never solve any human problem. Men may improve, they may invent better airplanes, and so on, but wars have never solved human problems and they never will. So let us forget for the moment that all of us might be destroyed through the craziness of superpowers, through the craziness of terrorists, or some demagogue in some country wanting to destroy his invented enemies. Let us forget all that for the moment. Let us consider what is your future, knowing that you are part of the rest of the world. What is your future? As I asked, to be a mediocre person? Mediocrity means to go half way up the hill, half way in anything, never going to the very top of the mountain or demanding all your energy, your capacity, never demanding excellence.

"Of course you must realize also that there will be all the pressures from outside—pressures to do this, all the various narrow religious sectarian pressures and propaganda. Propaganda can never tell the truth; truth can never be propagated. So I hope you realize the pressure on you—pressure from your parents, from your society, from the tradition to be a scientist, to be a philosopher, to be a physicist, a man who undertakes research in any field; or to be a businessman. Realizing all this, which you must do at your age, what way will you go? We have been talking about all these things for many terms, and probably, if one may point out, you have applied your mind to all this. So as we have some time together to go around the hill and come back, I am asking you, not as a teacher but with affection as a friend genuinely concerned, what is your future? Even if you have already made up your mind to pass some exams and have a career, a good profession, you still have to ask, is that all? Even if you do have a good profession, perhaps a life that is fairly pleasant, you will have a lot of troubles, problems. If you have a family, what will be the future of your children? This is a question that you have to answer yourself and perhaps we can talk about it. You have to consider the future of your children, not just your own future, and you have to consider the future of humanity, forgetting that you are German, French, English, or Indian. Let us talk about it, but please realize I am not telling you what you should do. Only fools advise, so I am not entering into that category. I am just questioning in a friendly manner, which I hope you realize; I am not pushing you, directing you, persuading you. What is your future? Will you mature rapidly or slowly, gracefully, sensitively? Will you be mediocre, though you may be first class in your profession? You may excel, you may be very, very good at whatever you do, but I am talking of mediocrity of the mind, of the heart, mediocrity of your entire being."

"Sir, I don't really know how to answer these questions. I have not given too much thought to it, but when you ask this question, whether I am to become like the rest of the world, mediocre, I certainly don't want to be that. I also realize the attraction of the world. I also see that part of me wants all that. I want to have some fun, some happy times, but the other side of me also sees the danger of all that, the difficulties, the urges, the temptations. So I really don't know where I will end up. And also, as you pointed out on several occasions, I don't know myself what I am. One thing is definite, I really don't want to be a mediocre person with a small mind and heart, though with a brain that may be extraordinarily clever. I may study books and acquire a great deal of knowledge, but I may still be a very limited, narrow person. Mediocrity, sir, is a very good word which you have used and when I look at it I am getting frightened—not of the word but of the whole implications of what you have shown. I really don't know, and perhaps in talking it over with you it may clear things up. I can't so easily talk with my parents. They probably have had the same problems as I have; they may be more mature physically but they may be in the same position as I am. So if I may ask, sir, may I take another occasion, if you are willing, to talk with me? I really feel rather frightened, nervous, apprehensive of my capacity to meet all this, face it, go through it and not become a mediocre person."

It was one of those mornings that has never been before: the near meadow, the still beeches, and the lane that goes into the deeper wood—all was silence. There wasn't a bird chirping and the nearby horses were standing still. A morning like this, fresh, tender, is a rare thing. There is peace in this part of the land and everything was very quiet. There was that feeling, that sense of absolute silence. It was not a romantic sentimentalism, not poetic imagination. It was and is. A simple thing is all this is. The copper beeches this morning were full of splendor against the green fields stretching to the distance, and a cloud full of that morning light was floating lazily by. The sun was just coming up, there was great peace and a sense of adoration. Not the adoration of some god or imaginative deity but a reverence that is born of great beauty. This morning one could let go of all the things one has gathered and be silent with the woods and the trees and the quiet lawn. The sky was a pale and tender blue and far away across the fields a cuckoo was calling, the wood pigeons were cooing, and the blackbirds began their morning song. In the distance you could hear a car going by. Probably when the heavens are so quiet with loveliness it will rain later on. It always does when the early morning is very clear. But this morning it was all very special, something that has never been before and could never be again.

"I am glad you have come of your own accord, without being invited, and perhaps if you are prepared, we can continue with our conversation about mediocrity and the future of your life. One can be excellent in one's career; we aren't saying that there is mediocrity in all professions; a good carpenter may not be mediocre in his work but in his daily, inward life, his life with his family, he may be. We both understand the meaning of that word now and we should investigate together the depth of that word. We are talking about inward mediocrity, psychological conflicts, problems and travail. There can be great scientists who yet inwardly lead a mediocre life. So what is going to be your life? In some ways you are a clever student, but for what will you use your brain? We are not talking about your career, that will come later; what we should be concerned about is the way you are going to live. Of course, you are not going to be a criminal in the ordinary sense of that word. You are not, if you are wise, going to be a bully; they are too aggressive. You will probably get an excellent job, do excellent work in whatever you choose to do. So let us put that aside for a moment; but inside, what is your life? Inwardly, what is the future? Are you going to be like the rest of the world, always hunting pleasure, always troubled with a dozen psychological problems?"

"At present, sir, I have no problems, except the problems of passing examinations and the weariness of all that. Otherwise I seem to have no problems. There is a certain freedom. I feel happy, young. When I see all these old people I ask myself, am I going to end up like that? They seem to have had good careers or to have done something they wanted to do but in spite of that they become dreary, dull, and they seem never to have excelled in the deeper qualities of the brain. I certainly don't want to be like that. It is not vanity, but I want to have something different. It is not an ambition. I want to have a good career and all that business but I certainly in no way want to be like these old people who seem to have lost everything they like."

"You may not want to be like them but life is a very demanding and cruel thing. It won't let you alone. You will have great pressure from society whether you live here or in America or in any other part of the world. You will be constantly urged to become like the rest, to become something of a hypocrite, say things you don't really mean, and if you do marry that may raise problems too. You must understand that life is a very complex affair—not just pursuing what you want to do and being pigheaded about it. These young people want to become something—lawyers, engineers, politicians, and so on; there is the urge, the drive of, ambition for power, money. That is what those old people whom you talk about have been through. They are worn out by constant conflict, by their desires. Look at it, look at the people around you. They are all in the same boat. Some leave the boat and wander endlessly and die. Some seek some peaceful corner of the earth and retire; some join a monastery, become monks of various kinds, taking desperate vows. The vast majority, millions and millions, lead a very small life, their horizon is very limited. They have their sorrows, their joys, and they seem never to escape from them or understand them and go beyond. So again we ask each other, what is our future, specifically, what is your future? Of course you are much too young to go into this question very deeply, for youth has nothing to do with the total comprehension of this question. You may be an agnostic; the young do not believe in anything, but as you grow older then you turn to some form of religious superstition, religious dogma, religious conviction. Religion is not an opiate, but man has made religion in his own image, blind comfort and, therefore, security. He has made religion into something totally unintelligent and impracticable, not something that you can live with. How old are you?"

"I'm going to be nineteen, sir. My grandmother has left me something when I am twenty-one and perhaps before I go to the university I can travel and look around. But I will always carry this question with me wherever I am, whatever my future. I may marry, probably I will, and have children, and so the great question arises—what is their future? I am somewhat aware of what the politicians are doing throughout the world. It is an ugly business as far as I am concerned, so I think I won't be a politician. I'm pretty sure of that but I want a good job. I'd like to work with my hands and with my brain but the question will be how not to become a mediocre person like ninety-nine percent of the world. So, sir, what am I to do? Oh, yes, I am aware of churches and temples and all that; I am not attracted to them. I rather revolt against all that—the priests and the hierarchy of authority, but how am I going to prevent myself becoming an ordinary, average, mediocre person?"

"If I may suggest, never under any circumstances ask 'how.' When you use the word *how* you really want someone to tell you what to do, some guide, some system, somebody to lead you by the hand so that you lose your freedom, your capacity to observe, your own activities, your own thoughts, your own way of life. When you ask 'how' you really become a secondhand human being; you lose integrity and also the innate honesty to look at yourself, to be what you are and to go beyond and above what you are. Never, never ask the question 'how.' We are talking psychologically, of course. You have to ask 'how' when you want to put a motor together or build a computer. You have to learn something about it from somebody. But to be psychologically free and original can only come about when you are aware of your own inward activities, watch what you are thinking and never let one thought escape without observing the nature of it, the source of it. Observing, watching. One learns about oneself much more by watching than from books or from some psychologist or complicated, clever, erudite scholar or professor.

"It is going to be very difficult, my friend. It can tear you in many directions. There are a great many so-called temptations—biological, social—and you can be torn apart by the cruelty of society. Of course, you are going to have to stand alone but that can come about not through force, determination, or desire but when you begin to see the false things around you and in yourself: the emotions, the hopes. When you begin to see that which is false, then there is the beginning of awareness, of intelligence. You have to be a light to yourself and it is one of the most difficult things in life."

"Sir, you have made it all seem so very difficult, so very complex, so very awesome, frightening."

"I am just pointing all this out to you. It doesn't mean that facts need frighten you. Facts are there to observe. If you observe them they never frighten you. Facts are not frightening. But if you want to avoid them, turn your back and run, then that is frightening. To stand, to see that what you have done may not have been totally correct, to live with the fact and not interpret the fact according to your pleasure or form of reaction, that is not frightening. Life isn't very simple. One can live simply but life itself is vast, complex. It extends from horizon to horizon. You can live with few clothes or with one meal a day, but that is not simplicity. So be simple, don't live in a complicated way, contradictory, and so on, just be simple inwardly. You played tennis this morning. I was watching and you seem to be quite good at it. Perhaps we will meet again. That is up to you."

"Thank you, sir."

September 15, 1973

It is good to be alone. To be far away from the world and yet walk its streets is to be alone. To be alone walking up the path beside the rushing, noisy mountain stream full of spring water and melting snows is to be aware of that solitary tree, alone in its beauty. The loneliness of a man in the street is the pain of life; he's never alone, far away, untouched and vulnerable. To be full of knowledge breeds endless misery. The demand for expression, with its frustrations and pains, is that man who walks the streets; he is never alone. Sorrow is the movement of that loneliness.

That mountain stream was full and high with the melting snows and the rains of early spring. You could hear big boulders being pushed around by the force of onrushing waters. A tall pine of fifty years or more crashed into the water; the road was being washed away. The stream was muddy, slate-colored. The fields above it were full of wild flowers. The air was pure and there was enchantment. On the high hills there was still snow, and the glaciers and the great peaks still held the recent snows; they will still be white all the summer long.

It was a marvelous morning and you could have walked on endlessly, never feeling the steep hills. There was a perfume in the air, clear and strong. There was no one on that path, coming down or going up. You were alone with those dark pines and the rushing waters. The sky was that astonishing blue that only the mountains have. You looked at it through leaves and the straight pines. There was no one to talk to and there was no chattering of the mind. A magpie, white and black, flew by, disappearing into the woods. The path led away from the noisy stream and the silence was absolute. It wasn't the silence after the noise; it wasn't the silence that comes with the setting of the sun, nor that silence when the mind dies down. It wasn't the silence of museums and churches but something totally unrelated to time and space. It wasn't the silence that mind makes for itself. The sun was hot and the shadows were pleasant.

He only discovered recently that there was not a single thought during these long walks, in the crowded streets or on the solitary paths. Ever since he was a boy it had been like that, no thought entered his mind. He was watching and listening and nothing else. Thought, with its associations, never arose. There was no image-making. One day he was suddenly aware how extraordinary it was; he attempted often to think but no thought would come. On these walks, with people or without them, any movement of thought was absent. This is to be alone.

Over the snow peaks clouds were forming, heavy and dark; probably it would rain later on but now the shadows were very sharp with the sun bright and clear. There was still that pleasant smell in the air and the rains would bring a different smell. It was a long way down to the chalet.

September 17, 1973

That evening, walking through the wood there was a feeling of menace. The sun was just setting and the palm trees were solitary against the golden western sky. The monkeys were in the banyan tree, getting ready for the night. Hardly anyone used that path and rarely you met another human being. There were many deer, shy and disappearing into the thick growth. Yet the menace was there, heavy and pervading: it was all around you, you looked over your shoulder. There were no dangerous animals; they had moved away from there; it was too close to the spreading town. One was glad to leave and walk back through the lighted streets. But the next evening the monkeys were still there and so were the deer and the sun was just behind the tallest trees; the menace was gone. On the contrary, the trees, the bushes and the small plants welcomed you. You were among your friends, you felt completely safe and most welcome. The woods accepted you and every evening it was a pleasure to walk there.

Forests are different. There's physical danger there, not only from snakes but from tigers that were known to be there. As one walked there one afternoon there was suddenly an abnormal silence; the birds stopped chattering, the monkeys were absolutely still and everything seemed to be holding its breath. One stood still. And, as suddenly, everything came to life; the monkeys were playing and teasing each other, birds began their evening chatter, and one was aware the danger had passed.

In the woods and groves where man kills rabbits, pheasants, squirrels, there's quite a different atmosphere. You are entering into a world where man has been, with his gun and peculiar violence. Then the woods lose their tenderness, their welcome, and here some beauty has been lost and that happy whisper has gone.

You have only one head and look after it, for it's a marvelous thing. No machinery, no electronic computers can compare with it. It's so vast, so complex, so utterly capable, subtle, and productive. It's the storehouse of experience, knowledge, memory. All thought springs from it. What it has put together is quite incredible: the mischief, the confusion, the sorrows, the wars, the corruptions, the illusions, the ideals, the pain and misery, the great cathedrals, the lovely mosques, and the sacred temples. It is fantastic what it has done and what it can do. But one thing it apparently cannot do: change completely its behavior in its relationship to another head, to another man. Neither punishment nor reward seem to change its behavior; knowledge doesn't seem to transform its conduct. The me and the you remain. It never realizes that the me is the you, that the observer is the observed. Its love is its degeneration; its pleasure is its agony; the gods of its ideals are its destroyers. Its freedom is its own prison; it is educated to live in this prison, only making it more comfortable, more pleasurable. You have only one head, care for it, don't destroy it. It's so easy to poison it.

He always had this strange lack of distance between himself and the trees, rivers, and mountains. It wasn't cultivated: you can't cultivate a thing like that. There was never a wall between him and another. What they did to him, what they said to him never seemed to wound him, nor flattery to touch him. Somehow he was altogether untouched. He was not withdrawn, aloof, but like the waters of a river. He had so few thoughts; no thoughts at all when he was alone. His brain was active when talking or writing but otherwise it was quiet and active without movement. Movement is time and activity is not.

This strange activity, without direction, seems to go on, sleeping or waking. He wakes up often with that activity of meditation; something of this nature is going on most of the time. He never rejected it or invited it. The other night he woke up, wide awake. He was aware that something like a ball of fire, light, was being put into his head, into the very center of it. He watched it objectively for a considerable time, as though it were happening to someone else. It was not an illusion, something conjured up by the mind. Dawn was coming and through the opening of the curtains he could see the trees.

September 20, 1973

The river was particularly beautiful this morning; the sun was just coming over the trees and the village hidden among them. The air was very still and there was not a ripple on the water. It would get quite warm during the day but now it was rather cool and a solitary monkey was sitting in the sun. It was always there by itself, big and heavy. During the day it disappeared and turned up early in the morning on the top of the tamarind tree: when it got warm the tree seemed to swallow it. The golden green fly-catchers were sitting on the parapet with the doves, and the vultures were still on the top branches of another tamarind. There was immense quietness and one sat on a bench, lost to the world.

Coming back from the airport on a shaded road with the parrots, green and red, screeching around the trees, one saw across the road what appeared to be a large bundle. As the car came near, the bundle turned out to be a man lying across the road, almost naked. The car stopped and we got out. His body was large and his head very small; he was staring through the leaves at the astonishingly blue sky. We looked up too to see what he was staring at and the sky from the road was really blue and the leaves were really green. He was malformed and they said he was one of the village idiots. He never moved and the car had to be driven round him very carefully. The camels with their load and the shouting children passed him without paying the least attention. A dog passed, making a wide circle. The parrots were busy with their noise. The dry fields, the villagers, the trees, the yellow flowers were occupied with their own existence. That part of the world was underdeveloped and there was no one or organization to look after such people. There were open gutters, filth and crowding humanity, and the sacred river went on its way. The sadness of life was everywhere, and in the blue sky, high in the air, were the heavy-winged vultures, circling without moving their wings, circling by the hour, waiting and watching.

What is sanity and insanity? Who is sane and who is insane? Are the politicians sane? The priests, are they insane? Those who are committed to ideologies, are they sane? We are controlled, shaped, pushed around by them, and are we sane?

What is sanity? To be whole, nonfragmented in action, in life, in every kind of relationship, that is the very essence of sanity. Sanity means to be whole, healthy and holy. To be insane, neurotic, psychotic, unbalanced, schizophrenic, whatever name you might give to it, is to be fragmented, broken up in action and in the movement of relationship, which is existence. To breed antagonism and division, which is the trade of the politicians who represent you, is to cultivate and sustain insanity, whether they are dictators or those in power in the name of peace or some form of ideology. And the priest: look at the world of the priesthood. He stands between you and what he and you consider truth, savior, God, heaven, hell. He is the interpreter, the representative; he holds the keys to heaven; he has conditioned man through belief, dogma, and ritual; he is the real propagandist. He has conditioned you because you want comfort, security, and you dread tomorrow. The artists, the intellectuals, the scientists, admired and flattered so much—are they sane? Or do they live in two different worlds—the world of ideas and imagination with its compulsive expression, wholly separate from their daily life of sorrow and pleasure?

The world about you is fragmented and so are you and its expression is conflict, confusion, and misery: you are the world and the world is you. Sanity is to live a life of action without conflict. Action and idea are contradictory. Seeing is the doing and not ideation first and action according to the conclusion. This breeds conflict. The analyzer himself is the analyzed. When the analyzer separates himself as something different from the analyzed, he begets conflict, and conflict is the area of the unbalanced. The observer is the observed and therein lies sanity, the whole, and with the holy is love.

September 27, 1973

It was a temple in ruins, with its roofless long corridors, gates, headless statues, and deserted courtyards. It had become a sanctuary for birds and monkeys, parrots and doves. Some of the headless statues were still massive in their beauty; they had a still dignity. The whole place was surprisingly clean and one could sit on the ground to watch the monkeys and chattering birds. Once, very long ago, the temple must have been a flourishing place with thousands of worshipers, with garlands, incense, and prayer. Their atmosphere was still there, their hopes, fears, and their reverence. The holy sanctuary was gone long ago. Now the monkeys disappeared as it was growing hot, but the parrots and doves had their nests in the holes and crevices of the high walls. This old ruined temple was too far away for the villagers to further destroy it. Had they come they would have desecrated the emptiness.

Religion has become superstition and image-worship, belief and ritual. It has lost the beauty of truth; incense has taken the place of reality. Instead of direct perception there is in its place the image carved by the hand or the mind. The only concern of religion is the total transformation of man. And all the circus that goes on around it is nonsense. That's why the truth is not to be found in any temple, church, or mosque, however beautiful they are. Beauty of truth and the beauty of stone are two different things. One opens the door to the immeasurable and the other to the imprisonment of man; the one to freedom and the other to the bondage of thought. Romanticism and sentimentality deny the very nature of religion, nor is it a plaything of the intellect. Knowledge in the area of action is necessary to function efficiently and objectively, but knowledge is not the means of the transformation of man; knowledge is the structure of thought and thought is the dull repetition of the known, however modified and enlarged. There is no freedom through the ways of thought, the known.

The long snake lay very still along the dry ridge of the rice fields, lusciously green and bright in the morning sun. Probably it was resting or waiting for some careless frog. Frogs were being shipped then to Europe to be eaten as a delicacy. The snake was long and yellowish, and very still; it was almost the color of the dry earth, hard to see, but the light of day was in its dark eyes. The only thing that was moving, in and out, was its black tongue. It could not have been aware of the watcher who was somewhat behind its head. Death was everywhere that morning. You could hear it in the village; the great sobs as the body, wrapped in a cloth, was being carried out; a kite was streaking down on a bird; some animal was being killed; you heard its agonizing cries. So it went on day after day: death is always everywhere, as sorrow is.

The beauty of truth and its subtleties are not in belief and dogma, they never are where man can find them for there is no path to its beauty; it is not a fixed point, a haven of shelter. It has its own tenderness, whose love is not to be measured; nor can you hold it, experience it. It has no market value to be used and put aside. It is there when the mind and heart are empty of the things of thought. The monk or the poor man are not near it, nor the rich; neither the intellectual nor the gifted can touch it. The one who says he knows has never come near it. Be far away from the world and yet live it.

The parrots were screeching and fluttering around the tamarind tree that morning; they begin early their restless activity, with their coming and going. They were bright streaks of green with strong, red, curved beaks. They never seemed to fly straight but always zigzagging, shrieking as they flew. Occasionally they would come to sit on the parapet of the veranda; then you could watch them, but not for long; they would be off again with their crazy and noisy flight. Their only enemy seemed to be man. He puts them in a cage.

October 4, 1973

As a young boy, he used to sit by himself under a large tree near a pond in which lotuses grew; they were pink and had a strong smell. [Krishnamurti is describing his own childhood.] From the shade of that spacious tree, he would watch the thin, green snakes and the chameleons, the frogs and the water snakes. His brother, with others, would come to take him home. It was a pleasant place under the tree, with the river and the pond. There seemed to be so much space, and in this the tree made its own space. Everything needs space. All those birds on telegraph wires, sitting so equally spaced on a quiet evening, make the space for the heavens.

The two brothers would sit with many others in the room with pictures; there would be a chant in Sanskrit and then complete silence; it was the evening meditation. The younger brother would go to sleep and roll over and wake up only when the others got up to leave. The room was not too large and within its walls were the pictures, the images of the sacred. Within the narrow confines of a temple or church, man gives form to the vast movement of space. It is like this everywhere; in the mosque it is held in the graceful lines of words. Love needs great space.

To that pond would come snakes and occasionally people; it had stone steps leading down to the water where grew the lotus. The space that thought creates is measurable and so is limited; cultures and religions are its product. But the mind is filled with thought and is made up of thought; its consciousness is the structure of thought, having little space within it. But this space is the movement of time, from here to there, from its center toward its outer lines of consciousness, narrow or expanding. The space which the center makes for itself is its own prison. Its relationships are from this narrow space but there must be space to live; that of the mind denies living. Living within the narrow confines of the center is strife, pain, and sorrow and that is not living.

The space, the distance between you and the tree, is the word, knowledge, which is time. Time is the observer who makes the distance between himself and the trees, between himself and *what is*. Without the observer, distance ceases. Identification with the trees, with another or with a formula, is the action of thought in its desire for protection, security. Distance is from one point to another and to reach that point time is necessary; distance only exists where there is direction, inward or outward. The observer makes a separation, a distance between himself and *what is;* from this grows conflict and sorrow. The transformation of *what is* takes place only when there is no separation, no time, between the seer and the seen. Love has no distance.

The brother died and there was no movement in any direction away from sorrow. This nonmovement is the ending of time. It was among the hills and green shadows that the river began and with a roar it entered the sea and the endless horizons. Man lives in boxes with drawers, acres of them, and they have no space; they are violent, brutal, aggressive, and mischievous; they separate and destroy each other. The river is the earth and the earth is the river; each cannot exist without the other.

There are no ends to words but communication is verbal and nonverbal. The hearing of the word is one thing and the hearing of no word is another; the one is irrelevant, superficial, leading to inaction; the other is nonfragmentary action, the flowering of goodness. Words have given beautiful walls but no space. Remembrance, imagination, are the pain of pleasure, and love is not pleasure.

The long, thin, green snake was there that morning; it was delicate and almost lost among the green leaves; it would be there, motionless, waiting and watching. The large head of the chameleon was showing; it lay along a branch; it changed its colors quite often.

April 10, 1975

In the silence of deep night and in the quiet still morning when the sun is touching the hills, there is a great mystery. It is there in all living things. If you sit quietly under a tree, you would feel the ancient earth with its incomprehensible mystery. On a still night when the stars are clear and close, you would be aware of expanding space and the mysterious order of all things, of the immeasurable and of nothing, of the movement of the dark hills and the hoot of an owl. In that utter silence of the mind this mystery expands without time and space. There's mystery in those ancient temples built with infinite care, with attention, which is love. The slender mosques and the great cathedrals lose this shadowy mystery for there is bigotry, dogma, and military pomp. The myth that is concealed in the deep layers of the mind is not mysterious; it is romantic, traditional, and conditioned. In the secret recesses of the mind, truth has been pushed aside by symbols, words, images; in them there is no mystery, they are the churnings of thought. In knowledge and its action there is wonder, appreciation, and delight. But mystery is quite another thing. It is not an experience, to be recognized, stored up, and remembered. Experience is the death of that incommunicable mystery; to communicate you need a word, a gesture, a look, but to be in communion with that, the mind, the whole of you, must be at the same level, at the same time, with the same intensity as that which is called mysterious. This is love. With this the whole mystery of the universe is open.

This morning there wasn't a cloud in the sky; the sun was in the valley and all things were rejoicing, except man. He looked at this wondrous earth and went on with his labor, his sorrow and passing pleasures. He had no time to see; he was too occupied with his problems, with his agonies, with his violence. He doesn't see the tree and so he cannot see his own travail. When he's forced to look, he tears to pieces what he sees, which he calls analysis, runs away from it or doesn't want to see. In the art of seeing lies the miracle of transformation, the transformation of *what is.* The "what should be" never is. There's vast mystery in the act of seeing. This needs care, attention, which is love.

April 14, 1975

A very large serpent was crossing a wide cart road just ahead of you—fat, heavy, moving lazily; it was coming from a largish pond a little way off. It was almost black and the light of the evening seen falling on it gave to its skin a high polish. It moved in a leisurely way with lordly dignity of power. It was unaware of you as you stood quietly watching; you were quite close to it; it must have measured well over five feet and it was bulging with what it had eaten. It went over a mound and you walked toward it, looking down upon it a few inches away, its forked black tongue darting in and out; it was moving toward a large hole. You could have touched it for it had a strange attractive beauty. A villager was passing by and called out to leave it alone because it was a cobra. The next day the villagers had put there on the mound a saucer of milk and some hibiscus flowers. On that same road further along there was a bush, high and almost leafless, that had thorns almost two inches long, sharp, grayish, and no animal would dare to touch its succulent leaves. It was protecting itself and woe to anyone that touched it. There were deer there in those woods, shy but very curious; they would allow themselves to be approached but not too close and if you did they would dart away and disappear among the undergrowth. There was one that would let you come quite close if you were alone, bright-eyed, with its large ears forward. They all had white spots on a russet-brown skin; they were shy, gentle and ever-watchful, and it was pleasant to be among them. There was a completely white one, which must have been a freak.

The good is not the opposite of the evil. It has never been touched by that which is evil, though it is surrounded by it. Evil cannot hurt the good but the good may appear to do harm and so evil gets more cunning, more mischievous. It can be cultivated, sharpened, expansively violent; it is born within the movement of time, nurtured and skillfully used. But goodness is not of time; it can in no way be cultivated or nurtured by thought; its action is not visible; it has no cause and so no effect. Evil cannot become good, for that which is good is not the product of thought; it lies beyond thought, like beauty. The thing that thought produces thought can undo, but it is not the good; as it is not of time, the good has no abiding place. Where the good is, there is order, not the order of authority, punishment, and reward; this order is essential, for otherwise society destroys itself and man becomes evil, murderous, corrupt, and degenerate. For man is society; they are inseparable. The law of the good is everlasting, unchanging and timeless. Stability is its nature and so it is utterly secure. There is no other security.

March 30, 1984

Walking down the straight road on a lovely morning, it was spring, and the sky was extraordinarily blue; there wasn't a cloud in it, and the sun was just warm, not too hot. It felt nice. And the leaves were shining and a sparkle was in the air. It was really a most extraordinarily beautiful morning. The high mountain was there, impenetrable, and the hills below were green and lovely. And as you walked along quietly, without much thought, you saw a dead leaf, yellow and bright red, a leaf from the autumn. How beautiful that leaf was, so simple in its death, so lively, full of the beauty and vitality of the whole tree and the summer. Strange that it had not withered. Looking at it more closely, one saw all the veins and the stem and the shape of that leaf. That leaf was all the tree.

Why do human beings die so miserably, so unhappily, with a disease, old age, senility, the body shrunk, ugly? Why can't they die naturally and as beautifully as this leaf? What is wrong with us? In spite of all the doctors, medicines, and hospitals, operations and all the agony of life, and the pleasures too, we don't seem able to die with dignity, simplicity, and with a smile.

Once, walking along a lane, one heard behind one a chant, melodious, rhythmic, with the ancient strength of Sanskrit. One stopped and looked around. An eldest son, naked to his waist, was carrying a terra-cotta pot with a fire burning in it. He was holding it in another vessel and behind him were two men carrying his dead father, covered with a white cloth, and they were all chanting. One knew what that chant was, one almost joined in. They went past and one followed them. They were going down the road chanting, and the eldest son was in tears. They carried the father to the beach where they had already collected a great pile of wood and they laid the body on top of that heap of wood and set it on fire. It was all so natural, so extraordinarily simple: there were no flowers, there was no hearse, there were no black carriages with black horses. It was all very quiet and utterly dignified. And one looked at that leaf, and a thousand leaves of the tree. The winter brought that leaf from its mother on to that path and it would presently dry out completely and wither, be gone, carried away by the winds and lost.

As you teach children mathematics, writing, reading, and all the business of acquiring knowledge, they should also be taught the great dignity of death, not as a morbid, unhappy thing that one has to face eventually, but as something of daily life—the daily life of looking at the blue sky and the grasshopper on a leaf. It is part of learning, as you grow teeth and have all the discomfort of childish illnesses. Children have extraordinary curiosity. If you see the nature of death, you don't explain that everything dies, dust to dust, and so on, but without any fear you explain it to them gently and make them feel that the living and the dying are one—not at the end of one's life after fifty, sixty, or ninety years, but that death is like that leaf. Look at the old men and women, how decrepit, how lost, how unhappy, and how ugly they look. Is it because they have not really understood either the living or the dying? They have used life, they waste away their life with incessant conflict, which only exercises and gives strength to the self, the "me," the ego. We spend our days in such varieties of conflict and unhappiness, with some joy and pleasure, drinking, smoking, late nights, and work, work, work. And at the end of one's life one faces that thing called death and is frightened of it. One thinks it can always be understood, felt deeply. The child with his curiosity can be helped to understand that death is not merely the wasting of the body through disease, old age, and some unexpected accident, but that the ending of every day is also the ending of oneself every day.

There is no resurrection; that is superstition, a dogmatic belief. Everything on earth, on this beautiful earth, lives, dies, comes into being and withers away. To grasp this whole movement of life requires intelligence, not the intelligence of thought, or books, or knowledge, but the intelligence of love and compassion, with its sensitivity. One is very certain that if the educator understands the significance of death and the dignity of it, the extraordinary simplicity of dying—understands it not intellectually but deeply—then he may be able to convey to the student, to the child, that dying, the ending, is not to be avoided, is not something to be frightened of, for it is part of one's whole life, so that as the student, the child, grows up he will never be frightened of the ending. If all the human beings who have lived before us, past generations upon generations, still lived on this earth, how terrible it would be. The beginning is not the ending.

And one would like to help—no, that's the wrong word—one would like in education to bring death into some kind of reality, actuality, not of someone else dying but of each one of us, however old or young, having inevitably to face that thing. It is not a sad affair of tears, of loneliness, of separation. We kill so easily, not only the animals for one's food but the vast unnecessary killing for amusement, called sport—killing a deer because that is the season. Killing a deer is like killing your neighbor. You kill animals because you have lost touch with nature, with all the living things on this earth. You kill in wars for so many romantic, nationalistic, political ideologies. In the name of God you have killed people. Violence and killing go together.

As one looked at that dead leaf with all its beauty and color, maybe one would very deeply comprehend, be aware of, what one's own death must be, not at the very end but at the very beginning. Death isn't some horrific thing, something to be avoided, something to be postponed, but rather something to be with day in and day out. And out of that comes an extraordinary sense of immensity.

PART 3

Life's Questions

As well as giving thousands of public talks and having many private discussions with individuals, Krishnamurti invited questions from those who attended the yearly gatherings in many countries. Even in later years, when the questions were written, rather than spoken from the audience, these were always explored afresh, spontaneously, "together as friends" as he often reminded his listeners.

He was involved in frequent meetings and seminars with scientists, educators, and the students and staff members of the schools founded by the various Krishnamurti Foundations. He held dialogues with psychiatrists and psychologists, professionals of almost every kind, and with the trustees of the foundations responsible for arranging his talks and travels, disseminating the teachings and maintaining the schools.

Krishnamurti considered the proper education of the young to be of crucial concern for each generation. He inspired the founding of schools which bore his name in India, England, and the United States. Visiting them often, and sitting informally with students and teachers, he would talk with them of the need to learn about themselves. Beyond their becoming academically capable, he stressed the need to be whole and integrated human beings with a concern for all humanity and the global environment.

This part includes questions taken from accounts in *The Collected Works, Beginnings of Learning, The Wholeness of Life,* forty years of public meetings, as well as dialogues with students and teachers, and trustees of the various foundations. Each of these extracts conveys Krishnamurti's eagerness to explore significant themes with openness, and his refusal to speak as an authority.

We are reminded that the answers are in the penetration of the questions themselves.

WHAT IS IT TO BE SERIOUS?

If we can begin by considering what it is to be serious, then perhaps our investigation into the whole process of our thinking and responding to the various challenges of life will have deeper significance.

What do we mean by being serious? And are we ever really serious? Most of us think very superficially; we never sustain a particular intention and carry it through because we have so many contradictory desires, each desire pulling in a different direction. One moment we are serious about something, and the next it is forgotten, and we pursue a different object at a different level. And is it possible to maintain an integrated outlook toward life? I think this is a fairly important question to consider because I wonder how many of us are serious at all? Or are we serious only about those things which give us satisfaction and have but a temporary meaning?

So I think it would be very interesting not merely to listen to a talk which I happen to be giving, but earnestly to try to find out together what it means to be serious. When a petty mind gives its effort to being serious, its seriousness is bound to be very shallow because it is without any understanding of the deeper significance of its own process. One may give one's energies to a particular object, spiritual or mundane, but as long as the mind remains petty, complex, without any understanding of itself, its serious activities will have very little significance. That is why it seems to me very important, especially at this time when there are so many complex problems, so many challenges, that a few of us at least should have a sustained interest in trying to find out if it is possible to be earnest or serious without being distracted by the superficial activities of the mind.

I don't know if you are interested in this problem, but it is surely quite important to find out why most people are not really serious because it is only a serious mind that can pursue a particular activity to its end and discover its significance. If one is to be capable of action which is integral, one must understand the ways of one's own mind, and without that understanding, merely to be serious has very little meaning. I wonder if any of you are following all this, and whether I am explaining myself?

We see the disintegrating process that is going on in the world. The old social order is breaking down, the various religious organizations, the beliefs, the moral and ethical structures in which we have been brought up, are all failing. Throughout our so-called civilization, whether Indian, European, or whatever it be, there is corruption, and every form of useless activity is being carried on. So, is it possible for you and me to be aware of this whole process of disintegration and, stepping out of it as individuals, be serious in our intention to create a totally different kind of world, a different kind of culture, civilization? Do you think we could discuss this instead of my giving a talk?

The problem is this: Being caught up in this social, religious, and moral disintegration, how can we as individuals break away and create a different world, a different social order, a different way of looking at life? Is this a problem to any of you, or are you content merely to observe this disintegration and respond to it in the habitual manner? Can we this evening discuss this problem together, think it right through, and resolve it in ourselves? Do you think it would be profitable to discuss what we mean by change?

QUESTIONER: Let us discuss seriousness.

KRISHNAMURTI: What do we mean by seriousness? To be serious, to be earnest, surely implies the capacity to find out what is true. Can I find out what is true if my mind is tethered to any particular point of view? If it is bound by knowledge, by belief, if it is caught in the conditioning influences that are constantly impinging upon it, can the mind discover anything new? Does not seriousness imply the total application of one's mind to any problem of life? Can a mind which is only partially attentive, which is contradictory within itself, however much it may attempt to be serious, ever respond adequately to the challenge of life? Is a mind that is torn by innumerable desires, each pulling in a different direction, capable of discovering what is true, however much it may try? And is it not, therefore, very important to have self-knowledge, to be serious in the process of understanding the self, with all its contradictions? Can we discuss that?

Q: Would you kindly tell us if life and the problems of life are the same?

K: Can you separate the problems of life from life itself? Is life different from the problems which life awakens in us? Let us take that one question and follow it right through.

Q: What about the atomic and the hydrogen bombs? Can we discuss that?

K: That involves the whole problem of war and how to prevent war, does it not? Can we discuss that so as to clarify our own minds, pursue it seriously, earnestly, to the end and thereby know the truth of the matter completely?

What do we mean by peace? Is peace the opposite, the antithesis, of war? If there were no war, would we have peace? Are we pursuing peace, or is what we call peace merely a space between two contradictory activities? Do we really want peace, not only at one level, economic or spiritual, but totally? Or is it that we are continually at war within ourselves and, therefore, outwardly? If we wish to prevent war, we must obviously take certain steps, which really means having no frontiers of the mind because belief creates enmity. If you believe in communism and I believe in capitalism, or if you are a Hindu and I am a Christian, obviously there is antagonism between us. So, if you and I desire peace, must we not abolish all the frontiers of the mind? Or do we merely want peace in terms of satisfaction, maintaining the status quo after achieving a certain result?

You see, I don't think it is possible for individuals to stop war. War is like a giant mechanism that, having been set going, has gathered great momentum, and probably it will go on and we shall be crushed, destroyed in the process. But if one wishes to step out of that mechanism, the whole machinery of war, what is one to do? That is the problem, is it not? Do we really want to stop war, inwardly as well as outwardly? After all, war is merely the dramatic outward expression of our inward struggle, is it not? And can each one of us cease to be ambitious? Because as long as we are ambitious, we are ruthless, which inevitably produces conflict between ourselves and other individuals, as well as between one group or nation and another. This means, really, that as long as you and I are seeking power in any direction, power being evil, we must produce wars. And is it possible for each one of us to investigate the process of ambition, of competition, of wanting to be somebody in the field of power, and put an end to it? It seems to me that only then can we as individuals step out of this culture, this civilization that is producing wars.

Let us discuss this. Can we as individuals put an end in ourselves to the causes of war? One of the causes is obviously belief, the division of ourselves as Hindus, Buddhists, Christians, communists, or capitalists. Can we put all that aside?

Q: All the problems of life are unreal, and there must be something real on which we can rely. What is that reality?

K: Do you think the real and the unreal can so easily be divided? Or does the real come into being only when I begin to understand what is unreal? Have you even considered what the unreal is? Is pain unreal? Is death unreal? If you lose your bank account, is that unreal? A man who says, "All this is unreal; therefore, let us find the real," is escaping from reality.

Can you and I put an end in ourselves to the factors that contribute to war within and without? Let us discuss that, not merely verbally, but really investigate it, go into it earnestly and see if we can eradicate in ourselves the cause of hate, of enmity, this sense of superiority, ambition, and all the rest of it. Can we eradicate all this? If we really want peace, it must be eradicated, must it not? If you would find out what is real, what is God, what is truth, you must have a very quiet mind, and can you have a quiet mind if you are ambitious, envious, if you are greedy for power, position, and all that? So, if you are really earnest, really serious in wanting to understand what is true, must not these things be put away? Does not earnestness, seriousness, consist in understanding the process of the mind, of the self, which creates all these problems, and dissolving it?

Q: How can we uncondition ourselves?

K: But I am showing you. What is conditioning? It is the tradition that has been imposed upon you from childhood, or the beliefs, the experiences, the knowledge, that one has accumulated for oneself. They are all conditioning the mind.

Now, before we go into the more complex aspects of the question, can you cease to be a Hindu, with all its implications, so that your mind is capable of thinking, responding, not according to a modified Hinduism, but completely anew? Can there be in you a total revolution so that the mind is fresh, clear, and, therefore, capable of investigation? That is a very simple question. I can give a talk about it, but it will have no meaning if you merely listen and then go away agreeing or disagreeing, whereas if you and I can discuss this problem and go through it together to the very end, then perhaps our talking will be worthwhile.

So, can you and I who wish to have peace, or who talk about peace, eradicate in ourselves the causes of antagonism, of war? Shall we discuss that?

Q: Are individuals impotent against the atomic and hydrogen bombs?

K: They are going on experimenting with these bombs in America, in Russia, and elsewhere, and what can you and I do about it? So what is the point of discussing this matter? You may try to create public opinion by writing to the papers about how terrible it is, but will that stop the governments from investigating and creating the H-bomb? Are they not going to go on with it anyhow? They may use atomic energy for peaceful as well as destructive purposes, and probably within five or ten years they will have factories running on atomic energy; but they will also be preparing for war. They may limit the use of atomic weapons, but the momentum of war is there, and what can we do? Historical events are in movement, and I don't think you and I living here in Banaras can stop that movement. Who is going to care? But what we can do is something completely different. We can step out of the present machinery of society, which is constantly preparing for war, and perhaps by our own total inward revolution, we shall be able to contribute to the building of a civilization which is altogether new.

After all, what is civilization? What is the Indian or the European civilization? It is an expression of the collective will, is it not? The will of the many has created this present civilization in India, and cannot you and I break away from it and think entirely differently about these matters? Is it not the responsibility of serious people to do this? Must there not be serious people who see this process of destruction going on in the world, who investigate it, and who step out of it in the sense of not being ambitious and all the rest of it?

What else can we do? But, you see, we are not willing to be serious, that is the difficulty. We don't want to tackle ourselves, we want to discuss something outside, far away.

Q: There must be some people who are very serious, and have they solved their problems or the problems of the world?

K: That is not a serious question, is it? It is like my saying that others have eaten when I myself am hungry. If I am hungry I will inquire where food is to be had, and to say that others are well-fed is irrelevant; it indicates that I am not really hungry. Whether there are serious people who have solved their problems is not important. Have you and I solved our problems? That is much more important, is it not? Can a few of us discuss this matter very seriously, earnestly pursue it and see what we can do, not merely intellectually, verbally, but actually?

Q: Is it really possible for us to escape the impact of modern civilization?

K: What is modern civilization? Here in India it is an ancient culture on which have been superimposed certain layers of Western culture like nationalism, science, parliamentarianism, militarism, and so on. Now, either we shall be absorbed by this civilization, or we must break away and create a different civilization altogether. It is an unfortunate thing that we are so eager merely to listen, because we listen in the most superficial manner, and that seems to be sufficient for most of us. Why does it seem so extraordinarily difficult for us seriously to discuss and to eradicate in ourselves the things that are causing antagonism and war?

Q: We have to consider the immediate problem.

K: But in considering the immediate problem you will find that it has deep roots; it is the result of causes which lie within ourselves. So, to resolve the immediate problem, should you not investigate the deeper problems?

Q: There is only one problem, and that is to find out what is the end of life.

K: Can we discuss that really seriously, go into it completely, so that we know for ourselves what is the end of life? What is life all about, where is it leading? That is the question, not what is the purpose of life. If we merely seek a definition of the purpose of life, you will define it in one way and I in another, and we shall wrangle and choose which is the better definition according to our idiosyncrasies. Surely that is not what the question means. He wants to know what is the end of all this struggle, this search, this constant battle, this coming together and parting, birth and death. What is the whole of existence leading to? What does it mean?

Now, what is this thing which we call life? We know life only through self-consciousness, do we not? I know I am alive because I speak, I think, I eat, I have various contradictory desires, conscious and unconscious, various compulsions, ambitions, and so on. It is only when I am conscious of these, that is, as long as I am self-conscious, that I know I am alive. And what do we mean by being self-conscious? Surely, I am self-conscious only when there is some kind of conflict; otherwise I am unconscious of myself. When I am thinking, making effort, arguing, discussing, putting it this way or that, I am self-conscious. The very nature of self-consciousness is contradiction.

Consciousness is a total process, it is the hidden as well as the active, the open. Now, what does this process of consciousness mean, and where is it leading? We know birth and death, belief, struggle, pain, hope, ceaseless conflict. What is the significance of it all? To find out its true significance is what we are trying to do.

And one can find out its true significance only when the mind is capable of investigation; that is, when it is not anchored to any conclusion. Is that not so?

Q: Is it investigation, or reinvestigation?

K: There is reinvestigation only when the mind is tethered, repetitive and, therefore, constantly reinvestigating itself. But to be free to investigate, to find out what is true, surely that requires a mind that is not held in the bondage of any conclusion.

Now, can you and I find out what is the significance of this whole struggle, with all its ramifications? If that is one's intention and one is serious, earnest, can one's mind have any conclusion about it? Must one not be open to this confusion? Must one not investigate it with a free mind to find out what is true? So, what is important is not the problem but to see if it is possible for the mind to be free to investigate and find out the truth of it.

Can the mind be free from all conclusions? A conclusion is merely the response of a particular conditioning, is it not? Take the conclusion of reincarnation. Whether reincarnation is factual or not is irrelevant. Why do you have that conclusion? Is it because the mind is afraid of death? Such a mind, believing in a certain conclusion which is the result of fear, hope, longing, is obviously incapable of discovering what is true with regard to death. So, if we are at all serious, our first problem, even before we ask what this whole process of life means, is to find out whether the mind can be free from all conclusions.

Q: Do you mean that for serious thinking the mind must be completely empty?

K: What do we mean by freedom? What does it mean to be free? You assume that if the mind is free, not tethered to any conclusion, it is in a state of vacuum. But is it? We are trying to find out the truth of what is a free mind. Is a mind free that has concluded? If I read Shankara, Buddha, Einstein, Marx—it does not matter who it is—and reach a conclusion or believe in a certain system of thought, is my mind free to investigate?

Q: Has comparison no place in the process of investigation?

K: Comparing what? Comparing one conclusion with another, one belief with another? I want to find out the significance of this whole process of life, with its struggle, its pain, its misery, its wars, its appalling poverty, cruelty, enmity; I want to find out the truth of all that. To do so must I not have a mind that is capable of investigation? And can the mind investigate if it has a conclusion, or compares one conclusion with another?

Q: Can a mind be called free if it has only a tentative conclusion?

K: Tentative or permanent, a conclusion is already a bondage, is it not? Do, please, think with me a little. If one wants to find out whether there is such a thing as God, what generally happens? By reading certain books or listening to the arguments of some learned person, one is persuaded that there is God, or one becomes a communist and is persuaded that there isn't. But if one wants to find out the truth of the matter, can one belong to either side? Must not one's mind be free from all speculation, from all knowledge, all belief?

Now, how is the mind to be free? Will the mind ever be free if it follows a method to be free? Can any method, any practice, any system, however noble, however new or tried out for centuries, make the mind free? Or does the method merely condition the mind in a particular way, which we then call freedom? The method will produce its own results, will it not? And when the mind seeks a result through a method, the result being freedom, will such a mind be free?

Look, suppose one has a particular belief, a belief in God, or what you will. Must one not find out how that belief has come into being? This does not mean that you must not believe, but why do you believe? Why does the mind say, "This is so"? And can the mind discover how beliefs came into being?

You see insecurity in everything about you, and you believe in a Master, in reincarnation, because that belief gives you hope, a sense of security, does it not? And can a mind that is seeking security ever be free? Do you follow? The mind is seeking security, permanency, it is moved by a desire to be safe, and can such a mind be free to find out what is true? To find out what is true, must not the mind let go of its beliefs, put away its desire to be secure? And is there a method by which to let go of the beliefs which give you hope, a sense of security? You see, this is what I mean by being serious.

Q: Are there periods of freedom in the conditioned mind?

K: Are there periods or gaps of freedom in the conditioned mind? Which is it that you are aware of, the freedom or the conditioned mind? Please take this question seriously. Our minds are conditioned, that is obvious. One's mind is conditioned as a Hindu, as a communist, this or that. Now can the conditioned mind ever know freedom, or only what it imagines to be freedom? And can you be aware of how your mind is conditioned? Surely, that is our problem, not what freedom is. Can you just be aware of your conditioning, which is to see that your mind functions in a particular manner? We are not talking of how to alter it, how to bring about a change; that is not the question. Your mind functions as a Hindu or a modified Hindu, as a Christian or a communist; it believes in something. Are you aware of that?

Q: Freedom is not an acquisition but a gift.

K: That is a supposition. If freedom were a gift it would only be for the chosen few, and that would be intolerable. Do you mean to say that you and I cannot think it out and be free? You see, sir, that is what I am saying: we are not serious. To know how one is conditioned is the first step toward freedom. But do we know how we are conditioned? When you make a red mark on your forehead, when you put on the sacred thread, do *puja*, or follow some leader, are not those the activities of a conditioned mind? And can you drop all that so that in dropping it you will find out what is true? That is why it is only to the serious that truth is shown, not to those who are merely seeking security and are caught in some form of conclusion. I am just saying that when the mind is tethered to any particular conclusion, whether temporary or permanent, it is incapable of discovering something new.

Q: A scientist has data. Is he prepared to give up those data?

K: Are you talking as a scientist or as a human being? Even the poor scientist, if he wants to discover anything, has to put aside his knowledge and conclusions, because they will color any discovery. Sir, to find out, we must die to the things we know.

Q: Can the unconditioning of the mind be done at the conscious or unconscious level, or both?

K: Sir, what is the mind? There is the conscious mind and the unconscious mind. The conscious mind is occupied with the everyday duties—it observes, thinks, argues, attends to a job, and so on. But are we aware of the unconscious mind? The unconscious mind is the repository of racial instinct, it is the residue of this civilization, of this culture, in which there are certain urges, various forms of compulsion. And can this whole mind, the unconscious as well as the conscious, uncondition itself?

Now, why do we divide the mind as the conscious and the unconscious? Is there such a definite barrier between the conscious and the unconscious mind? Or are we so taken up with the conscious mind that we have never considered or been open to the unconscious? And can the conscious mind investigate, probe into the unconscious, or is it only when the conscious mind is quiet that the unconscious promptings, hints, urges, compulsions come into being? So, the unconditioning of the mind is not a process of the conscious or of the unconscious; it is a total process which comes about with the earnest intention to find out if your mind is conditioned.

Please look at this and experiment with it. What is important is the total, earnest intention to find out if your mind is conditioned so that you discover your conditioning, and do not just say that your mind is or is not conditioned. When you look into a mirror you see your face as it is; you may wish that some parts of it were different, but the actual fact is shown in the mirror. Now, can you look at your conditioning in a similar way? Can you be totally aware of your conditioning without the desire to alter it? You are not aware of it totally when you wish to change it, when you condemn it, or compare it with something else. But when you can look at the fact of your conditioning without comparison, without judgment, then you are seeing it as a total thing, and only then is there a possibility of freeing the mind from that conditioning.

You see, when the mind is totally aware of its conditioning, there is only the mind: there is no "you" separate from the mind. But when the mind is only partially aware of its conditioning, it divides itself, it dislikes its conditioning or says it is a good thing; and as long as there is condemnation, judgment, or comparison, there is incomplete understanding of conditioning and, therefore, the perpetuation of that conditioning, whereas, if the mind is aware of its conditioning without condemning or judging, but merely watching it, then there is a total perception, and you will find, if you so perceive it, that the mind frees itself from that conditioning.

This is what I mean by being serious. Experiment with this, not just casually, but seriously watch your mind in action all the time—when you are at the dinner table, when you are talking, when you are walking—so that your mind becomes entirely aware of all its activities. Then only can there be freedom from conditioning and, therefore, the total stillness of the mind in which alone it is possible to find out what is truth. If there is not that stillness, which is the outcome of a total understanding of conditioning, your search for truth has no meaning at all, it is merely a trap.

Banaras, India, January 9, 1955

CAN WE CREATE A NEW CULTURE?

I think that one of the greatest problems confronting man at this present time is the question of creativeness, how to bring about the creative release of the individual, and if we can consider the question, not merely verbally, but go into it very deeply, perhaps we shall be able to discover the full significance of that word *creativeness.* It seems to me that this is the real issue, not what kind of political reform to work for, or what kind of religion to follow. How is it possible to bring about the creative release of the individual, not only at the beginning of his existence, but throughout life? That is, how is the individual to have abundant energy rightly directed so that his life will have expansive and profound significance?

I feel that revolution is necessary at the most profound level, not fragmentary revolution, but integrated revolution, a total revolution starting not from the outside but from within; and to bring about that total revolution, surely we must understand the ways of our own thought, the whole process of our thinking, which is self-knowledge. Without the foundation of self-knowledge, what we think has very little meaning. So it is important, is it not, that from the very beginning we should understand the process of our thinking, the ways of our mind; and the revolution must take place, not in any given department of thought, but in the totality of the mind itself. But before we go into that, I think it is essential to find out what it means to listen.

Very few of us listen directly to what is being said, we always translate or interpret it according to a particular point of view, whether Hindu, Muslim, or communist. We have formulations, opinions, judgments, beliefs through which we listen, so we are actually never listening at all; we are only listening in terms of our own particular prejudices, conclusions, or experiences. We are always interpreting what we hear, and obviously that does not bring about understanding. What brings about understanding, surely, is to listen without any anchorage, without any definite conclusion, so that you and I can think out the problem together, whatever the problem may be. If you know the art of listening, you will not only find out what is true in what is being said, but you will also see the false as false and the truth in the false; but if you listen argumentatively, then it is fairly clear that there can be no understanding, because argument is merely your opinion against another opinion, or your judgment against another, and that actually prevents the understanding or discovery of the truth in what is being said.

So, is it possible to listen without any prejudice, without any conclusion, without interpretation? Because it is fairly obvious that our thinking is conditioned, is it not? We are conditioned as Hindus, or communists, or Christians, and whatever we listen to, whether it is new or old, is always apprehended through the screen of this conditioning; therefore, we can never approach any problem with a fresh mind. That is why it is very important to know how to listen, not only to what is being stated, but to everything. It is clearly necessary that a total revolution should take place in the individual, but such a revolution cannot take place unless there is effortless comprehension of what is truth. Effort at any level is obviously a form of destruction, and it is only when the mind is very quiet, not making an effort, that understanding takes place. But with most of us, effort is the primary thing; we think effort is essential, and that very effort to listen, to understand, prevents comprehension, the immediate perception of what is true and what is false.

Now, being aware of your conditioning, and yet being free of it, can you listen so as to comprehend what is being said? Can you listen without making an effort, without interpreting, which is to give total attention? For most of us, attention is merely a process of concentration, which is a form of exclusiveness, and as long as there is the resistance of exclusive thinking, a total revolution obviously cannot take place, and it is imperative, I feel, that such a revolution should take place in the individual, for only in that revolution is there creative release.

So, the mind is conditioned by modern education, by society, by religion, and by the knowledge and the innumerable experiences which we have gathered; it is shaped, put into a mold, not only by our environment, but also by our own reactions to that environment and to various forms of relationship.

Please bear in mind that you are not merely listening to me, but are actually observing the process of your own thinking. What I am saying is only a description of what is taking place in your own mind. If one is at all aware of one's own thinking, one will see that a mind that is conditioned, however much it may try to change, can only change within the prison of its own conditioning, and such a change is obviously not revolution. I think that is the first thing to understand—that as long as our minds are conditioned as Hindus, Muslims, or what not, any revolution is within the pattern of that conditioning and is, therefore, not a fundamental revolution at all. Every challenge must always be new, and as long as the mind is conditioned, it responds to challenge according to its conditioning; therefore, there is never an adequate response.

Now, we all know that there is a great crisis in the world at the present time; there is enormous poverty and the constant threat of war. That is the challenge, and our problem is to respond adequately, completely, totally to this challenge, which is impossible if we do not understand the process of our own thinking. Our thinking is obviously conditioned; we always respond to any challenge as Hindus, Muslims, communists, socialists, Christians, and so on, and that response is fundamentally inadequate; hence the conflict, the struggle, not only in the individual, but between groups, races, and nations. We can respond totally, adequately, fully, only when we understand the process of our thinking and are free from our conditioning, that is, when we are no longer reacting as Hindus, communists, or what you will, which means that our response to challenge is no longer based on our previous conditioning. When we have ceased to belong to any particular race or religion, when each one of us understands his background, frees himself from it, and pursues what is true, then it is possible to respond fully, and that response is a revolution.

It is only the religious man who can bring about a fundamental revolution, but the man who has a belief, a dogma, who belongs to any particular religion, is not a religious man. The religious man is he who understands the whole process of so-called religion, the various forms of dogma, the desire to be secure through certain formulas of ritual and belief. Such an individual breaks away from the framework of organized religion, from all dogma and belief, and seeks the highest; and it is he who is truly revolutionary because every other form of revolution is fragmentary and, therefore, inevitably brings about further problems. But the man who is seeking to find out what is truth, what is God, is the real revolutionary because the discovery of what is truth is an integrated response and not a fragmentary response.

Is it possible, then, for the mind to be aware of its own conditioning and thereby bring about freedom from its conditioning? The mind's conditioning is imposed by society, by the various forms of culture, religion, and education, and also by the whole process of ambition, the effort to become something, which is itself a pattern imposed on each one of us by society, and there is also the pattern which the individual creates for himself in his response to society.

Now, can we as individuals be aware of our conditioning, and is it possible for the mind to break down all this limitation so that it is free to discover what is truth? Because it seems to me that unless we do free the mind from its conditioning, all our social problems, our conflicts in relationship, our wars and other miseries, are bound to increase and multiply, which is exactly what is happening in the world, not only in our private lives, but in the relationship between individuals and groups of individuals, which we call society.

Taking that whole picture into consideration and knowing all the significance of it, is it possible for the mind to be aware of its conditioning and liberate itself? Because it is only in freedom that there can be creativeness, but freedom is not a reaction to something. Freedom is not a reaction to the prison in which the mind is caught; it is not the opposite of slavery. Freedom is not a motive. Surely, the mind that is seeking truth, God, or whatever name you like to give it, has no motive in itself. Most of us have a motive because all our life, in our education and in everything that we do, our action is based on a motive, the motive either of self-expansion or self-destruction. And can the mind be aware of and liberate itself from all those bondages which it has imposed upon itself in order to be secure, to be satisfied, in order to achieve a personal or a national result?

I think the revolution of which I am talking is possible only when the mind is very quiet, very still. But that quietness of the mind does not come through any effort—it comes naturally, easily, when the mind understands its own process of action, which is to understand the whole significance of thinking. So the beginning of freedom is self-knowledge, and self-knowledge is not in the withdrawal from life but is to be discovered in the relationships of our everyday existence. Relationship is the mirror in which we can see ourselves factually, without any distortion, and it is only through self-knowledge, seeing ourselves exactly as we actually are, undistorted by any interpretation or judgment, that the mind becomes quiet, still. But that stillness of mind cannot be sought after, it cannot be pursued; if you pursue and bring about stillness of mind, it has a motive, and such stillness is never still because it is always a movement toward something and away from something.

So there is freedom only through self-knowledge, which is to understand the total process of thinking. Our thinking at present is merely a reaction, the response of a conditioned mind, and any action based on such thinking is bound to result in catastrophe. To discover what is truth, what is God, there must be a mind that has understood itself, which means going into the whole problem of self-knowledge. Only then is there the total revolution, which alone brings about a creative release, and that creative release is the perception of what is truth, what is God.

I think it is always important to ask fundamental questions: but when we do ask a fundamental question, most of us are seeking an answer, and then the answer is invariably superficial, because there is no yes or no answer to life. Life is a movement, an endless movement, and to inquire into this extraordinary thing called life, with all its innumerable aspects, one must ask fundamental questions and never be satisfied with answers, however satisfactory they may be, because the moment you have an answer, the mind has concluded, and conclusion is not life—it is merely a static state. So what is important is to ask the right question and never be satisfied with the answer, however clever, however logical, because the truth of the question lies beyond the conclusion, beyond the answer, beyond the verbal expression. The mind that asks a question and is merely satisfied with an explanation, a verbal statement, remains superficial. It is only the mind that asks a fundamental question and is capable of pursuing that question to the end that can find out what is truth.

QUESTIONER: In India today we see a growing disregard of all sensitive feeling and expression. Culturally we are a feeble, imitative country; our thinking is smug and superficial. Is there a way to break through and contact the source of creativity? Can we create a new culture?

KRISHNAMURTI: Sir, this is not only a question for Indians, it is a human question; it is asked in America, in England, and elsewhere. How to bring about a new culture, a creativity that is explosive, abundant, so that the mind is not imitative? A poet, a painter longs for that, so let us inquire into it.

What is civilization, what is culture as we know it now? It is the result of the collective will, is it not? The culture we know is the expression of many desires unified through religion, through a traditional moral code, through various forms of sanction. The civilization in which we live is the result of the collective will, of many acquisitive desires and, therefore, we have a culture, a civilization, which is also acquisitive. That is fairly clear.

Now, within this acquisitive society, which is the result of the collective will, we can have many reformations, and we do occasionally bring about a bloody revolution, but it is always within the pattern because our response to any challenge, which is always new, is limited by the culture in which we have been brought up. The culture of India is obviously imitative, traditional; it is made up of innumerable superstitions, of belief and dogma, the repetition of words, the worship of images made by the hand and by the mind. That is our culture, that is our society, broken up into various classes, all based on acquisitiveness; and if we do become nonacquisitive in this world, we are acquisitive in some other world, we want to acquire God, and so on. So our culture is essentially based on acquisitiveness, worldly and spiritual; and when occasionally there is an individual who breaks away from all acquisitiveness and knows what it is to be creative, we immediately idolize him, make him into our spiritual leader or teacher, thereby stifling ourselves.

As long as we belong to the collective culture, collective civilization, there can be no creativeness. It is the man who understands this whole process of the collective, with all its sanctions and beliefs, and who ceases to be either positively or negatively acquisitive—it is only such a man who knows the meaning of creativeness, not the *sannyasi* who renounces the world and pursues God, which is merely his particular form of acquisitiveness. The man who realizes the whole significance of the collective, and who breaks away from it because he knows what is true religion, is a creative individual, and it is such action that brings about a new culture. Surely, that is always the way it happens, is it not?

The truly religious man is not the one who practices so-called religion, who holds to certain dogmas and beliefs, who performs certain rituals or pursues knowledge, for he is merely seeking another form of gratification. The man who is truly religious is completely free from society, he has no responsibility toward society; he may establish a relationship with society, but society has no relationship with him. Society is organized religion, the economic and social structure, the whole environment in which we have been brought up, and does that society help man to find God, truth—it matters little what name you give it—or does the individual who is seeking God create a new society? That is, must not the individual break away from the existing society, culture, or civilization? Surely, in the very breaking away he discovers what is truth, and it is that truth which creates the new society, the new culture.

I think this is an important question to ponder over. Can the man who belongs to society—it does not matter what society—ever find truth, God? Can society help the individual in that discovery, or must the individual, you and I, break away from society? Surely, it is in the very process of breaking away from society that there is the understanding of what is truth, and that truth then creates the ripples which become a new society, a new culture. The *sannyasi,* the monk, the hermit renounces the world, renounces society, but his whole pattern of thinking is still conditioned by society; he is still a Christian or a Hindu, pursuing the ideal of Christianity or of Hinduism. His meditations, his sacrifices, his practices, are all essentially conditioned and, therefore, what he discovers as truth, as God, as the absolute, is really his own conditioned reaction. Hence, society cannot help man to find out what is truth. Society's function is to limit the individual, to hold him within the boundary of respectability. Only the man who understands this whole process, whose action is not a reaction, can find out what is truth, and it is the truth that creates a new culture, not the man who pursues truth.

I think this is fairly clear and simple; it sounds complicated, but it is not. Truth brings about its own action. But the man who is seeking truth and acting, however worthy and noble he may be, only creates further confusion and misery. He is like the reformer who is merely concerned with decorating the prison walls, with bringing more light, more lavatories, or what you will, into the prison, whereas, if you understand this whole problem of how the mind is conditioned by society, if you allow truth to act and do not act according to what you think is truth, then you will find that such action brings about its own culture, its own civilization, a new world which is not based on acquisitiveness, on sorrow, on strife, on belief. It is the truth that will bring about a new society, not the communists, the Christians, the Hindus, the Buddhists, or the Muslims. To respond to any challenge according to one's conditioning is merely to expand the prison, or to decorate its bars. It is only when the mind understands and is free from the conditioning influences which have been imposed upon it, or which it has created for itself, that there is the perception of truth, and it is the action of that truth which brings into being a new society, a new culture.

That is why it is very important for a country like this not to impose upon itself the superficial culture of the West nor, because it is confused, to return to the old, to the Puranas, to the Vedas. It is only a confused mind that wants to return to something dead, and the important thing is to understand why there is confusion. There is confusion, obviously, when the mind does not understand, when it does not respond totally, integrally to something new, to any given fact.

Take the fact of war, for example. If you respond to it as a Hindu who believes in *ahimsa,* you say, "I must practice nonviolence," and if you happen to be a nationalist, your response is nationalistic, whereas the man who sees the truth of war, which is the fact that war is destructive in itself, and who lets that truth act, does not respond in terms of any society, in terms of any theory or reform. Truth is neither yours nor mine, and as long as the mind interprets or translates that truth, we create confusion. That is what the reformers do, what all the saints have done who have tried to bring about a reformation in a certain social order. Because they translate truth to bring about a given reform, that reform breeds more misery and hence needs further reform.

To perceive what is truth there must be a total freedom from society, which means a complete cessation of acquisitiveness, of ambition, of envy, of this whole process of becoming. After all, our culture is based on becoming somebody, it is built on the hierarchical principle—the one who knows and the one who does not know, the one who has and the one who has not. The one who has not is everlastingly struggling to have, and the one who does not know is forever pushing to acquire more knowledge, whereas the man who does not belong to either, his mind is very quiet, completely still, and it is only such a mind that can perceive what is truth and allow that truth to act in its own way. Such a mind does not act according to a conditioned response; it does not say, "I must reform society." The truly religious man is not concerned with social reform, he is not concerned with improving the old, rotting society because it is truth and not reform that is going to create the new order. I think if one sees this very simply and very clearly, the revolution itself will take place.

The difficulty is that we do not see, we do not listen, we do not perceive things directly and simply as they are. After all, it is the innocent mind—innocent though it may have lived a thousand years and had a multitude of experiences—that is creative, not the cunning mind, not the mind that is full of knowledge and technique. When the mind sees the truth of any fact and lets that truth act, that truth creates its own technique. Revolution is not within society but outside of it.

Q: The fundamental problem that faces every individual is the psychological pain which corrodes all thinking and feeling. Unless you have an answer and can teach the ending of pain, all your words have little meaning.

K: Sir, what is teaching? Is teaching merely communication, words? Why do you want to be taught? And can another teach you how to end pain? If you could be taught how to end pain, would pain cease? You may learn a technique for ending pain, physical or psychological, but in the very process of ending one particular pain, a new pain comes into being.

So what is the problem, sirs? Surely, the problem is not how to end pain. I can tell you not to be greedy, not to be ambitious, not to have beliefs, to free the mind from all desire for security, to live in complete uncertainty, and so on, but those are mere words. The problem is to experience directly the state of complete uncertainty, to be without any feeling of security, and that is possible only if you understand the total process of your own thinking, or if you can listen with your whole being, be completely attentive without resistance. To end sorrow, pain, either one must understand the ways of the mind, of desire, will, choice, going into that completely, or else listen to find the truth. The truth is that as long as there is a point in the mind which is moving toward another point, that is, as long as the mind is seeking security in any form, it will never be free from pain. Security is dependency, and a mind that depends has no love. Without going through all the process of examination, observation, and awareness, just listen to the fact, let the truth of the fact operate, and then you will see that the mind is free from pain. But we do neither; we neither see, observe to find out what is truth, nor do we listen to the fact with our whole being, without translating, twisting, interpreting it. That is, we neither pursue self-knowledge, which also brings an end to pain, nor do we merely observe the fact without distortion, as we look at our face in the mirror. All that we want is to know how to end pain, we want a ready-made formula by which to end it, which means, really, that we are lazy, there is not that extraordinary energy which is necessary to pursue the understanding of the self. It is only when we understand the self—not according to Shankara, Buddha, or Christ, but as it actually is in each one of us in relation to people, to ideas, and to things—that there is the cessation of pain.

Bombay, February 16, 1955

CAN YOU UNDERSTAND THE FACT OF EMPTINESS?

QUESTIONER: Beyond all superficial fears there is a deep anguish, which eludes me. It seems to be the very fear of life—or perhaps of death. Or is it the vast emptiness of life?

KRISHNAMURTI: I think most of us feel this; most of us feel a great sense of emptiness, a great sense of loneliness. We try to avoid it, we try to run away from it, we try to find security, permanency, away from this anguish.

Or, we try to be free of it by analyzing the various dreams, the various reactions. But it is always there, eluding us, and not to be resolved so easily and so superficially. Most of us are aware of this emptiness, of this loneliness, of this anguish. And, being afraid of it, we seek security, a sense of permanency, in things or property, in people or relationship, or in ideas, beliefs, dogmas, in name, position, and power. But can this emptiness be banished by merely running away from ourselves? And is not this running away from ourselves one of the causes of confusion, pain, misery, in our relationships and, therefore, in the world?

So, this is a question not to be brushed aside as being bourgeois, or stupid, or merely for those who are not active socially, religiously. We must examine it very carefully and go into it fully. As I said, most of us are aware of this emptiness, and we try to run away from it. In running away from it, we establish certain securities, and then those securities become all-important to us because they are the means of escape from our particular loneliness, emptiness, or anguish. Your escape may be a Master, it may be thinking yourself very important, it may be giving all your love, your wealth, jewels, everything, to your wife, to your family; or it may be social or philanthropic activity. Any form of escape from this inward emptiness becomes all-important and, therefore, we cling to it desperately. Those who are religiously-minded cling to their belief in God, which covers up their emptiness, their anguish; and so their belief, their dogma, becomes essential—and for these they are willing to fight, to destroy each other.

Obviously, then, any escape from this anguish, from this loneliness, will not solve the problem. On the contrary, it merely increases the problem and brings about further confusion. So, one must first realize the escapes. All escapes are on the same level;

there are no superior or inferior escapes, there are no spiritual escapes apart from the mundane. All escapes are essentially similar; and if we recognize that the mind is constantly escaping from the central problem of anguish, of emptiness, then we are capable of looking at emptiness without condemning it or being afraid of it. As long as I am escaping from a fact, I am afraid of that fact, and when there is fear, I can have no communication with it. So, to understand the fact of emptiness, there must be no fear. Fear comes only when I am trying to escape from it, because in escaping, I can never look at it directly. But the moment I cease to escape, I am left with the fact. I can look at it without fear, and then I am able to deal with the fact.

Can You Understand the Fact of Emptiness?

So, that is the first step—to face the fact, which means not to escape through money, through amusement, through the radio, through beliefs, through assertions, or through any other means, because that emptiness cannot be filled by words, by activities, by beliefs. Do what we will, that anguish cannot be wiped away by any tricks of the mind, and whatever the mind does with regard to it will only be an avoidance. But when there is no avoidance of any kind, then the fact is there, and the understanding of the fact does not depend on the inventions or the projections or calculations of the mind. When one is confronted with the fact of loneliness, with that immense anguish, the vast emptiness of existence, then one will see whether that emptiness is a reality or merely the result of naming, of terming, of self-projection. Because, by giving it a name, by giving it a term, we have condemned it, have we not? We say it is emptiness, it is loneliness, it is death, and these words, *death, loneliness, emptiness,* imply a condemnation, a resistance, and through resistance, through condemnation, we do not understand the fact.

To understand the fact that we call emptiness, there must be no condemnation, no naming, of the fact. After all, the recognition of the fact creates the center of the "me," and the "me" is empty, the "me" is only words. When I do not name the fact, give it a term, when I do not recognize it as this or that, is there loneliness? After all, loneliness is a process of isolation, is it not? Surely, in all our relationships, in all our efforts in life, we are always isolating ourselves. That process of isolation must obviously lead to emptiness, and without understanding the whole process of isolation, we shall not be able to resolve this emptiness, this loneliness. But when we understand the process of isolation, we shall see that emptiness is merely a thing of words, mere recognition; and the moment there is no recognition, no naming of it, and hence no fear, emptiness becomes something else, it goes beyond itself. Then it is not emptiness, it is aloneness—something much vaster than the process of isolation.

Now, must we not be alone? At present we are not alone—we are merely a bundle of influences. We are the result of all kinds of influences—social, religious, economic, hereditary, climatic. Through all those influences, we try to find something beyond, and if we cannot find it, we invent it, and cling to our inventions. But when we understand the whole process of influence at all the different levels of our consciousness, then, by becoming free of it, there is an aloneness which is uninfluenced; that is, the mind and heart are no longer shaped by outward events or inward experiences. It is only when there is this aloneness that there is a possibility of finding the real. But a mind that is merely isolating itself through fear can have only anguish; and such a mind can never go beyond itself.

With most of us, the difficulty is that we are unaware of our escapes. We are so conditioned, so accustomed to our escapes, that we take them as realities. But if we will look more deeply into ourselves, we will see how extraordinarily lonely, how extraordinarily empty, we are under the superficial covering of our escapes. Being aware of that emptiness, we are constantly covering it up with various activities, whether artistic, social, religious, or political. But emptiness can never finally be covered—it must be understood. To understand it, we must be aware of these escapes, and when we understand the escapes, then we shall be able to face our emptiness. Then we shall see that the emptiness is not different from ourselves, that the observer is the observed. In that experience, in that integration of the thinker and the thought, this loneliness, this anguish, disappears.

Paris, May 7, 1950

WHAT IS OUR BASIC PROBLEM?

I think most of us are easily satisfied with explanations, and we do not seem able to go beyond mere words and directly experience something original for ourselves. We are always repeating like gramophone records, merely following some authority who promises a certain result.

Now, it seems to me that religion is something entirely different. It is not this worship of words, nor is it the projection of symbols and the experiencing of those symbols. Religion is the experiencing of that which lies beyond the measure of the mind; but to experience that state, to realize the immensity of it, one really has to understand the process of one's own thinking. Most of us are indifferent to the impressions, to the pressures, to the vitality of existence; we are easily satisfied, and some of us dare not even look at the problems about us and within ourselves.

So I think it would be worthwhile if we could look at our problems, not theoretically or abstractly, but actually, and see what our problems really are. Not that we are going to resolve the problem of war, or put an end to the butchery that is going on, but we are easily led away by the very enormity of these issues, and there is not that clarity of thinking which can come into being only when we begin with ourselves, not with somebody or something else. The world problem is our problem because we are the world. What we think does affect the world; what we do does affect society. The individual problem is directly related to the world problem, and I do not think we are giving sufficient importance to the power of individual thinking and action. Historically I am sure you will find that it is always individuals who produce the great movements that are brought about.

So we have to look first and foremost at our own problems because they are directly related to world problems, and then perhaps we shall come out of it with a different outlook, a fresh impulse, an explosive vitality.

Now, what is our basic problem? As students, or businessmen, as politicians, engineers, or so-called seekers of the truth, whatever that may be, what fundamentally is our problem?

First of all, it seems to me that the world is rapidly changing and that the Western civilization, with its mechanization, its industrialization, its scientific discoveries, its tyranny, parliamentarianism, capital investment, and so on, has left a tremendous imprint on our minds. And we have created through the centuries a society of which we are a part and which says that we must be moral, righteous, virtuous, that we must conduct ourselves in accordance with a certain pattern of thought which promises the eventual achievement of reality, God, or truth.

So there is a contradiction in us, is there not? We live in this world of greed, envy, and sexual appetites, of emotional pressures, mechanization, and conformity, with the government efficiently controlling our various demands, and at the same time we want to find something greater than mere physical satisfaction. There is an urge to find reality, God, as well as to live in this world. We want to bring that reality into this world. We say that to live in this world we have to earn money, that society demands that we be acquisitive, envious, competitive, ambitious; and yet, living in this world, we want to bring the other thing into being. We may have all our physical needs provided, the government may bring about a state in which we have a great measure of outward security, but inwardly we are starving. So we want the state which we call religion, this reality which brings a new impulse, an explosive vitality to action.

Surely, that is my problem, that is your problem. How are we to live in this world, where living implies competition, acquisitiveness, ambition, the aggressive pursuit of our own fulfillment, and also bring into being the perfume of something which is beyond? Is such a thing possible? Can we live in this world and yet have the other? This world is becoming more and more mechanized; the thoughts and actions of the individual are increasingly controlled by the State. The individual is being specialized, educated in a certain pattern to follow a daily routine. There is compulsion in every direction, and living in such a world, can we bring into being that which is neither outward nor inward, but which has a movement of its own and requires a mind that is astonishingly swift, a mind that is capable of intense feeling, intense inquiry? Is that possible? Unless we are neurotic, unless we are mentally peculiar, surely that is our problem.

Now, any intelligent man can see that going to temples, doing *puja,* and all the other nonsense that goes on in the name of religion is not religion at all; it is merely a social convenience, a pattern which we have been taught to follow. Man is educated to conform to a pattern, not to doubt, not to inquire; and our problem is how to live in this world of envy, greed, conformity, and the pursuit of personal ambition, and at the same time to experience that which is beyond the mind, call it God, truth, or what you will. I am not talking about the God of the temples, of the books, of the gurus, but of something far more intense, vital, immense, something which is immeasurable.

So, living in this world with all these problems, how am I to capture the other? Is that possible? Obviously not. I cannot be envious and yet find out what God or truth is; the two are contradictory, incompatible. But that is what most of us are trying to do. We are envious, we are carried along by the old momentum, and at the same time we dream of finding out whether there is God, whether there is love, truth, beauty, a timeless state. If you observe your own thinking, if you are at all aware of the operation of your own mind, you will see that you want to have one foot in this world and one foot in that other world, whatever it may be. But the two are incompatible, they cannot be mixed. Then what is one to do?

Do you understand, sirs? I realize that I cannot mix reality with something which has no reality. How can a mind that is agitated by envy, that is living in the field of ambition, greed, understand something which is completely still and which has a movement of its own in that stillness? As an intelligent human being I see the impossibility of such a thing. I also see that my problem is not to find God because I do not know what that means. I may have read innumerable books on the subject, but such books are merely explanations, words, theories which have no actuality for a person who has not experienced that which is beyond the mind. And the interpreter is always a traitor, it does not matter who that interpreter is.

My problem, then, is not to find truth, God, because my mind is incapable of it. How can a stupid, petty mind find the immeasurable? Such a mind can talk about the immeasurable, write books about it; it can fashion a symbol of truth and garland the symbol, but that is all on the verbal level. So, being intelligent and aware of this fact, I say, "I must begin with what I actually am, not with what I should be. I am envious, that is all I know."

Now, is it possible for me, while living in this society, to be free of envy? To say it is or is not possible is an assumption and, therefore, has no value. To find out if one can do it requires intensity of inquiry. Most of you will say it is impossible to live in this world without envy, without greed. Our whole social structure, our code of morality is based on envy, so you assume it is not possible and that is the end of it, whereas a man who says, "I don't know if there is a reality or not, but I want to find out; and to find out my mind must obviously be free of envy, not just in patches, but totally, because envy is a movement of agitation"—it is only such a man who is capable of real inquiry. We shall go into that presently.

So my problem is not to inquire into reality, but to find out whether, living in this world, I can be free of envy. Envy is not mere jealousy, though jealousy is part of it, nor is it merely being concerned because someone else has more than I. Envy is the state of a mind which is demanding more and more all the time—more power, more position, more money, more experience, more knowledge. And demanding the "more" is the activity of a mind which is self-centered.

Now, can I live in this world and be free of self-centered activity? Can I cease to compare myself with somebody else? Being ugly, I want to be beautiful; being violent, I want to be nonviolent. Wanting to be different, to be "more," is the beginning of envy—which does not mean that I blindly accept what I am. But this desire to be different is always in relation to something which is comparatively greater, more beautiful, more this or more that, and we are educated to compare in this way. It is our daily craving to compete, to surpass, and we are satisfied with being envious, not only consciously but also unconsciously.

You feel that you must become somebody in this world, a great man or a rich man, and if you are fortunate you say it is because you have done good in the past—all that nonsense about karma, and so on. Inwardly also you want to become somebody—a saint, a virtuous man—and if you observe this whole movement of becoming, this pursuit of the "more," both outwardly and inwardly, you will see that it is essentially based on envy. In this movement of envy your mind is held, and with such a mind, can you discover the real? Or is that an impossibility? Surely, to discover the real, your mind must be completely free of envy; there can be no demand for the "more," either openly or in the hidden recesses of the unconscious. And if you have ever observed it, you will know that your mind is always pursuing the "more." You had a certain experience yesterday, and you want more of it today; or, being violent, you want to be nonviolent, and so on. These are all the activities of a mind which is concerned with itself.

Now, is it possible for the mind to be free from this whole process? That is my inquiry, not whether there is or there is not God. For an envious mind to seek God is such a waste of time; it has no meaning except theoretically, intellectually, as an amusement. If I really want to find out whether there is God or not, I must begin with myself; that is, the mind must lie totally free from envy, and I can assure you, that is an enormous task. It is not just a matter of playing with words.

But you see, most of us are not concerned with that; we do not say, "I will free my mind from envy." We are concerned with the world, with what is happening in Europe, with the mechanization of industry—anything to get away from the central point, which is that I cannot help to bring about a different world until I as an individual have changed fundamentally. To see that one must begin with oneself is to realize an enormous truth; but most of us overlook it; we easily brush it aside because we are concerned with the collective, with changing the social order, with trying to bring about peace and harmony in the world.

Few people are concerned with themselves except in the sense of achieving success. I do not mean that kind of concern. I mean being concerned with the transformation of oneself. But first of all, most of us do not see the importance, the truth, of change; and secondly, we do not know how to change, how to bring about this astonishing, explosive transformation within ourselves. Changing in mediocrity, which is to change from one pattern to another, is no change at all.

This explosive transformation is the result of all one's energy coming together to solve the fundamental problem of envy. I am taking that as the central issue, though there are many other things involved in it. Have I the capacity, the intensity, the intelligence, the swiftness, to pursue the ways of envy, and not just say, "I must not be envious"? We have been saying that for centuries, and it has no meaning. We have also said, "I must follow the ideal of non-envy," which is equally absurd, because we project the ideal of non-envy and are envious in the meantime.

Please observe this process. The fact is that you are envious, while the ideal is the state of non-envy, and there is a gap between the two that has to be filled through time. You say, "Eventually I shall be free of envy"—which is an impossibility, because it has to happen now or never. You cannot set some future date on which you will be non-envious.

So, is it possible for me to have the capacity to inquire into and be totally free from envy? How does that capacity arise? Does it arise through any method or practice? Do I become an artist by practicing a particular technique day after day? Obviously not. The desire to have that capacity is a selfish movement of the mind, whereas if I do not try to cultivate it, but begin to inquire into the whole process of envy, then the means of totally dissolving envy is already there.

Now, in what manner do I inquire into the process of envy? What is the motive behind that inquiry? Do I want to be free of envy in order to be a great man, in order to be like Buddha, Christ, and so on? If I inquire with that intention, with that motive, such inquiry projects its own answer, all of which will only perpetuate the monstrous world which we have now. But if I begin to inquire with humility, that is, not with a desire to achieve success, then an entirely different process is taking place. I realize that I have not got the capacity to be free of envy, so I say, "I shall find out," which means that there is humility from the very beginning. And the moment one is humble, one has the capacity to be free of envy. But the man who says, "I must have that capacity, and I am going to get it through these methods, through this system"—such a man is lost, and it is such people who have created this ugly, treacherous world.

A mind that is really humble has an immense capacity for inquiry, whereas the mind that is under the burden of knowledge, that is crippled with experience, with its own conditioning, can never really inquire. A humble mind says, "I do not know, I shall find out"—which means that finding out is never a process of accumulation. Not to accumulate you must die every day, and then you will find, because you are fundamentally, deeply, humble, that this capacity to inquire comes of itself, it is not a thing that you have acquired. Humility cannot be practiced, but because there is humility, your mind has the capacity to inquire into envy, and such a mind is no longer envious.

A mind which says, "I do not know," and which does not want to become something has totally ceased to be envious. Then you will find that righteousness has quite a different meaning. Righteousness is not respectability; it is not conformity; it has nothing to do with social morality, which is mere convenience, a manner of living made respectable through centuries of compulsion, conformity, pressure, and fear. A mind that is really humble, in the sense

I have explained, will create its own righteousness, which is not the righteousness of a pattern. It is the righteousness of living from humility and discovering from moment to moment what is truth.

So your problem is not the world of newspapers, ideas, and politicians, it is the world within yourself—but you have to realize, to feel the truth of this, and not merely agree because the Gita or some bearded gentleman says it is so. If you are aware of that inner world and are watching yourself without condemnation or justification from day to day, from moment to moment, then in that awareness you will find there is a tremendous vitality. The mind that is accumulating is frightened to die, and such a mind can never discover what is truth. But to a mind that is dying every minute to everything that it has experienced, there comes an astonishing vitality because every moment is new; and only then is the mind capable of discovery.

It is good to be serious, and we are very rarely serious in our life. I do not mean just listening to somebody who is serious, or being serious about something, but having the feeling of seriousness in ourselves. We know very well what it is to be gay, flippant, but very few of us know the feeling of being deeply serious without an object to make us serious—that state in which the mind approaches every situation, however gay, happy, or exciting, with serious intent. So it is good to spend an hour together in this way, being serious in our inquiry, because life for most of us is very superficial, a routine relationship of work, sex, worship, and so on. The mind is always on the surface, and to go below the surface seems to be an enormously difficult task. What is necessary is this state of explosiveness, which is real revolution in the religious sense, because it is only when the mind is explosive that it is capable of discovering or creating something original, new.

Bombay, February 10, 1957

HOW DO YOU APPROACH THE PROBLEMS OF LIVING?

I think it might be worthwhile if we went into the question of how quickly the mind deteriorates and what are the primary factors that make the mind dull, insensitive, quick to respond. I think it would be significant if we could go into this question of why the mind deteriorates, because perhaps in understanding that, we may be able to find out what is really a simple life.

We notice as we grow older that the mind—the instrument of understanding, the instrument with which we probe into any problem, to inquire, to question, to discover—if misused, deteriorates, disintegrates, and it seems to me that one of the major factors of this deterioration of the mind is the process of choice.

All our life is based on choice. We choose at different levels of our existence. We choose between white and blue, between one flower and another flower, between certain psychological impulses of like and dislike, between certain ideas, beliefs, accepting some and discarding others. So our mental structure is based on this process of choice, this continuous effort at choosing, distinguishing, discarding, accepting, rejecting. And in that process there is constant struggle, constant effort. There is never a direct comprehension, but always the tedious process of accumulation, of the capacity to distinguish, which is really based on memory, on the accumulation of knowledge and, therefore, there is this constant effort made through choice.

Now, is not choice ambition? Our life is ambition. We want to be somebody, we want to be well thought of, want to achieve a result. If I am not wise, I want to become wise. If I am violent, I want to become nonviolent. The "becoming" is the process of ambition. Whether I want to become the biggest politician or the most perfect saint, the ambition, the drive, the impulse of becoming is the process of choice, is the process of ambition, which is essentially based on choice.

So, our life is a series of struggles, a movement from one ideological concept, formula, desire, to another, and in this process of becoming, in this process of struggle, the mind deteriorates. The very nature of this deterioration is choice, and we think choice is necessary, choice from which springs ambition.

Now, can we find a way of life which is not based on ambition, which is not of choice, which is a flowering in which the result is not sought? All that we know of life is a series of struggles ending in result; and those results are being discarded for greater results. That is all we know.

In the case of the man who sits alone in a cave, in the very process of making himself perfect there is choice, and that choice is ambition. The man who is violent tries to become nonviolent; that very becoming is ambition. We are not trying to find out whether ambition is right or wrong, whether it is essential to life, but whether it is conducive to a life of simplicity. I do not mean the simplicity of a few clothes; that is not a simple life. The putting on of a loincloth does not indicate a man that is simple; on the contrary, it may be that by the renunciation of the outer things, the mind becomes more ambitious, for it tries to hold on to its own ideal, which it has projected and which it has created. So if we observe our own ways of thinking, should we not inquire into this question of ambition? What do we mean by it, and is it possible to live without ambition? We see that ambition breeds competition—whether in children, in school, or among the big politicians, all the way up. This ambition produces certain industrial benefits, but in its wake, obviously there is the darkening of the mind, the technological conditioning, so that the mind loses its pliability, its simplicity and, therefore, is incapable of directly experiencing. Should we not inquire, not as a group but as individuals, you and I, should we not find out what this ambition means, whether we are at all aware of this ambition in our life?

When we offer ourselves to serve the country to do noble work, is there not in it the fundamental element of ambition, which is the way of choice? And is not, therefore, choice a corruptive influence in our life because it prevents the flowering? The man who flowers is the man who is, who is not becoming.

Is there not a difference between the flowering mind and the becoming mind? The becoming mind is a mind that is always growing, becoming, enlarging, gathering experience as knowledge. We know that process full well in our daily life, with all its results, with all its conflicts, its miseries and strife, but we do not know the life of flowering. And is there not a difference between the two which we have to discover—not by trying to demarcate, to separate, but to discover—in the process of our living? When we discover this, we may perhaps be able to set aside this ambition, the way of choice, and discover a flowering, which is the way of life, which may be true action.

So if we merely say that we must not be ambitious without the discovery of the flowering way of life, the mere killing of ambition destroys the mind also because it is an action of the will, which is the action of choice. So is it not essential for each one of us to find out in our lives the truth of ambition? We are all encouraged to be ambitious; our society is based on the strength of the drive toward a result. And in that ambition there are inequalities which legislation tries to level out, to alter. Perhaps that way, that approach to life, is essentially wrong, and there might be another approach, which is the flowering of life, which could express itself without accumulation. After all, we know when we are conscious of striving after something, of becoming something; that is ambition, the seeking of a result.

But there is an energy, a force in which there is a compulsion without the process of accumulation, without the background of the "me," of the self, of the ego; that is the way of creativity. Without understanding that, without actually experiencing that, our life becomes very dull; our life becomes a series of endless conflicts in which there is no creativity, no happiness. And perhaps if we can understand not by discarding ambition but by understanding the ways of ambition—by being open, by comprehending, by listening to the truth of ambition—perhaps we may come upon that creativity in which there is a continuous expression which is not the expression of self-fulfillment but is the expression of energy without the limitation of the "me."

QUESTIONER: In the worst of misery, most of us live on hope. Life without hope seems dreadful and inevitable, and yet very often this hope is nothing but illusion. Can you tell us why hope is so indispensable to life?

KRISHNAMURTI: Is it not the very nature of the mind to create illusion? Is not the very process of thinking the result of memory, of verbalized thought, which creates an idea, a symbol, an image to which the mind clings?

I am in despair; I am in sorrow; I have no way of resolving it; I do not understand how to resolve it. If I understand it, then there is no need for hope. It is only as long as I do not understand how to bring about the dissolution of a particular problem that I depend on a myth, on an idea of hope. If you observe your own mind, you will see that when you are in discomfort, in conflict, in misery, your mind seeks a way away from it. The process of going away from the problem is the creation of hope.

The mind going away from the problem creates fear; the very movement of going away, the flight from the problem, is fear. I am in despair because I have done something which is not right, or some misery comes upon me, or I have done a terrible wrong, or my son is dead, or I have very little to eat. My mind, not being able to resolve the problem, creates a certainty, something to which it can cling, an image which it carves by the hand or by the mind. Or the mind clings to a guru, to a book, to an idea which sustains me in my difficulties, in my miseries, in my despair, and so I say I shall have a better time next life, and so on and on and on.

As long as I am not capable of resolving my problem, my sorrow, I depend on hope; it is indispensable. Then I fight for that hope. I do not want anyone to disturb that hope, that belief. I make that belief into an organized belief, and I cling to that because out of that, I derive happiness; because I have not been able to solve the problem which is confronting me, hope becomes the necessity.

Now, can I solve the problem? If I can understand the problem, then hope is not necessary; then depending on an idea or an image or a person is not necessary because dependence implies hope, implies comfort. So the problem is whether hope is indispensable, whether I can resolve my problem, whether there is a way to find out how not to be in sorrow—that is my problem, not how to dispense with hope.

Now, what is the factor essential to the understanding of a problem? Obviously, if I wish to understand the problem, there must be no formula, there must be no conclusion, there must be no judgment. But if we observe our minds we will see that we are full of conclusions; we are steeped in formulas with which we hope to resolve the problem. And so we judge, we condemn. And so, as long as we have a formula, a conclusion, a judgment, a condemnatory attitude, we shall not understand the problem.

So the problem is not important, but how we approach the problem. The mind that is wishing to comprehend a problem must not be concerned with the problem, but with the workings of its own machinery of judgment. Do you follow?

I started out with the establishment of a hope, saying that it is essential because without hope I am lost. So my mind is occupied with hope, I occupy it with hope. But that is not my problem; my problem is the problem of sorrow, of pain, of mistakes. Is even that my problem, or is my problem how to approach the problem itself? So what is important is how the mind regards the problem.

I have altogether moved away from hope because hope is illusory, it is unreal, it is not factual. I cannot deal with something which is not factual, which has been created by the mind. It is not something real; it is illusory, so I cannot grapple with it. What is real is my sorrow, my despair, the things that I have done, the crowded memories, the aches, and the sorrows of my life. How I approach the aches and sorrows and miseries in my life is important, not hope, because if I know how I approach them, then I shall be able to deal with them.

So what is important is not hope but how I regard my problem. I see that I always regard my problem in the light of judgment—either condemning, accepting, or trying to transform it—or looking at it through glasses, through the screen of formulas of what somebody has said in the Bhagavad Gita, what the Buddha or the Christ has said. So my mind, being crippled by these formulas, judgments, quotations, can never understand the problem, can never look at it. So can the mind free itself from these accumulated judgments?

Please follow this carefully—not my words, but how you approach your problem. What we are always doing is pursuing the hope and everlastingly being frustrated. If I fail with one hope, I substitute another and so I go on and on. And as I do not know how to approach, how to understand the problem itself, I resort to various escapes. But if I knew how to approach the problem, then there is no necessity for hope. So what is important is to find out how the mind regards the problem.

Your mind looks at a problem. It looks at it, obviously, with a condemnatory attitude. It condemns it in distinguishing it, in reacting to it, or it wants to change it into something which it is not. If you are violent, you want to change into nonviolence. Nonviolence is unreal, it is not factual; what is real is violence. Now to see how you approach the problem, with what attitude—whether you condemn it, whether you have the memories of what the so-called teachers have said about it—that is what is important.

Can the mind eradicate these conditions, free itself from these conditions, and look at the problem? Can it be unconcerned with how to free itself from these conditions? If it is concerned with it, then you create another problem out of it. But if you can see how these conditions prevent you from looking at the problem, then these conditions have no value because the problem is important, pain is important, sorrow is important. You cannot call sorrow an idea and brush it aside. It is there.

So, as long as the mind is incapable of looking at the problem, as long as it is not capable of resolving the problem, there must be various escapes from the problem, and the escapes are hopes; they are the defense mechanism.

The mind will always create problems. But what is essential is that when we make mistakes, when we are in pain, to meet these mistakes, these pains, without judgment, to look at them without condemnation, to live with them and to let them go by. And that can only happen when the mind is in the state of noncondemnation, without any formula; which means, when the mind is essentially quiet, when the mind is fundamentally still; then only is there the comprehension of the problem.

Q: Will you please tell us what you mean by the words *our vocation?* I gather you mean something different from the ordinary connotation of these words.

K: Each one of us pursues some kind of vocation—the lawyer, the soldier, the policeman, the businessman, and so on. Obviously, there are certain vocations which are detrimental to society—the lawyer, the soldier, the policeman, and the industrialist who is not making other men equally rich.

When we want, when we choose a particular vocation, when we train our children to follow a particular vocation, are we not creating a conflict within society? You choose one vocation and I choose another, and does that not bring about conflict between us? Is that not what is happening in the world because we have never found out what is our true vocation? We are only being conditioned by society, by a particular culture, to accept certain forms of vocations which breed competition and hatred between man and man. We know that, we see it.

Now, is there any other way of living in which you and I can function in our true vocations? Is there not one vocation for man? Are there different vocations for man? We see that there are: you are a clerk, I polish shoes, you are an engineer, and I am a politician. We see innumerable varieties of vocations and we see they are all in conflict with each other. So man, through his vocation, is in conflict, in hatred, with man. We know that. With that we are familiar every day.

Now let us find out if there is not one vocation for man. If we can all find it, then the expression of different capacities will not bring about conflict between man and man. I say there is only one vocation for man. There is only one vocation, not many. The one vocation for man is to find out what is real.

If I and you are finding out what is truth, which is our true vocation, then in the search of that we will not be in competition. I shall not be competing with you, I shall not fight you, though you may express that truth in a different way; you may be the Prime Minister; I shall not be ambitious and want to occupy your place because I am seeking equally with you what is truth. Therefore, as long as we do not find out that true vocation of man, we must be in competition with each other, we must hate each other; and whatever legislation you may pass, on that level you can only produce further chaos.

So, is it not possible from childhood, through right education, through the right educator, to help the boy, the student, to be free to find out what is the truth about everything—not just truth in the abstract, but to find out the truth of all relationships—the boy's relationship to machinery, his relationship to nature, his relationship to money, to society, to government and so on? That requires, does it not, a different kind of teacher, who is concerned with helping or giving the boy, the student, freedom—so that he begins to investigate the cultivation of intelligence, which can never be conditioned by a society which is always deteriorating.

So, is there not one vocation for man? Man cannot exist in isolation, he exists only in relationship, and when in that relationship there is no discovery of truth, the discovery of the truth of relationship, then there is conflict.

There is only one vocation for you and me. And in the search of that, we shall find the expression wherein we shall not come into conflict, we shall not destroy each other. But it must begin surely through right education, through the right educator. The educator also needs education. Fundamentally, the teacher is not merely the giver of information, but brings about, in the student, the freedom, the revolt, to discover what is truth.

Q: When you answer our questions, what functions—memory or knowledge?

K: It is really quite an interesting question, is it not? Let us find out.

Knowledge and memory are the same, are they not? Without knowledge, without the accumulation of knowledge, which is memory, can you reply? The reply is the verbalization of a reaction, is it not? There is this question asked: What is functioning, memory or knowledge? I am only saying memory and knowledge are the same thing essentially, because if you have knowledge but have no memory of it, it will have no value.

You are asking what functions when I answer a question. Is knowledge functioning? Is memory functioning? Now what is it that is functioning with most of us? Please follow this. What is functioning with most of us when you ask a question? Obviously knowledge. When I ask you the way to your house, knowledge is functioning, memory is functioning. And with most of us that is all that functions because we have accumulated knowledge from the Bhagavad Gita or from the Upanishads or from Marx or from what Stalin has said or what your pet guru says or your own experience, your own accumulated reactions, and from that background, you reply. That is all we know. That is the actual fact. In your business that is what is functioning. When you build a bridge, that is what is functioning.

When you write a poem, there are two functions going on—the verbalization, the memory; and the creative impulse. The creative impulse is not memory, but when expressed it becomes memory.

So without memory, verbalization, the verbalizing process, there is no possibility of communication. If I do not use certain words, English words, I could not talk to you. The very talking, the verbalization, is the functioning of memory. Now the question is: What is functioning when the speaker is answering, memory or something else? Memory, obviously, because I am using words. But is that all?

Am I replying from the accumulated memories of innumerable speeches I have made during the last twenty years, which I keep on repeating like a gramophone record machine? That is what most of us are. We have certain actions, certain patterns of thought, and we keep on repeating them. But the repetition of words is entirely different to that because that is the way of communication.

By the repetition of experience, the experiences are gathered and stored away and, like a machine, I repeat from that experience, from that storehouse. Here again, there is repetition, which is again the memory functioning.

So you are asking if it is possible, while I am speaking, that I am really experiencing, not answering from experience? Surely there is a difference between the repetition of experience and the freedom of experiencing, which is being expressed through memory, which is the verbalization. Please listen. This is not difficult to understand.

I want to find out what ambition means, all that it implies. Do I really, now as I am speaking, investigate afresh the whole process of ambition? Or do I repeat the investigation which I have made yesterday about ambition, which is merely repetition? Is it not possible to investigate, to experience anew all the time, and not merely rely on a record, on memory, on the experience of yesterday? Is it not possible to flower, to be, all the time, now as I am speaking, without the repetitious experience of yesterday, though I use words to communicate?

Your question is: What is functioning when I am speaking? If I am repeating merely what I have said ten days ago, then it is of very little value. But if I am experiencing as I am talking, not an imaginative feeling, but actually, then what is functioning? The flowering is functioning, not through self-expression, not the "me" functioning, which is memory.

So it is very important, not for me alone but for all of us, to find out if we can keep our minds from being this storehouse of the past, and whether the mind can be stable on the waters of life and let the memories float by without clinging to any particular memory, and when necessary to use that memory as we do use it when we communicate. Which means the mind constantly letting the past float by, never identifying itself with it, never being occupied with it; so that the mind is firm, not in experience, not in memory, not in knowledge, but firm, stable in the process, in the way of experiencing continuously.

So, that is the factor which brings about no deterioration, so that the mind constantly renews. A mind that accumulates is already in decay. But the mind that allows memories to go by and is firm in the way of experiencing—such a mind is always fresh, it is always seeing things anew. That capacity can only come when the mind is very quiet. That quietness, that stillness, is not induced, cannot come about through any discipline, through any action of will, but when the mind understands the whole process of accumulation of knowledge, memory, experience. Then it establishes itself on the waters of life, which are always moving, living, vibrant.

Q: With what should the mind be occupied? I want to meditate. Would you please tell me on what I should meditate?

K: Now, let us find out what meditation is. You and I are going to find out. I am not going to tell you what meditation is. We are both going to discover it afresh.

The mind that has learned to meditate, which is to concentrate, the mind that has learned the technique of shutting out everything and narrowing down to a particular point—such a mind is incapable of meditation. That is what most of us want. We want to learn to concentrate, to be occupied with one thought to the exclusion of every other thought, and we call that meditation. But it is not meditation. Meditation is something entirely different, which we are going to find out.

So our first problem is why does the mind demand that it should be occupied? Do you understand? My mind says, "I must be occupied with something, with worry, with memory, with a passion, or with how not to be passionate, or how to get rid of something, or to find a technique which will help me to build a bridge." So the mind, if you observe, demands constant occupation, does it not? That is why you say, "My mind must be occupied with the word *Om,*" or you repeat *"Ram Ram"*; or you are occupied with drinking. The word *Om,* the words *Ram Ram,* or drinking are all the same because the mind wants to be occupied, because it says if it is not occupied it will do some mischief, if it is not occupied it will drift away. If the mind is not occupied, then what is the purpose of life? So you invent a purpose of life—noble, ignoble, or transcendental—and cling to that, and with that you are occupied. It is the same whether the mind is occupied with God or whether it is occupied with business, because the mind says consciously or unconsciously it must be occupied.

So, the next thing is to find out why the mind demands occupation. Please follow this. We are meditating now. This is meditation. Meditation is not a state at the end. Freedom is not to be got at the end; freedom is at the beginning. If you have no freedom in the beginning, you have no freedom at the end. If you have no love now, you will have no love in ten years. So what we are doing now is to find out what meditation is. And the very inquiry into what meditation is is to meditate.

The mind says, "I must be occupied with God, with virtue, with my worries, or with my business concern," so it is incessantly active in its occupation. The mind can only exist as long as it is active, as long as it is conscious of itself in action, not otherwise. The mind knows itself as being when it is occupied, when it is acting, when it has results. It knows itself as existing when it is in motion. The motion is occupation toward a result, toward an idea, or denial of that idea negatively.

I am conscious of myself only when there is motion, in and out. So consciousness is this motion of action, outward and inward, this breathing out of responses, of reactions, of memories, and then collecting them back again. So my mind is—I am—only when I am thinking, when I am in conflict with a thing, when there is suffering, when there is occupation, when there is strain, when there is choice.

So the mind knows itself as in motion when it is ambitious and drags itself there, and seeing that ambition is dull, it says, "I will occupy myself with God." The occupation of the mind with God is the same as the occupation of the mind with money. We think that the man whose mind is occupied with God is more sacred than the man who is thinking of money, but they are factually both the same; both want results, both need to be occupied. So, can the mind be without occupation? That is the problem.

Can the mind be blank, without comparing, because the "more" is the way of the mind knowing that it exists? The mind that knows it exists is never satisfied with *what is;* it is always acquiring, comparing, condemning, demanding more and more. In the demand for, in the movement of, the "more," it knows itself as existing, which is what we call self-consciousness, the conscious on the surface and the unconscious. This is our life, this is the way of our everyday existence.

I want to know what meditation is, so I say I want to be occupied with meditation. I want to find out what meditation is, so my mind is again occupied with meditation. So, can the occupied mind ever be capable of meditation? Meditation, surely, is the understanding of the ways of the mind. If I do not know how my mind operates, functions, works, how can I meditate? How can I really find out what is truth? So the mind must find out how it is occupied; then it begins to see with what it is occupied, and then finds that all occupations are the same because the mind then is filling itself with words, with ideas, with constant movement, so that there is never a quietness.

When the mind occupies itself with the discovery of what love is, it is another form of occupation, is it not? It is like the man who is occupied with passion.

When you say you must find out the truth, will you find truth? Or does truth come into being only when the mind is not occupied, when the mind is empty to receive, not to gather, not to accumulate. Because you can only receive once. But if what you have received you make into memory with which you are occupied, then you will never receive again. Because the receiving is from moment to moment. Therefore, it is of timelessness.

So the mind, which is of time, cannot receive the timeless. So the mind must be completely still, empty, without any movement in any direction. And that can only take place with a mind that is not occupied—not occupied with the "more," with a problem, with worry, with escapes; not conditioned in any belief, in any image, in any experience. It is only when the mind is totally free, then only is there a possibility of immense profound stillness; and in that stillness that which is eternal comes into being. That is meditation.

Bombay, March 11, 1953

WHAT IS THE CENTRAL CORE OF YOUR THINKING?

1

KRISHNAMURTI: What is the central core of your thinking? You know there is peripheral thinking, which is not really important, but at the center, what is the momentum, the movement of that thinking? What is that "me" that is so concerned with itself? I think about myself, that is the core, the heart of my thinking. And on the periphery I think about various things, the people here, the trees, a bird flying by, but these things don't really very much matter unless there is a crisis on the periphery that affects the "me," and the "me" reacts. Now what is that center from which you think, which is the "me"? And why is there this continual occupation about oneself? I am not saying it is right or wrong, but we see that we are occupied with ourselves. Why?

STUDENT: Because we think it is important.

K: Why do you give it importance?

S: When you are a child you have to.

K: Why do you think about yourself so much? See what is involved in this. Thinking about oneself isn't just a very small affair. You think about yourself in relation to another with like and dislike; and you think about yourself, identifying yourself with another. I think about the person I have just left, or the person I think I like, or the person with whom I have quarreled, or the person whom I love. I have identified myself with all those people, haven't I?

S: What do you mean by identify?

K: I love you, I have identified myself with you. Or I have hurt her and you identify yourself with her and get angry with me. See what has happened: I have said something to her which is harmful and unpleasant; you are her friend and you identify yourself with her and get angry with me. So that is part of the self-centered activity, isn't it? Are you sure?

S: But isn't it the other person who is identifying with you?

K: Is it or is it not? Let's inquire. I like you, I am very fond of you—what does that mean? I like your looks, you are a good companion and so on. It means what?

S: It means you are a better companion than other people and so I like being with you.

K: Go a little deeper. What does it mean?

S: You keep that person to yourself and exclude others.

K: That is part of it, but go on further.

S: It is pleasing to be with that person.

K: It is pleasing to be with that person and it is not pleasing with another person. So my relationship with you is based on my pleasure. If I don't like you I say, "I'll be off!" My pleasure is my concern, as is my hurt, my anger. So self-concern isn't just thinking about myself and identifying with this or that possession, person, or book. There is the peripheral occupation, and also I am comparing myself with you; that is going on all the time, but from a center.

S: You read about the refugees in India and you haven't a personal relationship with them but you do identify with them.

K: Why do I identify myself with those people who have been killed and chased out of East Pakistan? I watched them the other day on television. This is happening everywhere, not only in Pakistan. It is appalling. Now you say you identify yourself with all those refugees; what do you feel?

S: Sympathy.

K: Go on, explore it, unravel it.

S1: Anger against the people who caused this.

S2: Frustration because you can't do anything about it.

K: You get angry with the people who do these things, who kill the young men and chase out old women and children. Is that what you do? You identify with this and reject that. What is the structure, the analysis, of this identification?

S: You don't feel secure.

K: Through identification you feel that you could do something? Move on.

S: Even by taking one side you feel that you have a certain chance to do something.

K: Say I am anti-Catholic; I identify myself with a group who are anti-clerical. Identifying myself with those, I feel I can do something. But go further, it is still me doing something about it, it is still the occupation with myself. I have identified myself with something I consider greater, like India, communism, Catholicism, and so on, or with my family, my God, my belief, my house, you who have hurt me. What is the reason for this identification?

S: I separate myself from the rest of the world and in identifying with something bigger, that something becomes my ally.

K: Yes, but why do you do this? I identify myself with you because I like you. I don't identify myself with him because I don't like him. And I identify myself with my family, with my country, with my God, with my belief. Now why do I identify with anything at all? I don't say it is right or wrong, but what is behind this identification?

S: Inward confusion.

K: Is it?

S: You are afraid.

K: Push further.

S: The confusion is caused by the identification.

K: Is it? I am questioning you and you must question me too. Don't accept what I am saying, inquire. This whole process of identification, why does it happen? And if I don't identify myself with you, or with something, I feel frustrated. Are you sure?

S: You feel unfulfilled, empty.

K: Go on. I feel sad, frustrated, not fulfilled, insufficient, empty. Now I want to know why I identify myself with a group, with a community, with feelings, ideas, ideals, heroes, and all the rest of it. Why?

S: I think it is in order to have security.

K: Yes. But what do you mean by that word *security?*

S: Alone I am weak.

K: Is it because you cannot stand alone?

S: It is because you are afraid to stand alone.

K: You are frightened of being alone so, therefore, you identify?

S: Not always.

K: But it is the core, the root of it. Why do I want to identify myself? Because then I feel safe. I have pleasant memories of people and places so I identify myself with that. I see that in identification I am much more secure. Right?

S: I don't know if you want to talk about this particular aspect, but if I see the killing in Vietnam is wrong, and there is a group of anti-war demonstrators in Washington, then I go and join them.

K: Now wait a minute. There is an anti-war group and I join them. I identify myself with them because in identifying with a group of people who are doing something about it, I am also doing something about it; by myself I cannot do anything. But belonging to a group of people who demonstrate, who write articles, I am actively taking part in stopping the war. That is the identification. We are not saying the results of that identification are good or bad, but why does the human mind want to identify itself with something?

S: When is it action and when is it identification?

K: I am coming to that. First, I want to be clear in myself and in talking it over find out why I should identify. And when necessary I will identify. That is, I must first understand what it means to cooperate. Then, when I am really deeply cooperating, then I will know when not to cooperate. Not the other way round. I don't know if you see this. If I know what is involved in cooperation, which is a tremendous thing—to work together, to live together, to do things together—when I understand that, then I will know when not to cooperate.

Now I want to know why I identify myself with anything. Not that I shouldn't identify if there is a necessity of identification in action, but before I find out how to act, or with whom I can cooperate, I want to find out why there is this urge to identify. To have security, is that the reason? Because you are far from your country, from your family, you identify with this house, with a group, to be safe, protected. The identification takes place because you feel, Here I am secure. So is the reason you identify because you are insecure? Is that it? Insecurity means fear, uncertainty, not knowing what to think, being confused. So you need protection; it is good to have protection. Is that the reason that you identify?

What is the next step? In myself I am uncertain, unclear, confused, frightened, and insufficient; therefore, I identify myself with a belief. Now what happens?

S: I find I am still insecure.

K: No. I have identified myself with certain ideologies. What happens then?

S: You try to make that your security.

K: I have given various reasons for this identification—because it is rational, it is workable, all the rest of it. Now what happens when I have identified myself with it?

S: You have a conflict.

K: Look what happens. I have identified myself with an ideology, with a group of people, or a person; it is part of me. I must protect that, mustn't I? Therefore, if it is threatened I am lost, I am back again to my insecurity. So what takes place? I am angry with anybody who attacks or doubts it. Then what is the actual thing that takes place?

S: Conflict.

K: I have identified myself with an ideology. I must protect it because it is my security and I resist anybody who threatens that with a contradictory ideology. So where I have identified myself with an ideology there must be resistance; I build a wall around what I have identified myself with. Where there is a wall, it must create division. Then there is conflict. I don't know if you see all this?

Now what is the next step? Go on.

S1: What is the difference between identification and cooperation?

S2: It seems there has to be more understanding of cooperation.

K: You know what it means to cooperate, to work together? Can there be cooperation when there is identification? Do you know what we mean by identification? We have examined the anatomy of it. Cooperation means to work together. Can I work with you if I have identified myself with an ideology and you are identified with another ideology? Obviously not.

S: But people have to work together.

K: Is that cooperation?

S: No.

K: See what is involved. Because of our identification with an ideology we work together; you protect it and I protect it. It is our security—in the name of God, in the name of beauty, in the name of anything. We think that is cooperation. Now what takes place? Can there be cooperation when there is identification with a group?

S: No, because there is division. I find myself in conflict with members of the group, because I keep identifying with them.

K: Look what is happening. You and I have identified ourselves with that ideology. Our interpretation of that ideology may be—

S: Different.

K: Of course. If you vary in the interpretation of that ideology, you are deviating; therefore, we are in conflict. Therefore, we must both agree about that ideology completely. Is that possible?

S: That is exactly what happens with a school. Instead of an ideology, you identify with a school and each person has his own concept.

K: Yes, quite right. Why?

S: I sense that sometimes there is conflict here for just the reason you were giving when talking about an ideology. If you and I identify with the school, we think we are cooperating, but there isn't that spirit.

K: Therefore, I am asking, can there be cooperation when there is identification?

S: No.

K: Do you know what you are saying? {Laughter.] That is how everything in this world is working. Is that the truth? That where there is identification there can be no cooperation? It is a marvelous thing to discover the truth of this. Not your opinion, or my opinion, but the truth, the validity of it. Therefore, we have to find out what we mean by cooperation. You see that there can be no cooperation when there is identification with an idea, with a leader, with a group, and so on. Then what is cooperation in which there is no identification?

S: Acting in response to the situation itself.

K: I am not saying you are not right, but can we work together when you and I think differently? When you are concerned with yourself and I am concerned with myself? And one of the reasons is that knowing we cannot cooperate when we are thinking of ourselves, we try to identify ourselves with an ideology, hoping thereby to bring about cooperation. But if you don't identify, what is cooperation?

Here we are at Brockwood, in a school. We see there cannot be cooperation when there is identification with the school, with an idea, with a program, with a particular policy of this and that. And also we see that identification is the cause of all division. Then, what is cooperation? To work *together*—not *about* something. Do you see the difference? So before you do something together, what is the *spirit* of cooperation—the feeling, the inwardness of it—what is that feeling?

S: Understanding, being completely open to it.

K: Go a little deeper. We said identification is not cooperation. Are you quite sure on that point? And are you quite clear that cooperation cannot exist when each of us is concerned with himself? When you are concerned with yourself, you have no spirit of cooperation, you only cooperate when it pleases you. So what does it mean to cooperate? What does it mean to cooperate when there is no "me"? Otherwise you can't cooperate. I may try to cooperate around an idea, but there is always the "me" that is trying to identify itself with the thing that I am doing. So I must find out why it is that I am thinking about myself all day long: how I look; that somebody is better than me; why somebody has hurt me, or somebody has said, "What a nice person you are." Why am I doing this all day long? And at night too, when I'm asleep this goes on: "I am better than you"; "I know what I am talking about"; "It is my experience"; "You are stupid, I am clever." Why?

S: It seems a lot of it becomes a habit.

K: What is habit?

S: Not being aware.

K: No. What is habit? Not how is it formed.

S: Repetition of a movement.

K: Right. Why is there a repetition of this movement? Why is habit formed? You will see something extraordinary if you go slowly. We have all got short hair or long hair; why? Because others do it?

S: Is that habit or imitation?

K: See what takes place. First you imitate others, then you say, "Short hair is square."

S: Is a custom a habit too?

K: Yes. I don't want to go too quickly into this. Isn't all thinking habit? You agree?

S: Well, it is something you do over and over again.

K: Go on, see what you can discover for yourself when we go into this whole question of habit.

S: It is really a situation with an old reaction, isn't it?

K: A new situation we meet with old responses. Is not identification a habit?

S: Yes.

K: Because you are insecure. So do you know the nature of this machinery that makes for habit? Are you aware that you are always operating by habit? To get up at six o'clock every day, to believe, to smoke, not to smoke, to take drugs. You follow? Everything is reduced to habit—it may be of a week, ten days, or fifty years, but the habit is formed. Why does the mind fall into this groove? Haven't you asked yourself why you have a habit? Have you watched your mind working in habit?

S1: It is easier.

S2: It takes really a lot of energy to live without habit.

K: I am coming to that. Don't jump, move from step to step. I am asking myself: Why does the mind always live in habit? I thought that yesterday, I still think that today, and I will think the same about it tomorrow—with slight modifications perhaps. Now why does the mind do this?

S: One is half asleep.

K: We said laziness is part of it. What else? It feels easier with habits.

S: One is afraid of the unknown.

K: I want to go a little deeper than that.

S: The mind is afraid that if it doesn't maintain thinking in the same way, it will itself be threatened.

K: Which means what?

S: It sees a certain kind of order in habit.

K: Is habit order?

S: You can form a certain structure with habit, but that is not necessarily order.

K: Which means that the mind functions in habit for various reasons, like a machine. It is easier, it avoids loneliness, fear of the unknown, and it implies a certain order to say, "I will follow that and nothing else." Now why does the mind function in a groove, which is habit?

S: Its nature is that.

K: But if you say that, then you stop inquiring. We know the reasons that the mind functions in habit; are you actually aware of it? The highly psychopathic person has a habit which is completely different from others. A neurotic person has certain habits. We condemn that habit but accept others. So why does the mind do this? I want to go into it deeper, I want to see why it does it and whether the mind can live without habit.

S: Because it feels it is the personality.

K: We said that the personality, the ego, the "me" which says, "I am frightened, I want order, laziness, all that are different facets of the 'me.'" Can the mind live without habit? Except for the biological habits, the regular functioning of the body, which has its own mechanism, its own intelligence, its own machinery. Why does the mind accept habit so quickly? The question, "Can it live without habit?" is a tremendous question. To say that there is God, that there is a savior, is a habit. And to say there is no savior, but only the State, is another habit. So the mind lives in habit. Does it feel more secure in habit?

S: Yes.

K: Go slowly. Which means what? Functioning in the field of the known, it feels safe. The known is habit, right?

S: Even then, we still say we don't feel safe.

K: Because the known may change or may be taken away or get something added to it. But the mind is always functioning in the field of the known because there it feels secure. So the known is the habit, the known is knowledge—that is, knowledge of science, of technology, and the knowledge of my own experiences. And in that there is mechanical habit. Now I am asking: Can the mind move from the known—not into the unknown, I don't know what that means—but be free and move away from the borders of the known?

Look. If I know everything about the internal combustion engine, I can continue experimenting in the same direction, but there is a limitation. I must find something new, there must be some other way to create energy.

S: Would the mind say that if it wanted the security of the known?

K: I am not talking about security at the moment.

S: Are you saying that there has to be a break in continuity in technology in order for something new to happen?

K: That's right. That is what takes place. Otherwise man couldn't have invented the jet engine; he had to look at the problem differently.

My mind always works in the field of the known, the modified, which is habit. In relationship with human beings, in thought—which is the response of memory and always within the field of the known—I am identifying myself with the unknown through the known. The mind must function with the known because otherwise one couldn't talk, but I am asking if it can also function without any habit.

S: Does the mind ask that question because acting out of habit is unsuccessful?

K: I am not thinking of success.

S: But what would make the mind ask this?

K: My mind says, this isn't good enough, I want more. It wants to find out more, and it can't find it within the field of the known, it can only expand that field.

S: But it has to realize the limitation.

K: I realize it, and I say to myself: I can function within the field of the known, I can always expand it or contract it, horizontally, vertically, in any way, but it is always within the field of the known. My mind says I understand that very well. And so, being curious, it says: Can the mind live, can it function, without habit?

S: Is that a different question?

K: Now I am talking psychologically, inwardly. Apparently all life, all the mental activity in the psyche, is a continuity of habit.

S: Is there really an impetus or something—

K: I am creating an impetus. The mind is itself creating the impetus to find out—not because it wants to find something.

S: This is a very touchy point. This seems to be the key to some difficulty. Why—if I may just ask the question—does the mind say: I see the need for living without psychological habit?

K: I don't see the need, I am not positing anything. I am only saying I have seen the mind in operation in the field of the known—contracting, expanding horizontally or vertically, or reducing it to nothing, but always within that area. And my mind asks, if there is a way of living—I don't know it, I don't even posit it—in which there is no habit at all.

So we come back. Do you know what you are thinking about all day? You say, "Yes, I am thinking about myself, vaguely or concretely, or subtly, or in a most refined manner, but always around that." Can there be love when the mind is occupied with itself all the time? You say no; why?

S: Because if you are thinking about yourself all the time, you can't—

K: Therefore, you can never say, "I love you," until you stop thinking about yourself. When a man feels ambitious, competitive, imitative, which is part of thinking about oneself, can there be love?

So we have to find a way of living in which habit is not. But habit can be used—the known can be used, I won't call it habit—in a different way, depending on the circumstances, the situation, and so on. So is love habit? Pleasure is habit, isn't it? Is love pleasure?

S: What do you mean by love, sir?

K: I don't know. I will tell you what it is not; and when that is not in you, the other is. Listen to this: Where the known is, love is not.

S: So one has to find out first what habit is, and then about non-habit.

K: We have found it. We have said that habit is the continuation of action within the field of the known. The known is the tomorrow. Tomorrow is Sunday and I am going out for a drive; I know that, I have arranged it. Can I say, "Tomorrow I will love"?

S1: No.

S2: I do.

K: What do you mean, "I will love you tomorrow"?

S: We promise that.

K: In a church, you mean? That means love is within the field of the known and, therefore, within time.

S: But if you love once, can you suddenly stop loving?

K: I loved you once; I am bored with you now!

S: If you love someone today, you can love him tomorrow.

K: How do you know? I love you today, but you want to be sure that I'll love you tomorrow. Therefore, I say, "I'll love you, darling, tomorrow."

S: That is something else.

K: I am asking: Has love a tomorrow? Habit has a tomorrow because it continues. Is love a continuity? Is love identification?—I love my wife, my son, my God?

Therefore, you have to really understand—not just verbally—the whole process, the structure and the nature of the known, the whole field of it inwardly, how you function always within that field, thinking from that field. The tomorrow you can grasp because it is projected from the known. To really understand this you have to understand all that we have said; you have to know what you think and why, and you have to observe it.

S: You can know what you think, but you don't always know why you think it.

K: Oh, yes, it is fairly simple. I want to know why I think, why thought comes in. Yesterday I went to the tailor and I forgot my watch there. Last night I looked for it and I thought about it and said, "How lazy of me, how inconsiderate on my part to leave it there, giving trouble." All that went through the mind.

S: When you say it was inconsiderate of you, you were identifying yourself.

K: No, I forgot the watch. Which means they have to take the trouble to look after it, someone might take it, they will be responsible, all that. And I thought about it, and I know why this whole momentum of thinking arose from that. I watched the whole flow of thought. You can know the beginning and the ending of thought. You look so mystified! I have thought about it and I can end it. I left the watch there and I thought it might get lost; I have had it for a long time, I have cared for it; I would give it away, but not lose it. And if it is lost, finished. I don't think any more about it.

Now, to watch every thought, to be aware of it! Any thought is significant if you penetrate it; you can see the origin of it and the ending of it—not go on and on.

S: And you say that if you see why the thought originated, you will be able to see the ending of it?

K: No, look. Is there an individual thought separate from another thought? Are all thoughts separate or are they interrelated? What do you say?

S: They are interrelated.

K: Are you sure?

S: Well, they all come from one another.

K: If I understand their interrelationship, or if there is an understanding of the background from which all thought springs—

S: That is the difficult point.

K: To watch without any question of wanting an answer means infinite watchfulness. Not impatience. Watch carefully, then everything comes out. If you and I quarrel, I don't want to carry it in my mind, in thought, I want to finish it. I'll come to you and say, "I am sorry, I didn't mean it"; and it is finished. But do I do that?

Have you learned a lot—not *have* learned, but are you learn*ing,* seeing what it means to learn?

Brockwood Park, June 19, 1971

2

STUDENT: We were talking about why one can't say that one loves someone.

KRISHNAMURTI: Can we approach it in a different way? Do you know what aggressiveness is? It means opposition, to go against. From that arises the question. How are you going to meet life when you have passed through here and are so-called educated? Do you want to be swallowed up by the society, the culture in which you live, or are you going to oppose it, revolt against it, which will be a reaction and not a total action? Are you going to step into the easy way of life, conform, imitate, adjust to the pattern, whatever that pattern be, whether it be the establishment, or an establishment of a different kind, and so on? Or are you going to be a totally different human being, who is aware and knows he has to meet adversity and opposition and that, therefore, there is no easy way of satisfaction? Because most of us want a life of ease, of comfort, without trouble, which is almost impossible. And if you do meet opposition, will you run away from it?

If you don't like some place, certain people, a job, will you move away, run away from it to do something else that will be satisfactory? Do you use others for your own satisfaction? And is love the use of others, either sexually or as companionship, or for one's own satisfaction—not superficially but much more deeply?

How are you going to meet all this, which is what life is? The so-called educated people in the world, who have been to college, to university, have good jobs, fit into a place and stay there and advance there, have their own troubles, their own adversities. One may pass some exam and get a job, or one may have been educated technologically. But psychologically, one doesn't know anything about oneself. One is unhappy, miserable because one can't get this or that. One quarrels with one's husband or wife. And they are all very educated people who read books but disregard the whole field of life. And uneducated people do the same.

You are going to be educated. I don't know why, but you are going to be. And then what? Lead a comfortable life? Not that one is against comfort, but if one is seeking comfort in life it becomes rather shoddy, rather shallow, and you have to conform to a tremendous extent to the structure of the culture in which you live. And if you revolt against the culture and join a group, which has its own pattern, you have to fit into that too.

Most human beings throughout the world want to be safe, secure, comfortable, lead a life of indulgence, a life in which they do not have too much opposition, where they conform superficially, but revolt against conforming, become superficially respectable but are inwardly rebellious, have a job, get married, have children and responsibility. But because the mind wants something much more than that, they are discontented, running from one thing to another. Seeing all of this—not just one segment, one fraction of it, but the whole of the map—what are you all going to do? Or is it a question that you cannot possibly answer at your age? You are too young, perhaps, with your own occupations, so the other can wait.

S: One knows what one would like to do.

K: Do you know what you want to do?

S: I know what I'd like to do.

K: What would you like to do? Like? I might like to be the Queen of England, or the greatest something or other, but I can't, I haven't got the capacity. So when you say you'd like to do something, that gives you pleasure, that gives you satisfaction. That is what everybody wants: comfort, pleasure, satisfaction. "This is what I want to do because I feel happy doing it." And when you find opposition along that path, you don't know how to meet it and then you try to escape from it.

You know, this is really a very difficult question; it is not easy to say what one would like to do. This is a very complex question. That is why I said, "Is this asking too much?" Or, at your age, are you already beginning to have an inkling of what you want to do, not only for the next year but for the rest of your life?

S: We are not too young.

K: I don't know. I don't know whether you are too old or too young. It is for you to answer, not for me. I am putting this to you, for you to find out.

S: Some of us are already too old. We are already shaped. Already we have had experiences that make us all very bored with life.

K: You know, the other day we were talking about the fact that we are always thinking about ourselves. And when you are thinking about yourself, isn't it generally around what gives you the greatest pleasure? "I want to do that, because it is going to give me tremendous satisfaction." So how do you meet all these things? Shouldn't you be educated not only in geography, history, mathematics, and all the rest of it, but also in this field, where you have to discover for yourself how to live in this monstrous world? Isn't that part of education? Now how could you set about educating yourself to meet this life? Do you expect somebody else to educate you, as they educate you in mathematics and other subjects?

S: No.

K: No? You are quite sure? If nobody is going to educate you in the psychological, inward, way of living, how are you going to do it? How are you going to educate yourself? You know what is happening in the world? Apart from the monstrosities and wars and butcheries and all the terrible things that are going on, people who think they know are trying to educate you—and not just in the technological world that is clear, simple, and factual.

The other day on television some bishop said: "The knowledge of God is love and if you don't have knowledge of God you can't live, life becomes meaningless." Now there is that statement made most emphatically by a well-known bishop, or whatever he was, and I listened to it and I said: I am learning, I want to find out. I want to be educated. He has reasonable explanations, and you look at his collar, or his coat, or his beret, and you say, "Oh, he is a priest, he is an old man, he is repeating old stuff, that is nothing," and you push him away. And then a man comes along and offers you a pattern of living which seems reasonable, logical; and because of his personality, the way he looks, dresses, walks—you know all the tricks—you say, "Yes, he has got something." And you listen to him. And through the very act of listening you are being conditioned by what he says, aren't you?

S: It depends how you listen.

K: If you don't know how to listen to that bishop, you will say, "How reasonable, he says we have lived this way for two thousand years, this is the right way, with the knowledge of God." I listen to him and there is something that appeals to me and I accept it. I have been influenced by him. And I am also influenced by a man who says, "Do this and you will have enlightenment." So I am being influenced all around. What shall I do? I want to educate myself because I see very well nobody is going to educate me in that field. Because they have never educated themselves, they have never gone into themselves and examined, explored, searched out, looked and watched; they have always conformed to a pattern. And they are trying to teach me how to live within that pattern, whether it is the Zen pattern, or the Christian, or the communist pattern. They have not educated themselves in the sense we are talking about, though they may be clever in argument and in dialectics.

So as nobody is going to help me to educate myself inwardly, how shall I begin? I see that if I don't do that I will become a lopsided human being. I may be very good at writing an essay and getting a degree, but then what? And the whole of the rest of my life is neglected. So how shall I educate myself, become mature in a field where very few people have taken the trouble to investigate, to inquire? Or they have done it and imposed their thinking on others, not helped them to find out for themselves.

Do you understand what I am talking about? Freud, Jung, Adler, and other analysts, who have gone into this and stated some facts, traced all behavior to childhood conditioning. They have laid down a certain pattern and you can investigate in that direction and get more information, but that is not you learning about yourself; you are learning according to somebody else. Knowing what life is, what is happening in the world—wars, antagonism, politicians, priests, hippies with their little bit of philosophy, people who take drugs, the makers of communes, and the hatred between various classes—how will you set about finding out for yourself? Take all that is there outwardly, and inwardly people are ambitious, greedy, envious, brutal, violent, exploiting each other. These are facts, I am not exaggerating.

Seeing all this, what shall I do? Shall I conform to some pattern, which is comforting, which is what I want to do, a fulfillment for myself? Because if you don't have a certain spark, a flame in you now at the age of fifteen, sixteen, twenty, or twenty-five, it is going to be very difficult when you are fifty. Then it is much more difficult to change. So, what shall I do? How shall I face all this, look at it, listen to all the terrible noise in the world—the priests, the technicians, the clever men, the workers, the strikes that are going on? Shall I choose a particular noise that appeals to me and follow that noise for the rest of my life? What shall I do? This is a tremendous problem, it is not a simple problem.

S: I want to experiment.

K: Experiment?

S: Well, let things come to me.

K: Listen to what I am saying. Seeing all this, I don't know what to do. Not knowing what to do, I am going to find an easy way out as I generally do. Don't fool yourself. This is a tremendously complex problem.

S: But to find the easy way out is still not real.

K: Wait, I am not at all sure. I face all this tremendous uproar that is going on, the shouting, the pushing, and I find there is an easy way out—I become a monk. That is what is happening in certain parts of the world, because people don't trust politicians, scientists, technicians, preachers, anymore. They say, "I am going to withdraw from all this and become a solitary monk with a begging bowl"; they are doing it in India. Or not knowing what to do, you drift, carrying on from day to day, not bothering. Or if you must find a way out you force yourself, or you join a group that thinks it is tremendously advanced. Is that what you are all going to do?

If I had a daughter or a son here, that would be my concern as a parent. I would feel tremendously concerned. And Brockwood is concerned; it is tremendously important. You can all go to colleges and universities and get degrees and jobs, but that is too simple. That is, a way out doesn't solve anything either. So if I had a son or a daughter, I would ask how they are going to be educated in the field where they themselves don't take an interest, and where others don't know how to help them to understand that enormous field that has been neglected.

So I would say to a daughter or son, "Look, listen to all this, listen to all the noise that is going on in the world. Don't take sides, don't jump to any conclusions, but just listen. Don't say one noise is better than another noise; they are all noises, so just listen first. And listen also to your own noise, your chattering, your wishes—'I want to be this and I don't want to be that'—and find out what it means to listen. Find out, don't be told. Discuss it with me and find out what it means first. Find out what it means to think, why you think, what is the background of your thinking. Watch yourself, but don't become self-centered in that watching. Be tremendously concerned, in watching, about further enlargement of yourself." If you watch yourself, there is a tremendous danger of self-centeredness.

If I were a parent I would be tremendously concerned with the problem, the question, of how to educate people in this field where there is no real understanding or help. I would discuss to find out how you think, why you think, and what you think. Not in order to change it, not to suppress it, not to overcome it, but to find out why you think at all. Question it! I don't know if you have noticed that most books, all the social, religious, moral, ethical structure, the relationship between man and man, are based on thinking. "This is right, this is wrong, this should be, this must not be"—it is based on the structure of thought. I want to find out if that is the way of living, to base everything on thought, on what I like and what I don't like, what I want to do, what I don't want to do.

Brockwood Park, June 24, 1971

WHAT IS THE RELATION BETWEEN KRISHNAMURTI'S TEACHING AND TRUTH?

1

QUESTIONER 1: Can we discuss the relation between Krishnamurti's teaching and truth?

QUESTIONER 2: Is there such a thing as a teaching at all, or is there only truth?

KRISHNAMURTI: Is it the expression of truth? There are two things involved. The speaker is either talking out of the silence of truth, or he is talking out of the noise of an illusion, which he considers to be the truth.

Q: That is what most people do.

K: So which is it that he is doing?

Q: There could be a confusion between the word and truth.

K: No, the word is not the truth. That's why we said either he is talking out of the silence of truth or out of the noise of illusion.

Q: But because one feels that he is speaking out of the silence of truth, there is a greater possibility for the word to be taken as truth.

K: No, let's go slowly, for this is interesting. Who is going to judge, who is going to see the truth of the matter? The listener, the reader? You who are familiar with Indian scriptures, Buddhism, the Upanishads, and know most of the contents of all that, are you capable of judging? How shall we find out? You hear him talking about these things and you wonder if he is really speaking out of this extraordinary silence of truth, or as a reaction and from a conditioned childhood, and so on. That is to say, either he is talking out of his conditioning or out of the other. How will you find out? How will you approach this problem?

Q: Is it possible for me to find out if what is meeting that teaching is the noise within myself?

K: That's why I am asking you. What is the criterion, the measure that you apply so you can say, "Yes, that is it"? Or do you say, "I don't know"? I am asking what you do. Or do you not know but are examining, investigating, not whether he is speaking out of silence or conditioning, but watching the truth of what he is saying? I would want to know whether he was speaking out of this or out of that. But as I don't know, I am going to listen to what he is saying and see if it is true.

Q: But what sees it as true?

K: Say one is fairly alive to things. One listens to this man and one wants to find out whether what he says is mere words or the truth.

Q: When I have come to the conclusion that it is the truth, then I am already not listening.

K: No, I don't know. My whole life is concerned with this problem; it is not just for a few years or a few days. I want to know the truth of this matter. Is he speaking out of experience or from knowledge, or not out of any of these things? Most people speak out of knowledge, so we are asking that question.

I don't know how you would find out. I'll tell you what I would do. I would put his personality, his influence, all that, completely aside. Because I don't want to be influenced; I am skeptical, doubtful, so I am very careful. I listen to him, and I don't say, "I know" or "I don't know," but I am skeptical. I want to find out.

Q: Skeptical means you are inclined to doubt it, which is already a bias—

K: Oh, no! I am skeptical in the sense that I don't accept everything that is being said.

Q: But you lean toward doubting. It's negation.

K: Oh, no. I would rather use the word *doubt,* in the sense of questioning. Let's put it that way. I say to myself, "Am I questioning out of my prejudice?" This question has never been put to me before, I am exploring it. I would put everything else aside, all the personal reputation, charm, looks. I am not going to accept or reject, I am going to listen to find out. Am I prejudiced? Am I listening to him with all the knowledge I have gathered about religion, of what the books have said, what other people have said, or what my own experience tells me?

Q: No. I may be listening to him precisely because I have rejected all that.

K: Have I rejected it? Or am I listening to him with all that? If I have rejected that, then I am listening very carefully to what he has to say.

Q: Or I am listening with everything that I already know of him?

K: I have said that I have put away his reputation. Am I listening to him with the knowledge that I have acquired through books, through experience and, therefore, I am comparing, judging, evaluating? Then I can't find out whether what he is saying is the truth. But is it possible for me to put aside all that? I am passionately interested to find out. So for the time being, while I am listening at least, I will put aside everything I have known. Then I proceed. I want to know, but I am not going to be easily persuaded, pulled into something by argument, cleverness, logic. Now am I capable of listening to what he is saying with complete abandonment of the past? It comes to that. Are you? Then my relationship to him is entirely different. Then I am listening out of silence.

This is really a very interesting question. I have answered for myself. There are a dozen of us here, how would you answer it? How do you know that what he is talking about is the truth?

Q: I wouldn't be concerned with that word *truth.* When you use the word *truth,* you indicate you have the ability to judge what is true, or you already have a definition of truth, or you know what truth is, which means you will not be listening to what somebody is saying.

K: Don't you want to know whether he is speaking falsehood, out of a conditioned mind, from a rejection and, therefore, out of a reaction?

Q1: I realize that in order to listen to anybody, I can't listen with a conditioned mind.

Q2: Another question which arises is: I reject all this knowledge and listen in silence. Is truth in that silence?

K: I don't know. That is one of the things I have got to find out. How would you answer this question?

Q: I think first of all you can be sensitive to what is false. In other words, to see if there is something false, something incoherent.

K: Logic can be very false.

Q: Yes, I don't mean just logic, but you can be sensitive to the whole communication to see if there is some deception. I think one of the questions implied here is: Are you deceiving yourself?

K: Again, forgive me for asking, but how do you know he is speaking the truth? Or is he deceiving himself and is caught in an illusion which gives him a feeling that he is telling the truth? What do you answer?

Q: One goes into it oneself. One cannot accept it without going deeply into it.

K: But one can deceive oneself so appallingly.

Q: You go through the layers of all those deceptions and beyond them.

K: If I were a stranger I might say: You have listened to this man for a long time, how do you know he is telling the truth? How do you know anything about it?

Q: I could say that I have looked at what you have said, and each time I was able to test it to see if it was right. I have not found anything that was contradictory.

K: No. The question was: How do you find out the truth? Not about contradiction, logic, all that. One's own sensitivity, one's own investigation, one's own delving, is that enough?

Q: If one goes all the way, if one goes through all the possible self-deceptions and then goes so far as to say that in the moments when one is listening one feels there is a change in oneself, it may not be a total revolution, but there is a change.

K: That can happen when you go for a walk and look at the mountains and are quiet, and when you come back to your home certain things have taken place. You follow what I am saying?

Q: Yes. We listen to people who speak from knowledge, and we listen to you, and there is something totally different.

K: Have you answered the question?

Q: Someone wrote to me and asked if I agreed with everything Krishnamurti said. "Didn't he tell you that you should doubt everything he said?" The only way I could answer was to say: "Look, to me it is self-evident."

K: It may be self-evident to you and yet an illusion. It is such a dangerous, delicate thing.

Q: I think that for thought it is not at all possible to be sure about this matter. It is typical of thought that it wants to be sure that it is not deceiving itself, that it is listening to truth. Thought will never give up that question, and it is right for thought never to give up questioning, but thought cannot touch it, cannot know about it.

K: Dr. Bohm and I had a discussion of this kind in a different way. If I remember rightly, we said: Is there such a silence which is not the word, which is not imagined or induced? Is there such a silence, and is it possible to speak out of that silence?

Q: The question was whether the words are coming from perception, from the silence, or from the memory.

K: Yes.

Q: The question is whether the words that are used are communicating directly and are coming out of the emptiness, out of the silence, or not.

K: That is the real question.

Q: As we used to say, like the drum which vibrates to the emptiness within.

K: Yes. Are you satisfied by this answer, by what the others have said?

Q: No.

K: Then how do you find out?

Q: The very words you are using deny the possibility of being satisfied and of working at it intellectually. It is something that has nothing to do with those things.

K: Look, suppose I love you and trust you. Because I trust you and you trust me, whatever you say won't be a lie and I know you won't deceive me under any circumstances. You won't tell me something which is not actual to you.

Q: I might do something out of ignorance.

K: But say you trust me and I trust you. There is a relationship of trust, confidence, affection, love; like a man and a woman when they are married, they trust each other. Now is that possible here? Because, as she points out, I can deceive myself with logic, with reason, with all these things. Millions of people have done it. I can also see the danger of loving the priest: he can play havoc with me.

Q: If one has affection for someone, one projects all kinds of illusions onto him.

Q: I think the trust, the investigation, logic, and all that, go together with love.

K: That is a very dangerous thing too.

Q: Isn't there any way to avoid danger?

K: I don't want to be caught in an illusion.

Q: So can we say that truth is in the silence out of which the teaching comes?

K: But I want to know how the silence comes! I might invent it. I might have worked to have a silent mind for years, conditioned it, kept it in a cage, and then say, "Marvelous, I am silent." There is that danger. Logic is a danger. Thought is a danger. So I see all the dangers around me. I am caught in all these dangers and I want to find out if what that man is saying is the truth.

Q: Are we saying that perception has to be pure and in the realm of silence—the real realm of silence, not a fantasy—in order to be able to even come close to this question?

K: Dr. Bohm is a scientist, a physicist; he is clear-thinking, logical. Suppose someone goes to him and asks, "Is what Krishnamurti says the truth?" How is he going to answer?

Q: Doesn't Dr. Bohm, or anybody, have to go beyond the limitations of logic?

K: Somebody comes to him and asks, "Tell me, I really want to know from you, please tell me if that man is speaking the truth."

Q: But you are then saying use the instrument of logic to find out?

K: No. I am very interested because I have heard so many people who are illogical and careless say he is speaking the truth. But I go to a serious thinker, careful with the use of words, and ask, "Please tell me if he is telling the truth, not some crooked thing covered up." How is he going to answer me?

Q: The other day when that man said you may be caught in a rut, and you looked at it, what happened then?

K: I looked at it in several different ways and I don't think I am caught in a groove, but yet I might be. So after examining it very carefully, I left it. Something takes place when you leave it alone after an examination; something new comes into it.

Now I am asking you: Please tell me if that man is speaking the truth.

Q: For me it is a reality. I can't communicate it to you. This is what I have found out and you have to find it out for yourself. You have to test it in your own mind.

K: But you may be leading me up the garden path.

Q: That is all I can say. I can't really communicate it.

K: You may be up the garden path yourself.

Q: It seems to me I would want to know what he is bringing to bear on the answer to this question. Is it science? Is it logic? Is it his own intelligence? I would want to know out of what he was going to answer me.

K: How do you in your heart of hearts, as a human being, know that he is speaking the truth? I want to feel it. I object to logic and all that. I have been through that before. Therefore if all that is not the way, then what is?

Q: There are people who are very clever, who speak of things which are very similar, who have grasped this intellectually very well and say they are speaking from truth.

K: Yes, they are repeating in India now: "You are the world." That is the latest catchword!

Q: In order to communicate that, I have to speak out of the silence you were referring to.

K: No, please be simple with me. I want to know if Krishnamurti is speaking the truth. Dr. Bohm has known Krishnamurti for several years. He has a good, trained mind so I go to him and ask him.

Q: All he can say is, "I know this man, this is how he affects me. He has changed my life." And suddenly a note may be struck in the other one.

K: No. I want it straight from the horse's mouth!

Q: But you said you wanted proof.

K: I don't. It is a very serious question, it isn't just a dramatic or intellectual question. This is a tremendous question.

Q: Can one ever get an answer? Or is that person asking a false question to begin with?

K: Is he?

Q: I think I could say to him that when we did discuss these things it was from the emptiness, and that I felt it was a direct perception.

K: Yes. Is direct perception unrelated to logic?

Q: It doesn't come from logic.

K: But you are logical all the same.

Q: That may come later, not at that moment.

K: So you are telling me: I have found out that man is telling the truth because I had a direct perception, an insight into what he is saying.

Q: Yes.

K: Now, be careful, because I have heard a disciple of some guru saying exactly the same thing.

Q: I have also heard a guru say this but a little later by looking at it logically I saw the thing was nonsense. When I was looking at the fact and the logic I saw that it did not fit. So I would say that in addition to direct perception I have constantly examined this logically.

K: So you are saying that perception has not blinded you and with that perception goes logic also.

Q: Yes, logic and fact.

K: So perception first, then logic. Not first logic, then perception.

Q: Yes. That is what it always has to be.

K: So through perception and then with logic, you see that it is the truth. Hasn't this been done by the devout Christians?

Q: Logic is not enough, because we have to see how people actually behave as well. I see that Christians say certain things, but when we look at the whole of what they do it doesn't fit.

K: Isn't there a terrible danger in this?

Q: I am sure there is a danger.

K: So you are now saying that one has to walk in danger.

Q: Yes.

K: Now I begin to understand what you are saying. One has to move in a field which is full of danger, full of snakes and pitfalls.

Q: Which means one has to be tremendously awake.

K: So I have learned from talking to him that this is a very dangerous thing. He has said you can only understand whether Krishnamurti is speaking the truth if you are really prepared to walk in a field which is full of pitfalls. Is that right?

Q: Yes.

K: It is a field which is full of mines, the razor's edge path. Are you prepared to do that? One's whole being says, "Be secure."

Q: That is the only way to do anything.

K: I have learned to be aware of the dangers around me and also to face danger all the time and, therefore, to have no security. The inquirer might say, "This is too much," and go away! So this is what I want to get at. Can the mind, which has been conditioned for centuries to be secure, abandon that and say, "I will walk into danger"? That is what we are saying. It is logical, but in a sense it is illogical.

Q: In principle that is the way all science works.

K: Yes, that is right. So it also means I don't trust anybody, any guru, any prophet. I trust my wife because she loves me and I love her, but that is irrelevant.

Q: The word *danger* has to be explained too. From one point it is dangerous, and from another it isn't. I have to investigate. My conditioning is very dangerous.

K: So we're saying: "I have walked in danger and I have found the logic of this danger. Through the perception of the danger I have found the truth of what Krishnamurti is saying. And there is no security, no safety in this, whereas all the others give me safety."

Q: Security becomes the ultimate danger.

K: Of course.

Q: What you have described is actually the scientific approach. They say every statement must be in danger of being false; it has been put that way.

K: That is perfectly right. I have learned a lot. Have you? A man comes from Seattle or Sheffield or Birmingham and is told, "I have found that what he says is the truth because I have had a perception and that perception stands logically." It is not outside of reason. And in that perception I see that where I walk is full of pitfalls, of danger. Therefore, I have to be tremendously aware. Danger exists when there is no security. And the gurus, the priests, all offer security. Seeing the illogic of it I accept this illogic too.

Q: I am not sure that you should call it illogical. It is not illogical but it is the way logic has to work.

K: Of course. Are we saying that direct perception, insight, and the working out of it demand great logic, a great capacity to think clearly? But the capacity to think clearly will not bring about insight.

Q: But if the logic does not bring about perception, what does it do exactly?

K: It trains, it sharpens the mind. But that certainly won't bring about an insight.

Q: It is not through the mind that the perception comes.

K: That all depends on what you mean by the mind. Logic makes the mind sharp, clear, objective, and sane. But that won't give you the other. Your question is: How does the other come about?

Q1: No. That was not my question. Logic clears the mind, but is the mind the instrument of perception?

Q2: Yes, that is what we said, that it clears the mind of confusion, of the debris.

Q1: The debris may come if you don't have logic.

K: You might remain in the debris if you don't have logic.

Q: If the perception is a real perception and so the truth, why does it then need the discipline of logic to examine it?

K: We said perception works out logically. It does not need logic. Whatever it does is reasonable, logical, sane, objective.

Q: It is logical without an intent to make it so.

K: That's it.

Q: It is like saying that if you see what is in this room correctly, you will not find anything illogical in what you see.

K: All right. Will the perception keep the confusion, the debris, away all the time so that the mind never accumulates it and doesn't have to keep clearing it away? That was your question, wasn't it?

Q: I think perception can reach the stage at which it is continually keeping the field clear. I say that it can reach that stage for a certain moment.

K: At a certain moment I have perception. But during the interval between the perceptions there is a lot of debris being gathered. Our question is: Is perception continuous so that there is no collection of the debris? Put it round the other way: Does one perception keep the field clear?

Q: Can one make a difference between insight and perception?

K: Don't break it up yet. Take those two words as synonymous. We are asking: Is perception from time to time, with intervals? During those intervals a lot of debris collects and, therefore, the field has to be swept again. Or does perception in itself bring about tremendous clarity in which there is no debris?

Q: Are you saying that once it happens it will be there forever?

K: That is what I am trying to get at. Don't use the words *continuous*, *never again*. Keep to the question of whether, once perception has taken place, the mind can collect further debris, confusion. It is only when that perception becomes darkened by the debris that the process of getting rid of it begins. But if there is perception why should there be a collecting, gathering?

Ojai, California, 22 March, 1977

2

KRISHNAMURTI: We were asking how one can know that what Krishnamurti is saying is true. He might be caught in his own conditioning, illusions, and not being able to free himself from them, have put together a series of observations, words, and calls them truth. How do you know whether what he is saying is actual, truthful, and lasting?

Dr. Bohm said that when one has an insight, a direct perception into what is being said, then there is no doubt that it is the truth. Having that insight you can work it out logically to show that the perception is true. But is that perception brief, only to be had at intervals and, therefore, gathering a lot of debris—those things that block perception—or is one perception enough? Does it open the door so that there is insight all the time?

QUESTIONER: Does that mean that you would never have any confusion?

K: Yes, we came to that point. One has a perception, an insight, and that insight has its own capacity for reason, logic, and action. That action is complete, because the perception is complete for the moment. Will further action confuse perception? Or, having perception, is there no further confusion?

Q: I think we were saying that there is danger in this. If you say, "My action is always right—"

K: Oh, that is dangerous!

Q: We also said that logic has its danger. One could think one has an insight when one has not.

K: Suppose I have the capacity to reason it out and act and then say: That is a perfect, complete action. Some people who read the Gita act according to it and they call that insight. Their action is patterned after their reading. They say this action is complete. I have heard many of them say this, as do Catholics and Protestants who are completely immersed in the Bible. So we are treading on very dangerous ground and, therefore, are greatly aware of it.

Q: You also said that the mind tries to find security in all this.

K: The mind has always been seeking security and when that security is threatened it tries to find security in insight, in direct perception.

Q: In the illusion of insight.

K: Yes, but it makes the insight into security. The next question is: Must there be a constant breaking of perception? That is, one day one sees very clearly, one has direct perception; then that fades away and there is confusion. Then again there is a perception and an action, followed by confusion, and so on. Is that so? Or is there no further confusion after these deep insights?

Q: Are we saying this perception is whole?

K: Yes, if the perception is complete, whole, then there is no confusion at any time. Or, one may deceive oneself that it is whole and act upon it, which brings confusion.

Q: There is also a possible danger that one has a genuine perception, an insight, and is not fooling oneself, and that out of that comes a certain action. But then one could fall into making whatever that action was into a formula and stop having the insight. Let's say that out of an insight which was real a certain action came. One then thinks that is the way things should be.

K: That is what generally happens.

Q: But isn't that a corruption of the perception, just making a pattern out of the action instead of continuing to look? It is like being able to really look at something; for instance, looking out of the window and seeing something. But then you don't look out again and you think everything is the way it was. It may have totally changed. The perception starts out being genuine, but you don't continue to look, have insight.

K: Yes. Scientists may have an insight in some specialized field and that insight is put into a category of science unrelated to their lives. But we are talking of a perception that is not only in the field of action but also in daily life.

Q: As a whole and so there is a continuity.

K: Yes.

Q: But I still don't think we have gone into the question of danger. You said that one day a man came to you and said maybe you were stuck in a groove.

K: Yes, caught in a rut.

Q: You didn't say immediately, "I know I am not because I have had a perfect insight."

K: Ah, that would be deadly!

Q: But rather, you said you looked at it for several days.

K: Of course.

Q: I am trying to find out what we are driving at. Perhaps we are saying that there may be an insight which never goes back into confusion. But we are not saying there is one.

K: Yes, that's right. Now would you say that when there is complete perception—not an illusory perception—there is no further confusion?

Q: It seems reasonable to say that.

K: That means from day to day there is no confusion at all.

Q: Then why did you feel it necessary to look into it?

K: Because I may deceive myself. Therefore, it is dangerous ground and I must be alert, I must watch it.

Q: Are we seeing as an insight now that when there is an insight of that kind there is no further confusion? But we may deceive ourselves nevertheless.

K: Yes. Therefore, we must be watchful.

Q: Do you mean after the real insight you could then deceive yourself?

K: No. You have a deep insight, complete, whole. Someone comes along and says: "Look, you are deceiving yourself." Do you instantly say, "No, I am not deceiving myself because my perception was complete"? Or do you listen and look at it all afresh? It doesn't mean that you are denying the complete perception; you are again watching if it is real or illusory.

Q: That is not necessarily an intellectual process?

K: No, no. I would say both. It is intellectual as well as nonverbal.

Q: Is perception something that is always there and it is only that we—

K: That leads to dangerous ground. The Hindus say that God is always there inside you, the abiding deep divinity, or soul, or *Atman,* and it is covered up. Remove the confusion, the debris, and it is found inside. Most people believe that. I think that is a conclusion. You conclude that there is something divine inside, a soul, the *Atman,* or whatever you like to call it. And from a conclusion you can never have a total, complete perception.

Q: But this leads to another problem, because if you deny that, then what makes one step out of the stream? Does it mean that the stepping out is for certain individuals only?

K: When you say "certain individuals" I think you are putting the wrong question, aren't you?

Q: No. If the possibility exists for everyone—

K: Yes, the possibility exists for human beings.

Q: For the totality?

K: For human beings.

Q: Then there is some energy, which—

K: Which is outside of them or which is in them.

Q: Yes. We don't know.

K: Therefore, don't come to any conclusion. If from a conclusion you think you perceive, then that perception is conditioned; therefore, it is not whole.

Q: Does that mean that there would not be the possibility of a deepening of perception?

K: You can't deepen insight. You can't deepen perception. You perceive the whole, that's all.

Q: What do you mean then by saying there was this mind into which you could continually go more deeply?

K: That is something else.

Q: Are you saying that perception, if it is partial, is not perception?

K: Of course, obviously not.

Q: You mentioned watchfulness after perception.

K: What happened was that a man came up to me and said, "You are getting old, you are stuck in a groove." And I listened to it. For a couple of days I thought about it. I looked at it and said to myself, "He may be right."

Q: You are almost suggesting that it could be possible.

K: No, I wanted to examine it. Not say it could or could not.

Q: To be caught in habit after a perception, could that not ever happen again, at certain levels?

K: There is partial perception and total perception; let's divide it into those two. When there is total perception, there is no further confusion.

Q: You don't get caught in habit?

K: There is no further confusion. Because it is so.

Q: What if something happens to the brain physically?

K: Then of course it is gone.

Q: So there seems to be a limitation to what you say, because one assumes that the brain remains healthy.

K: Of course, it assumes that the whole organism is healthy. If there is an accident, your brain suffers concussion and something is injured, then it is finished.

Q: The major danger is that we would mistake a partial perception for the total.

K: One has to go into the question of what perception is. How do you come to it? That is very important, isn't it? You cannot have perception if your daily life is in disorder, confused, contradictory. That is obvious.

Q: Doesn't this perception mean that there is constant renewal?

K: No. Is that energy outside or inside? She is asking that question all the time.

Q: Isn't outside and inside an artificial division? Is that a real thing, or is it just an illusion?

K: She said that this perception needs energy. That energy may be an external energy, a mechanical energy, or a nonmechanistic energy which may exist deeply inside you. Both are mental concepts. Would you agree to that? Both are conclusions which one has either accepted because tradition has said so, or one has come to that conclusion by oneself. Any form of conclusion is detrimental to perception. So what does perception mean? Can I have perception if I am attached to my position, to my wife, to my property?

Q: It colors the act of perceiving.

K: Yes, but take the scientists. They have their families, their attachments; they want position, money, and all the rest of it, but they have an insight.

Q: It is not total.

K: So we are saying that total perception can only take place when in your daily life there is no confusion.

Q: May we look more closely into that, because couldn't it be that a total perception can take place in spite of that and wipe it away?

K: I can see if the windows are not clean my view is confused.

Q: Would that mean that there is a conditioned insight?

K: If I am in fear, my perception will be very partial. That is a fact.

Q: But don't you need perception to end fear?

K: Ah, but in investigating fear I have a total perception of fear.

Q: Surely if there is fear or attachment, even one's logic would be distorted.

K: One is frightened; as we said, that distorts perception. But in investigating, observing, going into fear, understanding it profoundly, in delving into it, I have perception.

Q: Are you implying that there are certain things you can do which will make for perceptions, which means although you have fear and it distorts, the distortion is not so total that you cannot investigate it. There is still that possibility, although you are distorting through fear?

K: I realize that I am distorting perception through fear.

Q: That's right, then I begin to look at fear.

K: I investigate it, look into it.

Q: In the beginning I am also distorting it.

K: Therefore, I am watching every distortion. I am aware of every distortion that is going on.

Q: But you see, I think the difficulty lies there. How can I investigate when I am distorting?

K: Wait, just listen. I am afraid and I see fear has made me do something that is a distortion.

Q: But before I can see that, the fear has to fade away.

K: No, I am observing fear.

Q: But I cannot observe fear if I am afraid.

K: Take a fact—that you are afraid. You are conscious of it. That means that you become aware of the fact that there is fear. And you observe also what that fear has done. Is that clear?

Q: Yes.

K: And you look more and more into it. In looking very deeply into it you have an insight.

Q: I may have an insight.

K: No, you will have insight, which is quite different.

Q: What you are saying is that this confusion due to fear is not complete, that it is always open to mankind to have insight.

K: To one who is investigating, who is observing.

Q: If you try to investigate something else while you are afraid, you get lost in fear. But it is still open to you to investigate fear.

K: Yes, quite right. One suffers and sees what it does. In observing it, investigating it, opening it up, in the very unrolling of it you have a certain insight. That is all we are saying. That insight may be partial. Therefore, one has to be aware that it is partial. Its action is partial and it may appear complete, so watch it.

Q: Very often it looks as if it is totally impossible to have an insight, since you say, "If you are distorting how will you look?" But you are also saying that, as a matter of fact, when you have a distortion, the one thing you can look at is the distortion.

K: That's right.

Q: That factually you have that capacity.

K: One has that capacity.

Q: You can look at that. The fear which creates the distortion can be looked at; so you can't say that no perception whatsoever is possible.

K: That's just it, then you have locked the door.

Q: Could one say that the fear can look at itself?

K: No, no. One is afraid. In looking at that fear—not having an insight, just watching it—you see what it does, what its action is.

Q: You mean by looking, being aware of it.

K: Without any choosing, being aware. And you see what fear does. In looking at it more extensively, deeply, widely, suddenly you have an insight into the whole structure of fear.

Q: But still, in that moment of fear, I am fear.

K: How you observe fear matters; whether you observe it as an observer or *the observer is that*. You perceive that the observer is the observed, and in this action there is distortion, confusion. And you examine that confusion, which is born of fear, and in the very process of examination you have an insight. Do it, you will see it—if you don't limit yourself; in saying, "I am too frightened, I can't look," you run away from it.

Q: To simplify it perhaps too much, when we said one can't see through the window because it is dirty and it distorts, the action of examining the fear, the distorting factor, is the cleansing of the window.

K: How you observe, how you investigate, that is the real thing. That is, perception can take place only when there is no division between the observer and the observed. Perception can take place only in the very act of exploring. To explore implies that there is no division between the observer and the observed. Therefore, you are watching the movement of fear and in the very watching of it there is an insight. I think that is clear.

And yet you see, Krishnamurti says, "I have never done this."

Q: Never gone through all this? Then how do you know somebody else can?

K: That's just it. Let's discuss it. Suppose you have not gone through all this, but you see it instantly. Because you see it instantly, your capacity to reason explains all this. Another listens and says, "I'd like to get that." I don't have to go through that whole process.

Q: Are you saying that all we have been discussing just now is merely a pointer to something else? We don't have to go through all that.

K: Yes. I want to get at that.

Q: In other words, that helps to clear the ground in some way?

K: Yes.

Q: It is not really the main point.

K: No.

Q: Are you saying there is a shortcut?

K: No, no shortcut. Must you go through fear, jealousy, anxiety, attachment? Or can you clear the whole thing instantly? Must one go through all this process?

Q: You previously said that you have never done this. And by having that immediate total perception you are able to see what those with the dirty windows can do to clean them. But that isn't necessary; there is perhaps a direct, an immediate, way for those who haven't—

K: No. First put the question, see what comes out of it. Dr. Bohm says to Krishnamurti, "You have probably not gone through all this. Because you have a direct, a total, insight you can argue with reason, with logic; you can act. You are always talking from that total perception; therefore, what you say can never be distorted." And another listens to all this and says: "I am frightened, I am jealous, I am this, I am that, and, therefore, I can't have total perception." So I observe attachment, or fear, or jealousy, and I have an insight.

Is it possible through investigating, through awareness and discovering that the observer is the observed and that there is no division, in the very process of investigation—in which we are observing without the observer and see the totality of it—is it possible to free all the rest? I think that is the only way.

Q: Is it possible not to have certain fears, jealousy, attachment? Could that be part of one's conditioning if one were raised in a certain way, or went to a certain school?

K: But there may be deeper layers. You may not be totally conscious of them, you may not be totally aware of the deeper fears. You may say, "Superficially I am all right, I have none of these things."

Q: But if one went to a certain school, would the kind of learning and investigation that would take place in such a school clear the way toward the possibility?

K: Obviously. What we are talking about is whether one must go through all this process.

Q: Couldn't we remove from the problem the personal aspect? We are discussing what is open to mankind rather than to any individual.

K: Yes. Is it open to any human being without going through all this process?

Q: By "this process," do you mean involvement with the fear?

K: With fear, sorrow, jealousy, attachment. Must you go through all that, step by step, or can a human being see the whole thing at a glance? And that very glance is the investigation and the complete, total perception?

Q: Which is what you mean when you say the first step is the last.

K: Yes, total perception.

Q: Then what would one's responsibility be toward someone who is in sorrow?

K: The response to that human being is the response of compassion. That's all. Nothing else.

Q: For instance, if you see an injured bird, it is very easy to deal with that because it really doesn't require very much of you. But when you come into contact with a human being, he has a much more complex set of needs.

K: What can you do actually? Somebody comes to you and says, "I am in deep sorrow." Do you talk to them out of compassion, or from a conclusion, or out of your own particular experience of sorrow, which has conditioned you? Do you answer according to your conditioning? A Hindu who is conditioned in a certain way says, "My dear friend, I am so sorry, but in the next life you will live better. You suffered because you did this and that," and so on. Or a Christian would respond from some other conclusion. And he takes comfort in it. Because a man who is suffering wants some sort of solace, someone on whose lap he can put his head. So what he is seeking is comfort and avoidance of this terrible pain. Will you offer him any of those escapes? Whatever comes out of compassion will help him.

Q: Are you saying that as far as sorrow is concerned you can't directly help anyone, but the energy of compassion itself may be of help?

K: That's right; that's all.

Q: But many such wounded spirits will come and I think it is going to be a problem to know how to deal with them.

K: There is no problem if you are compassionate. Compassion doesn't create problems. It has no problems; therefore, it is compassionate.

Q: You are saying that total compassion is the highest intelligence?

K: Of course. If there is compassion, that compassion has its own intelligence and that intelligence acts. But if you have no compassion and no intelligence, then your conditioning makes you reply according to whatever another wants. I think that is fairly simple.

To go back to the other question, must a human being go through the whole process? Has no human being said, "I won't go through all this; I absolutely refuse to go through all this"?

Q: But on what basis does one refuse? It wouldn't make sense to refuse to do what is necessary.

K: Of course. You see, we are such creatures of habit. Because my father is conditioned, generations after generations are conditioned, and I am conditioned. And I accept it; I work in it and I operate with it. But if I say, "I won't ever operate in my conditioned responses," something else may take place. Then, if I realize I am a bourgeois, I don't want to become an aristocrat or a militant, I refuse to be a bourgeois, which doesn't mean I become a revolutionary, or join Lenin or Marx; those are all bourgeois to me. So something does take place. I reject the whole thing. You see, a human being never says, "I will reject the whole thing." I want to investigate that.

Q: Do you mean that even to say, "I am going to get rid of the whole thing," is not necessary?

K: Of course. I mean saying, "I won't be a bourgeois," is just words.

Q: But isn't the key to this somewhere in desire? There is some sort of desire for continuity, for security.

K: That's right. Bourgeois implies continuity, security, it implies belonging to something, a lack of taste, vulgarity, all that.

Q: But Krishnaji, if you are saying that Krishnamurti never said this, never had the need to say it, we can only conclude that you are some kind of freak.

K: No, no. You can say he is a freak, but it doesn't answer the question. Krishnamurti says, "I have not touched all this." Somebody asks, "Why should I go through all this?" Don't say Krishnamurti is a freak, but how it happens.

Q: In saying, "I won't be a bourgeois," you are discovering it in yourself.

K: No, no. That is a different matter. If somebody says to you, "I have never been through all this," what do you do? Do you say he is a freak? Or would you say, "How extraordinary; is he telling the truth? Has he deceived himself?" You discuss with him. Then your question is, "How does it happen?" You are a human being, he is a human being; you want to find out.

Q: You ask in what way we are different. He is a human being that has never been through all that, and yet he points out.

K: No, he has never been through it. Don't say he points out. Don't you ask that question: "How does it happen; must I go through all this?" Do you ask that?

Q: You are taking two widely separate things. One is the uncontaminated person who never had to go through the process because he was never in the soup.

K: Leave out why he didn't go through it.

Q: But most other people, apparently, are in some form of—

K: Conditioning—

Q: —in some form of contamination—it may be fear or something else. Therefore, the person who has already got this sickness—let's call it that—says "This man has never been sick for a day in his life." What good is it to examine that, because one is already sick in some form.

Q: The question is, how can a human being who is sick in some way get out of it directly without going through endless self-exploration?

K: Can we put the whole thing differently? Do you seek excellence, not excellence, for instance, in a building, but the essence of excellence? Then everything falls away, doesn't it? Or do you seek excellence in a certain direction and never the essence of excellence? As an artist I seek excellence in my painting and get caught in that. A scientist gets caught in something else. But an ordinary human being, not a specialist, just an average intelligent human being who does not take drugs, does not smoke, is fairly intelligent and decent; if he sought the essence of excellence, would this happen? The essence would meet all this. I wonder if I am conveying something?

Q: Does it exist apart from this manifestation?

K: Listen carefully first. Don't object or reject and say if and but. That very demand for excellence, how you demand it, brings the essence of it. You demand it passionately. You demand the highest intelligence, the highest excellence, the essence of it, and when fear arises, then you—

Q: Where does the demand come from?

K: Demand it! Don't say, "Where does it come from?" There may be a motive, but the very demand washes it all away. I wonder if I am conveying anything?

Q: You are saying to demand this excellence, which we don't know.

K: I don't know what is beyond it, but I want to be morally excellent.

Q: Does that mean goodness?

K: I demand the excellence of goodness, I demand the excellent flower of goodness. In that very demand there is a demand for the essence.

Q: Does perception come from this demand?

K: Yes, that's right.

Q: Could you go into what you call this demand?

K: It is not a demand which means asking, a demand that means imploring, wanting. Cut out all those.

Q: It doesn't mean those?

K: No, no.

Q: But then you are back with prayer.

K: Oh, no. Leave out all that.

Q: You are really saying that the impossible is possible to the average intelligent human being?

K: We are saying that, yes, which is not a conclusion, which is not a hope. I say it is possible for the average human being, who is fairly clean, who is fairly decent, fairly kind, who is not a bourgeois.

Q: Traditionally we are conditioned to believe that there are special people with no conscious content of consciousness, so it is very difficult for someone like me to feel that one could really be completely free of it.

K: You see, you have not listened. K says to you, please listen first, don't bring in all these objections. Just listen to what he is saying. That is, what is important in life is the supreme excellence, which has its own essence. That's all. And to demand does not mean begging or praying, getting something from somebody.

Q: The point is, we find we confuse demand with desire.

K: Of course.

Q: There must be no beliefs.

K: No beliefs, no desire.

Q: You see, when people feel that they want to give up desire then there is a danger of giving up this demand as well.

K: How can we put this? Let's find a good word for it. Would the word *passion* be suitable? There is passion for this, passion for excellence.

Q: Does it imply that this passion has no object?

K: You see how you immediately form a conclusion. *Burning* passion, not *for* something. The communists are passionate about their ideas. That passion is very, very petty and limited. The Christians have passion for missionary work; that passion is born of the love of Jesus. That again is not passion, it is very narrow. Putting all that aside, I say, "Passion!"

Q: As you were just saying, people have had some vision, or a dream of something, and that has developed a great energy. But you are saying it is not a dream, it is not a vision, but it is nevertheless some perception of this excellence.

K: All those passions feed the ego, feed the "me," make "me" important, consciously or unconsciously. We are cutting out all that. There is a young boy who has a passion to grow up into an extraordinary human being, into something original.

Q: He sees that it is possible.

K: Yes.

Q: And, therefore, he has the passion.

K: Yes, that's right. It is possible. Is that what is missing in most human beings? Not passion, but the welling up of . . . I don't know how to put it. There is this passion in a human being who demands the supreme excellence, not in what he writes in his books, but the feeling of it. You know this, don't you? That may shatter everything else. Again, that human being didn't demand it. He says, "I never even asked for it."

Q: Perhaps that is due to conditioning. We are conditioned to mediocrity, not to make this demand. That is what you mean by mediocrity.

K: Yes, of course. Mediocrity is lack of great passion—not for Jesus, or for Marx, or whatever it is.

Q: We are not only conditioned to mediocrity but to direction, so the demand is always to have some direction.

K: The demand is a direction, quite right.

Q: To have a demand without any direction—

K: That's right. I like the word *demand* because it is a challenge.

Q: Doesn't a demand without direction imply that it is not in time?

K: Of course. It demands no direction, no time, no person. So, does total insight bring this passion? Total insight *is* the passion.

Q: They can't be separate.

K: Total insight is the flame of passion that wipes away all confusion. It burns away everything else. Don't you then act as a magnet? The bees go toward the nectar. In the same way don't you act as a magnet when you are passionate to create? Is it that there is this lack of fire? That may be the thing that is missing. If there is something missing, I would ask for it.

Q1: Could we talk about the relationship between the conditioned and the unconditioned mind, and whether it is only possible to ask for small things, or can we somehow leap beyond that into something bigger?

Q2: Whatever the "me" asks for, the asking in a direction is the small thing.

K: Quite right.

Q: We have to ask for the unlimited, for the unconditioned.

K: She is really asking what the relationship is between the conditioned and the unconditioned. Also, what is the relationship between two human beings when one is unconditioned and the other is not? There is no relationship.

Q: How can you say that there is no relationship between the unconditioned and the conditioned human being?

K: There is no relationship from the conditioned to the unconditioned. But the unconditioned has a relationship to the other.

Q: But logically one could ask if there is an essential difference between the unconditioned and the conditioned. Because if you say there is, then there is duality.

K: What do you mean by essential difference?

Q: Let's say difference in kind. If there is an essential difference between the conditioned and the unconditioned there is duality.

K: I see what you mean. X is conditioned, Y is not conditioned. X thinks in terms of duality, his very conditioning is duality. But duality has no relationship with Y, yet Y has a relationship with X.

Q: Because there is no duality.

K: Yes. Y has no duality; therefore, there is a relationship. You also asked another question: Essentially, deeply, is there a difference? Are not both the same?

Q: Could one ask the question in another way? Is the conditioning only superficial?

K: No. Then we are lost.

Q: The world couldn't be unconditioned, could it?

K: The world is "me" and "I" am the world.

Q: That is an absolute fact only to the unconditioned.

K: Oh, not at all. Be careful, it is so. It is an obvious fact.

Q: You mean that only the unconditioned can perceive that?

K: I am refuting it. I say it isn't quite like that.

Q: I mean it in the sense that I may say, "I am the world, the world is me," but I revert to an action that is a contradiction to that. Therefore, it is not an absolute fact for me. There may be moments when the fact of it is seen by me.

K: Yes. Do you mean: I say to myself very clearly, "I am the world and the world is me"?

Q: I see it.

K: I feel it.

Q: I feel it, yes.

K: And I act contrary to that, which is, I act personally, selfishly—"my," "me." That is a contradiction to the fact that the world is me and I am the world. A person can say this merely as an intellectual conclusion, or a momentary feeling.

Q: It is not an intellectual conclusion, because I am stating my position, but I accept that for you the position is totally different.

K: No, you don't even have to accept that. See the fact, which is, when one says, "I am the world and the world is me," there is no me. But one's house has to be insured; I may have children; I have to earn a living. But there is no me. See the importance of it. There is no me all the time. I function, but there is no me which is seeking a higher position and all that. Though I am married, I am not attached, I don't depend on a wife or husband. The appearances may give you the impression that the me is operating, but actually, to a man who feels, "The world is me and I am the world," to him there is no me. To you, looking at him, there is. That human being lives in this world, he must have food, clothes and shelter, a job, transportation, all that, yet there is no me.

So when the world is me and I am the world, there is no me. Can that state, that quality operate in all directions? It must operate in all directions. When you say, "I am the world and the world is me," and there is no me, there is no conditioning. Then I don't put the question: In that unconditioned state does the conditioned exist? When a human being says, "I am the world and the world is me," there is no I.

Q: Therefore, the other person also is not there. There is no you.

K: There is no me, there is no you. When you ask if the conditioned exists in this state you are asking a wrong question. That is what I was getting at. Because when there is no I there is no you.

Q: The question is: How does that person see the kind of confusion that arises around "I" and "you"? He sees what is going on in the world, that people are generally confused about this.

K: I exist; there is you and me. And you also think the same thing. So we keep this division everlastingly. But when you and I really realize, have profound insight, that the world is me and I am the world, there is no me.

Q: There is no me and no you. No means everything.

K: The world of living, everything.

Q: Then the question whether there is an essential difference between this and that, the unconditioned and the conditioned, doesn't arise because there is no "between."

K: Yes, that's right. There is no "you," there is no "I" in that state, which doesn't include the conditioned state. Is this too abstract?

Q: Why do you have to say, "I am the world" first, and then deny this?

K: Because it is an actuality.

Q: But then you imply that the "I" is still there if I say, "I am the world."

K: That is merely a statement. It is an actual fact that I am the world.

Q: Whatever I mean by the word *I,* I also mean by the word *world.*

K: Yes.

Q: So we don't need those two words.

K: Yes, you and I, remove that.

Q: There is just everything.

K: No, this is very dangerous. If you say I am everything—

Q: I am trying to find out what you mean by "the world."

K: If you say, "I am everything," then the murderer, the assassin, is part of me.

Q: Suppose I say, "I am the world" instead, does that change it?

K: [laughing] All right. I see the actual fact that I am the result of the world. The world means killing, wars, the whole of society. I am the result of that.

Q: And I see everybody is the result of that.

K: Yes. I am saying the result is "I" and "you."

Q: And that separation.

K: When I say, "I am the world," I am saying all that.

Q: You mean to say I am generated by the world, I am identified with everything.

K: Yes. I am the product of the world.

Q: The world is the essence of what I am.

K: Yes. I am the essence of the world. It is the same thing. When there is a deep perception of that, not verbal, not intellectual, not emotional, not romantic, but profound, there is no you or me. I think that holds logically. But there is a danger. If I say, "The world is me, I am everything," I'll accept everything.

Q: You are really saying that one is the product of the whole of society.

K: Yes.

Q: But I am also of the essence of the whole of society.

K: Yes. I am really the essential result of all this.

Q: Does it help to use the word *ego?*

K: It is the same thing, it doesn't matter. You see, when you say "me," or "ego," there is a possibility of deception that the "I" is the very essence of God. You know about that superstition.

Q: The Atman.

K: Yes.

Q: But there is still another question. Is the unconditioned mind also a product of all this? Then we come to a contradiction.

K: No, there is no contradiction. Without using the word *I,* it can be said the result of the world is this. The result of the world is that also. We are two human beings, which means the result has created the "I" and the "you." When there is an insight into the result there is no "result."

Q: The result changes and vanishes when we see it.

K: That means there is no result. Therefore, "you" and "I" don't exist. That is an actual fact for a man who says, "I am not the result." You see what it means? There is no causation in the mind and, therefore, there is no effect. Therefore, it is whole, and any action born of it is causeless and without effect.

Q: You have to make that clear, in the sense that you still use cause and effect concerning ordinary, mechanical things.

K: Quite. This human being, X, is a result. And Y is a result. X says, "I," and Y says, "I"; therefore, there is "you" and "I." X says, "I see this," and investigates, goes into it, and he has an insight. In that insight the two results cease. Therefore, in that state there is no cause.

Q: There is no cause and no effect although it may leave a residue in the mind.

K: Let's go into it. In that state there is no result, no cause, no effect. That mind acts out of compassion. Therefore, there is no result.

Q: But in some sense it would look as if there were a result.

K: But compassion has no result. A is suffering; he says to X, "Please help me to get out of my suffering." If X really has compassion his words have no result.

Q: Something happens, but there is no result.

K: That's it.

Q: But I think people generally are seeking a result.

K: Yes. Let's put it another way. Does compassion have a result? When there is result there is cause. When compassion has a cause then you are no longer compassionate.

Q: But compassion also acts.

K: Compassion is compassion, it doesn't act. If it acts because there is a cause and an effect, then it is not compassion: it wants a result.

Q: It acts purely.

K: It wants a result.

Q: What makes it want a result is the idea of separation. Somebody says, "There is a person suffering, I would like to produce the result that he is not suffering." But that is based on the idea that there is "me" and "he."

K: That's it.

Q: There is no "he" and no "I." There is no room, no place, to have this result.

K: It is a tremendous thing! One has to look at it very, very carefully. Look, the world is me and I am the world. When I say "me," "you" exist; both of us are there. The "you" and the "I" are the results of man's misery, of selfishness, and so on; it is a result. When one looks into the result, goes into it very, very deeply, the insight brings about a quality in which "you" and "I"—who are the result—don't exist. This is easy to agree to verbally, but when you see it deeply there is no "you" and no "me." Therefore, there is no result; which means compassion. The person upon whom that compassion acts wants a result. We say, "Sorry, there is no result." But the man who suffers says, "Help me to get out of this," or, "Help me to bring back my son, my wife." He is demanding a result. This thing has no result. The result is the world.

Q: Does compassion affect the consciousness of man?

K: Yes. It affects the deep layers of consciousness. The "I" is the result of the world; the "you" is the result of the world. And to the man who sees this deeply, with a profound insight, there is no "you" or "I." Therefore, that profound insight is compassion, which is intelligence. And the intelligence says, if you want a result I can't give it to you, I am not the product of a result. Compassion says, this state is not a result; therefore, there is no cause.

Q: Does that mean there is no time either?

K: No cause, no result, no time.

Ojai, California, March 24, 1977

PART 4

You Are the World

In the last two decades of his life, Krishnamurti continued to divide his time between India, Europe, and the United States, giving public talks, holding dialogues with small groups, and meeting with individuals. An extremely important feature of this period were the gatherings at Saanen, in Switzerland. Held for twenty-five consecutive years, these were perhaps the strongest international focus of his work.

Krishnamurti's life for over sixty years was always public; except for brief periods of illness and withdrawal for rest, his talks and meetings continued until his death in Ojai, California, in February 1986. In all that time the message of his talks was in essence as it had been in the early years: Truth is a pathless land; each of us represents all humanity and one needs to be a light to oneself, free of all authority. In conveying these teachings, Krishnamurti explored the abiding themes of thought, time, suffering, death, space, silence, and the sacred. In his talks and writings too, he touched, sometimes almost reluctantly because it might become stimulation or escape, on the inner wellspring of his life's work.

Krishnamurti provided a religious language that was extremely appropriate for the twentieth century. Ranging from the poetic to the meticulously precise, this language conveys nuances and insights for which previously accepted "mystical" language was frequently inadequate. From the beginning of his life until the end, his talks—remarkable in their range and universality—were always a process of joint exploration.

When Mary Lutyens, one of Krishnamurti's biographers, asked him to convey the core of his message, he did so, and this one page summation, *The Core of Krishnamurti's Teaching*, begins the final part of the book. It is followed by selections from public talks given in Ojai, California; Saanen, Switzerland; Brockwood Park, England; New Delhi; and Washington, D.C.

This part of the book expresses the work of the final decade of his long life. The themes are quintessentially what they have been since the outset; there is, however, an evolution of expression, which underpins the relevance of Krishnamurti's teachings for all time.

THE CORE OF KRISHNAMURTI'S TEACHING

The core of Krishnamurti's teaching is contained in the statement he made in 1929 when he said "Truth is a pathless land." Man cannot come to it through any organization, through any creed, through any dogma, priest, or ritual, nor through any philosophical knowledge or psychological technique. He has to find it through the mirror of relationship, through the understanding of the contents of his own mind, through observation, and not through intellectual analysis or introspective dissection. Man has built in himself images as a sense of security—religious, political, personal. These manifest as symbols, ideas, beliefs. The burden of these dominates man's thinking, relationships, and daily life. These are the causes of our problems, for they divide man from man in every relationship. His perception of life is shaped by the concepts already established in his mind. The content of his consciousness *is* this consciousness. This content is common to all humanity. The individuality is the name, the form, and superficial culture he acquires from his environment. The uniqueness of the individual does not lie in the superficial but in the total freedom from the content of consciousness.

Freedom is not a reaction; freedom is not choice. It is man's pretense that because he has choice he is free. Freedom is pure observation without motive; freedom is not at the end of the evolution of man, but lies in the first step of his existence. In observation one begins to discover the lack of freedom. Freedom is found in the choiceless awareness of our daily existence.

Thought is time. Thought is born of experience, of knowledge, which are inseparable from time. Time is the psychological enemy of man. Our action is based on knowledge and, therefore, time, so man is always a slave to the past.

When man becomes aware of the movement of his own consciousness he will see the division between the thinker and the thought, the observer and the observed, the experiencer and the experience. He will discover that this division is an illusion. Then only is there pure observation, which is insight without any shadow of the past. This timeless insight brings about a deep radical change in the mind.

Total negation is the essence of the positive. When there is negation of all those things which are not love—desire, pleasure—then love is, with its compassion and intelligence.

London, October 21, 1980

TOTAL ACTION WITHOUT REGRET

1

Thought has created this world, the world of politics, the world of economics, the world of business, of social morality and all the religious structures. All our problems and all our desires to find answers to problems are within that consciousness, within the field that thought has created. So thought is trying to find answers to the mess it has made in our personal relationships, in our relationship with the community. Even your meditations, even your gods, your Christs, and your Buddhas are the creations of thought, which is matter, which can only operate within the field of time. We think that through thought, through will, through ambition, through drive and aggression, through substituting new religions for the old traditions, we can solve all the problems of personal relationship.

Is there an answer to all the problems through the operation of thought? If thought will give no answer to all the problems, then what will?

What is consciousness? What is the operation of thought? All your meditations are in that area; all your pursuits of pleasure, fear, greed, envy, brutality, violence, are within that field. And thought is always endeavoring to go beyond that, asserting the ineffable, the unnamable, unknowable. The content of consciousness is consciousness. Your consciousness or another's consciousness is its content. If it is born in India, then all the traditions, superstitions, hopes, fears, sorrows, anxieties, violence, sexual demands, aggression, the beliefs, dogmas, and creeds of that country are the content of its consciousness. Yet the content of consciousness is extraordinarily similar, whether one is born in the East or in the West.

Look at your own consciousness, if you can. If you are brought up in a religious culture as a Christian, you believe in saviors, rituals, creeds, and dogmas on one side and, on the other side, you accept social immorality, wars, nationalities and their divisions that restrict economic expansion and deny consideration for others. The content of your consciousness is your personal unhappiness, your ambitions, your fears, your greeds, your aggressiveness, your demands, your loneliness, your sorrow, your lack of relationship with another, the isolation, frustration, confusion, misery.

All that is consciousness whether you are of the East or the West—with variations, with joys, with more knowledge or less knowledge. Without that content, there is no consciousness as we know it.

All education is based on the acquiring of more knowledge, more information, but functioning always within this area. Any political reformation based on a new philosophy is an invention still within that area. And so man goes on suffering, unhappy, lonely, fearful of death and of living, hoping for some great leader to come and take him out of his misery, a new savior, a new politician. In this confusion we are so irresponsible that out of our own disorder we are going to create tyrants, hoping they will create order within this area. This is what is happening outside of us and inside. Any leader we choose will be like us; we will not choose a leader who is totally different from us. That is the actual picture of our life: conflict inside and outside, struggle, opposition to one another, appalling selfishness.

When there is so much sorrow in the world it is necessary to find out for oneself—through careful, slow, patient, hesitating investigation—if there is any other way of solving all these problems other than through the operation of thought. Is there an action which is not based on thought? Is there an intelligence which is not the function or the result of thought, which is not put together by thought, which does not come about through cunning, through friction and struggle, something entirely different?

To communicate one has to listen not just to the speaker but to the very action of listening. How does one listen? Does one ever really listen at all? Is one free to listen, or does one always listen with the cunning operations of thought, with interpretation or prejudice? One has to listen, if one is free, to the content of one's consciousness, to listen not only to what is at the surface, which is fairly simple, but to the deeper layers of it. That means to listen to the totality of consciousness.

How does one listen to and look at one's consciousness?

The speaker was born in a certain country where he absorbed all the prejudices, the irrationalities and the superstitions, the beliefs, the class differences, as a Brahmin. There the young mind absorbed the tradition, the rituals, the extraordinary orthodoxy, and the tremendous discipline imposed by that group upon itself. And then he moves to the West; and again he absorbs from all that is there. The content of his consciousness is what has been put into it, what he has learned, what his thoughts are, and its own emotions, which thought recognizes. That is the content and the consciousness of this person. Within that area he has all the political, religious, personal, communal problems. All the problems are there. And not being able to solve them himself, he looks to books, to others, asking what to do, how to meditate, what to do about personal relationship with his wife, or his girlfriend, his parents. Should he believe in Jesus or in Buddha or the new guru who comes along with a lot of nonsense? He is searching for a new philosophy of life, a new philosophy of politics, and so on, all within this area.

Man has done this from time immemorial, but there is no answer within that area. You may meditate for hours, sitting in a certain posture, breathing in a special way, but it is still within that area because you want something out of your meditation.

So there is this content of consciousness: dull, stupid, traditional thought, recognizing all its emotions—otherwise they are not emotions. Always it is thought, which is the response of memory, knowledge, and experience operating. Now, can the mind look at it? Can you look at the operation of thought?

When you look, who is the observer who is looking at the content? Is it different from the content? This is really a very important question to ask, and to which to find an answer. Is the observer different from the content and, therefore, capable of changing it and going beyond it? Or is the observer the same as the content? First, look. If the observer—the "I" that looks, the "me" that looks—is different from the observed, then there is a division between the observer and the observed and, therefore, conflict: "I must not do this; I should do that"; "I must get rid of my particular prejudice," and I adopt a new prejudice; "I must get rid of my old gods," and I take on new gods. So when there is a division between the observer and the observed, there must be conflict. That is a principle, that is a law. So, do I observe the content of my consciousness as if I were an outsider looking in, altering the pieces and moving the pieces to different places? Or am I the observer, the thinker, the experiencer, the same as that which is observed, experienced, thought?

If I look at the content of my consciousness as an outsider observing, then there must be conflict between what is observed and the observer. There *must* be conflict, and in that conflict we live: the "me" and the "not me," "we" and "they." If "I," the observer, am different from anger, I try to control it, suppress it, dominate it, overcome it, and there is conflict. But is the observer different at all? Or is he essentially the same as the observed? If he is the same, then there is no conflict, is there? The understanding of that is intelligence. Then intelligence operates and not conflict.

It would be a thousand pities if you did not understand this simple thing. Man has lived in conflict. He wants peace through conflict. And there can never be peace through conflict; however many armaments you may have against another's equally strong armaments, there will never be peace. Only when intelligence operates will there be peace, the intelligence that comes when one understands that there is no division between the observer and the observed. The insight into that very fact, that very truth, brings this intelligence.

This is a very serious thing, for then you will see that you have no nationality; you may have a passport but you have no nationality. You have no gods. There is no outside authority, nor inward authority. The only authority then is intelligence. It is not the cunning intelligence of thought, which is mere knowledge operating within a certain area, and that is not intelligence.

So this is the first thing to understand when you look at your consciousness: the division between the thinker and the thought, between the observer and the observed, between the experiencer and the experienced is false, for they are one. There is no thinker if you do not think. Thought has created the thinker. That is the first thing to understand, to have an insight into the truth of, the fact of, as palpable as you sitting there, so that there is no conflict between the observer and the observed.

So, what is the content of your consciousness, the hidden as well as the open? Can you look at it—*and not make an effort?*

You can find this out, not just sitting there, but in your relationships. That is the mirror in which you will see, not by closing your eyes, or by going off into the woods and thinking up some dreams. In the actual fact of your relationship with man, woman, your neighbor, your politician, your gods, your gurus, you will observe your reactions, your attitudes, your prejudices, your images, your constant groping. The content is in that. What you are doing now is merely ploughing, and you can only sow when you observe your relationships and see what actually is taking place. You can look as much as you like and begin to distinguish various qualities and tendencies, but if you look as an observer different from the observed then you are bound to create conflict and, therefore, further suffering. When you have an insight, see the truth that the observer is the observed, then conflict ceases altogether. Then a totally different kind of energy comes into operation.

There are different kinds of energy. There is physical energy from good food; there may be energy created by emotionalism, sentimentality; there is energy created by thought through various conflicts and tensions. Within that field of energy we have lived, and we are still trying to find greater energy within that field to solve our problems. There is a different kind of energy, or the continuation of this energy in a totally different form, when the mind is operating completely, not in the field of thought but intelligently.

Can the mind observe its content without any choice as to the content, not choosing any part of the content, any part of the piece, but observing totally? Now, how is it possible to observe totally? When I look at a map of France, as I come from England and cross the Channel, I see the road leading to Gstaad. I can tell the mileage, I can see the direction. All that is very simple because it is marked on the map and I follow it. In doing that, I do not look at any other part of the map; I know the direction in which I want to go and that direction excludes all others. In the same way, a mind that is seeking in a given direction does not see the whole. If I want to find something that I think is real, then the direction is set and I follow that direction and my mind is incapable of seeing the totality. Now, when I look at the content of my consciousness, which is the same as yours, I have set a direction—to go beyond it. A movement in a particular direction, seeking a certain pleasure, not wanting to do this or that, makes one incapable of seeing the whole. If I am a scientist, I see only in a certain direction. If I am an artist, there again. If I have a certain talent or gift, I see only a certain direction. So the mind is incapable of seeing the totality and the immensity of that totality if there is a movement in a particular direction. So can the mind have no direction at all?

This is a difficult question. Please listen to it. Of course, the mind has to have direction when I go from here to the house, or when I have to drive a car, when I have to perform some technical function; but I am talking of a mind that understands the nature of direction and, therefore, is capable of seeing the whole. When it sees the whole, it can then also operate in direction. If I have the whole picture in mind, then I can take in the detail; but if my mind only operates in details, then I cannot take in the whole. If I am concerned with my opinions, with my anxieties, with what I want to do, with what I must do, I cannot see the whole. Obviously. If I come from India with my prejudices, superstitions, and traditions, I cannot see the whole. So can the mind be free of direction? Which does not mean that it is without direction. When it operates from the whole, the direction becomes clear, very strong and effective; but when the mind only operates in a direction according to the pattern it has set for itself, then it cannot see the whole.

There is the content of my consciousness. The content makes my consciousness. Now, can the mind look at it as a whole? Can it just look without any direction, without any judgment, without any choice? That implies no observer at all, for the observer is the past. Can it look with that intelligence which is not put together by thought? For thought is the past. Do it. It requires tremendous discipline; not the discipline of suppression, control, imitation, or conformity, but a discipline that is an act in which the truth is seen. The operation of truth creates its own action, which is discipline.

Can your mind look at its content when you talk to another, in your gestures, in the way you walk, in the way you sit and eat, in the way you behave? Behavior indicates the content of your consciousness, whether you are behaving according to pleasure, reward, or pain, which are part of your consciousness. The psychologists say that, so far, man has been educated on the principle of punishment and reward, hell and heaven. Now, they say that we must be educated only on the principle of reward, that we must not punish but reward—which is the same thing. To see the absurdity of punishment and reward is to see the whole. When you see the whole, intelligence functions when you act, and you are not then behaving according to reward or punishment.

Behavior exposes the content of your consciousness. You may hide yourself behind a polished behavior, a behavior that is very carefully drilled, but such behavior is merely mechanical. From that arises another question: Is the mind entirely mechanical, or is there any portion of the brain that is not mechanical at all?

To go over what has been said: Outside of us, in the political world, in the economic world, in the religious world, in the social world, and so on, mankind is searching. There are gods, new gurus, new leaders. And when you observe all this very clearly you see that man is functioning within the field of thought. Thought, essentially, is never free. Thought is always old because thought is the response of memory as knowledge and experience. Thought is matter. It is of the material world, and thought is trying to escape from that material world into a nonmaterial world. But trying to escape into the nonmaterial world by thought is still material. We have all the moral, social, and economic problems of the individual and the collective. The individual is essentially, intrinsically, part of the collective. The individual is not different from the collective; he may have different tendencies, different occupations, different moods, and so on, but he is intrinsically part of the culture, which is society.

Now, those are facts as to what is going on about us. The facts as to what is going on inside us are very much the same. We are trying to find an answer to the major problems of our human life through the operation of thought—thought which the Greeks imposed upon the West, with their political philosophy, with their mathematics, and so on. Thought has not found an answer and it never will. So we must go then into the whole structure of thought and the content that it has created as consciousness. We must observe the operation of thought in relationship, in our daily life. That observation implies having an insight as to whether it is a fact that the observer is different from the observed, for if there is a difference there must inevitably be conflict, just as there is between two ideologies. Ideologies are the inventions of thought, conditioned by the culture in which they have developed.

Now, can you, in your daily life, observe this? In such observation you will find out what your behavior is, whether it is based on the principle of reward and punishment—as most of our behavior is, however polished and refined. From that observation one begins to learn what real intelligence is. Not the intelligence that is obtained from a book, or out of experience; that is not intelligence at all. Intelligence has nothing whatsoever to do with thought. Intelligence operates when the mind sees the whole, the endless whole—not my country, my problems, my little gods, my meditations. It sees the whole implication of living. And this quality of intelligence has its own tremendous energy.

Saanen, July 14, 1974

2

We were saying that the world outside us and inside us is in a chaotic condition and that the politicians, the leaders, the priests, are all trying to solve our problems in the field of thought. This has been so for centuries upon centuries. But one sees that suffering still goes on: there are endless wars, governments are more or less corrupt, politicians play a crooked game, and ideologies and systems have taken the place of morality and intelligence. Seeing all this, objectively, without any prejudice, without being dedicated to any particular ideology or any system, one observes that thought is divisive and that excellence in thought is not necessarily excellence in conduct.

We are concerned with something that one has to go through, investigate deeply, as deeply as one can, verbally and nonverbally. That demands a great deal of care, affection and consideration, a sense of intimate communication with each other. It demands that you and I share the thing together. You share it not by just listening to a series of words or ideas or concepts—because they are not ideas or concepts with which to agree or disagree—but rather, by really taking part in it with all your heart, with all your mind, with all your energy. Such serious concern and commitment do reveal a great deal, not only the source of our thought and its mischief, but also the source of action.

We live by action; we cannot possibly avoid action. You may withdraw from the world into a monastery, take vows, but that is still action. You may specialize in a particular field which gives you an opportunity for your talent and a career—that is action. Action is also in relationship between you and another. The movement of life is action.

Thought, in civilizations so far, has produced actions which are conflicting, contradictory, opposing; therefore, breeding great mischief and misery. Is excellence in thought and, therefore, action, possible? Or is there always conflict when thought produces action? This is your life, and if you would understand your life, your behavior, your conduct, your relationship, your confusion, to find out what to do so that action is excellent at all levels, then you must ask if there is an action that is not fragmented by thought. Thought is fragmentary in its very nature and yet through thought you are trying to find at all levels an action which will not be contradictory, which will not be regretful, which will be whole, total, complete. Is there an action that is supremely excellent yet is not based on the movement of thought?

Why is thought—upon which we live, upon which our whole social morality is dependent—divisive? Thought is matter. It is the response of the past. It creates the movement of time as yesterday, today, and tomorrow. Thought has its source and root in the past and, having its root in the past, it must create time as movement. One sees that by its very nature, by its very function and structure, thought has its being essentially in the past. It lives in tradition, in the accumulated knowledge that society has acquired, and in the great accumulation of scientific knowledge, all of which is in the past. Thought is essentially a movement from the past. Therefore, it must be divisive. It can pretend, or speculate, or conceive, that it is beyond time; it can imagine a timeless state, but it is still thought. It can pretend that it is going beyond its own limits, but it is still thought. So thought creates a boundary of time around itself, and that is the factor of division.

We are all reared in the field of thought. Education is a movement in thought, the getting of more and more knowledge, the refinement of thought. Thought, being divisive, whatever action it creates must be fragmented, which therefore gives rise to conflict. This is a principle. Man has lived, historically as we know it, in a series of crises and responses, which inevitably breed more conflict. One sees it in the modern world. There is a crisis: thought tries to answer it and, in the very answering of it, more problems are created. One country supplies arms to another knowing well that that is going to create more trouble, and so on, and so on.

So can thought ever bring about an action that is total, whole, sane, not contradictory? Our life *is* contradictory: we live at different levels—at the business level, the family level, the scientific level, the religious level, or at the artistic level—each opposing the other, each specializing in his own department. Specialization becomes exclusive and, therefore, contradictory and, therefore, destructive. Thought, trying to be excellent in its action, specializes and brings about more conflict, more division. Each specialization has its own ambitious end; each career has its own reward, which is contradictory, opposed to affection, care, consideration, and love. Looking at it, one asks if there is an action that is whole, not fragmentary, an action in which there is no regret, no sense of fulfillment, no sense of frustration.

Is there such an action? That is what we are asking all our life, for whatever we do brings a certain pain, a certain confusion, or a certain reward in the pursuit of which we create more division. It is inevitable and natural and logical to ask if there is an action that is not born out of the movement of thought.

I will go into something which may appear to be different, but which is not. We need energy. We have physical energy, emotional energy, the energy of hate, the energy of lust, the energy of great passion, and the energy of great tension that is brought about through the sense of frustration, division, and lack of fulfillment. As one gets older, the body becomes rather worn out, disease and pain come, and energy wastes away. Most of our energy is the product of conflict—I am this, I *should* be that—or of fright and the aggressive desire to continue in a given direction. There is the energy that is brought about through commitment to an ideal—the whole communist world is based on that, from Lenin until now, destroying people by the millions to get what it thinks is right. That gives one tremendous energy. The saint, dedicated to an ideal, to a picture, to an imagination, to a formula, has an extraordinary energy. The idealists have an extraordinary energy. In any form of specialization, energy is required. The more you specialize, the more energy you have. This is what one sees not only in oneself but also outside.

Thought creates its own energy. To produce such a marvelous machine as a submarine, one must have tremendous energy and cooperation, energy that is brought about through an idea, through organized thought. And this kind of energy is always—in the deep sense of that word—destructive, because it is divisive.

Now, is there an energy that is not destructive, that is not divisive, that is not mechanical, not based on idea or a commitment to an ideology? Is there an energy that is not in any way involved in the field of time as thought, movement?

Life is action. In the very living, all relationship is action, movement in action. And that movement, that action, is based on thought. At present, all political, religious, social, and economic life, and moral relativism, are based on thought, which is divisive, contradictory, and breeding misery. Is there an action totally unrelated to all that? To find out, one must have energy. It is not mere intellectual energy, with all its accumulated knowledge, nor emotional energy, which is recognizable by thought and, therefore, still part of thought, but an energy that can bring about a total transformation in the very process of the mind. To inquire very deeply into whether there is an action that is not based on the movement of thought, you need a great deal of energy, not the energy of trying to find an end, not the energy that you have when you are moving in a particular direction, but the energy that can change the content of consciousness.

To put it differently, one knows what the content of one's consciousness is—if one is at all awake and aware, attending to one's behavior, watching, listening. The desire to change that content is a movement in a particular direction. That does give energy but it is divisive. Yet one realizes that the content *must* be totally changed because we cannot go on as we are unless we want to destroy the whole of humanity. The content makes consciousness. Therefore, when there is total transformation of the content there is a different kind of—I won't call it consciousness—a different level altogether. To bring about that change, one needs tremendous energy.

So there must be freedom from direction. Please see the logic of it, the sanity of it. There must be freedom from a conclusion. Although a conclusion may give one a great deal of energy, it is a kind of energy that is wasteful. The mind must be free of the response of thought. It must be free of ideals because they again have direction. The mind must be free of all the divisive movements of thought, as nationality, as race, as religion.

Now, can your mind be free of all that? If it cannot, then do what you will—stand on your head for ten thousand years, or meditate sitting in a posture breathing rightly for another ten thousand years—you will never find the other.

So, can the mind see how stupid, how unintelligent, ideals are? Can it see the truth of it, not just say that they are wrong and put them away? For when you see the truth of it, you are free of it—not as when you logically or historically examine something, but as when you see something poisonous and you drop it. There is no conflict because intelligence sees that it is stupid to go the way of ideals. Can you free your mind from all this?

Do you free it one thing at a time, or do you free it totally? If you free it one thing at a time, that takes energy—looking at how stupid nationality is and dropping it; looking at ideals and seeing that they do not lead anywhere, that they breed conflict, and dropping them. Will you free the mind layer by layer, which will take time, which will take analysis? Traditionally it is said that you must go step by step, that first you must get rid of this, control your body, breathe rightly. Not only traditional but modern psychology says to go step by step, analyze, tear away layer by layer. You can spend years until you die doing that. Will you go through that process taking long years? Now, is that not a wastage of energy? If it is, then how shall the mind empty itself of its content so that it has a totally different kind of energy, a totally different existence? Is there a way of looking at all this totally and, therefore, being totally free of it?

The content of my mind is the content of your mind. The content of your consciousness is the content of my consciousness, slightly modified, with a little more or a little less color, a little more or a little less elaboration, more artistry and less something else, but more or less the same. The mind becomes aware of this and it says, "How can I be aware of the totality of it, not only of the conscious but the unconscious?" I know I can strip layer after layer, both of the conscious as well as of the unconscious; I know I can go through that process, taking time, analyzing, knowing the danger of analysis. I can do that. That is the traditional, accepted way to do this. And I see that that takes infinite time, because every step in analysis must be accurate, otherwise the next step will be corrupted by the previous analysis. So, each analysis must be complete, true, and final, otherwise I am lost. And who is the analyzer? Is not the analyzer the analyzed? So I see that that is not going to do a thing.

So what am I to do? What is my mind to do when it has seen the absurdity of this?

Now, has it actually seen the absurdity of it, or does it imagine it has seen it because somebody has said that it is absurd? We are secondhand people, so am I accepting the authority of another when I say it is absurd? That is a *verbal* assertion without any reality. That acceptance has no validity; it does not produce results. So the mind discards authority, whether it is traditional or the authority I have cultivated out of my own desires and selfishness, my authority which asserts that I know. The mind totally discards authority. Not the authority of law, obviously, but the psychological authority of someone who tells you what to do because you are in confusion and look to somebody who will free you from that confusion, out of your disorder creating the authority. It is historically so. Wherever there is disorder, a man springs up and tyrannically brings about some kind of order, which is total disorder. So, can the mind put away authority because it sees the truth about it, the significance of it, the nature of it? Not just as a reaction against authority, as we do, because when you react against authority you are creating another authority. That is obvious.

Can the mind, your mind, be free of the traditional approach of analysis, introspectively trying to improve? Because you see the truth of being free of authority; therefore, there is no guru, no savior, there are no steps through meditation to come upon something extraordinary. There is something extraordinary, but not through this way. Can the mind put away all this, deny all this, without any resistance? To do that you must look. You must look outwardly and inwardly; hear the music of the world and the discord of the world and the music inwardly and the discord outwardly, because both are the same. We are an intrinsic part of the world. To do this we require energy and this energy is not brought about by concepts, by words. This energy comes when you have insight into the disorder of a mind that functions mechanically in the movement of thought. So, no belief, no idea, no concept, no ideal, no commitment of any kind in that field. Then, through negation of what is false—not through resistance or reaction to the false—through choiceless rejection of what is false, you have a different kind of energy.

It is simple enough. If you climb a mountain you must discard all the things that you have been carrying on the plain, you must put them all aside. It is far more important to understand attachment and the corrupting factors of thought—which are attachment and power, domination in different forms, the corruption of property and possessions—than to search, or to take vows.

Most of us are attached to possessions, whether it is an antique table, which you look after and polish very carefully, or a house, or a person, a group, an idea, or a particular form of experience. Why is the mind attached—to our looks, our hair, our worries? There are so many things we are attached to. Why? And then, knowing that possessions in any form are one of the major corrupting factors in life we say, "Do not possess, have a few clothes that are necessary, but do not possess, take a vow of nonpossession." In that there is a lot of travail: "I want that; I must give it up, I have taken a vow." Possessions corrupt, and we say we must be detached from possessions, so then there is all the conflict involved in that. Understanding attachment is much more important than detachment.

Why is there attachment? Not how to be detached, but why is the mind attached? Why are you attached to your house, to your wife, to your girl, to your ideas, to your meditations, to your systems? Why? What would happen if you were not attached?

Attachment gives a certain occupation to the mind; you constantly think about something. The brain and the mind say, "I must be occupied with something"—with my god, with my sex, with my drink; "I must be occupied"—with the kitchen, or with some social order, or commune, or whatever it is. Out of this demand for occupation there is attachment, holding on to something. Why must the mind be so occupied? What would happen if it were not so occupied? Would it go astray? Would it disintegrate? Would it feel utterly naked, empty? Does the fear of that emptiness demand occupation and, therefore, give importance to the furniture, the book, the idea, and so on? It is out of the empty feeling and loneliness, from not being totally whole, that the mind is attached. Can the mind live, be vital, energetic, full of depth, without attachment? Of course it can.

Is love attachment? Not that love is detachment. When love is attached or detached then it is painful, which we all know; we go through that ugly state.

Power is another form of corruption—political power, religious power, power in the business world, power in the exercise of a certain talent that one has. When you dominate somebody, your cook or your servant, your wife or your husband, there is tremendous pleasure. That is another factor of corruption. That energy, which is so necessary to bring about a transformation in the content of consciousness, is dissipated in all these ways. Can you see all this as fact, as a dangerous fact? Not a relative danger, but a total danger for human beings.

Now, if you see that as real danger, as you would see the danger of a falling rock, you move away from it instantly and you are free of it. To observe this, you need a certain sensitivity, physical as well as psychological, and you cannot have this sensitivity if you are indulging in all kinds of things—drink, sex, overworking. So, if you are at all serious, if you give your attention, your care, your affection to this, then you will see for yourself that out of this freedom from the division that thought has created, there is another kind of energy, which is intelligence. That intelligence is not put together by thought. It is not the cunning intelligence of a politician or a priest or a businessman. It comes out of the freedom that is perceiving the falseness, the unreality of all that. Can your mind see it totally? It cannot see it totally if it has any direction at all.

An intelligent mind acts in the field of thought intelligently, sanely, without resistance. It is free from the structure and implications of attachment, from the action of attachment, from the pursuit of power with all its complications, the ruthlessness of it. It sees the dividing process of thought, and seeing that clearly, totally, it has energy. That energy is intelligence. Having that energy, that intelligence, it can operate in the field of thought, not the other way round.

One can see that there is no division between the outside and the inside, it is an interrelationship. One sees that, and one also sees that one needs energy to transform the mind. So one discards everything that is wasteful, everything that is psychological, everything that breeds division and conflict within the mind. It can be done only when there is an observation of it, not a resistance to it. There is such observation only when the observer is the observed. The observer is the past, put together by thought in terms of experience, knowledge, memory, tradition; they are the essence of the observer. What it observes, which is the result of thought, is still thought. The chaos in the world, the misery, the starvation, the poverty, the brutality, the violence, the mess that is going on, the madness that is going on, is created by thought. And it is the observer who says, "I must change all that"—if he is at all intelligent, if he is at all awake and not concerned with his own little pattern of life. But is the observer different from what he observes? He is put together by thought also, so he *is* the observed. Now when the understanding of that takes place, not as a verbal statement but as a reality, conflict ceases and the mind goes beyond the limitations that thought has imposed on action.

Now can you do this? If you cannot, why not? Is it because you are indolent, lazy, indifferent, not only to your own sorrow, to your own suffering, to your own misery, but to the misery of millions of people, to what is going on in Russia, in India, and elsewhere? Are you totally indifferent to all that, because you want to find God, you want to meditate, you want to learn how to breathe properly, how to have the right kind of sexual relationship, and so on? If you are concerned with the whole of humanity, not just your neighbor or your wife but with the whole of humanity, then when you see that whole you can put the detail in order. But without the perception of the whole you cannot put the detail in order. The politicians, the analysts, the priests, fail to see this. It is only you and I, if we are utterly responsible, concerned, serious, committed, who will be able to meet these problems because we have seen the whole and, therefore, are extraordinarily alive and intelligent and yet able to function in detail.

Saanen, July 16, 1974

3

We have talked of understanding our actions, of our behavior and the content of consciousness. Unless we understand the nature and the structure of this consciousness in which we act, through which all our behavior and all our thinking takes place, it seems to me we shall always be floundering, confused, always living in constant battle within ourselves and outside. We shall never be able to find peace, a sense of deep inward tranquility. In a world that is getting madder and madder every day, where there is so much brutality, violence, deception, and chicanery, it is so necessary that all of us should understand this immense problem of living.

We are going to concern ourselves now with what is called materialism. Materialism means evaluating life as matter, matter in its movement and modification, also matter as consciousness and will. We have to go into it to find out if there is anything more than matter and if we can go beyond it. This is not merely an intellectual amusement and investigation but rather a deep inquiry as to whether our minds and our whole social, economic, and religious life is entirely material. Is all existence, including consciousness and will, the movement and modification of matter?

We are ruled by our senses—taste, smell, touch, and so on; they play a great part in our life. The brain, if you examine it, if you are rather aware of its activities, holds in its cells memory as experience and knowledge. What these cells hold is material; so thought, the capacity to think, is matter. And you can imagine, or construct through thought, as thought, "otherness"; that is to say, other than matter—but it is still matter as imagination. We know that we live in a material world, based on our sensations, desires, and emotions, and we construct a content of consciousness that is essentially the product of thought. We know that, if we do not just romanticize but go into it very deeply and seriously; yet, knowing that, we say there must be "otherness," something beyond that. So thought begins to investigate "the other." But when thought investigates "the other," it is still material. It is important to understand this because we are all so romantically minded; all our religions are sentimental and romantic. Living in this very small field of materialism, we want to have something much greater beyond. That is a natural desire. So thought constructs a verbal or nonverbal structure of God, otherness, immensity, timelessness, and so on. But it is still the product of thought, so it is still material.

So thought creates the form outside, thinking that that form, that image, that prototype, is not material. But that form is the product of thought; the ideal is still the product of thought, so it is still material. If you go to India or elsewhere in the East, they will tell you they accept that, but they say there is a higher self, there is a superconsciousness, which dominates the material, or encloses the material—as in the West you have the soul. They call it by a Sanskrit word, *Atman.* But the *Atman,* the superconsciousness, the soul, is still the product of thought. Thought is matter; whatever its movements, inside, outside, in trying to go beyond itself, it is still material.

So the question arises: Is the mind mechanical? That is, in your mind, are your thoughts, your feelings, your reactions, your responsibilities, your relationships, your ways, your opinions, and so on, merely mechanical; that is, responding according to conditioning, according to environmental influence? If that is the totality of the mind, then we live in a tremendous, inescapable prison.

This has been the problem of man right through the ages. He knows he lives by the senses, by his desires, by touch, by appetites—sexual, intellectual, and otherwise—and he questions: "Is that all?" Then he begins to invent the gods, the supergods, superconsciousness, and so on and so on. Having invented and projected a form, he pursues it, thinking he is tremendously idealistic or tremendously religious. But his pursuit of what he calls "God" or truth is still the pursuit of the product of thought, which is material. See what he has been doing. See what his churches, temples, and the mosques have done to him, to each one of us. Sense this great deception on which he has been fed, which he thinks is extraordinarily idealistic. When one realizes that, in seriousness, it is rather a shock, because one is stripped of all illusion.

If one has gone that far, one then begins to ask if there is a movement other than the movement of thought. How does one find out? If one is trying to find out if there is something beyond the material, then one must examine what is the cause of one's search. Is the cause of one's search an escape from this? Cause means motive. Is all one's inquiry motivated? Because if it is, the root of that is either the seeking of pleasure or the escape from fear. Or, if it is from total dissatisfaction with *what is,* then it projects its own answer. Therefore, to inquire into "the other," my mind must be without cause.

We said, and we are saying again, that there must be a transformation in the mind, not peripheral reformation but a revolution deep in the mind, to solve the problems that thought has created, whether they are religious, economic, social, or moral. If one is really serious, not flippant, not merely amused by intellectual theories or philosophies that are invented by thought, then one must be concerned and totally committed to this question of transforming the content of consciousness. For it is the content that makes up consciousness, as we said. And we asked who the entity is that is to change it. We said that the observer is the observed and that when there is a division between the observer and the observed, the "me" and the "not me," then there is conflict. That conflict is essentially a waste of energy. And when you look into it and find that the observer is the observed, you remove conflict altogether and you have enormous energy because it is no longer wasted in conflict.

Now this energy is either in the field of thought or it is an energy totally different from thought. For a mind that is burdened, conditioned, and shaped by materialistic thought, is there a movement other than that of thought? To find that out, we must look into the cause of this search. Where there is a cause there is time. The cause produces an effect and that effect again becomes a cause. It is not really difficult because this is our life; it becomes difficult when you treat it, or look at it, as something apart from our daily life.

Put it differently. What is virtue, morality? Is morality transient? Is morality relative? Or is it absolute? For us, in the modern world, morality is relative, and that relativism is nearly destroying us. So one asks: What is virtue? Is there an absolute virtue, a sense of no hate under any circumstances? Is there a complete peace, an absolute peace, which can never be disturbed? Can one live without any sense of violence? Or is violence relative, hate modified, and so on? So what is virtue? If you hit me and I hit you back and apologize for it later, that becomes relative. If I have a cause for hating you, or disliking you, or being violent, that cause makes my action not complete and, therefore, relative. Is there a way of living which has no cause? Because the moment you have a cause, living becomes relative. If I have cause to love you—because you give me comfort, psychologically, physically, sexually, morally—it is not love. So where there is a cause, action must be relative. But when there is no cause, action will be absolute.

See what takes place in your life, not in the explanation I am giving. If I depend on you, if I am attached to you, that dependence and attachment have a cause. It is because I am lonely, or I am unhappy, or I want companionship; I want your love, your affection, your care, and so I am attached to you. From that attachment there is great sorrow, there is pain. Because you do not love me, or you only tolerate me, or give me a little of your affection and turn to somebody else, there is jealousy, antagonism, hate, and all the rest that follows. Where there is a cause, then action, morality, must be relative.

Can the mind be free of form, free of the ideal, of form as a cause, so that the mind is capable of going beyond itself? It is very simple really; words make it so difficult. Words are necessary in order to communicate, but if you merely live at the verbal level they are absolutely useless. It is like ploughing, ploughing, ploughing—and you destroy the earth by merely ploughing.

We have this problem, which man right from the beginning has sought to solve, which is: Is all life mechanical? Is all life material? Is all existence, including mind and consciousness and will, matter? Is your whole life that? You may pretend it is not, but actually it is that. Being enclosed in that, thought creates a form, the ideal of the supreme, the highest form of excellence, great nobility, the gods, as well as all the other things that thought has put together in the world, the immense technological movement. It is all matter. And living on this shore as we are, with our wars, our hatreds, our appalling politics—living on this side of the river, which is matter, the mind says, "I want to go across; there must be something there because this life is too stupid." And it is stupid: just to go to the office, to earn money, to take responsibility, to struggle, compete, worry, to despair, to have anxieties, immense sorrows, and then die. We say that is not good enough. We may put it more philosophically, in more extravagant or romantic language, but we see it is stupid and we want something more.

Then we say: "How are we to cross this river to the other shore?" We ask, "Who will take us across?" When we ask that question, there is the priest, the guru, the man who knows, and he says, "Follow me"—and then we are done, because he is exactly like us, because he still functions within the field of thought. He has created the gods, Jesus, Buddha, Krishna. He has created the form and that form is as materialistic as your sensations; it is the product of thought. Now, if that is absolutely clear and there is no romantic escape, no ideological washing of the hands, no seeking comfort and all the other things that lead to illusions, if it is absolutely clear that any modification within the field of consciousness is merely moving from one object to another within the field of thought, then what is the mind to do? Or not to do?

First, such a mind must be in total order, material order, because if it is in disorder it cannot go away from itself. Thought is matter and all its activity within consciousness has created extraordinary confusion and disorder. Politically, religiously, socially, morally, in relationships, in every direction it has created disorder. And that is your life. Unless there is absolute order—and I am using the word *absolute* not *relative*—unless there is absolute order within that area, any cause to move away from that area is still the product of disorder. So there must be order.

Now, how does this order come about politically, religiously, intellectually, morally, physically, in relationships—an absolute order, not a convenient order, not a relative order? How is the mind, which has been trained, educated, conditioned, to live in disorder and to accept disorder, to bring order in itself? Bear in mind, that if you say there is an outside agency which will bring order, then that outside agency is the product of thought and, therefore, it will create contradiction—and, therefore, *disorder*. If you say the action of will will bring about order, then what is will? "I *will* do that"—look at it, find out. When you are aggressive, when you say, "I must do that," what is that will that is in action? Is it not desire, a projected end to be achieved, the achieving of an end projected by thought as an ideal, as a form, as an original pattern? Can thought bring order? That is the way the politicians and the priests and all the so-called reformers are trying to achieve it. *Thought has created disorder*. So what is one to do?

Can the mind, your mind, observe, see, this disorder? One is in disorder. One sees that the exercise of will, the following of another, having desire to overcome disorder, is still within the field of disorder. So one says to oneself, "What am I to do; what is the mind to do?" First of all, does one know disorder? Does the mind see disorder, or does it know only the description of disorder? You describe to me a mountain, its beauty, its snow, its lines against the blue sky, the depth of shadows in the forest, the running waters, the murmur of trees, the beauty of it all. You describe it to me and the description catches my mind and I live with that description. But the description is not that which is described. So one asks oneself, "Am I caught in the description, or am I actually seeing disorder?" One is intellectual, the other is factual. Now, is the mind observing its disorder, which means no word, not being caught in the description, but merely observing this enormous disorder? Can the mind so observe? And in observing its own disorder, is there an "observer" looking at it, or is there no observer at all, but merely the observing?

I observe you, I see you. I met you last year; you were pleasant or unpleasant to me; you flattered or insulted me, or neglected me. The memory of that remains. This year I meet you and the memory responds. That memory is the past and also that memory is the observer. Of course. Can the mind observe all the disorder, social and moral and so on, which is created by thought, in which I am, which is part of me? Can it observe this disorder without the observer? If the observer is there looking at disorder, then there is a division between the observer and the observed. In that division, conflict takes place: "I must control it, I must change it, I must suppress it, I must overcome it," and so on. Now when the observer is not, and there is only observation, then there is no conflict, there is merely observing. Then there is energy to go beyond disorder.

Where there is division, there must be disorder. The observer, rooted in the past, is essentially the factor of division. Now can the mind see the truth of that and observe the actual disorder of your life, not the description? Can it observe your disorder, your confusion, your anxieties, your contradictions, your selfish demands, all that? Observe. And if it observes without the observer there is then the going beyond it, which means total order, not relative order but mathematical order that is essential before you can go any further. Without order in the material world, in the world of matter, in the world of thought, the mind has no basis, no foundation on which to move.

Therefore, there must be observation of behavior. Do I behave according to a motive, according to circumstances? Is my behavior pragmatic, or is it under all circumstances the same? Not the same in the sense of copying a pattern; is it a behavior that is never relative, that is not based on reward and punishment? Inquire into it, observe it and you will find how terrible your behavior is, how you look to a superior and inferior and all the other things you do. There is never a constant movement free of the motive of reward and punishment.

Then also you have to inquire into relationship in the material world. Relationship is of the highest importance, because life *is* relationship. What is your relationship? Have you any relationship? Relationship means to respond adequately to any challenge. As I inquire into relationship, is my relationship with another personal and intimate, or not so intimate? Is it based on my opinions, my memories, my hurts, my demands, my sexual appetites? If my relationship to you is relative, it changes: I am moody one day, not moody the next day, the next day I am affectionate, and the third day I hate you, and the fourth day I love you, and so on, and so on. If that relationship is not satisfactory, I will go to somebody else. This is the game that we have been playing for centuries. Now it is more open, more extravagant, more vulgar, that is all.

So my mind has to find out what its relationships actually are. Unless there is complete harmony in the material world in which I live, which is part of me, in me, which is my consciousness, the mind cannot possibly go beyond itself. That is why your meditations, your postures, your breathing exercises, your going to India and searching, are so utterly meaningless.

So, is my relationship relative? Is all relationship relative? Or is there no relationship at all except when the division as the "me" and the "you" does not exist? I am related to you because I love you, because you give me food, clothes, shelter, you give me sex, you give me companionship. I have built a marvelous image about you; we may get annoyed with each other, irritated, but that is trivial. And I hold on to you; I am attached to you, and in that attachment there is great pain, there is great sorrow, suffering, torture, jealousy, antagonism. And then I say to myself, "I must be free of that." And in freeing myself from that I attach myself to somebody else. And the game begins again. So I say to myself, "What is this relationship? Is there a relationship? Can there ever be a relationship?" There is the "me" that is pursuing my appetites, my ambitions, my greed, my fears, my wanting to have more prestige, greater position, and so on; and there is the other also pursuing his or her own demands. Is there any relationship possible at all between two human beings, each functioning with and pursuing his own exclusive, selfish, demands?

There may be no relationship in that direction, but there may be relationship when there is no "me" at all. When the "me," as thought, is nonexistent, I am related; then I am related to you, the trees, the mountains, to the rivers, to human beings. That means love—does it not?—which has no cause.

Consciousness, with its content, is within the field of matter. The mind cannot possibly go beyond that unless it has complete order within itself and conflict in relationship has come totally to an end—which means a relationship in which there is no "me."

This is not just a verbal explanation: the speaker is telling you what he lives, not what he talks about; if he does not live it, it is hypocrisy, a dirty thing to do.

When the mind has order and the sense of total relationship, then what takes place? Then the mind is not seeking at all, it is not capable of any kind of illusion. That is absolutely necessary, because thought can invent any experience, any kind of vision, any kind of superconsciousness and all the rest of it. There is no ideal, there is no form, there is only behavior, which is order and the sense of relationship for the whole of man. There you have the foundation.

Now another question arises from this: Is the brain totally conditioned? This brain of mankind has had thousands and thousands of experiences; it is educated with a great deal of accumulated knowledge from books and elsewhere, and that is there in the brain. And thought operates only within that field of the known. It can invent a field that says, "Apart from knowing, 'I' am there," but that is too silly. So my mind is asking: Is the whole brain conditioned by the economic, social, environmental, religious, culture it has lived in? Is the mind, in which is included the brain, totally conditioned within the borders of time? Is the mind a complete slave?

Do not say yes or no, for then you have settled it, then there is nothing more into which to inquire. But a mind that is asking, groping, looking, without any motive, without any direction, says, "Is the mind totally conditioned and, therefore, mechanical?" And you see that it is mechanical when it is functioning in the field of knowledge, whether scientific, technological, or the priestly tradition. It is mechanical; there is repetition, repetition, repetition. That is what is going on—the repetition of desire, sexual or otherwise, repeating, repeating, repeating. Therefore, the mind asks itself, "Is the totality of this thing mechanical, or is there, in this field of the mind, an area that is not mechanical?" Can the mind be free of causation, for where there is causation, all movement as thought must be mechanical.

Saanen, July 18, 1974

4

Our chief concern is the transformation, the radical change, of the human mind. The human mind includes the brain, the heart, the organism as a whole, the mind that has created this world around us, the world of corruption, violence, brutality, vanity, and all the structures that bring about war. We are concerned with the change of the content of consciousness because the content makes consciousness. Unless that radical revolution, that psychological change, comes about, there will be no end to conflict, no end to suffering and all the violence that is going on throughout the world.

This change cannot possibly be brought about without knowing oneself, self-knowledge. This is not knowledge of the "higher self" or knowledge of some "supreme consciousness," for they are still within the field of thought. Unless one understands one's self, the self of every day—what it thinks, what it does, its devotions, its deceptions, its ambitions, all its self-centered activities, its identification with something noble or ignoble, the state or some ideal—one is still within the field of the "me." Unless one understands that narrowing field, of which one is so little aware—the field in which there is the unconscious as well as the conscious, which is concerned with the individual ego, its individual ambitions and reactions, which are essentially a part of the whole, part of the community, part of the culture in which it lives—unless we understand that radically, the content of consciousness cannot possibly be transformed.

"Understanding" is not an intellectual, an emotional, or a passing, thing. It is something that comes with action and, therefore, it is a complete understanding and not a partial understanding. In understanding oneself, one's consciousness and its content—for there is no consciousness without content—one sees there are two principal factors, pleasure and fear. They cannot be separated. Where there is the pursuit, the insistence on, and the demand for pleasure, there must be in its wake fear. In understanding fear, one must not disregard the fact of pleasure.

Thought is the measure of fear. Thought is the response of memory, which is experience and knowledge stored up in the brain cells and tissues. Thought is matter. The whole world is constructed from thought, is based in its very nature and substance and activity on thought. One has to find out whether it is thought that has bred fear. Not how to be free of fear; freedom from fear will inevitably come about when one understands the structure, the nature, and the functioning of thought.

When one observes the whole process of thought—which has created the world with all its religions, with all its gods, with its saviors, which has created the materialistic world in which we live—one sees that, as long as we function there and remain there, fear must continue. Fear is the cause of loneliness, of deprivation, both physical and psychological; it is the cause of attachment to property, to people, ideas, concepts, nationalities, families. As long as there is this functioning of thought within the material world—and it has to function in that world—fear must remain. What else has one if one lives in that world, for there one must seek security, physical or psychological! As long as the mind seeks material security, as long as the mind asserts a permanency, there must be fear. Yet the brain can only function effectively, objectively, rationally, if it has complete security. That is obvious. When it has no security, it seeks security in belief in gods, in symbols, in ideologies, in nationalities, which leads to neurotic action. As long as I call myself a nationalist of a particular country, I am behaving neurotically; I bring about conflict and division between people. That is one of the causes of fear. When you realize that, when you are aware of its whole nature, are you still a nationalist? If you are, there must be the continuance of pleasure and of fear.

If the mind lives totally in the material world, then nothing exists but matter, which is thought, consciousness and will. If the mind lives there, fear will go on, because there, there is nothing else but the demand for material security and permanency. Where there is that demand, there must be fear.

There are all the various fears concealed in the very recesses of one's consciousness: racial, collective, the fear of famine, and so on. There are hidden fears and extraordinarily subtle forms of pleasure. There is fear, both conscious and unconscious, the fear of death, of loneliness, of losing a job, the fear of what people will say, the fear of your own attachments and of losing them, the fear of not succeeding, not becoming great. Can they all be exposed—and without analysis? We have seen the futility of analysis, how the analyzer and the analyzed are the same. So, what is a mind to do when it realizes the absurdity, the falseness, of analysis or introspective examination?

To understand what the mind is to do, we must go into the question of meditation. When we use the word *meditation,* hear it as though you have never heard the word before. What is meditation? Not how to meditate; that is irrelevant, because the moment you understand what meditation is, it happens naturally, like breathing. To find out what meditation is, the real meaning, can you learn from another? Volumes have been written about it. People have meditated according to a particular system—Zen or the many, many varieties and methods of the Hindu systems. They all imply an end to be achieved through control. Control implies a controller. And is the controller different from the controlled? The meditative groups, with their systems and their philosophies, say, "Control your thought!" Thought wanders about and that wandering about is a wastage of energy; therefore, they say thought must be absolutely held, disciplined, subjugated in the pursuit of that thing called enlightenment, God, truth, what you will, the nameless. That implies a controller, obviously. And who is the controller? Is he different in quality, in nature, from that which he says he is going to control? This is very important to understand.

The speaker wants to point out that one can live completely in daily life, without any control, against all the traditions, against all your education, your social and moral behaviors. To live a life absolutely without any controls means you have to understand very, very deeply who is the controller and what is the controlled, for this is part of meditation. Is the controller different from that which he is controlling, which is thought? Some say the controller is different, that he is the higher self, that he is part of the higher consciousness, that he is the essence of understanding or the essence of the past, which has accumulated so much knowledge. But the controller is still within the field of thought; and however much that thought may be elevated, it is still within the area of time and measure.

Do you see the truth of this? Not the verbal acceptance of it, or the intellectual comprehension of it, but the truth that all the gods, Christian or Hindu, all of them, are the invention of thought. Thought can project itself into all kinds of states, into all kinds of illusions, and when thought says there is the higher self, it is still within the field of thought and, therefore, that higher self is still matter.

When you see that the controller is the controlled, the whole aspect of meditation changes. Meditation means the emptying of consciousness of its content. Then only can the mind and the brain be absolutely quiet. That absolute—not relative—that absolute quietness is necessary to observe. Not to experience! Experiences we have had, of every kind, and thought desires more experience, including the experience of another state, another dimension. We are fed up with this world and its experiences; they are boring, they are limited, confined, narrow, and we want an experience which is totally different. Now, to experience involves recognition. If I do not recognize, is there an experience? I have had the experience of looking at a mountain, the beauty of it, the shadow, the lovely deep blue of an early morning, the whole sense of something extraordinary and magnificent. That experience cannot exist if there is no relationship to the past. And so experience implies recognition from the past. And the mind wants to experience something supreme. *But to recognize it, it must already have had it.* Therefore, it is not the supreme, it is still the projection of thought.

Meditation is that in which there is no experience. In that there is no element of time, which implies movement and direction. Direction implies will. Can the mind empty itself of time, direction, and movement, which implies the ending of thought? That is the whole problem.

We need knowledge to function; to speak any language, we need knowledge; to drive a car, we need knowledge; to do anything, we need knowledge. What place has knowledge in meditation? Or has it no place at all? It has no place because knowledge is merely a continuation of the past, it is still the movement of time. So can the mind empty itself of the past and come upon that area of itself that is not touched by thought? We have only operated, so far, within the area of thought as knowledge. Is there any other part, any other area of the mind, which includes the brain, which is not touched by human struggle, pain, anxiety, fear and all the violence, all the things that man has made through thought? The discovery of that area is meditation.

That implies the discovery of whether thought can come to an end yet still operate when necessary in the field of knowledge. We need knowledge, otherwise we cannot function, we would not be able to speak, nor be able to write, and so on. Knowledge is necessary to function and its functioning becomes neurotic when status becomes all important, which is the entering of thought as the "me." So knowledge is necessary and yet meditation is to discover, or come upon, or to observe, an area in which there is no movement of thought. Can the two live together, harmoniously, *daily?*

Yoga exercises are excellent to keep the body healthy, and so on. But through them you can never come upon the other, never! Because if you give them all importance, you are not giving importance to the understanding of yourself, which is to be watchful, to be aware, to give attention to what you are doing, every day of your life. That is, to give attention to how you speak and what you say, to what you think, how you behave, whether you are attached, whether you are frightened, whether you are pursuing pleasure, and so on, to be aware of the whole movement of thought. If you are and you are really serious about it, then you will have established right relationship. Obviously. When all things about us are chaotic, when the world is going to pieces, as it is, relationship becomes extraordinarily important. When there is the establishing of total relationship, whole relationship—not between you and me, but human relationship with the whole of the world—then you have the basis for meditation.

From there you can go on to behavior, how you behave. If your behavior is based on pleasure or on reward, it is not behavior. It is merely the pursuit of pleasure, and from that fear arises. Relationship, behavior, and order are absolutely essential if you want to go into the question of meditation. If you have not laid this foundation, then do what you like, stand on your head and breathe in and out for the next ten thousand years and repeat words, words, but there will be no meditation. If you have the money, you can go to India. But I do not know why you go, you will find no enlightenment there. *Enlightenment is where you are.* And where you are, you have to understand yourself. Having established that, laid the foundation there of order—not mechanical order but order which is virtue from moment to moment, which is not following a pattern, not the order of the establishment, not the order or the virtue of society, which is immoral—then you can go into the question of finding out what meditation is.

Meditation implies a quality of mind that is absolutely silent. Not *made* silence, not a contrived act brought about through will, but a silence that comes naturally when you have established order, relationship, and behavior. Silence is necessary. If my mind is chattering, as most minds are, in that chatter there may be a period of silence. Between two chatterings there may be a period of silence. But that is not silence. Silence is not the absence of noise; it is not the absence of conflict. Silence comes only when the content of consciousness has been completely understood and gone beyond, which means the observer and the observed are one and there is no controller. When there is no controller—which does not mean that you live a life of nondiscipline—when there is no controller, no observer, then action is instantaneous and it brings a great deal of energy.

Meditation means the emptying of consciousness of its content and that happens only when you observe your consciousness and its content without the observer. Can you look at your wife, your husband, your girl, your boy, or the mountain, without the observer? The observer is the past. As long as there is the observer, he will inevitably translate everything he observes in terms of the past; therefore, he is the maker of time. He divides the observed and the observer. In that there is conflict. When there is observation without the observer, there is no conflict, no past; there is only the fact and you have the energy to go beyond it. Do it and you will find out.

Meditation implies a gathering of all energy. You have established order, relationship, behavior; therefore, you are not dissipating energy in that field. That energy is necessary to look without the observer and you have the energy to go beyond. With that energy, which has not been dissipated, the mind sees that there is an area which is not touched by thought. But all this requires tremendous attention and discipline. It is not just a plaything for immature people. Meditation requires tremendous discipline. The word *discipline* means to learn—not control, subjugate, imitate, and conform. Discipline means to learn. From the word *discipline* comes "disciple," one who is willing to learn from the master, *to learn*. But here there is neither a disciple nor a master but only the act of learning, all the time. And that requires a great deal of attention, a great deal of energy, so that you are watching and thus, you create no illusions. It is so easy to create illusions; they come when you are pursuing, demanding, wanting, an experience. Desire creates illusions.

All this implies a mind that is very, very serious and a heart that is of love, that has never been hurt. We human beings, from childhood on, are hurt. Our parents hurt us, and in the business world we are hurt. We are hurt in every direction, and when we are hurt we cannot possibly love. So is it possible for a mind that has been hurt to be free of all that hurt, which is part of consciousness? You will find, when you look at it, that it is utterly and irrevocably possible to empty all hurts and, therefore, to love, to have compassion. To have compassion means to have passion for all things, not just between two people, but for all human beings, for all things of the earth, the animals, the trees, everything the earth contains. When we have such comparison we will not despoil the earth as we are doing now, and we will have no wars.

To a mind that is serious, totally dedicated, concerned, meditation means something extraordinary, something immense. In meditation, mind discovers space. Space is held within a room and there is space outside it. Thought as the "me" creates the narrow space in which it acts; it has created, through hurt, through all kinds of reasons, walls within which it lives. There is that narrow space and the space which thought has created outside of itself. Is there a space which has no frontiers, which has no boundaries and, therefore, no center? This is meditation, to find out.

As long as there is a center, the "me" or the idea of the "me," with all its attachments, that very center creates a space around itself. Where there is a center, there must be a border. The border may be extended, but it is still limited by the space that the center has created. Meditation means to come upon that space in which there is no center; therefore, no direction; therefore, no time. Without meditation and the coming upon that thing which is not able to be experienced, which is not to be put into words, which has no time, which has no continuity, life has very little meaning. You may have a lot of money, or no money; you may be attached to your property, to your wife, to your friend, or you may worship your particular little god, which thought has invented, but as long as you live there, there will be suffering, pain, anxiety, and violence. And that has no meaning in itself, obviously. Only when you come upon this space—not invent it, not project it, not bring it about through any system—then only does life have an extraordinary sense of beauty and meaning.

Saanen, July 28, 1974

A RELATIONSHIP WITH THE WORLD

1

We are the world. The world is you and me, the world is not separate from you and me. We have created this world—the world of violence, the world of wars, the world of religious divisions, sex, anxieties, the utter lack of communication with each other, with no sense of compassion, consideration for another. Wherever one goes in any country throughout the world, human beings, that is, you and another, suffer; we are anxious, we are uncertain, we don't know what is going to happen. Everything has become uncertain. Right through the world as human beings we are in sorrow, fear, anxiety, violence, uncertain of everything, insecure. There is a common relationship between us all. We are the world essentially, basically, fundamentally. The world is you, and you are the world. Realizing that fundamentally, deeply, not romantically, not intellectually but actually, then we see that our problem is a global problem. It is not my problem or your particular problem, it is a human problem.

So we are dealing with the human, global problem, which is that you as a human being are living in a disintegrating world. So when we talk about relationship, we are talking about the relationship of man to man. When you understand *that* relationship, then you can come very much closer, which is the relationship between you and your neighbor, you and your wife, you and your son, and so on. Unless you have a global, universal, sense of the whole human being, you will live merely in fragments, as an American, or a European, a communist, a socialist, a Hindu, or a Buddhist—and all the rest of the divisions that man has made. We are concerned with mankind, which is you. Wherever you go, man is suffering, man is afraid, man wants to find out if there is some truth anywhere—if there is any god, if there is anything sacred, whether there is an eternity or only the ending of life and whether man can ever be free from fear, find an end to sorrow.

When we say man we mean woman also; let us not quarrel about words, it becomes rather childish.

In our examination together, there is no authority, there is no teacher and the taught, there is no guru and the disciple; therefore, there is no authority. In the psychological world, in the world of the spirit, there is no authority. You are not following the speaker or accepting what he is saying. It is good to have a great deal of skepticism, but that skepticism must be kept on a leash, and you must know when to let it go and when to hold it. In examining this vast problem of existence, both of us must be very clear and understand that there is no authority, the one who knows and the other who does not know. Together we are looking into this. Whether you are capable of looking is a different matter. Whether you are intensely, consistently, pursuing the investigation depends on you. If you do not have the energy, the intention, the necessary persistence, then you make authority. If you are lazy, indolent, then you give authority to another. Or if you are disorderly in your life and you see orderliness in another then you make him into an authority. So, please, we are going together to examine without any sense of authority, which means there is freedom to look. Because one of the causes of this disintegrating society in which we live is that we are followers; we accept spiritual authority, the intermediary, the priest, the analyst, as our guide in matters of the spirit. We become incapable when we give ourselves over to another to find out about ourselves. We don't seem to be able to look into ourselves and examine very closely the whole of human existence—which is yourself. If we are examining, investigating together, and there is no authority, only freedom to examine, see the beauty of it: then you and I have a relationship.

In the human being and in the society in which he lives, one of the basic causes of this disintegration, this breaking up, is the utter lack of religious spirit. Religion means accumulating all your energy to investigate truth; to find out, to come upon that state of mind or consciousness in which there is truth that is not invented by thought. One of the factors of disintegration is the utter lack of the religious mind, and another is the lack of morality—not a Christian morality, or Hindu morality, or the morality of permissiveness; morality implies orderliness, basic order. It is not order according to a pattern, according to the convenience of environment, but an order that comes when you understand the nature of disorder, and that morality is a thing that is living.

This disintegrating world is your mind. You are the essence of society, you are the basis of society in your relationships. And when there is no relationship then there is disintegration. So what is relationship? Relationship is the basis of our existence, the basis of our society, and unless there is deep understanding of that and a transformation in that relationship, we cannot go further into the question of meditation, what is religion, what is truth, and so on. So that is the bedrock upon which we must stand clearly.

We must find out what it means to have right relationship, accurate relationship. The word *accurate* means factually correct. What is relationship? What does it mean to be related to another—at the physical level, sexual level, psychological level, emotional level, intellectual level, and at the level of what one calls love? If that whole nature and structure of relationship is not understood clearly and lived daily, to go to meditate is utterly infantile, has no meaning, because then meditation becomes merely a futile escape. Unless you establish right relationship between you and another, that being the very basis of existence, trying to meditate becomes an evasion of the actual that leads to all kinds of neurotic, destructive results.

So what is actual relationship in our daily life with each other? If you examine it very closely, and are not afraid, see what is taking place. You have an image about yourself, don't you? You have a picture, an idea, a concept of yourself, and the person you are related to has his or her concept, her image, her picture about herself. Please, you are looking at yourself, you are not merely listening to these words. Words are a mirror, and the mirror becomes useless when you are looking at yourself actually. So you and the other, man and woman, boy or girl, or husband and wife, and so on, each human being, has a picture, an image, a conclusion, an idea about herself or himself.

If you have lived with another for a week, or a hundred weeks, you have made a picture of the other, and the other has made a picture of you. That is a fact, isn't it? Are you afraid to look at that picture? That picture has been built through many days, many years, many incidents: nagging, pleasure, comfort, fear, domination, possession, attachment, and so on and so on and so on. Each person has an image of the other. That is an actuality, isn't it? And you call that relationship. That is a relationship between two pictures, between two images. Right? You are not agreeing with the speaker, you are looking at the fact. These pictures or images or conclusions are memories, which each has put together, stored up in the brain. And they are reacting to each other according to those images. You have been hurt, and that hurt is a memory, stored up in the brain, and that reacts. So our relationship is not actual but from memories. If you are married, you have built a picture about your wife, and the wife has built a picture, an image about you. Those pictures, those images are the nagging, the casual remarks, the hurts, the pleasures, the comforts, the sexual memories, all that. And the relationship is between these two verbal pictures in memory; it is not actual; and, therefore, there is always division and conflict. When you have been hurt in that relationship, it is the image you have built about yourself that has been hurt.

I wonder if you are actually observing it in yourself, or listening to the speaker and agreeing with the speaker. They are two different facts. If you are agreeing with the speaker, that has very little significance. Do you actually see that you have built an image about yourself and that hurt exists because of that image?

So in this relationship of human beings, hurt has taken place. The image has been hurt. Unless you heal that image totally there must always be conflict. There are past hurts and you may receive further hurts. You have been hurt in the past; unfortunately this happens from childhood—in school, in college, at home. Right throughout life one is hurt, and because one is hurt, one builds a wall around oneself to resist, not to be hurt anymore. And when one builds a wall around oneself, division takes place. You may say, "I love you," but it is just words, because a division exists.

Is it possible not to be hurt at all? Which doesn't mean build a wall of resistance so that nothing can touch you, but to live without resistance, which means never to be hurt.

Do you know what it means to be hurt? When a child is compared with another, that is a hurt. Any form of comparison hurts. Any form of imitation, conformity, hurts, not only verbally but deeply. And when one is hurt, out of that hurt there is violence. So is it possible never to be hurt? How are we to deal with past hurts and prevent future hurts? We will find out.

When you say, "I am hurt," what is this "I" that is hurt? You say, "You have hurt me"—by your word, by a gesture, by discourtesy, and so on and so on—what is hurt? Is it not the image that you have built about yourself? Please, do look at it. That image is one of the factors that society, education, and environment have built in you. "You" are that picture, that image, the name, the form, the characteristics, the idiosyncrasies, and so on. All that is you, the picture, the image which you are. And that image has been hurt. You have a conclusion about yourself, that you are this or that, and when that conclusion is disturbed you are hurt. So can you live without a conclusion, without a picture, without an image about yourself? As long as you have an image about yourself, you are everlastingly hurt. You may resist it, you may build a wall around yourself, but when there is a wall around yourself, when you withdraw, there is a division, and where there is a division there must be conflict—as with the Arab and the Jew, the Hindu and the Muslim, the communist and the noncommunist. Where there is a division, it is the law that there must be conflict.

So is it possible not to be hurt at all? That is, to have an innocent mind, a mind that is incapable of being hurt. It is very important to find out if one can live that in daily life. Not go off to some monastery or some community where you all agree together, becoming mushy and sentimental, but actually *in daily life* to find out if you can live without an image and, therefore, never be hurt, which means never to have conflict, never to have psychological division. We are going to find out. We are going to examine whether it is possible to live that way.

First be aware that one has this image. When I have an image about myself and that is hurt, and my wife has an image about herself and she is hurt, how can we have any kind of relationship? So is it possible not to have an image, which means not to be hurt? One has been hurt in the past, and one has resisted it, built a wall around oneself, is frightened of being hurt more; therefore, withdraws, becomes isolated. Now how will you deal with the past hurts? Will you analyze why you have been hurt, the causes of your hurt. Will you go into it analytically?

Look at the analytical tradition. We have accepted analysis as part of our life. If you cannot analyze yourself you go to the professional. What is the process of analysis? There is the analyzer and the analyzed. See the division already. But is not the analyzer the analyzed? So you have created an artificial division between the analyzer and the analyzed, but in actuality the analyzer is the analyzed. So there is a fundamental error in the process of analysis. And in the process of analysis you take time—days, months, years—playing the game and enriching each other in your own peculiar ways, financially and emotionally, and all the rest of it. So, realizing that fundamental error in the process of analysis, how is one to be free of all the past hurts, and any hurts that may come in the future?

The speaker and you are sharing this question, to find out actually, in daily life, whether it is possible to live without a single hurt, because then you will know what love is.

Hurt and flattery are the same, aren't they? Both are different forms of hurts. You are flattered, and you like it, and the flatterer becomes your friend. So that also is another form of encouraging the image. The one you want, the other you don't want. We are now dealing only with what we don't want, which is not to be hurt; but we want the other, which is pleasurable, which is comforting, pleasing to the images that we have. So both are the same. Now how am I, how is a human being, to be free of hurt? So we have to go into the question of what it is to be attentive.

What does it mean to attend? If you know what it means to attend, it may solve the problem. Have you ever given total attention to anything? Complete attention in which there is no center from which you attend? When there is a center from which you attend then there is a division. Let's put it differently. You know what it is to be aware. One is aware of the trees under which we are sitting, aware of the branches, the color of the branches and their thickness, of the leaves, the shadows, aware of all the nature, the beauty of it. [The Ojai talks took place in the open in a grove of oaks.] Then you are also aware of sitting on the ground, the color of the carpet, the microphone. And can you be aware of all this, the microphone, the carpet, the earth, the color of the leaves, and so on, the blue shirt, be aware of all that without any choice? To look at it without any choice, judgment, just to look.

If you can look without any judgment, without any choice, just observe, in that observation there is no observer. The moment the observer comes in prejudice begins, the like and the dislike, "I prefer this, I don't prefer that," division takes place. So there is attention only when there is no entity who says, "I am attending." Please, it is important to understand this. Because if there is attention, when there is an awareness in which there is no choice, no judgment, merely observation, then you will see you will never be hurt again, and the past hurts are wiped away. But the moment the observer comes in then the observer gets hurt.

So, when there is complete attention, there is no hurt. If someone says the speaker is a fool or arrogant; in listening to the word and giving complete attention to it, there is no past hurt or future hurt because there is no entity who is observing. Please, this is very important, because as long as there is a division there must be conflict. It is very important, in dealing with fear, with pleasure, with sorrow, with death, to see that as long as there is a division between the observer, the experiencer, the thinker and the thought, there must inevitably be conflict, division, fragmentation and, therefore, disintegration. So can you observe the tree, yourself, your neighbor, observe life completely attentively? Then can you observe with total attention the picture that you have about yourself? And when you give that complete attention is there a picture at all?

When there is no image, no picture, no conclusion, then what is the relationship between two human beings? Now our relationship is based on division, which is an obvious fact. The man goes to the office where he is brutal and ambitious, greedy; then he comes home and he says, "Darling, how lovely you are." So there is contradiction in our life and, therefore, our life is a constant battle and, therefore, there is no relationship. To have real human relationship is to have no image whatsoever, no picture, no conclusion. And it is quite complex, because you have memories. Can you be free of memories of yesterday's incidents? All that is implied. Then what is the relationship between two human beings who have no images? You will find out if you have no image. That may be love.

So can one live, actually in daily life, without division; which means without war, without conflict?

Ojai, April 3, 1976

2

All our life is based on thinking. All our actions are the result of thought, either from the deep past, or from immediate necessities according to environment. Thought guides our whole life. Thought has divided us into nations, classes, into religious sects, beliefs—with their dogmas, rituals. Thought has built the churches—Catholic, Protestant, Hindu, and the various Eastern religious structures and propaganda. I think this is irrefutable fact.

What is thought? Why has it become such an extraordinarily important factor in our life? Our education, our relationship is based on thought, on image, verbal structure. It is all put together by thought. Why is it that thought has become so persistent, continuous, and divisive?

In examining why thought has become so extraordinarily important, we have also to go into the question of consciousness.

Consciousness is filled with thought and the things of thought. Whether it is conscious or unconscious, deep down it is still the movement of thought, from the past, meeting the present, and creating the future. All that is the movement of thought. Movement implies time. Thought implies measurement. So thought is a movement, time and measure. What is the process of thought? What is the nature and the structure of thought? That is our life: we act, we live according to certain patterns laid down by thought, consciously or unconsciously, deep down. It seems extraordinarily important to understand thought because thought has divided people, nationally, geographically, according to their beliefs, according to their dogmas. Thought has built up the whole memorial structure as the "me" and the "you," the ego, the personality, and so on.

We are trying to find out if there is another consciousness that is not put together by thought and, therefore, we must examine this consciousness as we know it, which is filled with the things of thought. What is the source of thinking? Why is thinking, thought, fragmentary? From where does thought come? What is the nature of consciousness, and why is that consciousness filled with all this movement of thought? One must discover for oneself what is the beginning of thought.

Isn't thought a reaction of memory? Memory is knowledge stored up as experience. There is an experience, knowledge of that experience as memory, and the response of that memory is thinking. So the source of thinking is in the past. So thought springs from the past. If you examine it, all our lives are based in the past, our roots are in the past. Knowledge is the past, there is no knowledge of the future, or of the present. There is knowledge of the present only when there is a complete understanding of what the structure and the nature of the past is—and ending it.

So thought is the response of the movement from the past. The past is stored up in the brain as experience and knowledge. And why is thought fragmentary? Why has thought built divisions between people—as Christians, Buddhists, communists, socialists, capitalists, believers and nonbelievers, and so on? Is there an action that is not based on thought, that is not divisive, that is not fragmentary, in which there is no regret, pain, sorrow? The fragmentary process is seen in our daily life as the "me" and the "you," "we" and "they," the Christian, the non-Christian, and so on and so on and so on. That fragment of thought may think there is God, but God then is still the product of a fragment.

Thought has filled our consciousness with its own fragments, and then thought says, "I must go beyond this fragment, I must find enlightenment, I must find God, I must find truth, I must find Nirvana," whatever you like to call it. A fragment is trying to understand that which is whole—that which is sane, healthy, holy—the word *whole* implies all that. So the fragment has been trying to grasp or come upon that which is whole. So it meditates, it controls, it tries to follow a system in order to arrive at that, but it is still the movement of time as a fragment in measure.

So why is thought a fragment? Why has it become a fragment? Why has thought divided you and me, we and they, the Buddhist, communist, socialist? Can thought see the whole? Can thought see itself as a fragment? Or can it never see itself, see its own limitation, see its own fragmentary movement and, therefore, never see the whole.

Now leave it there for the moment and we will come to it in a different way.

Does one realize, see that one's consciousness is its content? The content of consciousness makes consciousness. If you are a Christian, the content of your consciousness, all the beliefs, the dogmas, the rituals, the reactions, the attachments, the anxieties, the fears, the sorrows, the aspirations, the images which you have built about yourself and about others, all your conclusions, your prejudices, all that is the content of your consciousness. It is so. So your consciousness is made up of the things it contains. And the content of consciousness is filled by the things of thought—your scholastic knowledge, the knowledge of your own experiences, prejudices, and so on. So your consciousness is fragmentary. And within that area we are trying to find reality, truth, by expanding it, trying to go beyond it.

Are you just accepting my words or are you observing for yourself, watching the content of your own consciousness, and seeing that it is filled with all the things that you have accumulated? Not only the things you have accumulated, but what the past generations have accumulated—the traditions, the manner of behaving. All that is your consciousness, and because it is fragmentary and, therefore, divisive, it must always be in conflict. Thought realizes this and then says to itself, "I must go beyond it"—through meditation, through control, through suppression, through various forms of enlarging consciousness. This is the game we are playing all the time, holding on to our content, and trying to go beyond it.

So thought cannot see the whole, because it is fragmentary. If thought could see the whole it would be the whole, it would not make an effort to be the whole—the whole being healthy, not divisive, sane, and holy. But it is not. Now, the observer is fragmentary; it says, "I am conscious of the limitations of my thought." That observer is the past and the past, which is fragmentary, makes every action fragmentary. The past is the knowledge, experience, all the things that human beings have gathered together for centuries and centuries. And we think the ascent of man lies through knowledge. One questions whether knowledge is the instrument of ascent, although various professors and experts say knowledge is the way because knowledge is the past. The movement of thought is time, and we think time will make us progress, evolve, grow, but time is also fragmentary.

There are two kinds of time: physical, chronological time by the watch—yesterday, today, and tomorrow—and the psychological time of "I will be," a psychological tomorrow, where I shall be able to achieve enlightenment, where I will be perfect. But is there psychological time at all, or is it still the invention of thought? We are trying to find out if there is an action that is not based on the past and, therefore, divisive. Is there an action that is complete, whole, not caught in the net of time?

After seeing the action, the movement that is going on in the world—and in ourselves, which is the world—one wants to find out if there is an action not based on a conclusion—because conclusion is the movement of thought—action that is not based on an ideal, which is again fragmentary, action not based on a prejudice, an action that is every moment whole, complete, so that in that action there are no regrets, no sorrows, no pain. Don't you want to find such an action? We live with action that is painful, in which there is always uncertainty, regrets—"I wish I hadn't done that." One knows the action that brings regret, pain, sorrow, confusion, and so on, and one wants to find out if there is an action that is whole and, therefore, complete; into which none of the regrets, or the poisonous movements, enter. I think this is what whatever is intelligent in a human being demands, and not being able to find it one invents an outside agency—if I can reach God, then I will know complete action. He will never reach God because God is his own invention! So we are going to find out if there is an action that is whole, sane, healthy, rational and, therefore, holy.

Why has thought invented an ideal? The ideal is the opposite of *what is.* The ideal is in the future, and *what is* is actual. One does not know how to deal with the actual, how to understand it, how to go beyond it and, therefore, not being able to understand it, one projects an ideal, which is fictitious, which is not actual. So there is the division between *what is* and the ideal and, hence, conflict. Thought, being fragmentary, is not capable of understanding *what is* actually in the present. It thinks it will understand by creating an ideal and trying to follow that ideal and, therefore, it brings more and more conflict. But if one is capable of looking at the present, the actual, the *what is,* without the principle, without the ideal, without the observer, who is the past, then one meets the actual.

Can one look at *what is* without a prejudice, without prejudgment? Can you look at *what is* without the observer, who is the past? Say you are envious of people, how do you look at that envy? Are you looking at it as an observer who is different from envy? You look at it as though you are separate from envy, but the fact is that *you are* envy. You are not the observer who is different; the observer himself is that. So the observer is the observed. Please, this is really very important to understand. When you have grasped the truth that the observer is the observed, then that which is observed undergoes radical change. What prevents a radical change of *what is* is the interference of the observer, who is the past. To understand this removes all conflict.

We are educated to conform to the division of the observer and the observed, and the observer is always trying to do something about the observed. He says, "I am envious; I will find it reasonable to be envious; if I am not envious what will happen in society?"; I suppress it, rationalize it, or justify it, which are all a process of conflict. Out of that conflict we have all kinds of violence. But the actual fact is that the observer *is* the observed. And, therefore, the division ends. When there is only observation of the fact, the fact undergoes radical transformation. So can one live a life in which there is no conflict whatsoever? That is to be perfectly sane. It is the unbalanced, the insane, who are always in conflict.

So one wants to find a way of living in which there is no conflict, in which thought, which is the movement in time as measure, which creates division, can realize its own limitation and function where it is absolutely necessary, and not enter into the psychological field at all. Thought has built the psyche, the psychological states, which is me, my ego. And thought is fragmentary; therefore, what it has created, the "me," is fragmentary. Then thought says, "I must integrate with the whole"—which is an impossibility. So can thought realize, itself, that it is a fragment, and that whatever movement it makes must be fragmentary? Can it realize that there is an action that is not fragmentary, which can only take place when the observer is the observed, and that in that, that which *is* undergoes a radical change.

Our consciousness is filled with the things of thought and, therefore, our consciousness is fragmentary. Is there a consciousness that is not fragmentary, and can thought find it? Is there a consciousness that is not put together by thought? We have divided the universe as the "me" and the "you," "we" and "they," good and evil. We have divided it, that is, thought has divided it. And then thought says to itself, "Is there a consciousness that is not put together by me?" Now how are you, a human being, going to find out if there is a consciousness that is not put together by thought? Man has tried this for millennia. It isn't just now that we are trying it. He has said there must be another consciousness that is not this kind of consciousness. And so he says, "I must control thought; there must be a system by which thought can be controlled, and then when thought is controlled, held, perhaps I will know what the other is." And this is the whole basis of meditation: control thought. But he doesn't ask who the controller is. The controller is still thought.

So, to find out, to come upon that which is not put together by thought, we have to understand the place of thought as knowledge and where thought has no place whatsoever, without suppressing it. Thought has a place as knowledge in our daily, superficial activities: driving a car, working in a factory, writing. It is only possible to give knowledge its right place when you have understood the whole nature of thinking. The psyche, the "me," has been put together by thought—my virtue, my temperament, my desires, my ambitions, my peculiar idiosyncrasies, my experience as opposed to your experience. Those are all the result of thought. Thought as knowledge has its right place, but it has no place in the psyche. That means, can the mind, can this whole structure of the psyche cease to be? Then only is there a totally different kind of consciousness—which you will never find through meditation.

All the things that thought has put together is reality. But thought has not put together the mountain or the tree, and that is also a reality. All the gods, all the rituals, all the mischief that is being made in the world by thought, is a reality—war is a reality, killing people is a reality, the violence, the brutality, the callousness, the destruction, is a reality made by thought, put together by thought. The mountains, the trees, the rivers, the beauty of the sky, is a reality but it is not put together by thought. Belief is a reality put together by thought but it is neurotic. The neuroticism is a reality. And truth is not reality. Thought can never touch truth. Then what is the relationship between truth and reality?

We have examined the nature of thought. We said thought is a material process, matter, because it is stored up in the brain, part of the cell, which is matter. So thought is a material process in time, in movement. And whatever that movement creates is reality—the neurotic as well as the so-called fragmentary are realities. The actual is a reality, like the microphone. And nature is also a reality. So what is truth? Can thought, which is fragmentary, which is caught up in time, mischievous, violent, find truth, truth being the whole, that which is sacred, holy? And if it cannot find it, then what is the relationship of thought, of reality, to that which is absolute?

You know, all this demands meditation. This *is* real meditation, not the things imported into this country by the gurus. Can consciousness, which is its content, ever expand to include consciousness of truth? Or does this consciousness of the psyche, the "me" with all its content, have to end before the perception of what is truth. One has to find out what is the nature of the psyche, which has been put together by thought. What is "me"—the vanity, the arrogance, the desire to achieve, to become successful—to which one clings so desperately? What is the nature of it? How has it come about? Because if that exists, the other cannot be. If I am egotistic, as long as that psychic center exists, truth cannot possibly be, because truth is the whole.

So how is the mind—the mind being all the senses, the emotions, the memories, the prejudices, the principles, the ideals, memories, experiences, the totality of that, which is the psyche, which is the me—how is that to end and yet act in *this* world? Is that possible?

To find that out one must go very deeply into the question of fear, the very complex problem of pleasure, and the question of sorrow and whether sorrow can ever end. Man has lived with sorrow for millennia upon millennia. He hasn't been able to end it. And one must also go into the question of what is death and love. Because all that is the matrix of the me. So this is a very, very serious affair, it is not just a thing to be played with. One must give one's whole life to understand this. To live in this world completely, sanely, without the psyche; not escape, not go off into some monastery or commune, but to live here, in this mad, insane, and murderous world where there is so much corruption, where politics are divorced from ethics. To live in this world sanely, without the psyche, the "me," is a tremendous challenge. That requires a mind that can think meticulously, correctly, objectively, having all the senses fully awakened, not drugged by alcohol, speed, and all the rest of it. You must have a very healthy mind, and when it is drugged or smoking, drinking, you do not have a healthy mind; all that destroys the mind, makes the mind dull.

Ojai, April 4, 1976

3

If one single human being understands radically the problem of fear and resolves it, not tomorrow or some other day but instantly, he affects the whole consciousness of mankind. That is a fact. As we have said, your consciousness is not your private property, it is the result of time, of thousands of incidents, experiences, that are put together by thought. That consciousness is in constant movement. It is like a stream, a vast river of which you are a part. So there is no particularization; and if you go into it very deeply, there is no individuality. You may not like that, but look at it. Individual means an entity who is undivided, indivisible, who is not fragmented, who is not broken up but is a whole being. But most of us, unfortunately, are fragmented, broken up, divided, like the rest of the world—unhappy, concerned, confused, miserable, aching, frightened.

So we are going together to explore the question of fear and whether it can end. We are sharing it together. Fear can be very little or an enormous burden. There is fear of losing a job, fear of not being successful, fear of death, fear of not being loved, fear of loneliness, isolation, fear of deep insecurity, the fear of being dependent, fear of not doing the right thing, or the fear of following the rest of the crowd, or being left behind. You know what fears are. Man has never been able psychologically to be free of fears. Fear has burdened his mind, darkened his outlook. He does not know how to deal with these fears; therefore, he escapes from them into violence, brutality, arrogance, bitterness.

What is the root cause of fear? Please look into yourself. Use the words as a mirror to discover your own fear and as you observe find out the root of it; not the branches, the leaves, the trivialities of fear, but the fundamental cause of fear. Because if there is fear psychologically, inwardly, every action becomes distorted, and there is no meticulous, clear observation.

What is the root of fear? Is it not being able to find complete security, psychologically, inwardly? Complete, total certainty, security. Is it that we are seeking permanency, something that will endure, that will last, that is final? Is there the uncertainty of not being? First let us see if there is security psychologically; because we may be seeking psychological security and, therefore, creating insecurity in the outward world. What is security, psychologically, inwardly? What do we mean by being secure, having firm, certain, enduring, unshakable, immovable, security so that nothing can shake it, break it down? Is that what you are seeking in relationship between each other? Having complete knowledge and depending on that knowledge to give us stability? That means seeking permanency, something that nothing can change and, therefore, eternity in the sense of putting an end to time.

So, is time one of the factors of fear? There is time by the watch, time as yesterday, today, and tomorrow. Chronological time is necessary, it is there. Is there psychological time? Is there for me, for you, psychologically, tomorrow? If there is not, there is immense fear. If you are confronted with the fact that there is no tomorrow psychologically, your whole foundation is shaken; because tomorrow you are going to have greater pleasure, tomorrow you will be better, tomorrow you will achieve, tomorrow you will get rid of your fear. So psychologically is there tomorrow?

Tomorrow means time. Tomorrow implies thought, which is in itself fragmentary; it has created psychological time, in which you will move from *what is* to "what should be." So is time a factor of fear? Time exists, but is there time at all psychologically: to make an effort to be something? Or, is fear of not being? What is this everlasting demand for self-expression, the "me" expressing itself, the "me" and the "you," the "I," the ego? Tackle this, because it is your life, and if you understand this and are free of fear, you open the door to heaven.

What is this "me" that says, "I must be," "I must meditate," "I must find God," "I must realize," "I must be happy," "I am lonely," "I must be successful," "I am frightened," "I must be told"? Is it not the name, Mr. So-and-so, the form, the form being the body that you see in the mirror, and all the associated memories, all the concepts about yourself, the image about yourself, the image that says, "I am much better than you are"? Are they not all put together by thought? Thought itself is a fragment, and the activity of that fragment is not only the "me," but the fragments it has created all round you—separate nations, separate classes, wars, the whole of that. And thought is a material process in time. Thought is the response of memory, experience, knowledge, stored up in the brain.

So the "me" to which we cling is fictitious. That may be the root cause of fear, clinging to something that is nonexistent. So, there is the fictitious, imagined me, a picture, a symbol, an idea, an image, put together by thought in time, which is a material process, measurement. And that "me," being uncertain of its very existence, deeply, in the very depths of one's being, may be the deep fundamental cause of fear. That doesn't mean that if you have no "me" you cannot live in this world. On the contrary.

Now can you look at the movement of time? Time is movement. The ending of that movement is putting a stop to time. That is one of the major factors of meditation, so that time comes to an end, psychologically. So deep rooted fear is the movement of thought in time, which is a material process, which has created an artificial structure called the "me," and having created it clings to it. Thought clings to a fragment that it has created, and thought itself is a fragment. There is fear in relationship, because in relationship we have created the image of you and me. The man and the woman each has an image of the other, a picture, a symbol, put together by time, of many days, many years, or an hour. And their relationship is between these two images. Look into it and you will see the actuality of it. We cling to the picture, to the image, and we are frightened of losing that image. So we are forced to look at each other totally differently if there is no image.

We have described in words the nature, the quality, the structure, of this thing called fear. Now, knowing that the description is not the described, can you look not at the description but at the fact? Can you look at it? That is, can you observe it?

It is very important to learn how to observe. There is an art in observation. "Art" means putting things in their proper place, putting everything where it belongs. Can you observe this thing called fear? Are you, the observer, different from the thing observed? When you are angry, or envious, or jealous, or whatever it is, are you different from that feeling which we have named as "jealousy"? Or you are jealousy? So the observer is the observed. To put it differently, is the thinker different from his thought? Or again differently, is the experiencer different from the experience? If he is not different, then why do you seek experiences? If there is no difference between the observer and the observed, then there is only the observed. Then there is only thinking, not the thinker different from thought.

You want experiences. You are bored with the experiences that you have had already, the daily experiences of sex, this, that, and the other, so you want other experiences—experience of god, experience of enlightenment, experience of Jesus, experience of Krishna consciousness. And you have never asked who the experiencer is, and whether he is different from the experienced. You want to experience Krishna consciousness, or the consciousness of Jesus, or something else, but to experience that, you must recognize it, mustn't you? *That means you have already known it.* Therefore, the experiencer is the experienced.

So can you look at fear without the observer? Because you are the fear, fear isn't different from you. When you are angry, is that anger different from you? If you say it is different, then you try to control it, then you try to rationalize it, then you try to do something about it. But if the observer is the observed, you can't do anything about it, you are that. So observe fear without the observer.

One realizes in observing that fear is not different from the observer. When the observer is the observed there is fundamental change in that which is observed. When there is division between the observer and the observed, in that division there is conflict. I say I must get rid of it, I must control it, or ask why should I not have fear, why should I not have neurotic actions out of those fears. There is always contradiction, division, and, therefore, conflict—which is a wastage of energy. It is a wastage of energy when there is conflict, trying to control, running away, going to somebody to tell me how to get rid of fear. All those are factors of wasting energy. If you don't waste energy—and that only takes place when the observer is the observed—then you have that immense energy to transform *what is*. The very observation is the energy which transforms "that which is." Get this, and then you will see that you are completely free from psychological fears.

If you have listened with all your heart and your mind, then when you get up you are free of fear. That means you have listened. That means it is your problem and it is absolutely necessary to solve it, not tomorrow, but instantly. That is, when you perceive something, then you act instantly, and that perception is only possible when the perceiver is the perceived, because there you have total energy. Total observation is only possible when there is no observer—the observer being the past. When there is that total attention given to observation, that which is observed undergoes a fundamental transformation. Got it? Do it!

Ojai, April 10, 1976

4

Why does the human mind pursue pleasure? We are not saying that there should not be pleasure, but we are going to investigate into the nature of pleasure because apparently human beings are everlastingly committed to pleasure. Why is there this great demand for pleasure, the easiest way of action, the most comfortable way of living, the pursuit not only of physical, sensory pleasures, but psychological pleasures? And the ultimate pleasure is God, enlightenment. What is pleasure? It may be the other side of the coin of fear. Most human beings disregard fear, do not know how to deal with fear, and pursue pleasure constantly.

Through culture, through tradition, through our habits, the environment, and so on, part of our brain has become mechanistic. Is pleasure mechanistic? Is it the repetition of a certain delight of yesterday, either sexual or otherwise, which becomes a memory, and we pursue the memory as pleasure? We are concerned with the transformation of the human mind. We cannot live as we are living. There must be a radical change in our minds, in our hearts, in our whole way of living, and so it is very important to find out why we human beings have been caught in this everlasting pursuit of pleasure.

Now look at it. Yesterday there were some delightful incidents, something that you liked immensely happened. That is registered in the brain, it becomes a memory. Then thought says, "I must have more of that." It is the repetition of an incident which is over, which was considered pleasure by thought, the pursuit of it today and tomorrow. That is mechanistic, mechanical, obviously.

What is the difference between pleasure, enjoyment, and joy? There are three things: pleasure, enjoyment, and joy. You can cultivate pleasure—taste, all sensory activities. Can you cultivate enjoyment? Or can you cultivate joy? Joy comes uninvited, by some curious chance. You find yourself suddenly, extraordinarily, unspeakably happy. Then thought takes it over and says, "I must have more of it." So the moment thought interferes with that thing called joy, which is uninvited, it becomes pleasure. Therefore, it becomes mechanistic.

So that is our life, a way of living, that is constantly repetitive, constantly going over something that was, that is already dead, making it live through thought and pursuing that as pleasure. You can look at something beautiful, the trees and the clouds and the light. But when thought comes in and says, "That was a most lovely thing," it is already finished. So can you watch the beauty of nature, the beauty of this world, with all your senses and not let thought come in? Then enjoyment is completely for the moment, but when thought takes it over, it becomes pleasure and it becomes mechanistic. Please, this requires a mind with a tremendous sense of alertness, watchfulness, awareness. Experiment with it now as we are talking. Look at the trees, the sunlight, the beauty of the hills, the shadows, the playing of those shadows among the hills, the valleys. It is a delight. Can you watch it without thought coming into it, and end it there, not wanting to continue it? What has continuity becomes mechanistic. In that which has an ending, there is a new beginning. Got it?

Now, you had an insight into this, didn't you? Please, watch it carefully. You had an insight; is that insight the product of thought? So you have found something. That is, when there is an insight and action through insight, it is not mechanistic. Insight or intelligence is not the product of thought; it is nonmechanistic action. Whenever thought takes over the moment of delight, it becomes mechanistic. You saw that. The perception of that is intelligence, isn't it? Can you act always according to that intelligence, not according to the repetitive movement of thought? Do you see the difference?

So we see the movement of pleasure, based upon desire, desire being sensation. To watch the trees, the clouds, the heavens and the stars and the moon, is a tremendous sensation if you watch it with all your senses. Then thought comes in. So where there is sensation plus thought there is a desire. That is, the sensations, the activity of the senses at their highest, plus thought, is desire. Do you see that? How do you see it? You see it because your intelligence is observing it. That intelligence is not the product of thought.

Have you considered why human beings suffer, both biologically as well as inwardly, why there are tears? What is this suffering, this sorrow? Can it ever end, or is it an everlasting movement from the beginning of mankind to our end? Must man put up with it, live with it?

Organized religions, based on authority and belief, have never solved this problem. Christianity says somebody suffered for you, and you carry on. Hindus and the Buddhists have their own explanations. So man has lived with sorrow from the most ancient days. Can sorrow end? If there is no ending to sorrow, there is no compassion, there is no love. We think suffering is necessary, or we think there is no solution to suffering; therefore, we must escape from it. And we have developed a marvelous network of escapes.

What is sorrow? There is this thing called sorrow, which is pain, grief, loneliness, a sense of total isolation, no hope, no sense of relationship or communication, total isolation. Mankind has lived with this great thing and perhaps cultivated it because he does not know how to resolve it. We are going to find out if there is an end to sorrow, because without the ending of sorrow there is no love. When there is love will you suffer for another? When there is love will there be sorrow? You might have sympathy, kindliness, generosity, sharing, but love is something totally different, a different dimension, which one can come upon only when sorrow ends.

There is sorrow when someone dies whom you "love." You feel utterly lonely when you have lost someone upon whom you have depended. When you feel that you cannot climb the ladder of success, when someone whom you think you love does not return it, when your beliefs, in which you have false security, are shattered; when your mother or father dies, or son or brother dies, there is sorrow.

What actually takes place when you suffer? Not biologically, physiologically, but psychologically, which is much more penetrating, much deeper, much more excruciating. You may shed tears, escape from it, never look at it, but it is always there. Sorrow is the lot of human beings, everyone knows it. We escape from it, rationalize it, justify it, or say that every human being suffers so I must suffer. Or if you are prejudiced religiously, you say it is the work of God. Now all those are ways and means of escaping from the fact of *what is,* which is sorrow. Now if you don't escape, that is, if there is no rationalizing, no avoiding, no justifying, just remaining with that totality of suffering, without the movement of thought, then you have all that energy to comprehend the thing that you call sorrow.

If you remain without a single movement of thought, with that which you have called sorrow, there comes a transformation in that which you have called sorrow. That becomes passion. The root meaning of sorrow is passion. When you escape from it, you lose that quality which comes from sorrow, which is complete passion, which is totally different from lust and desire. When you have an insight into sorrow and remain with that thing completely, without a single movement of thought, out of that comes this strange flame of passion. And you must have passion, otherwise you can't create anything.

Out of passion comes compassion. Compassion means passion for all things, for all human beings. So there is an ending to sorrow, and only then you will begin to understand what it means to love.

So one has to have an insight into fear, insight into relationship, insight into the whole structure and nature of thought, thought that breeds fear, that pursues pleasure, and into the ending of sorrow. If you have an insight into all that, you have that intelligence that transforms your mechanistic activity into something totally nonmechanistic. Don't go away and think about it! You have no time. When you think about what has been said, then your thinking becomes traditional, mechanistic, and empty, but as you are sitting there, sharing this thing, it is happening now. It must happen now, otherwise it will not ever happen, because thought will prevent it. Thought has no insight. Have an insight into what we have pointed out, knowing the description is not the described, and it must take place instantly, now. Thinking about it is just a waste of time. When you are sharing something, you are sharing it now.

Ojai, April 11, 1976

5

We have loaded the word *love* with so much meaning, mostly sensual. Using that word, knowing all the complications of that word, the meaning of that word, we must explore together the structure and the nature of that thing called love.

Is love desire or pleasure? What is desire and how does it arise? How does it flower? What is the root of it? How does it come into being? Apparently for most of us love is intimately connected with desire—sexually, psychologically, biologically, and spiritually. The objects of desire vary, but the root of desire is the same. So how does desire come into being in each one of us?

Religions based on belief, religions of authority, which are not religion at all, have said that to serve God you must be free of desire. So the monks, the Indian *sannyasis,* try to suppress desire, and in the process of repression identify themselves with an image, with a name, and thereby think they have solved the problem. They are burning inside with desire but they suppress it through rituals, through discipline, through every form of conformity, effort. This has been a great problem for human beings who are very serious to find out if there is truth, because desire breeds illusion. Desire breeds experiences, and when you cling to an experience, that becomes an illusion. We have identified love with desire.

Is not desire sensation—that is, the activity of the senses, plus thought? Sensations plus thought is desire. Is that fact or just a statement of an idea? Can you look at something with all your senses completely? And in that looking end it and not let thought come into the activity of sensation? That is, when you look at the trees, the mountains, the face of a human being, the endless movement of the sea, with all your senses, all your eyes and ears and nerves, can you look at it completely and not allow thought to come in, to interfere with it? Then your perception is whole, whereas when thought interferes with that perception, it becomes fragmentary. So desire is fragmentary.

Unfortunately, or fortunately—it is up to you—we have identified desire with that thing called love. Is love desire? Is love attachment? When you are attached to something you are that. When you have totally identified with something, you are that. Why is there this urge to identify, to be attached? Why is one human being attached to another? Does not attachment breed fear, fear of losing what one is attached to? Being attached, you may become jealous, frightened, anxious, which are obvious phenomena. You are attached because of your own insufficiency, loneliness. And so out of your own insufficiency, loneliness, a sense of lacking, you cling to another. So is attachment love? Where there is attachment there must be exploitation. And we use that word *love* to cover up all this. And is love jealousy?

None of these things exist as attachment when you have understood that that emptiness in yourself can never be filled by something else. You have to look at it. You have to not escape from it, observe it totally. Then you will see that loneliness goes completely away. Then there is not that lonely attachment. Then perhaps one will know what love is. In attachment there is fear, there is anxiety, there is hate, all the conflicts in relationship; and where there is conflict can there be love? Where there is ambition, can there be love? When you strip yourself of ambition, anxiety, attachment, and understand deeply the meaning and the significance of pleasure and desire, then you perhaps come upon that strange thing called love. And out of that comes compassion. Compassion is the highest form of intelligence. When you have compassion and, therefore, intelligence, you will do the right thing at the right moment. I hope you are following, not verbally, but actually in your hearts, in your minds, doing it.

And there is the question of what death is. It is rather strange to talk about it on a lovely morning, but it is part of life. Not to go into the full meaning of that word, and know what it implies, to shut ourselves away from it, to escape from it, to avoid it, not to talk about it, is to divide life, which is a total movement. We must go into this question. Not only for the aged, but also for the young; we are all involved in this. So what does living mean, and what does dying mean? What do we mean by living, our daily living? An effort, a struggle, a conflict, pleasure, anxiety, uncertainty, fear of losing a job, or having a job, trying to get a better job, and so on, constant struggle, constant effort, fear, anxiety, with occasional joy—this is our life, if you are honest about it. This is our everyday existence. To that endless struggle we cling, and say that is living.

And what then is dying? The ending of this so-called living? Is it a biological ending? Or the ending of this immense stream which man has created of conflict, sorrow, pain, anxiety? Please, it is your life we are talking about, not a description of the speaker's life, or somebody else's life. It is your life, your daily life with which we are concerned. Unless there is a radical transformation in that daily life we are going to create more and more misery for ourselves and for other human beings, which is actually what is going on. So what is dying?

There is a biological death through accident, through disease. And the body, the organism, wears itself out and comes to an end. The body has its own intelligence, but we have destroyed that intelligence through drink, through drugs, through constant effort, battle. Through various drugs and chemicals, medicines, we have destroyed that innate intelligence of the organism, and so the body dies by constant strain, usage.

Is it possible for the organism, this biological instrument with its brain, never to deteriorate? Our brain as it gets older deteriorates. Can the brain be young all the time and not deteriorate? When there is constant friction, constant effort, constant struggle, biologically as well as psychologically, the brain must deteriorate. Is there a way of living without effort and so the brain is always young, fresh, active, decisive. It is possible. Is one aware daily of the constant battle in oneself—trying to be something, trying to imitate, trying to conform, becoming the ideal, which is the mechanical process? Do you know, are you conscious that you are doing this? Don't ask how to stop it, how to break the mechanical routine, but be aware of it without any choice, just look at it, because if you introduce an effort you have already destroyed it. Can you observe without any choice the mechanical movement of the brain, or rather one part of the brain that has been cultivated for centuries upon centuries to act mechanically? Just be aware of it, not try to correct it, not try to alter it, because from trying to alter it comes conflict. As we said, where there is duality, difference between the observer and the observed, there must be conflict. When there is no observer but merely observation then there is no conflict.

If you are totally aware during the day of all the mechanical movement, the ways of your thinking, desire, then you will find at night when you go to sleep, in spite of what all the scientists say, there are no dreams. The mind, the brain is quiet because all your problems, all your activities have been dissolved during the day, if you are attentive, are watchful, aware. Then when you go to sleep there is peace; the brain may be in movement but it is a quiet movement, it is not an agitated, anxious movement. Therefore, the brain brings order in itself, so the brain becomes young, fresh. It cannot be young and fresh and decisive if there is any form of hurt. When it is free of hurt, the brain has no resistance.

Apart from the biological ending of the organism, what is death? What is it that you are so frightened of? Is it the ending of your experiences? The ending of your knowledge? The ending of all the things that you are attached to, psychologically? Biologically, when death takes place, whatever you are attached to does end. You are not going to carry your house, your furniture, your books and even your gurus—the Catholic guru, or the Protestant guru, or the Indian guru—with you. So what is it that human beings are so dreadfully frightened of? They are frightened of something ending, of ending psychologically, inwardly.

And knowing it *is* going to end we want comfort, so we say there must be a continuity. The ancient Hindus said there is a continuity, which is called reincarnation. They said you will be reborn next life according to what you have done in this life. If you have behaved properly, decently, morally, in the next life you are going to be better, and through a series of incarnations, and depending on your behavior, you will ultimately come to the highest principle. That is a very comforting theory, and millions believe in that. The Buddhist attitude is that life is a constant flux, a constant movement and when that manifests, an enclosure takes place which becomes the "you," the "me," which through time, through constant movement, undergoes change. And of course the Christians have their own belief in the resurrection; they believe that their own deity woke up from death physically.

We are saying something entirely different. Please listen because you will see, if you really understand this thing, that there is a timeless movement, a timeless state. First, we said, the world is you, and you are the world. All human beings, radically, basically, are afraid, anxious, in sorrow, confused, unhappy, with occasional joy; psychologically it is a constant movement, wherever human beings are it is the same stream. It is the same stream; therefore, you are the world and the world is you. That is a fact. You may have different temperament, different gifts, capacities, idiosyncrasies, but those are the responses of the culture in which you have lived. But the basic stream is the same.

Therefore, there is no individuality. Individuality implies a wholeness, an indivisible entity, and you are not that indivisible entity. You are divided, broken up; therefore, you are not actually an individual, indivisible. You become totally individual in the complete sense of that word when you are whole, in which there is no fragmentary action. The word *whole* means healthy, sane, holy. You are the world and the world is you, and you are caught in that constant stream. But sorrow can be ended, fear can be ended—not tomorrow, actually now; then you are out of that stream—not you, there is a manifestation, which is out of that stream or freed from that stream, because that stream is time.

That stream is time. So you have to find out whether time has a stop. Time has a stop when there is no longer the movement of that stream. That stream is fear, that stream is conflict, that stream is sorrow, and all the confusion man has built through thought. So that is the stream of time. When there is an ending to that stream, time has stopped; therefore, there is a totally different dimension.

So the thing that we are afraid of losing when death takes place is the structure that thought has built as "me," the form, the name, and the attachment to the form and to that name, which are pain, pleasure, anxiety. All that is the "me," the "you." You can say there is a higher me, but that is still the product of thought. So that movement in which human beings are caught is the movement of time, driven by thought. The greater the volume of that stream the greater is the volume of thought. And when that stream, which is our consciousness with all its content, comes to an end, then time has a stop and, therefore, there is a totally different dimension. And when you understand this, not verbally, but deeply, and live it daily—and it *can* be done—then you will see that death has a totally different significance.

Ojai, April 17, 1976

6

One has been talking for the last fifty years and more, seeing a lot of people, talking over not only their personal problems, but the global problems of human beings, the vast confusion, the misery, the extraordinary lack of clarity. And through all these days and years it becomes more and more clear that unless human beings radically transform themselves, we may destroy not only ourselves but the earth. So it seems to us that there must be a group of people who are utterly serious, who are concerned, not superficially, not adjusting themselves to environment and circumstances, but deeply, and who will live a life that is whole, complete, noble, full of intensity and clarity. Otherwise we waste the short years we have.

So we have talked about various things, like the utter lack of relationship between human beings; we have talked about the process of thought as a material movement in time and said that thought is totally inadequate to solve our human problems because thought has created them. Thought cannot solve them because thought is a fragment, a material process and a movement of measure. We also talked about fear and the ending of it, about understanding the whole complex problem of pleasure and of the ending of sorrow, and we talked about love and death.

As we are concerned with the very deep problem of existence, we must not put aside the whole question of religion, meditation, and whether there is anything sacred, holy.

To hear correctly is an art. To see things as they are is also an art. And to learn, not from others, the whole content of one's human consciousness, which is the result of millennia of human endeavor, human sorrow, human agony, anxiety. It is all there in us. In learning to look at, to listen to all the content of that consciousness, in the observation of that consciousness, is action.

We are going to discuss religion together, because religion is the creative factor of a new culture. If there is no religion then the culture dies, civilization goes to pieces. Considering what the world is like, with all its brutality, violence, wars, divisions, class hatreds, and so on, which all indicate degeneration of the human mind, it behooves us to discover for ourselves what religion is. Is it a gathering of beliefs? Is it performing rituals, repeating endless words which have really no meaning at all? Is it going on Sunday morning to a church, or to a temple, or to a mosque, and repeating some chant, some words. If one asks oneself seriously, what is the necessity of any belief, of any conclusion? Beliefs, conclusions, divide people. In this little village there are five or six divisions of Christianity. And throughout the world there is much division brought about by so-called religions—the Hindu, the Buddhist, the Muslim, and the Christian, and their innumerable sects. So what is the importance of any belief at all? Or does belief prevent the understanding of what truth is?

Is religion divorced from daily life, or is religion a movement that brings order in our life? If religion is divorced from our daily life it can only create further confusion, further conflict.

To find out the meaning of religion, one must have order in one's life. Our life is confused, contradictory, disorderly, fragmented, broken up; how can such a life have order? Order is not the acceptance of a blueprint. Order comes only when one realizes, is aware fully, without any choice, of one's own confusion, one's own daily disordered life. From awareness without any choice of disorder comes order; that is, from the understanding, from the observation of our daily life, which is disorderly. Such observation is not based on condemnation, rationalization, judgment. From that choiceless awareness comes order and this order is a living thing; therefore, it is constantly moving. Although to the modern generation, morality means nothing, morality in essence is order. And without order how can there be clarity?

Part of this touches the question of meditation; without order in one's life, without being totally moral in one's daily activity, how can you even think of meditating? You may sit cross-legged for the rest of your life, for the next ten incarnations or a million incarnations, breathe in a certain way that you have learned in India, but you will never come upon that which is truth because your life is disorderly. Therefore, you must bring order into that life before you even think of meditating; if you "meditate" without having order, it is a marvelous escape and, therefore, without any significance, without any meaning. Please do realize this. Meditation is the most marvelous thing, but not your kind of meditation. There must be order in our relationship, and that can only exist when there is no fear. Order is not put together by thought. If it is put together by thought then it will create further disorder.

To find, or come upon, that which is most sacred, most holy, there must be a life based solidly on order. And the importance of all meditations is to come upon that silence. Even biologically, physiologically, to see anything clearly, to look at the trees, the light on the leaves, the green grass, and the hills and to see them clearly your mind must be quiet, mustn't it. It is so simple, we make it so complex. To see anything clearly, to observe clearly, you must have a quiet mind, mustn't you? If you are chattering, chattering, you won't see the tree, you won't see the depth of the shadow, the beauty of a trunk or a limb. You can only see it when your mind is quiet.

See the fact of it, the reason of it, the logic of it, that you can see something clearly only when your mind is silent. You cannot hear what somebody else is saying if you are talking to yourself all the time. So if you want to hear somebody clearly you must be quiet. So silence is absolutely necessary to perceive outwardly and inwardly. The outward and the inward are the same movement, they are not different. It is one unitary movement, but we have divided it as the inner and the outer. By observing the outer clearly, you then discover the inner, and then see that it is one movement. To see this clearly you must look, observe silently.

We are investigating together the meaning and the depth of that thing called religion, to find out if there is anything incorruptible, untouched by thought, which is not an illusion, which is not the projection of one's own desire, or an experience, but something that has never been touched by thought, something totally original. And to come upon that we said there must be order in daily life, which is the essence of virtue.

There are different kinds of silence, aren't there? There is the silence between two noises—is that silence? There is silence between two thoughts—is that silence? There is so-called peace between two wars—is that peace? So what is silence? Is it put together by thought? Is it contrived? Is it something that is manufactured because you understand that if you want to see "heaven" you must be silent? Then you say, "How am I to be silent? Teach me how to be silent." Out of the desire to find out what silence is, people begin to invent systems, methods, ways to come upon that.

Now if once you understand this you will never touch any system; because what is implied in a system and a practice? Repetition, practice, practice, practice, control, make an effort, which is, become mechanical. As we have said, part of our brain has become mechanical. We said thought in its essence is mechanical, because thought is the repetition, or the reaction, of memory. And when you already live a life that is mechanical and try to go beyond that mechanical life by introducing another mechanical process, which is systems, methods, practices, you are still mechanical. So when once you see the truth of this, the logic, the reason of this, you will never touch systems, methods, practices. Anything that is contrived, put together by thought—however beautiful, however logical, however ancient, traditional—makes the mind more mechanical and eventually dull. The very seeing of the truth of that ends the demand for systems, methods.

If silence is not put together by thought, then what is it? To see clearly you must be silent, to hear clearly the mind must not be chattering. If you see the truth of it, then it happens. You do not have to make an effort to be silent.

So what is that which is silent? We will look at it by examining awareness. What is awareness, to be aware? When you are sitting there you are aware of the trees, the shadows, the light on the leaves, the movement of the leaves. [The talk is taking place in the open in an oak grove.] If you are looking at the tree you are aware of it. Can you look at it without verbalization? Just look without naming it, without giving it a quality, or description, just observe.

We never just observe: we look and say, "How beautiful," "How ugly," "How useful," depending on our conditioning. So we never observe things as they are. Now can you observe, see the beauty of this whole land, all the hills, their quietness, their shadows, just observe without any reaction of thought, without any reaction of like and dislike? Just to observe, that is awareness. Be aware of the universe around you, then be aware of the universe inside. The universe inside is much more complex. The universe inside is our whole consciousness. And the consciousness is its content. The universe inside is much more complex, much more subtle, and if one has the energy, the capacity, the intensity, and the clarity, to go into it, there is a tremendous depth in that. So, be aware first of the outer, look at it, and be aware of all your reactions to it, and then go beyond your reactions and observe. Now in the same way go into the universe of yourself, which is your consciousness, with all its content, with its experiences, with its knowledge, with its likes, with its fears, anxieties, sorrow, pain. Be conscious of that enormous content that man has added to for thousands of years, be aware of that.

Can one be aware totally? Or must one take one segment after another, one layer after another, one fragment after another? The content of consciousness makes up consciousness; if there is no content there is no consciousness, as we know it. Will you understand the content of consciousness bit by bit? Or is there an understanding of it totally? The content of your consciousness is your conditioning—as a Christian, as a socialist, by the climate, by the food, by all the things that man has done to himself and to others, his identifications, his beliefs. All that is consciousness. To understand that consciousness, will you examine it portion by portion? Or is there a way of looking at it wholly, so that you don't have to take time?

There is a way of looking at it wholly, not fragment by fragment. And that is only possible if you understand awareness. So there is awareness of the world outside you, watching your reactions to the world outside you, and observing without reactions the world outside you. And move from the outer to the inner with all the content, which is your consciousness, to observe it. First you will react to it, naturally: "I don't like," "I like," "How beautiful this is," "How pleasurable that was," "I wish I could keep a little bit of this," and so on and so on and so on. Watch that reaction and then go beyond it. If you go beyond it then, you see the whole content instantly.

This is part of meditation: to see the outer actually as it is, not what you wish it to be, the wars, the antagonisms, the hatreds, the innumerable insults and hurts that human beings receive, the sorrow, the pain, the anxiety, the loneliness, lack of love, to observe all that. Then what takes place? Then you will see that energy is being gathered, because there is order and, therefore, there is no wastage of energy. When there is mathematical order in your daily life, there is no wastage of energy. It is only when there is no order that there is wastage of energy. When there is order, there is the accumulation of energy. And with that energy observe the world and yourself, and realize the world out there and here are the same movement. There is the accumulation of energy when there is an observation without the observer. The observer is the past, the past being all your prejudices, your opinions, your conclusions, your traditional responses. The observer is the past and the observer meets the present, the *what is,* and tries to translate it according to his past conclusions. Right? That gives to the past further movement in time as the future. You are the result of the past. That is a fact. Part of your brain is the result of a series of adventures, happenings, incidents, experiences, as knowledge, and knowledge is always the past. That movement of the past meets the present and translates the present, or modifies the present according to the past and so gives a further movement into the future. The past meeting the present is a movement; the present is also a movement; if the past meeting the present ends there, which means no movement, then time has a stop.

So meditation then is bringing about order in life, and thereby gathering great energy, and ending conflict between the observer and the observed, which adds further energy. When there is a division between the observer and the observed there must be conflict. When you are angry, at the moment of anger, at the second of anger, there is no division; but a second later a division takes place: "I must not be angry," or, "Why shouldn't I be angry?" Where there is a division, there must be conflict. Conflict with all its violence is a wastage of energy. The gathering of total energy is the beginning of silence.

We live confused lives, our consciousness is in turmoil, constantly in battle, constantly choosing, denying, asserting, dominating, being attached. It is in constant struggle, boiling all the time; and that boiling is a wastage of energy. For that turmoil to come to an end is part of meditation. Not by control. The moment you control, who is the controller? Please, go into this yourself. The controller is part of thought. When the controller tries to control thought that is a wastage of energy. But if you see the truth, that the controller is the controlled, then the conflict comes to an end. That means you have further energy, and this energy is necessary, this complete energy, which is not put together by friction. Friction has its own energy, but this energy that we are talking about is not put together by thought and, therefore, it is not the result of friction. This energy is necessary to come upon that which is sacred, which is the religious mind.

Meditation then is the emptying of the content of consciousness—which means the fears, the anxieties, the conflicts in relationship—the ending of sorrow and, therefore, compassion. The ending of the content of consciousness is complete silence. Then that silence is full of energy. It is not vacant silence. It is not a silence that wants something more.

So meditation is not the repetition of mantras, not merely sitting down breathing carefully. Meditation must be totally uninvited, not contrived, not put together. Which means there is no measurement. If one has gone that far—no, it is not far or near—if one has done this, then there is that emptiness.

Now wait a minute. Scientists say in this emptiness there is energy. We are saying that when there is this meditative process, movement, there is a totally different kind of consciousness of a dimension in which there is all this energy which has been gathered through meditation, order in life. You have total energy—*there is* total energy. And in that emptiness there is not a thing. There is nothing. Nothing means not a thing. Thing means thought. Thought is a material process. So in that emptiness thought does not exist at all. And, therefore, there is no experiencer who is experiencing this total nothingness.

What is beauty? That is also part of our life. Is it the shadow? The line of an architectural building? The painting? The marvelous cultures that exist in the world? The mountains? The running waters? The beautiful face? What is beauty? Does not beauty exist when there is not a center of conflict? When you say, "How beautiful it is," what is the feeling behind that? What is the nature, the quality of emotion, the surging of something? Is that beauty? Or is beauty the total absence of the observer? When there is only complete observation, in which there is no choice, no division, there must be this sense of beauty. That may be that which is sacred. Not the beauty of form of a woman or a man. There is the beauty of woman and man, the beauty of a tree, the beauty of a line, of a sheet of water, the running sea, but to find out, or come upon that sense of total absence of anything that is contradictory, something that is whole, complete, sane, rational. Such a mind is a beautiful mind, which is the religious mind. Because there you have total energy embodied.

So there is such a thing as something sacred that is not touched by thought, that is not touched or made corrupt by human beings, with their desires and frights and quarrels and mischief. And to come upon that is not only part of meditation, but the ending of sorrow, which is the beginning of wisdom. So wisdom is not learning from books or going to a school. When there is an ending of sorrow in yourself as a human being, then out of that comes wisdom.

And when a human being transforms himself, when *you* transform yourself radically, you are affecting the whole consciousness of mankind. You are mankind, you are the movement of mankind. This is a fact, this is actual. If you change, you affect the world. So it is your tremendous responsibility. We must be very skeptical of all psychological experiences, subjective experiences, because they are most destructive.

So meditation implies a life of great order and, therefore, great virtue, morality. And it implies the understanding and the depth of beauty. And it implies the emptying of that consciousness which is you, with all your attachments, fears, hopes, despairs, the emptying of all that by observing.

Then you have energy which alone can discover that which is eternal, which has no beginning and no ending.

Ojai, April 18, 1976

One wonders, observing what is going on in the world, why there is so much disorder, why man is destroying man. Why is there such enormous expenditure on armaments? Why have people divided themselves into tribal romantic nationalities? Why have the organized religions, the accepted religions, throughout the world, divided themselves? Why is there such division in the world? We are inclined to think that an outside agency has created all this mess, that "God," or some other supreme entity, having created man, has let him loose on the earth. What mankind has done is quite incredible and shocking, not only toward other human beings, but also in himself. Why in the world are there are so many neurotic people? Why is there this constant battle between man and woman? Why is there this inward disorder, which naturally must express itself in outward disorder?

Our lives have produced the society in which we live. Society is not created by some extraordinary events but by the extraordinary lives we lead, not only we, but also past generations. Could we go together into it, think it out together, not only think it out but also go beyond the realm of thought? We have pointed out over and over again that thought is born of memory, memory is the result of knowledge and experience. And thought, therefore, is always limited, for knowledge is everlastingly limited because there can be no complete knowledge about anything. And thought born out of that must also be very, very limited. And the world in which we live, our daily life, our careers, our anxieties, fears, and sorrows, are the result of our thinking, are the product of our daily activity.

Could we together look at life as a whole, our education, our occupations, our hobbies, work, and all the travail that exists inwardly, the psychological conflicts, the anxieties, the fears, the pleasures, the sorrows? Could we take all that as a whole and not let thought occupy itself with one particular part, with one particular pattern, or cling to one particular experience, looking at life from only that point of view? Why do we live the way we are living? Why is there so much disorder in the world and in ourselves? Is the world disorder different from our disorder?

Why is there disorder outwardly and disorder inwardly? Are they two separate disorders? Or are they one unitary process? The disorder out there is not different from the disorder in me, but rather this disorder is a movement which goes outward and comes inward. It is like a tide going back and forth endlessly. Can we begin to bring about order in our life? Because without order there is no freedom. Complete order, not occasionally or once a week, but in our daily life, not only brings freedom; there is then in that order love. A disordered, confused, mind that is in conflict cannot have or be aware of what love is.

Can there be absolute order? We are using the word *absolute* in its right sense, complete, total, not an order that is intellectually brought about, an order that is based on values, not order that is the outcome of environmental pressures, or adaptation to a certain norm, a certain pattern. We are talking about absolute total order in which there is no division as disorder at all. We are asking whether there is an order in which there can never be disorder.

Why does our mind, which includes the brain, our emotional responses, sensory responses, and so on, accept and live in disorder? If you observe your own mind, that is, your own life, which is based on your mind, your thoughts, your emotions, your experiences, your memories, regrets, apprehensions, why does that mind, which has all this in its consciousness, accept disorder? Not only the neurotic disorder, the acceptance of disorder and living with disorder, getting used to disorder, but why does the mind have this sense of division, this sense of order and disorder, this constant adjustment? Is this inevitable? Is this our natural state? If it is natural then one must live with this conflict, in this disorder, from the moment you are born until you die. And if it is unnatural, which obviously it is, what is the cause of it? What is the basis of it, what is the root of all this? Does the basis depend on our particular attitudes, on our particular desires?

One wants to find out what is the basis of this disorder, the root of it. To find out, how do we approach it? How do we approach the problem of disorder in order to resolve it totally? What is your approach? Are you approaching to find order out of disorder and, therefore, your approach is already directed? Suppose I am in disorder and I have the desire to bring about order. That very desire dictates what the order must be, whereas if I approach the problem of disorder as though I want to find the root of it, then my direction is not diverted, wasted in various intellectual, verbal, and emotional directions, but my whole attention is directed to the cause of it. So how do you, as a human being, living in this world, both outwardly and inwardly in disorder, approach this? We must be very clear what our approach is.

If it is clear then let us find out together what is the root of disorder. Is it self-contradiction? Is it desire that has created this division in us? Wherever there is division there must be conflict, and conflict means disorder. Conflict is disorder, whether it is minor, or conflict that brings about a great crisis. So is our conflict self-contradiction, saying one thing, doing another, having ideals and always trying to accommodate ourselves to those ideals? Is it our desire to become something? Or is this conflict created by thought? Because thought in itself, as we said, is limited and, therefore, it divides as the outer and the inner, the "you" and the "me." Thought struggles to become something which it is not. Are these constant divisions, becoming, contradicting, conforming, comparing, imitating psychologically, the various expressions of a central cause?

So what is the central cause, the root of all this? You are exercising your mind; therefore, you are aware of how you approach the problem, you are aware of your own contradictions, your own conflicts, your own divisions, your own apprehensions. Is one aware of all that? Or is one aware only of a fragment of it, a fragment that demands an immediate response? If I am concerned about my livelihood, I am not concerned about anything else because that is an immediate demand. I need money, food; I have children, responsibility; therefore, my approach to this whole problem will be directed by my desire to have a job. Or if I have been thinking along a certain pattern, along a certain direction, and I am unaware that I am caught in that pattern, then when I approach this question I am always approaching it according to the pattern that my mind has established. Or if I am emotional, romantic, then my approach will be sloppy, not precise, not exact.

So one must be very clear for oneself how one approaches this problem, because if we approach it with any pattern at all we shall not be able to solve it. Therefore, is our mind free from patterns? From ideals? From a direction? Are you aware of the confusion of the world, which is becoming worse every day? And of the confusion in us which we have inherited, to which we have added? Of the society in which we live, which is so utterly confused, where there is such great injustice: millions starving and the affluent society; tyranny and democratic freedom to think what you like, to express what you like?

Our mind and our consciousness is the consciousness and the mind of the world. Wherever you go man is suffering, anxious, uncertain, lonely, desperate in his loneliness, burdened with sorrow, insecure. Psychologically, you are the humanity, you are not separate from the rest of mankind. The idea that you are an individual with a mind that is specially yours is an absurdity because this brain has evolved through time. It is the brain of mankind, and that brain is part of mankind, genetically, and so on, and so on. So you are the world and the world is you. It is not an idea or a concept, a utopian nonsense; it is a fact. And that mind is utterly confused. And we are trying to discover for ourselves the root of it.

What is the cause of these divisions between man and woman, between nation and nation, between one group and another group, these divisions of belief, ideals, concepts, historical conclusions, and materialistic attitudes? Division must inevitably create conflict. That is a fact. Through division we think that there can be security; where there is division as British, French, German, each group holding together as an idea, as a concept, under a flag, they think there is security. And this isolation must inevitably create division. So do we understand very deeply the truth that as long as there is division there must be conflict? Obviously there is no security in this isolation, this seclusion. You can build a wall around yourself as a nation but that wall is going to be broken down.

So what is the cause, the root, of this division? Each human being in the world thinks, lives according to the pattern, that he is separate from another, with *his* problems, *his* anxieties, *his* neurosis, *his* particular way of thinking. The center of this is the idea that I am separate from you. Now, is that a fact? Is it a fact that we are separate individuals, totally different from another? You may be tall, you may be short, have black hair, white hair, but inwardly are we different? Inwardly we all go through the same, or similar, things. So there is no division psychologically. And as long as we accept that idea that we are separate you must have conflict and, therefore, division and confusion.

You hear a statement like this, that as long as you think you are separate from another human being psychologically, there must be conflict and disorder. That is a fact. When you hear that, do you make an abstraction of it as an idea and then see how that idea can be carried out? Or it is a fact? If it is a fact, then you can do something about it. But if you are merely making an abstraction of that fact into an idea then we are getting lost, because you have your idea and I have my idea. But it is a common fact upon which we stand as human beings, that as long as there is division inside me and you, there must be conflict and disorder and confusion. But our minds are so conditioned; for thousands of years we have been conditioned by what other people have said to think that we are separate. Religions have said that we are separate, that each individual must save himself; that whole pattern is repeated over and over and over again. Being so conditioned it is very difficult to accept something which perhaps is true. I am using the word *perhaps* because I am not being dogmatic; but it is a fact. Going into it analytically with you, if you are willing, with argument, intellectually, reasoning, at the end of it, we come to the same fact.

If we want to understand the nature of confusion and the ending of confusion—completely, not relatively—are we aware of this fact? If we are aware, then the question arises: What shall I do? I know I am divided, now how am I to put away this division?

Is the fact of this division different from the observer who is observing the fact? I will explain a little. I observe greed. I am greedy. Is that greed which I observe different from me, from the observer who says, "I am greedy"? Or greed is the observer? Right? So there is no division between the observer who says, "I am greedy" and who acts upon greed, saying, "I must not be greedy. I must control it. I must suppress it. I must go beyond it." So there is a division, and that division is conflict and, therefore disorder. But the fact is, that the observer who says "I am greedy," that observer *is* greed himself. Have you gone that far? If you have gone that far, then I am asking: Is this confusion, this division, different from the observer who is me observing it? Or is this confusion, this division, me? My whole being is that, right? I wonder if you come to that point, otherwise you can't go much further. Please come! This is really important if you can really understand this once and for all as a fact. If you understand it, it will make life totally different, because in that there is no conflict. I will point it out.

Suppose I am attached to a person. In that attachment and in the consequences of that attachment are innumerable pains, jealousy, anxiety, dependency, the whole consequence of attachment. In that attachment to the person there is division immediately. Now is that attachment, the feeling of dependence, clinging, holding on to somebody, different from me? Or I am that? *I am attachment*. If one realizes that, conflict ends. It is so. Not that I must get rid of it, not that I must be independent, detached; detachment is attachment; if I try to become detached I am attached to that detachment.

So now am I very clear that there is no division: When I say I am attached, I am attachment, I am the state of attachment. Therefore, I have removed completely all conflict, haven't I? Do you realize that? I am that.

So I, me, is confusion. It is not that I realize I am confusion, or that I have been told that I am confusion, but the fact is that I, as a human being, *am* in a state of confusion. Any action I do will bring more confusion. So I am in a state of total confusion. And all the struggle to overcome it, suppress it, to be detached, all that is gone, all movement of escape has completely come to an end. If it has not, don't move from there. Be free first of all escapes, of all verbal, symbolic escapes, and remain totally with the fact that you are, as a human being, in a state of confusion. Then what has taken place?

We are two friends talking this over, this is not therapy or any of that nonsense, or psychological analysis. We are two people talking this over together, saying how we have come to that point, logically, rationally, unemotionally, and, therefore, sanely. Because to be sane is the most difficult thing. So we have come to that point: that is, I am that. What has taken place in the mind?

Before, I wasted energy in suppressing, trying to find how not to be confused, going to some guru or someone else. All that I have done is a wastage of energy. Now when there is the realization that I am confused, what has happened? Come with me! My mind then is completely attentive to confusion. My mind is in a state of complete attention with regard to confusion. Right? Therefore, what takes place? When there is complete attention, there is no confusion. It is only when there is no attention that confusion arises. Confusion arises when there is division, which is inattention.

Where there is total attention there is no dissipation of energy. When I am saying, "How am I to get this total attention?" that is a wastage of energy. When you see that where there is confusion it is brought about by inattention, then that very inattention is attention.

Now with that attention we are going to examine fear, pleasure, suffering. It is important to be free of fear. The mind has never been free of fear. You may cover it, you may suppress it, you may be unaware of it, you may be so enchanted by the world outside that you are never aware of your own deep-rooted fears. Where there is fear there is no freedom, there is no love, there is discontent. To see this, you must have the capacity to run—not physically but inwardly run, jump—not go step by step like a snail.

One sees what fear does in our life. Fear brings darkness to the mind. We are not talking of a particular neurotic fear, but about fear itself. When we understand the root of fear, fear about something particular disappears. If I am afraid of the dark, that is my particular fear and I want that particular fear to be resolved; I am not concerned with the whole field of fear. But if I understand the whole field of fear, the other thing doesn't exist. We are concerned with the whole field of fear. Can that fear be dissolved completely, so that the physical fear and the complex fears of the psyche, the inward fears, dissolve? The physical fears one can deal with fairly simply, but if you are attached to physical fears and are concerned only with resolving the physical fears then you are attached to that which will then create division and, therefore, conflict. If we understand first the psychological fears, then you can deal with the physical fears, not the other way round. First deal with the wider fear, the depth and the nature and the darkness of fear, then you will yourself resolve the particular physical fears. Don't start the other way, with the physical fear, which is what we all want to do.

The psychological fears are far more important; they make us such ugly human beings. When there is fear, we become violent, we want to destroy in the name of God, in the name of religion, in the name of social revolution, and so on, and so on. Now, can we as human beings, who have lived with this fear for immeasurable time, be free of it? We have asked that question; now how do you approach the problem of fear? Do you approach it with the desire to resolve it? If you do, you are again separating yourself from the fact of fear. So are you approaching it as an observer who is afraid and wants to resolve it, or do you realize that you are fear?

Have you given your total attention to this fact? That you, as a human being, who is the rest of humanity, are frightened, live in fear, consciously or unconsciously, with superficial fears or deep hidden fears? The hidden fear becomes completely open when you are attentive.

You are investigating, you are looking at yourself, not agreeing with the speaker, the speaker is not important. And I mean it, he is not important. What is important is that you walk away without a single shadow of fear. So when you become aware of fear, do you escape from it? Do you try to find an answer for it? Do you try to overcome it? If you do, you are dissipating energy; therefore, you are dividing and, therefore, there is conflict about fear and how to be free of it. All that arises. But if you realize that fear is you, there is no movement to be made. There is no movement to be made, you are that and, therefore, all your attention is directed, is that; in that attention fear is held.

It is up to you. You see, as long as we try to overcome, the very overcoming has to be overcome. But if you say, "Yes, it is a fact and I won't move from that," then the thing dissolves—completely, not relatively, not gone one day and then the next day is full of fears. It is gone when you have given complete attention to it.

It is similar with regard to pleasure. Be careful now! We have to be very careful here.

I don't know if you have noticed that right from the earliest time of man, one thing that has driven him everlastingly forward is pleasure, the pursuit of pleasure and the avoidance of sorrow. You can see it in the pictures, the paintings, the ancient writings, the symbols. Everything says, Pursue this, avoid that. Thought can divide life into fear, pleasure, sorrow, job; but they are all one, aren't they? See what we have done: our mind has been conditioned, accepting, living in this norm of constant pursuit of pleasure. God, if you have that image, is the essence of pleasure. You name it differently but your urge is to attain that ultimate sublime pleasure so that you will never be disturbed, you will never be in conflict, and so on, and so on, and so on. And we must understand it, not suppress it, not run away from it.

Why has pleasure, like sorrow, like fear, become so all important in life? Do you understand the word *sorrow,* the suffering of man, the suffering of centuries, war after war, destroying human beings, destroying nature, destroying animals, whales, everything. Man not only suffers but causes suffering. That is part of us, part of our consciousness. And we try to avoid that because we have not solved it. We think the pursuit of pleasure is the main thing, that in that at least we can have something accurate, something real that will go on. So that becomes dominant, and fear, sorrow, anxiety, are all in the background—not only sexual pleasures, but the remembrances, the pictures, and all the rest that goes on in the mind. If you watch it, you see what is happening, that your own minds become full of that. Not the actual act but the whole build-up, and that building-up is called love. So pleasure, love, suffering, fear are all entangled, all interrelated.

So will you take fear, pleasure, sorrow, separately, one by one? Or will you have the capacity to deal with the whole of it? Our minds are being broken up, so we take one by one, hoping to resolve one by one and come to the end of the breaking up, the fragments. Now how will you deal with the whole of it? Deal with your disorder, pleasure, fear, sorrow as a total movement of life? Not as something separate, but as a whole. Can you do it? That is, can you look at yourself as though it were in a mirror, psychologically, as a whole being? Or can you only look at a part?

How do you look at yourself? Can you take your job, your wife and children, your religion, your particular way of thinking, your experiences, your ideas, your intentions, your ambitions, as one unitary movement? That is the only way to solve the whole thing, not through fragments.

Now how will a mind, the brain, the emotions, that have been broken up for generations upon generations, approach or realize the totality? Will you approach the whole of life fragmentarily, business first, money first, house first, wife, children, sex, bit by bit? Or can your mind see the whole of existence? Is it capable of that? Or are you striving to see the whole of it? If you are striving to see the whole of it, it is finished, you will never have it, because then you create a division, conflict, confusion. To see that life is one movement, you need really to learn. Learn—not from me! Learn from yourself by observing. Learn to observe the division and see the futility of approaching that; see the obvious fact that you can't through one fragment approach the whole universe. You must have a mind that is capable of receiving the whole universe, and that is possible only when the mind is clear of confusion, fear. Then there is no shadow of division, as the "me" and "you," my country, your country, my dogma, and so on. That means, when there is complete freedom then there is the perception of the whole. And from that comprehension, from that intelligence, one can act in the world, to get a job, to get no job, to do anything. But now we approach it as parts and we are creating havoc in the world.

Why does the mind live in time? It has evolved in time. The present mind that we have has evolved through thousands of years. And that is normal and healthy, obviously. But we are asking why time has become so important psychologically, inwardly. Please ask yourself. Is it because we are always avoiding *what is* in order to become something else, moving from this to that? Psychologically I am this, but I should not be this but that. Psychologically I am unhappy, but I must be happy. The "must" or "will" or "shall be" is the movement of time. So the mind is caught in time because it is always moving away from this, from *what is.* It will change in time: "I will be good, give me time." That is like developing a muscle. Your muscle may not be sufficiently strong but if you keep on doing something to strengthen it, it will become strong. With the same mentality we say, "I am this, I will be that, so give me time." But will *what is* be changed through time? When I have great anxiety, can that anxiety be changed through time? That is, will I become, or be in, a state where I have no anxiety? See what I have done? I have anxiety; I have projected a state of not being anxious; and to arrive at that state I must have time. But I never ask if this anxiety I have can be changed immediately without allowing time. See what happens: I am anxious; I hope to be not anxious; there is a time interval, a lag, and in that lag of time all other activities are going on, other pressures, negligence; so anxiety is never solved. I think I will come to a state when I have no anxiety, so I am struggling, struggling. It is like a man who is violent. He has invented nonviolence, but in that time interval he is violent, so he never reaches nonviolence.

So the question is then: Can *what is* be transformed immediately, which means never allowing time to interfere? Listen to this, you will find out, it is really simple. If we apply our mind we can solve anything. They have been to the moon, built marvelous submarines, done incredible things. Here, psychologically, we are so reluctant, so incapable, or have made ourselves incapable. If you do not allow time, or never think in terms of time, then the fact is not. Because we allow time the fact becomes important. If there is no time it is resolved. Suppose I died this second, there is no problem. When I allow time, I am afraid of death. If I live completely without psychological time, it is an extraordinary thing. Time means accumulation. Time means remembrance. Time means accumulating knowledge about oneself. But when there is no time at all, psychologically, there is nothing.

Because we have allowed time as a factor to intervene between living and dying, fear arises. The nature of dying can be found in the living. That is, death is the ending, the ending of my possessions, my wife, my children, my house, my bank account. In that ending there is no argument. I don't say to death, "Please hold on a minute." So where there is ending, there is a beginning. I will go into it.

When there is an ending to attachment—completely, not just to persons and ideas but the whole process of attachment, with all the consequences of that—there is a totally different state of mind. Isn't there? I have been attached to my furniture and that attachment has been a burden. With the ending of that burden there is freedom. So ending is more important than beginning. So can I, living, end? End my anxiety, end my fears. End, not the bank account, I am not talking of that, but ending psychologically. Ending my uncertainty. When I am confused, to end it, not say, "I must find out why I am confused, what is the cause of confusion, and I must be free from confusion." All that is time. That is negligence, whereas diligence is to be aware of the whole movement of time and to end anxiety immediately. Therefore, there is no accumulation psychologically as knowledge.

Now death is ending. Ending of everything. Death is an ending and I am living. We are living, active. Can we psychologically end everything? Can you end your attachment instantly, immediately—your anger, your violence, your greed, your this and that, end while living? Then living is dying. Not living and ultimately dying. Living means the dying, otherwise you are not alive. And most of us are frightened of dying because we have never been able to live properly, we have never lived. We have lived in conflict, in struggle, in pain, in anxiety, and we call that living. Living is not all that. If all that can be ended, then there is living. So you are then living and dying. They go together, like a flower with perfume; the perfume is not apart from the flower, it is there.

This is the actual ending of senility, if you go into it very deeply, so the mind never gets old like a machine that is always wearing itself out because of friction. But it is not your mind, it is the human mind. The mind is the result of a million years, it is the mind of the Indian, of the Chinese, the Russians, all other human beings, because they go through similar pain, anxiety, sorrow, pleasures, occasional joys and occasional love. So our brain, our mind, is the mind of humanity. If you can understand that one real fact then we will live without any division, which is causing such disaster in the world.

Because their minds are everlastingly chattering, everlastingly moving from one thing to another, driven by desire, driven by seeking reward and avoiding pain, human beings have always sought some kind of quietness, some kind of peace in which at least for ten minutes it can be quiet. Man has sought this. Go to the church, sit there quietly. Go to a marvelous cathedral, when there is no circus going on, and be quiet. And it is a strange fact that in all these churches there is never a moment of quietness, except when it is empty. Because if you are quiet, you might inquire. If you are quiet, you might begin to doubt. But if you are occupied all the time, you never have time to look around, to question, to doubt, to ask. That may be one of the great tricks of the human mind.

What is meditation and why should one meditate? Is it natural? Like breathing, like seeing, like hearing, is it natural? And why have we made it so unnatural? Taking postures, following systems of Buddhist meditation, Tibetan meditation, Christian meditation, Tantric meditations, and the meditations set by your favorite guru. Aren't all those really abnormal? Why should I take a certain position to meditate? Why should I practice, practice, practice? To arrive where? Can I follow a system—twenty minutes in the morning, twenty minutes in the evening—to have a quiet mind? Having achieved a little quiet mind I can go off and do other mischief all day long.

Is there a way of meditating that is none of these things? People say meditation is to quiet the mind, to have a mind that is capable of observation, to have a mind that is completely centered, completely concentrated, so that there is no thought except one thought, one picture, one image, one center upon which you are looking. Right? I don't know if you have gone through all this? The speaker has played with them for half an hour for each of these meditations, for ten minutes, five minutes, and they meant nothing.

You have to go into the question of who is the controller and who is the controlled. Our whole life, if you observe, is this: controlling and not controlling: I must control my emotions, I must control my thinking; I can only control my thinking by constant practice; and to practice I must have a system. A system implies a mechanical process, making the mind more and more mechanical. It is already mechanical now but we want to make it much more dull. Why do we go through all this? You want to have an experience, and you know drugs do you harm; therefore, you put them aside, but hope that by practicing something you will experience something else.

Why do human beings demand experience? Is the mind asleep, and experience means a challenge? Or is the mind awake and so does not need an experience. You have to find out if your mind is asleep, or bored with the experiences that you have had: sex, drugs, and all the rest. You want something far beyond all that; you are always craving for more delightful, more extravagant, experience. Why does the mind demand experience? Ask yourself, please.

There is only one thing. A mind that is very clear is free from all entanglements of attachment. Such a mind is a light to itself. Therefore, it does not want an experience, there is nothing to experience. You cannot experience enlightenment. The very idea of experiencing it is a stupid thing to say; to say, "I have achieved enlightenment," is really dishonest. You cannot experience truth because there must be an experiencer to experience. If there is no experiencer, there is no experience at all. But we are attached to our experiencer and, therefore, we are always asking for more and more and more.

Meditation generally as it is accepted now is the practice of a system, breathing properly, sitting in the right position, wanting or craving greater experience, or the ultimate experience. This is what we are doing. And all that is a constant struggle, a never-ending struggle. This is a never-ending struggle, which is hoping to end all struggles! See what we have done. I am struggling, struggling, struggling to end struggling sometime in the future. See what tricks I have played on myself. I am caught in time. I don't say, "Why should I struggle at all?" If I can end this struggle *that* is enlightenment. To have no shadow of conflict. But we do not want to give up all those efforts; we are caught in time. And to be free of time is to be free to have pure observation, and then the mind becomes extraordinarily quiet. You don't have to make the mind quiet. If you end all conflict, the mind naturally becomes quiet. And when the mind is absolutely silent, without any movement of thought, then perhaps you will see something, perhaps there is something sacred beyond all words. And this man has sought everlastingly, something that is beyond measure, beyond thought, which is incorruptible, unnameable, eternal. That can only take place when the mind is absolutely free and completely silent.

So one must begin very near, very near. And when you begin very near, there is no far. When you begin near, there is no distance and, therefore, there is no time. And it is only then that that which is most holy can be.

Brockwood Park, September 6 and September 7, 1980

My friends, if you have listened to yourself, the speaker is only a mirror in which you see yourself as you are. If you see yourself as you are, then you can throw away the mirror, break it. The mirror is not important. It has no value. What has value is that you see clearly in that mirror yourself as you are, the pettiness, the narrowness, the brutality, the anxieties, the fears. When you begin to understand yourself then you go profoundly into something that is beyond all measure. But you must take the first step. And nobody is going to help you to take that first step.

We are thinking together, walking down a lane full of quietness and a great sense of beauty. One wonders what beauty is. You may see some statue or picture or a lovely head of the Buddha in a museum, or in a house, and you say how marvelous it is; but behind the words, behind the structure of a painting, the shadows, the proportions, what is beauty? Is it in the way you look at it? Is it in the picture? Is it in the face of a person? When you see a marvelous mountain against a blue sky, with the great depth of a valley and snowcapped peaks, when you look at all that great beauty, for a moment you have forgotten yourself. The mountain is so vast, so extraordinarily lighted by the morning sun catching the highest peaks, and your whole brain is struck by the grandeur, by the greatness of that sight, and for a second you forget all about yourself, forget all about your worries; you forget your wife, your husband, your children, your country. And you look at that with all your being, and have no sense of contradiction, duality. Its splendor is there and the self, the "me" is for a second put aside by the greatness of that beauty.

As one came in, one looked at the moon, very young, new, extraordinarily simple. And, therefore, one thought, what is the point of talking at all? What is the point of reading books, attending meetings, what is the point of all this existence when one cannot look at this simple thing clearly, with great love and affection, a simple thing, to approach life with all its complexity, simply, without all the accumulated knowledge of our past, our traditions? Just to look at this vast movement of life, simply, with a brain that is not burdened, a brain that is active, alive, full of energy, with clarity, simplicity.

Having said that, let us proceed together. We human beings have suffered a great deal. There have been incessant wars. For the last five thousand years there has been a war practically every year, human beings killing each other, destroying what they have built, great monuments being destroyed overnight. This has been the history of man, perpetual conflict, war. And through wars man has suffered enormously. How many people have shed tears—for their sons, their husbands left maimed for life, one arm, no legs, blind. Mankind has shed tears endlessly. And we too are shedding tears, because our life is rather empty, lonely. And we suffer too, all of us, not only watching the suffering of others but also the grief, the pain,. the anxiety, of our own life, the poverty of people, not the poverty of the poor only but also the poverty of our own minds and hearts. And when we begin to discover this enormous poverty, in spite of our vast information and knowledge, that breeds also great sorrow.

There is the sorrow of loneliness, the sorrow brought about by man's inhumanity to man, the sorrow of losing your friend, your son, your brother, your mother, and so on. We have carried this sorrow throughout our lives for centuries upon centuries. And we have never asked if that sorrow can ever end. We are asking now, together, looking at this sorrow of the world and the sorrow in which one lives, in your own heart, in your own mind, in your own brain. We are asking whether that sorrow can ever end, or must men and women always carry it throughout the future from the past. Can that sorrow ever end?

As there is an art in love and so on, there is also an art in questioning, doubting; doubting one's own conclusions, one's own opinions, to question why we tolerate this vast burden of sorrow. Sorrow is also self-pity, the feeling of utter loneliness, and the sorrow that is brought about through great failures, through comparison, through the whole movement of feeling a sense of lack of relationship to anybody. But we never go to the very end of it. We would rather escape from it, seek some form of comfort, some form of drug that gives us solace.

So, could we not try to find an answer, not ask whether sorrow can be conquered, but be aware to see the full meaning of that word *sorrow.* Sorrow also means, etymologically, passion—not lust, passion. Without passion, life becomes rather dull, meaningless. And the ending of sorrow brings about passion. So together we are looking at this word, the content of that word, the significance of that thing called *sorrow,* which man has carried throughout his life—looking at it, not explaining it away, not finding the cause. There are many causes of sorrow—the death of a son, the failure of not being successful, not being able to fulfill, having no identification, and so on and so on—but if you are inquiring into the causes of sorrow then you are also preventing yourself from looking at the word, the beauty, the strength of that word.

Sorrow means grief, pain, anxiety, desperate loneliness, the meaninglessness of this existence. All that and more is contained in that word. Can you look at it wholly, as you would hold a precious jewel, a marvelous piece of sculpture? Hold it, remain with it, and not in any way allow thought to come and interfere with that actuality. If you can so remain with that, then that very word, the significance of that word, is totally ended. But we never stay with anything. We always want to find an end, and so we are always moving away from that very jewel that would give us great vitality, great strength, great passion.

Are we walking together, or are you merely listening to these words and getting emotional, romantic and, therefore, never looking at that thing, the pain of it, the grief, the emptiness of one's own being? If one can really completely hold that jewel, it is a great jewel, but man has tried to do everything he can to escape from it; volumes have been written about it. But the books, the explanations, the words, are not the actual. Remain with the actual, then that very attention brings an end to that thing that we call sorrow.

Where there is sorrow there cannot be love. Love is not related to any activity of the human brain. Love is something that comes into being when there is no fear, when there is an end to sorrow. Then that very love becomes compassion, which is passion, with its immense intelligence.

We are all going to die, but we human beings put that as far away as possible from us; and so there is duality: living and dying. Have you ever considered what duality is and whether duality, the opposite, exists at all? We have been brought up by tradition, by education, by the books, to think that there is duality, contradiction, man and woman, anger and not being angry, violence and nonviolence, and so on. So we have divided the whole of life into duality. Is there such a thing as duality, is there an opposite, psychologically? Of course, there is an opposite between man and woman, between daylight and darkness, sunrise and sunset. You are taller than another, someone is fairer than another, one person is more learned than another; there is that physical duality, the opposites, dark hair, fair hair, the beautiful and the ugly.

Now, psychologically, inwardly, is there an opposite? Your tradition says there is. Books have been written about it saying that it is only the liberated who are free from duality—which is such utter nonsense. Sorry. You and I can look at this problem very simply—simply, not with all the complications of philosophers. There is duality outwardly, but inwardly, psychologically, inside the skin there is only one thing. There is anger, for example, and when you say, "I must not be angry," it becomes duality, the ideal which thought has projected, has structured from the pain it has. So there is only that fact. Violence is a fact, nonviolence is nonfact. So why do we give such importance to the nonfact, which then becomes the opposite? We are caught in this ugly business of duality, which means choice, to choose.

Is there an opposite, psychologically, in anything at all? There is violence, anger, hatred, dislike. Those are facts. But to invent a nonfact like nonviolence, that you must like people, and so on and so on, is just unreal. Therefore, there is only the fact. And a fact has no opposite. When we live with fact, then there is no conflict involved. Have you understood anything of this? But our whole condition is based on duality: I am this, I must not be that; I am a coward, I must be brave; I am ignorant about myself, so I must learn that. We are caught up in this. And we are saying there is no opposite psychologically at all actually. The opposite is structured, or put together, by thought to escape from the actual. I am violent, that's actual; but there are a great many people telling me that I must be nonviolent. The nonviolence is totally unreal, because I am violent. But if I remain with the actuality then I can do something about it, or not do anything about it, not pretend. To pursue the ideal of nonviolence is just playing games with yourself. While you are pursuing nonviolence, you are actually violent. So we are saying there is no psychological opposite, there is only *what is.* And if you understand that, then does the conflict of duality exist at all?

With that quality of brain that has understood this question of duality, let us look at what is called living and dying. We are trying to eliminate altogether this conflict between *what is* and "what should be." Then the brain is free and full of energy to face things as they are. So there is the living and the dying as two opposites. To understand both, the living and the dying, one must approach this nondualistically. What is living, what do you call living? Going to the office from nine o'clock in the morning to six o'clock in the evening every day of your life for the next sixty years, being bossed, being bullied, and you bullying somebody else? Or you are a businessman always wanting more and more money, more power, better position, and then go home and quarrel with your wife, sleep with her, and beat her up verbally, or actually. And this constant struggle, constant conflict, the utter despair, hopelessness, goes on. This is what we call living. And in your heart of hearts there is fear, despair, anxiety, grief. This is actuality, isn't it? And you are frightened to leave that, because death is coming. One is deeply identified with this so-called living, has taken roots in that, and is frightened to end all that.

And so you say there will be a next life. Next life is the continuity of the same old pattern, only perhaps in a different environment. If you believe in the next life, then you must live rightly now—morally, ethically, have some sense of humility. But you really do not believe in the next life, you talk about it, you write volumes about it. If you actually believe, then you must live now rightly, because what you are now, your future will be the same. If you do not change now your future will be the same. This is logical. This is sane.

For us, death is total ending, the ending of your attachment, ending all that you have collected. You cannot take it with you. You may like to have it until the last minute, but you cannot possibly take it with you. We have divided life into dying and living, and this division has brought about great fear. Out of that fear we invent all kinds of theories that are very comforting; they may be illusory, but they are very comforting. Illusions are comfortably neurotic. But is it possible, as we live, to die to things that we are attached to? If I am attached to my reputation, and death is coming along, I am getting older and I am frightened, because I am going to lose everything. So can I be totally free of the image, of the reputation, that people have given me? So that I am dying as I am living. So the division between the living and dying is not miles apart, it is together. Do you understand the great beauty that each day, or each second, there is no accumulation, no psychological accumulation? You have to accumulate clothes, money, and so on, that's a different matter, but psychologically there is no accumulation as knowledge, as attachment, saying, "It's mine."

Will you do it? Will you actually do this thing so that this conflict between death and living, with all its pain and fear and anxiety, comes totally to an end? So that you are—the brain is—incarnated. *Then* the brain is being reborn afresh, so that it has tremendous freedom. So, when living, be with death, so that you are a guest in this world, so that you have no roots anywhere, so that you have a brain that is amazingly alive. Because if you carry all the burdens of yesterday, your brain becomes mechanical, dull. If you leave all the psychological memories, hurts, pains, behind, every day, then it means dying and living are together. In that there is no fear.

What happens to the person who does not do any of this? Please, this is being said with great humility, with great compassion and affection. I hear from you of a totally different way of living. I see the logic of it, the sanity of it, the clarity of it. I see it intellectually, verbally I have accepted it. But I pursue my old ways, the ways of my life, to which I am accustomed. And I am going to die and I am frightened, as most people are frightened. So I ask what is going to happen? Will I be reborn?

My consciousness accepts this old way of life and hopes that perhaps next life it will have a better chance. But is that consciousness, which I have said is "mine," my consciousness at all? That consciousness is the consciousness of humanity. Each one of us shares this consciousness, so it is not mine. Please, you must question whether your consciousness is your individual consciousness or is shared by all humanity. All humanity goes through what you are going through, in a different environment, in a different ambiance. So you are not actually an individual. You may have a different body from another, you may have a better bank account. One may be lame, one may be healthy, but inwardly your being is shared by all the rest of humanity. Therefore, you are humanity. So as long as you think you are an individual, you are living in illusion, because your consciousness, your life, is shared by everybody on this earth. So when you die, your consciousness, which is shared by all humanity, will continue. And that consciousness manifests itself, through someone, and then he says. "It is mine," "I am an individual," *"Atman,"* "soul," and so on.

So there is a way of living that is totally different. Then you are no longer concerned with dying, but with living—living which contains, which moves with, death. I leave it to you. If you don't understand, please don't deny it, find out, question, doubt your own individuality. It is possible to live a life psychologically in which there is never a continual recording, there is the ending of recording. Say you are flattered, or insulted, that is recorded.

Now, not to record flattery or insult is to have a brain that is free, not burdened by a thousand records of a thousand yesterdays.

The religions which exist throughout the world accept dogmas, some fantastic beliefs, some meaningless rituals. To find out what religion is, one must doubt the accepted thing, have the vitality, the strength, to wipe it out. One must question, doubt, wipe away all the structure put together by thought. When you question all this, to find out the nature of a religious brain, religious mind, there must be freedom to inquire. If you have a hypothesis, it must be proved under a microscope, or under the clarity of your own attention. If a human being, you, has the intention, the drive, the energy, the passion to find out if there is something sacred, holy, to do that there must be no fear, there must be no sense of anxiety, there must be complete freedom. And that is meditation.

Meditation can only be actual, truthful, honest, when there is no fear, no hurt, no anxiety, no sorrow. Meditation can only take place when there is no conscious effort made to meditate. I am afraid it goes against everything you believe.

How do you come upon that which is sacred? Is there anything sacred? Man has sought throughout the ages something beyond. From the times of the ancient Sumerians, the Egyptians, Romans, people have sought. And they worshiped light, worshiped the sun, worshiped the tree, worshiped the mother, never finding anything. So can we together discover or rather, come upon, that thing which is most holy?

That can only take place when there is absolute silence, when the brain is absolutely quiet. You can discover for yourself—if you are attentive, watchful, watchful of your words, the meaning of the words, never saying one thing and doing anther, if you are watchful all the time—that the brain has its own natural rhythm. But upon that natural rhythm thought has placed all kinds of things. For us, knowledge is tremendously important. To do anything physical *requires* knowledge, but psychological knowledge, the knowledge you have accumulated about your hurts, about your vanity, your arrogance, your ambition, all that knowledge is you. And with that knowledge we try to find out if there is anything most holy. You can never find out through knowledge, because knowledge is limited, and it will always be—physically, technologically, and psychologically.

So the brain must be absolutely quiet, not through control, not through following some method, system, not by cultivating silence. Silence implies space. Have you noticed how little space we have in our brain? It is cluttered up, full with so many thousands of things; it has very little space. And for silence there must be space because that which is immeasurable, that which is unnameable, cannot exist or be perceived or seen by a narrow little brain. If you take a journey into yourself, empty all the content that you have collected and go very, very deeply, then there is that vast space, that so-called emptiness, that is full of energy.

And in that state alone there is that which is most sacred, most holy.

New Delhi, November 13, 1983

TRUTH MOST HOLY

1

We are going to talk together about the whole of our existence—from the moment we are born until we die. In that period of time, whether it be fifty years, ninety years, or a hundred years, we go through all kinds of problems and difficulties. We have economic, social, and religious problems, problems of personal relationship, problems of individual fulfillment, wanting to find roots in some place or other. We have innumerable psychological wounds, fears, pleasures, sensations. There is a great deal of fear in all human beings, a great deal of anxiety, uncertainty; and there is the pursuit of pleasure. All human beings on this beautiful earth suffer a great deal of pain, loneliness. We are going to talk about all that together, and about what place religion has in modern life. We are also going to talk over together the question of death, what is a religious mind, and what is meditation. Is there anything that is beyond thought and is there anything sacred in life, or is everything matter, so that we lead only a materialistic life?

This is a conversation between you and the speaker in which there is no implication of conversion, or propaganda, or of introducing new theories, ideas, and exotic nonsense. That would be too terrible. We are going to, if you will kindly, talk over together our problems as two friends. Though we don't know each other, we are going to talk, discuss, have a conversation—which is much more important than being lectured at or being told what to do, what to believe, what to have faith in, and so on. On the contrary, we are going to observe dispassionately, impersonally, not anchored to any particular problem or theory, what mankind has done to the world and what we have done to each other. We are going to take a very long, complex journey together, and it is your responsibility, as well as that of the speaker, that we walk together, investigate together, look together at the world we have created.

The society in which we live is put together by man. Each one of us has contributed to it. Life is very complex. We like to look at complexity and get more and more complex. We never look at anything simply, with our brains, with our hearts, with our whole being. We have lived on this earth for many millennia, and during those long periods of time mankind has suffered loneliness, despair, uncertainty, confusion, multiple choices and, therefore, multiple complexities. There have been wars—not only physical bloody wars but also psychological wars. And mankind has asked if there can be peace on earth. But apparently this has not been possible. There are about forty wars going on at the present time, ideological, theoretical, economic, social. During historical times, perhaps about five thousand to six thousand years, there have been wars practically every year. We are preparing for wars now. Two ideologies, the communist and the so-called democratic, are at war over what kind of implements we should use, control of armaments. War seems to be the common lot of mankind. One observes all over the world the piling up of armaments, from the tiny little nation or tribe to the highly sophisticated affluent society like yours. How can we have peace on earth? Is it at all possible?

It has been said that there is no peace on earth, only in heaven. This is repeated in different ways, both in the East and the West. Christians have killed more than anybody else on earth. We are observing these facts, these actualities, not taking sides. And then there are the different religions. In Buddhism there is no god; in Hinduism somebody calculated that there are about three hundred thousand gods—that's rather fun, you can choose whichever god you like. In Christianity and Islam there is only one god, based on two books, the Bible and the Koran. So religions have divided man. Just as nationalism, which is a glorified form of tribalism, has divided man, so has religious ardor. Fundamentalists in India, here, and in Europe, are reviving their religious traditions. I wonder if you have ever looked at the word *reviving?* You can only revive something that is dead or dying. You can't revive a living thing.

Man has always been in conflict. Everyone in this world goes through all kinds of misery, all kinds of sorrow, pain, desperate loneliness; and we long to escape from all that. We are observing together this extraordinary phenomenon: how man, after these thousands of years, still remains a barbarian—cruel, vulgar, full of anxiety and hatred. Violence is increasing in the world, so one asks if there can be peace on this earth, because without peace, inwardly, psychologically, the brain cannot flower; human beings cannot live completely, holistically.

Why are we human beings, after this long evolution in which we have gathered immense experience, knowledge, a great deal of information, still perpetually in conflict? That's the real question. Because when there is no conflict there is naturally peace. Without getting angry or irritated with what we are investigating together it is the responsibility of men and women to inquire, not merely intellectually, verbally, but with your hearts, with your brains, with all your being, and find out why we are what we are.

We have tried various religions, various economic and social systems, and yet we live in conflict. Can this conflict in each one of us end—completely, not partially, not occasionally? It's a very serious question. It demands a serious answer. Why do human beings, including you, and the speaker perhaps, live in perpetual conflict, with problems and divisions? Why have we divided the world into nationalities, religious groups, social behaviors? Can we seriously inquire into whether it is possible to end conflict? First psychologically, inwardly, because if there is a certain quality of freedom inwardly, then we shall produce a society in which there will be no conflict. It is our responsibility as human beings, as so-called individuals, seriously to put our brains, our energy, our passion, into discovering for ourselves—not according to any philosopher or psychiatrist, but find out for ourselves—whether this conflict between human beings can end.

What is conflict? Why have we lived with conflict? Why have we problems? Please inquire with the speaker into these questions. What is a problem? The etymological meaning of that word is "something thrown at you," a challenge, something you have to answer. When you are a child, you are sent to school, where you have the problems of writing, mathematics, history, science, chemistry, and so on. So from childhood you are trained to have problems. Look at it carefully. Your brain is conditioned, trained, educated to have problems. Observe it for yourself. We are together investigating, looking into the problems that we have. From childhood we are trained, educated, conditioned to have problems. And when new problems arise, as they inevitably do, it is our brains, full of problems, that try to solve them and thereby increase them, which is what is happening in the world. The politicians all over the world are increasing problem after problem. And they have found no answers.

Is it possible to have a brain that is free, so that you can solve problems, instead of a brain cluttered with problems? Is that possible? If you say it is or is not possible, you have stopped investigating. What is important in this inquiry is that one must have a great deal of doubt, skepticism, never accepting anything at its face value or according to pleasure or gratification. Life is much too serious.

We should inquire not only into the nature of conflict and problems, but also perhaps into something which may be much more important: all over the world, go where you will, every human being on this earth goes through all kinds of sorrow. Millions have had tears, and occasional laughter. Like you, every human being on this earth has had great loneliness, despair, anxiety, has been confused, uncertain. Psychologically, this is a fact, an actuality. This is observable; you can see it on every face on this earth. And so psychologically you are the rest of mankind. You may be tall, short, black, or white, but psychologically you are mankind. Please understand this—not intellectually or ideologically or as a hypothesis, but as an actuality, a burning reality—that you psychologically are the rest of mankind. Therefore, psychologically you are not individuals. Although religions, except perhaps parts of Hinduism and Buddhism, have entertained, encouraged, the sense of individual growth, of saving individual souls and all that business, in actuality your consciousness is not yours. It is the rest of mankind's, because we all go through the same mill, the same endless conflict. When you realize this, not emotionally, not as an intellectual concept but as something actual, real, true, then you will not kill another human being. You will never kill another, either verbally or intellectually, ideologically or physically, because then you are killing yourself.

But individuality has been encouraged all over the world. Each one is struggling for himself, his success, his fulfillment, his achievement, pursuing his desires and creating havoc in the world. Please understand this very carefully. We are not saying that each individual is not important; on the contrary, if you are really concerned with peace—globally, not just in your own little backyard—as most serious people must be concerned, as you are the rest of humanity, that is a great responsibility.

So we must find out for ourselves why human beings have reduced the world to what it is now. What is the cause of all this? Why have we made such a mess of everything we touch? Why is there conflict in our personal relationships? Why is there conflict between your god and the other's god? We must inquire together into whether it is possible to end conflict. Otherwise we will never have peace in this world. Peace on earth was talked about long before Christianity. Long before Christianity, people worshiped trees, stones, animals, lightning, the sun; there was no sense of "God" because they considered the earth as the mother to be worshiped, to be preserved, spared, not destroyed as we are doing now.

Without agreeing or disagreeing, can all of us look at things as they are; not as you think they are, not from your idea or concept of *what is,* but just look? Look nonverbally, if that's possible; that's much more difficult.

First of all, this is the actual world we live in. You cannot possibly escape from it through monasteries, through religious experiences. One must doubt all one's experiences. Man has done everything on earth possible to run away from the actuality of daily living with all its complexities. Why do we have conflict in relationship between man and woman, sexual division? In this peculiar relationship, the man is pursuing his own ambition, his own greed, his own desires, his own fulfillment, and the woman is doing the same. So there are two ambitious, driving beings, driven by desire, two parallel lines never meeting, except perhaps sexually. How can there be a relationship between two people when each one is pursuing his own desires, ambitions, greeds? In this relationship, because there is this division, there is no love. That word *love* is spoiled, spat upon, degraded; it has become merely sensuous, pleasurable. Love is not pleasure. Love is not something put together by thought. It is not something dependent on sensation. So how can there be right, true relationship between two people when each one considers his own importance? Self-interest is the beginning of corruption, destruction, whether it be in the politician or the religious man. Self-interest dominates the world and, therefore, there is conflict.

There is separation, as the Jew and the Arab, as the Christian who believes in some savior and the Hindu who doesn't. There is national division, religious division, individual divisions. Where there is division there must be conflict. That is a law. So we live our daily life in a little circumscribed self, a limited self. Self is always limited and that is the cause of conflict. That is the central core of our struggle, pain, anxiety.

One becomes aware of it, as most people must naturally, not because you're told to or because you read some book of philosophy or psychology, but because it's an actual fact. Each one is concerned with himself. He lives in a separate world all to himself.

And, therefore, there is division between you and another, between you and your religion, between you and your god, between you and your ideologies. So is it possible to understand, not intellectually but deeply, that you are the rest of mankind? Whatever you do, good or bad, affects the rest of mankind because you *are* mankind.

Your consciousness is not yours. Your consciousness is made up of its content. Without the content there is no consciousness. Your consciousness, like that of the rest of humanity, is made up of beliefs, fears, faith, gods, personal ambitions. Your whole consciousness is made up of all this, put together by thought.

One hopes that we have taken the journey together, that together we are walking the same road, not that you are listening to a series of ideas. We are not pursuing ideas or ideologies, but facing actuality, because in actuality and going beyond that actuality is the truth. And when there is truth it is the most dangerous thing. Truth is very dangerous because it brings a revolution in oneself.

Have you ever gone into the question of why we ask questions? Not that you should not, but we are inquiring. Suppose you ask the speaker a question and he answers it; either you accept it or deny it. If it is satisfactory to you according to your conditioning or your background, then you say, "Yes, I agree with you entirely." Or if you don't agree, you say, "What nonsense." But if you begin to inquire into the question itself, is the answer separate from the question? Or does the answer lie in the question itself? The perfume of a flower is the flower. The very flower is the essence of that perfume. But we depend on others so much to be helped, to be encouraged, to solve our problems; therefore, out of our confusion we create authority, the gurus, the priests.

It is good to ask questions. You know, we have lost the art of investigation, discussion, not taking sides but looking at things. It is very complex.

We should also ask why, from childhood, we are hurt psychologically. Most of us are wounded psychologically, and from that wound, whether one is conscious of it or not, many of our problems arise. A child is wounded by a scolding, by hearing something ugly, brutal, violent. When you say "I am wounded," who is it that is wounded? Is it the image that you have built about yourself that is wounded, the psyche? The psyche is the "me" and the me is the image I have built about myself. There is nothing spiritual about it. That's another ugly word, *spiritual.* So that image gets hurt and we carry that image right through our life. If one image is not pleasant, we put together another image which is pleasant, encouraging it as worthwhile, significant, giving intellectual meaning to our life.

Is it possible to live on this earth not having a single image about anybody—including god, if there is such an entity—no image about your wife and your children and your husband, or anyone? Not to have a single image? Then it is possible never to be hurt.

Just to observe without any distortion is entirely different from analysis, as you observe your neighbor's dress, face, how he talks; just to observe, not to criticize, not to evaluate, judge, but to observe. Observe a tree, observe the moon and the swift-running waters. When you so observe then you ask yourself, what is beauty?

They talk a great deal about beauty in the magazines: how you must be beautiful, your face, your hair, your complexion. What is beauty? Is beauty in the picture, in the painting, in the strange modern structure? Is beauty in a poem? Is beauty merely in the physical face and body? Have you ever asked this question? If you are an artist or a poet or a literary person, you may describe something very beautiful, paint something that is lovely, write a poem that really stirs your very being. So what is beauty? Have you ever noticed that when you give a nice toy, a complicated toy, to a child who is being naughty, he gets completely absorbed in it and all his naughtiness stops because he is absorbed? Is being absorbed in a poem, in a face, in a picture, beauty? When you look at a marvelous mountain with a cap of eternal snows, its line against the blue sky, for a second the immensity of that mountain drives away the self, the "me," with all my problems, all my anxiety. In seeing the majesty of the great rocks and the lovely valleys and the rivers, at that moment, that second, the self is not. So the mountain has driven away the self, as the toy quiets the child. That mountain, that river, the depth of the blue valleys, dispel for a second all your problems, all your vanities and anxieties. Then you say, "How beautiful that is." But is there beauty without being absorbed by something outside? That is, beauty is where the self is not.

So beauty is when the self is not. That requires great meditation, great inquiry, a tremendous sense of discipline. The word *discipline* means the disciple who is learning from the master;

learning, not disciplining as in conforming, imitating, adjusting. Learning brings its own tremendous discipline, and for an inward sense of austerity discipline is necessary.

We must also inquire carefully into whether it is possible to be free of fear. This is really an important question to ask. I am not asking it for you, but you are asking this of yourself. Is it possible, living in modern society with all the brutality, with all the tremendous violence that is on the increase, to have freedom from fear? What is fear? Humanity has put up with fear, has never been able to solve fear. Never. There are various forms of fear. You may have your own particular fear: fear of death, fear of gods, fear of the devil, fear of your wife, fear of your husband, fear of the politicians. God knows how many fears humanity has. What is fear? Not the mere experience of fear in its multiple forms, but the reality, the actuality, of fear? How is it brought about? Why has humanity, which is each one of us, accepted fear as a way of life—violence on television, violence in our daily life, and the ultimate violence of organized killing, which is called war? Is not fear related to violence? We are inquiring into fear, the actual truth of fear, not the idea of fear. The idea of fear is different from the actuality of fear.

So what is fear? How has it come about? What is the relationship of fear to time, to thought? One may be frightened of tomorrow, or of many tomorrows, or have fear of what has happened before, in the past, or be in fear of what is actually going on now. And the fear of death is the ultimate fear. Is fear brought about by time? Someone has done something in the past to hurt you, and the past is time. The future is time. The present is time. So we are asking, is time a central factor of fear? Fear has many, many branches, many leaves, but it's no good trimming the branches. We are asking what the root of fear is; not the multiple *forms* of fear, because fear is fear. Out of fear you have invented gods, saviors. If you have absolutely no fear psychologically, then there is tremendous relief, a great sense of freedom. You have dropped all the burdens of life.

So we must inquire very seriously, closely, hesitantly, into this question: Is time a factor? Obviously. I have a good job now; I may lose it tomorrow, so I'm frightened. When there is fear, there is jealousy, anxiety, hatred, violence. So time is a factor of fear. Time is a factor and thought is a factor, thinking about what has happened, what might happen. Isn't thinking a factor in fear? Has thinking brought about fear? One sees that time has brought fear. Time is not only time by the clock, but psychological time, the inward time: "I am going to be—"; "I am not good, but I will be"; "I will get rid of my violence," which is again the future. All that implies time.

Are you prepared for all this? Do you want to go into all this? If you do, I'm rather surprised, because you have all been instructed, informed, you have been told what to do by the psychologists, by the priests, by your leaders; you are always seeking help and finding new ways of being helped. So one has become a slave to others. One is never free to inquire, to stand psychologically completely by oneself.

We are now going to inquire into time. What is time? Apart from the clock, apart from the sunrise and the sunset, apart from the light and the dark, what is time? Please, if you really understand the nature of time inwardly, you will find for yourself an extraordinary sense of having no time at all.

Time is the past, time is the future, and time is the present. The whole cycle is time. The past is your background, what you have thought, what you have lived through, your experiences, your conditioning as a Christian, a Hindu, a Buddhist. Without the past you wouldn't be here. You have been programmed like a computer, repeating, repeating, repeating, for two thousand years, and the Hindus for three to five thousand years. So the past is the present; what you are now is the result of the past. And tomorrow, or a thousand tomorrows, is what you are now, so the future is now. In the now, all time is contained. This is a fact too, an actuality, not a theory. What you are is the result of the past and what you will be tomorrow is what you are now. If I am violent now, tomorrow I will be violent. So tomorrow is in the now, in the present, unless I radically, fundamentally, bring about a mutation. Otherwise I will be what I have been. We have had a long evolution, evolving to what we are now. And if we carry on that game, we will be violent, we will be barbarous the next day. So as all time is contained in the now—which is a fact, an actuality—can there be total mutation *now* in all our behavior and our way of living, thinking, feeling? Because if we don't radically, psychologically bring about a mutation, then we will be exactly what we have been in the past. Is it possible to bring about this psychological mutation at all?

You know, when you have been going north all your life, following a particular direction, or no direction, just wobbling as most people do, if somebody comes along and tells you most seriously that going north leads nowhere, there is nothing at the end of it, you listen seriously, not only with the hearing of the ear but deeply. "Go east or south," you are told, and you say, "I will do it." At that moment you have taken a new turn and there is a mutation. The speaker is making it very simple, but it is a very complex problem: to realize deeply that we have been going on this way for centuries and we have not changed at all. We are still violent, brutal, and all the rest of it. If we actually perceive that, not intellectually or verbally but deeply, then we turn in another direction. At that second there is the mutation in the very brain cells themselves.

We said time is important because we live by time, but we don't live time as a whole, which is the present. In the present all time is contained, the future and the past. If I am violent today, I will be violent tomorrow. But can I end that violence today completely, not partially? I can. And is fear brought about by thought? Of course it is. Don't accept the speaker's word for it, look at it. I am secure today, but I am frightened of what might happen tomorrow: there might be war, there might be some other catastrophe. So time and thought are the root of fear.

Now what is thinking? If time and thought are the root of fear—which they are in actuality—what is thinking? Why do we live, act, do everything, on the basis of thought? The marvelous cathedrals of Europe, their beauty, structure, architecture, have been put together by thought. All religions and their paraphernalia, their medieval robes, are put together by thought. All the rituals are contrived, arranged, by thought. And our relationship with each other, man and woman, is based on thought. When you drive a car, it is based on thought. Recognition is thought. So one has to inquire into what thinking is.

Probably very few people have asked this question. The speaker has been asking this question for sixty years. What is thought? If you can find out what is the origin, the beginning of thought, why thought has become so extraordinarily important in our life, there may be in that very inquiry a mutation taking place. So we are asking what is thought, what is thinking? Don't wait for me to answer. Look at it, observe it.

Thinking is the word. The word is important, the sound of the word, the quality of the word, the depth, the beauty of a word. Especially the sound. Thinking is part of memory, isn't it? If we had no memory at all, would we be able to think? We wouldn't. Our brain is the instrument of memory—memory of things that have happened, experience, and so on, the whole background of memory. Memory arises from knowledge, from experience. So experience, knowledge, memory, and the response of memory, is thought. This whole process of experiencing, recollecting, holding, becomes our knowledge. Experience is always limited, naturally. Is experience different from the experiencer? Give your brain to this, find out! If there is no experiencer, is there an experience? Of course not. So the experience and the experiencer are the same, like the observer and the observed. The thinker is not separate from his thoughts. The thinker is the thought.

So experience is limited, as you can observe in the scientific world or any other field. They are adding more and more and more every day to their knowledge through experience, through experiments on animals and all that horror that is going on. And that knowledge is limited because it can be added to. So memory is limited. And from that memory thought is limited. So thought, being limited, must invariably bring about conflict. Just see the pattern of it; don't accept what the speaker is saying. That's absurd; he is not an authority, he is not a guru. We can observe this fact together, that thought and time are the root of fear. Time and thought are the same, they are not two separate movements. See this fact, this actuality, that time and thought, time-thought, are the root of fear. Just observe it in yourself. Don't move away from the reality, from the truth that fear is caused by time and thought. Hold it, remain with it, don't run away from it. It is so. Then it is like holding a precious jewel in your hand. You see all the beauty of that jewel. Then you will see for yourself that fear psychologically completely ends. And when there is no fear you are free. And when there is that total freedom you don't have gods, rituals, you are a free man.

When you yourself become both the teacher and the disciple—disciple being a man who is learning, learning, learning, not accumulating knowledge—then you are an extraordinary human being.

Washington, D.C., April 20, 1985

2

We are going to face the truth of things, not live in delusions. With delusions it is very difficult to observe. If you are deluding yourself and not facing actualities, then it becomes impossible to look at oneself as one is. But we like delusions, illusions, every form of deception, because we are frightened to look at ourselves. To look at ourselves very clearly, accurately, precisely, is only possible in the mirror of relationship; that is the only mirror we have. In the mirror of relationship you see what you are, if you allow yourself to see what you are.

We want everlasting pleasure in different ways: sexual, sensory, intellectual, the pleasure of possession, the pleasure of acquiring a great skill, the pleasure one derives from having a great deal of information, knowledge, and the ultimate gratification of what we call "God." Man has pursued pleasure endlessly, in the name of God, in the name of peace, in the name of ideology. And then there is the pleasure of power, having power over others, political power. Have you noticed that power is an ugly thing, when one dominates another in any form? Power is one of the evil things in life. And pleasure is the other side of the coin of fear. When one understands deeply, profoundly, seriously, the nature of fear, then pleasure is delight, seeing something beautiful, seeing the sunset or the morning light, the dawn, the marvelous colors, the reflection of the sun on the waters. That is delight; but we cultivate that memory as pleasure.

What is action? We are all so active from morning till night, not only physically but psychologically, the brain everlastingly chattering, going from one thing to another endlessly. During the day and during the night in dreams the brain is never at rest, it is perpetually in motion. What is action, the doing? The very word *doing* is in the present, it is not having done or "I *will* do." Action means the doing now, accurately, completely, holistically, if I can use that word, action that is whole, complete, not partial. When action is based on some ideology, it is not action, is it? It is conformity to a certain pattern that you have established and, therefore, it is incomplete, action according to some memory, some conclusion. If you act according to a certain ideology, pattern, or conclusion, it is incomplete; there is a contradiction in it.

Is action related to disorder or to order? We live in disorder, our life is disorderly, confused, contradictory—saying one thing, doing another; thinking one thing and doing quite the opposite. What is order and what is disorder and what is the relationship of action to order and disorder?

What is disorder? Look at the world, if you will; the world is in disorder. Terrible things are happening. Very few of us know actually what is happening in the scientific world, in the world of the art of war, all the terrible things that are going on in other countries; the poverty in all countries, the rich and the terribly poor, always the threat of war, one political group against another political group. So there is this tremendous disorder. That is an actuality, not an invention or an illusion. We have created this disorder, because our very living is disorderly. And we are trying to bring about order through the social reforms. Without understanding and bringing about the end of disorder, we try to find order. It is like a confused mind trying to find clarity. A confused mind is a confused mind; it can never find clarity. So can there be an end to disorder in our life, *our daily life?* Not order in heaven or in another place, but in our daily life can there be order? Can there be the end of disorder? When there is the end of disorder there is naturally order. That order is living that is not according to a pattern or mold.

We are investigating, looking at ourselves and learning about ourselves. Learning is different from acquiring knowledge. If you will please kindly give your attention to this a little bit, learning is an infinite process, a limitless process, whereas knowledge is always limited. And learning implies not only observing visually, optically, but also observing without any distortion, seeing things exactly as they are. That requires the discipline of one who is learning, not the terrible discipline of orthodoxy, tradition, or following certain rules, dictates. It is learning through clear observation, hearing exactly what the other fellow is saying without any distortion. And learning is not accumulative because you are moving. In learning what disorder is in ourselves, order comes about very naturally, easily, unexpectedly. And when there is order, order is virtue. There is no other virtue except complete order; that is *complete* morality, not some imposed or dictated morality.

Every human being, whether rich or poor, intellectual or just ordinary laymen like us, goes through every form of suffering. Have you ever looked at people who have cried through centuries? Through thousands of wars? There is immense sorrow in the world. Not that there is not also pleasure, joy, and so on, but in understanding and perhaps ending sorrow we will find something much greater. Can sorrow ever end or is mankind doomed forever to suffer, to suffer not only physically but psychologically? Inwardly we have suffered enormously without perhaps saying a word about it, or crying our hearts out. During all this long evolution of man from the beginning of time until now, every human being on this earth has suffered. Suffering is not merely the loss of someone you think you like or love, but also the suffering of the very poor, the illiterate. If you go to India or other parts of the world, you see people walking miles and miles to go to a school, little girls and little boys. They will never be rich, they will never ride in a car, probably never have a hot bath. They have one sari and that is all. And that is sorrow. And the man who goes by in a car, who looks at this, is in sorrow, if he is at all sensitive, aware. And there is the sorrow of ignorance; not ignorance of writing and literature, and so on, but the sorrow of a man who does not know himself. There are multiple ways of sorrow.

Can this sorrow end for each one? There is the sorrow in oneself and the sorrow of the world. There have been thousands of wars, people maimed, appalling cruelty. Every nation on earth has committed cruelties. It is appalling and we're still perpetuating that cruelty. Cruelty brings enormous sorrow. As human beings, just observing, being aware sensitively of all this, we see sorrow is a terrible thing, and ask if that sorrow can end. Please ask yourself whether sorrow can ever end? Because, as with hatred, when there is sorrow there is no love. When you are suffering, concerned with your own suffering, how can there be love? So one must ask this question, however difficult it is, to find not the answer but the ending of sorrow.

What is sorrow? Is sorrow self-pity? Please, investigate. We're not saying it is or it is not, we are asking. Is sorrow brought about by self-pity? Is that one of the factors? Is sorrow brought about by loneliness, feeling desperately isolated, and in that isolation having no relationship with anything?

Is sorrow merely an intellectual affair to be rationalized, explained away? Or can one live with it without any desire for comfort? That is, to *live* with sorrow, not escape from it, not rationalize it, not find some exclusive comfort, some religious or illusory romantic escape, but to live with something that has tremendous significance. Sorrow is not only a physical shock; when one loses one's son or husband, wife or girl, that is a tremendous biological shock; one is almost paralyzed with it. Can we look at sorrow as it actually is in us, and remain with it, hold it, and not move away from it? Sorrow is not different from the one who suffers. The person who suffers wants to run away, escape, do all kinds of things. But to look at it as you look at a beautiful child, to hold it, never escape from it, then you will see for yourself, if you really look deeply, that there is an end to sorrow. And when there is an end to sorrow, there is passion. Not lust, not sensory stimulation, but passion. Very few have this passion, because we are so consumed with our own griefs, with our own pains, with our own pity and vanity. We have tremendous energy, but we dissipate it by conflict, through fear, through endless chattering about nothing. And passion has tremendous energy. That passion is not stimulated. It doesn't seek stimulation; it is there, like a burning fire. It only comes when there is the end of sorrow.

When you have the ending of this sorrow, it is not personal, because you are the rest of humanity. We all suffer; we all go through loneliness; every human being on this earth, rich or poor, learned or ignorant, goes through tremendous anxieties, conscious or unconscious. Your consciousness is not yours, it is human consciousness. In the content of that consciousness are all your beliefs, your sorrows, your pities, your vanities, your arrogance, your search for power, position. All that is your consciousness, which is shared by all human beings. Therefore, it is not your particular consciousness. And when you really realize that—not verbally or intellectually or theoretically or as a concept, but as an actuality—then you'll not kill another, hurt another. You will have some other thing which is totally different, of a different dimension altogether.

What is love? We use the word *love* so loosely. It has become merely sensuous, sexual; love is identified with pleasure. And to find that perfume one must go into what is not love. Through negation you come to the positive, not the other way round. Through negation of what is not love you come to that which is immensely true, which is love.

Love is not hate, that is obvious. Love is not vanity, arrogance. Love is not in the hand of power: wanting power, whether over a small child or over a group of people or a nation, surely is not love. Love is not pleasure. Love is not desire. Love is certainly not thought. When you are ambitious, aggressive—as you are all brought up to be successful, to be famous, to be known, which is all so utterly childish—how can there be love?

So love is something that cannot be invited or cultivated. It comes about naturally, easily, when the other things are not. And in learning about oneself, one comes upon this. Where there is love, there is compassion; and compassion has its own intelligence.

That is the supreme form of intelligence, not the intelligence of thought, of cunning and deception. It is only when there is complete love and compassion that there is that excellence of intelligence that is not mechanical.

Shall we talk about death? Are you interested in finding out what death is? What is the meaning of that word *death,* the dying, the ending? Not only the ending but what happens after death? Does one carry the memories of one's own life? The whole Asiatic world believes in reincarnation; that is, I die, having led a miserable life, perhaps done a little good here and there, and next life I will be better, I will do more good. It is based on reward and punishment, like everything else in life. And in Christianity there is resurrection, and so on.

If we put all that aside for the moment, really put it aside, not cling to one thing or the other, then what is death? What does it mean to die? Not only biologically, physically, but also psychologically. You have acquired all the accumulation of memories, one's tendencies, skills, idiosyncrasies, the things that one has gathered, whether it be money, knowledge, friendship; and death comes and says, "Sorry, you can't take anything with you." What does it mean to die? What is death? How do we inquire into it? I am living, I go along every day; it is routine, mechanical, miserable, happy, unhappy. And death comes, through accident, through disease, through old age, senility. We are frightened of death, we never see the greatness of this extraordinary thing. A child is born, a new human being comes into being. That is an extraordinary event. And that child grows and becomes whatever you have all become, and then dies. Death is also something most extraordinary; it must be; and you won't see the depth and the greatness of it if you are frightened.

Death means surely the ending of everything, the ending of my relationships, the ending of all the things I have put together in my life, all the knowledge, all the experience. I've led an idiotic life, a meaningless life, or I have tried to find intellectually a meaning to life; then death comes and says, "That's the end." But I am frightened, it can't be the end. I've got so much, I've collected so much, not only furniture or pictures. I identify myself with the furniture or the pictures or the bank account so *I am* the bank account, the pictures, the furniture. When you identify with something so completely, you are that. I have established roots. I have established a great many things round me. And death comes and makes a clean sweep of all that. So I ask myself, is it possible to live with death all the time? Not at the end of ninety or a hundred years, not at the end of my life but with all my energy, vitality, and all the things that go on, can I live with death all the time? Not commit suicide, I don't mean that, that's too silly, but live with death, which means the ending every day of every thing I've collected. The *ending*.

Have you gone into the question of what continuity is and what ending is? That which continues can never renew itself, be reborn. So can I live with death, which means that everything that I have done and collected ends? Ending is more important than continuity. The ending means the beginning of something new. If you merely continue, it is the same pattern being repeated in a different mold. So can I live with death? That means freedom, complete, total, holistic freedom. And in that freedom there is great love and compassion, and that intelligence which has not an end, which is immense.

Man has always sought something beyond all this pain, anxiety, and sorrow. Is there something that is sacred, eternal, that is beyond all the reaches of thought? This has been a question from the most ancient of times. What is sacred? What is that which has no time, that which is incorruptible, that which is nameless, that which has no quality, no limitation, the timeless, the eternal? Is there such a thing? Man has asked this for thousands and thousands of years. So he has worshiped the sun, the earth, nature, the trees, the birds; everything that's living on this earth man has worshiped since ancient times. The Vedas and the Upanishads never mention God. That which is supreme, they said, is not manifested.

So are you asking that question too? Are you asking if there is something sacred? Is there something that is not put together by thought, as all organized religions are? What is religion? Not only what is religion, but what is the religious brain, religious mind? To inquire into that deeply, not superficially, there must be total freedom. Not freedom *from* one thing or the other, but freedom as a whole, per se. Is it possible, living in this ugly world, to be free from pain, sorrow, anxiety, loneliness?

If there is order in one's life, real order, then what is meditation? Is it following certain systems, methods: the Zen method, the Buddhist meditation, the Hindu meditation, and the methods of the latest gurus? If meditation is determined, if it is following a system, a method, practiced day after day, what happens to the human brain? It becomes more and more dull. Is meditation something entirely different? It has nothing whatever to do with method, system, practices; therefore, it can never be mechanical. It can never be conscious meditation. It is like a man consciously wanting money and pursuing money: consciously you meditate, wanting to achieve peace, silence. The man who pursues money, success, power, and the man who pursues so-called spirituality are both the same.

Is there a meditation which is not determined, practiced? There is, but that requires enormous attention. That attention is a flame and that attention is not something that you come to; it is attention *now* to everything, every word, every gesture, every thought; it is to pay complete attention, not partial. If you are listening partially now, you are not giving complete attention. When you are completely attentive there is no self, there is no limitation.

The brain now is full of information, cluttered up, there is no space in it, and one must have space. Space means energy. When there is no space, your energy is very limited. The brain is now so heavily laden with knowledge, with theories, with power, position, so everlastingly in conflict and cluttered up, that it has no space. And freedom, complete freedom, is to have that limitless space. The brain is extraordinarily capable, has infinite capacity, but we have made it small and petty. When there is that space and emptiness and, therefore, immense energy—energy is passion, love and compassion and intelligence—then there is that truth which is most holy, most sacred, that which man has sought from time immemorial. That truth does not lie in any temple, in any mosque, in any church. And it has no path to it except through one's own understanding of oneself, inquiring, studying, learning. Then there is that which is eternal.

Washington, D.C., April 21, 1985

Part 1

What I Want to Do: The report of the first public talk in Mexico City, October 20, 1935, page 221 in volume II of *The Collected Works of J. Krishnamurti*, © 1991 Krishnamurti Foundation of America.

What Are You Seeking?: The report of the first public talk at Ojai, California, June 16, 1934, page 52 in volume II of *The Collected Works of J. Krishnamurti*, © 1991 Krishnamurti Foundation of America.

The Significance of Environment: The report of the second public talk at Ojai, California, June 17, 1934, page 57 in volume II of *The Collected Works of J. Krishnamurti*, © 1991 Krishnamurti Foundation of America.

A Dynamic Society: The report of the third public talk at Ojai, California, June 18, 1934, page 62 in volume II of *The Collected Works of J. Krishnamurti*, © 1991 Krishnamurti Foundation of America.

Living in Ecstasy: The report of the tenth public talk at Ojai, California, June 29, 1934, page 94 in volume II of *The Collected Works of J. Krishnamurti*, © 1991 Krishnamurti Foundation of America.

To Be a True Human Being: The report of the eleventh public talk at Ojai, California, June 30, 1934, page 99 in volume II of *The Collected Works of J. Krishnamurti*, © 1991 Krishnamurti Foundation of America.

Being Vulnerable to Truth: The report of the twelfth public talk at Ojai, California, July 1, 1934, page 104 in volume II of *The Collected Works of J. Krishnamurti*, © 1991 Krishnamurti Foundation of America.

Part 2

The First and Last Freedom: Introduction to *The First and Last Freedom*, © 1954 Krishnamurti Foundation of America.

Ambition: Number 79 in *Commentaries on Living*, © 1956 Krishnamurti Foundation of America.

The Individual and the Ideal: Number 19 in *Commentaries on Living, Second Series*, © 1958 Krishnamurti Foundation of America.

Fear and Escape: Number 75 in *Commentaries on Living*, © 1956 Krishnamurti Foundation of America.

Time and Transformation: Number 20 in *The First and Last Freedom*, © 1954 Krishnamurti Foundation of America.

Sorrow from Self-Pity: Number 55 in *Commentaries on Living, Third Series*, © 1960 Krishnamurti Foundation of America.

Education and the Significance of Life, © 1953 Krishnamurti Foundation of America.

Life Ahead, © 1963 Krishnamurti Foundation of America.

Freedom from the Known, © 1969 Krishnamurti Foundation Trust, Ltd.

Krishnamurti's Journal, © 1982 Krishnamurti Foundation Trust, Ltd.

Krishnamurti To Himself, © 1987 Krishnamurti Foundation Trust, Ltd.

Part 3

What Is It to Be Serious? From the report of the first public talk at Rajghat, Banaras, India, January 9, 1955, page 259 in volume VIII of *The Collected Works of J. Krishnamurti*, © 1991 Krishnamurti Foundation of America.

Can We Create a New Culture? From the report of the first public talk in Bombay, February 16, 1955, page 207 in volume VIII of *The Collected Works of J. Krishnamurti*, © 1991 Krishnamurti Foundation of America.

Can You Understand the Fact of Emptiness? From the report of the fifth public talk in Paris, May 7, 1950, page 172 in volume VI of *The Collected Works of J. Krishnamurti*, © 1991 Krishnamurti Foundation of America.

What Is Our Basic Problem? From the report of the second public talk in Bombay, February 10, 1957, page 239 in volume X of *The Collected Works of J. Krishnamurti*, © 1991 Krishnamurti Foundation of America.

How Do You Approach the Problems of Living? From the report of the tenth public talk in Bombay, March 11, 1953, page 241 in volume VII of *The Collected Works of J. Krishnamurti*, © 1991 Krishnamurti Foundation of America.

What Is the Central Core of Your Thinking? Meetings with students at Brockwood Park School, Hampshire, England; from *Beginnings of Learning*, © 1975 Krishnamurti Foundation Trust, Ltd.

What Is the Relation Between Krishnamurti's Teaching and Truth? Meetings with the international trustees of the Krishnamurti Foundations at Ojai, California, in 1977; from *The Wholeness of Life*, © 1979 Krishnamurti Foundation Trust, Ltd.

Part 4

The Core of Krishnamurti's Teaching, © 1981 Krishnamurti Foundation Trust, Ltd.

Total Action Without Regret: From *Talks in Saanen 1974*, © 1975 Krishnamurti Foundation Trust, Ltd.

A Relationship with the World: From the recordings of the public talks in Ojai, California, 1976, © 1976/1996 Krishnamurti Foundation Trust, Ltd.

The Wholeness of Life: From the recordings of the public talks at Brockwood Park, 1980, © 1980/1996 Krishnamurti Foundation Trust, Ltd.

The Ending of Sorrow: From the recordings of the public talks in New Delhi, 1983, © 1983/1996 Krishnamurti Foundation Trust, Ltd.

Truth Most Holy: *Washington, D.C., Talks, 1985*, © 1988 Krishnamurti Foundation Trust, Ltd.

INDEX

INDEX